T0344950

Ten Laws of Operational Risk

Founded in 1807, John Wiley & Sons is the oldest independent publishing company in the United States. With offices in North America, Europe, Australia and Asia, Wiley is globally committed to developing and marketing print and electronic products and services for our customers' professional and personal knowledge and understanding.

The Wiley Finance series contains books written specifically for finance and investment professionals as well as sophisticated individual investors and their financial advisors. Book topics range from portfolio management to e-commerce, risk management, financial engineering, valuation and financial instrument analysis, as well as much more.

For a list of available titles, visit our Web site at www.WileyFinance.com.

Ten Laws of Operational Risk

Understanding its Behaviours to Improve its Management

MICHAEL GRIMWADE

WILEY

Library of Congress Cataloging-in-Publication Data is Available:

ISBN 9781119841357 (Hardback)
ISBN 9781119841364 (ePDF)
ISBN 9781119841371 (ePub)

Cover Design: Wiley
Cover Image: © themacx/Getty Images

SKY6A37E639-0121-49A9-9B86-2DFA6C8253BA_111921

To Karen, Charlotte and Olivia.

My thanks go to the management of ICBC Standard Bank for their ongoing encouragement and support.

I would also like to thank my friends and colleagues in the world of Operational Risk for helping me by reviewing drafts of this book, in particular Professor Elizabeth Sheedy, Dr Patrick McConnell, Dr Peter Mitic, Dr Ariane Chapelle, Dr Luke Carrivick, Dr Peter McCormack, Siraj Ahmed, Mia Pollock and Wayne McLaughlin.

Contents

MICHAEL GRIMWADE first worked on Operational Risk management during the early years of the profession in the mid-1990s, a decade before Basel II was finalised. He is Head of Operational Risk for ICBC Standard Bank and has previously held senior Operational Risk management roles at MUFG Securities, RBS and Lloyds TSB. Prior to this Michael was a management consultant with PwC and Deloitte Consulting, and he has also been a Director of the Institute of Operational Risk.

Michael has written a number of articles on the setting of appetite for Operational Risk; scenario analysis techniques; the quantification of emerging risks; how Climate Change may impact Operational Risk; and the modelling of Operational Risk capital. His book *Managing Operational Risk: New Insights and Lessons Learnt* was published in 2016. Michael received an award in 2014 from the Institute of Operational Risk for his contribution to the profession. He has a degree in Zoology from Oxford University and is a member of the ICAEW.

He lives in West London with his wife Karen and their two daughters, Charlotte and Olivia, and a very curious Bengal cat, called Milo. Any typos in this book are most likely caused by Milo's habit of walking across his keyboard.

The contents of this book are the Author's own views rather than those of ICBC Standard Bank.

"Unlike credit and market risk, operational risk is lacking in basic theory as to why, where and when operational risk losses occur."

Dr Patrick McConnell
Operational Risk Executive, Academic and Author

"You can know the name of a bird in all of the languages of the world, but when you're finished, you'll know absolutely nothing whatsoever about the bird ... so let's look at the bird and see what it's doing – that's what counts."

Professor Richard P. Feynman
Winner of the Nobel Prize in Physics in 1965

Introduction

Understanding Operational Risk is intuitively fundamental to its effective management. But a review of the profession's literature, regulations and training reveals that whilst there are many thousands of words on the subject of integrated frameworks for managing Operational Risk, specific behaviours and quantification, there is a lack of an overarching theory that might explain and predict its behaviour. This observation was made very clearly in a paper written by Dr Patrick McConnell, which opens with the statement that "Unlike credit and market risk, operational risk is lacking in basic theory as to why, where and when operational risk losses occur" (McConnell, 2017).

The challenge is that Market and Credit Risk are respectively defined as risks of losses arising from external events, i.e. the movement of market prices or the failure of a customer/counterparty to meet its obligations, whilst Operational Risk is primarily defined as losses arising from internal causal factors. In his brief paper McConnell proposes that Operational Risk losses arise when formal information channels are corrupted, interrupted or disrupted and that the scale of any losses can be linked to the quantum of data involved. In this book, I adopt a different approach, as I have set out Ten Laws of Operational Risk that describe how inadequacies or failures; business profiles; human and institutional behaviours and biases; and internal and external causes combine to result in events. The nature of the impacts drives both the rapidity and the scale of any resulting losses. Whilst this is different from McConnell's approach, his paper was both my inspiration for this book, and also influenced my ideas.

Part One of the book begins by following Professor Richard Feynman's advice and observing that over the last two decades there are distinct patterns and trends in the behaviour of Operational Risk loss data, systematically collected by either the Basel Committee[1] or the Operational Riskdata eXchange Association (ORX).[2] For example, whilst the vast majority of Operational Risk loss events have relatively low impacts, a very small number of loss events, primarily Conduct Risks, have disproportionately high impacts.[3] Additionally, whilst some categories of Operational Risk remain quite stable, others show persistent trends over time. Finally, the risk profiles of firms vary by business line and also by bank. All of these observations suggest that Operational

---

[1]Tranches 1 and 2 of the Basel Committee's Quantitative Impact Study 2 (QIS-2).
[2]ORX Association's (www.orx.org) annual reports from 2010 to 2020.
[3]During the period 2010 to 2018, 38 very large losses (≥\$1 billion) suffered by ORX members, represented just over 50% of losses by value, despite constituting only 0.01% of loss events by number (Figure 6.1).

Risk is far from random, and hence, Chapters 2 to 4 describe Ten Laws that explain these various behaviours.

The first five laws are described in Chapter 2 and relate to the occurrence, detection and the financial significance of individual loss events. Specifically, they identify the nature of the inadequacies or failures that constitute Operational Risk events: the business profiles of firms, and the underlying internal and external causes, and assess their varying relevance to different categories of Operational Risk. Business profile is systematically defined in terms of a firm's strategy (both past and present), culture and infrastructure, including governance; processes; people and systems, and its external relationships with authorities, e.g. regulators; its sources of capital, funding and revenues; third (and fourth) party service providers; and society (this is set out in the diagram below).

The first five laws also cover the nature of control failures; the rapidity (velocity) with which different categories of impacts accrete; the duration of events; and the lags between the detection of events and their subsequent crystallisation into losses.

The final five laws describe the interactions between Operational Risk and other factors. Chapter 3 covers the concentration of losses in firms driven by either internal

FIGURE I.1 The business profile of a firm (Grimwade, 2020)

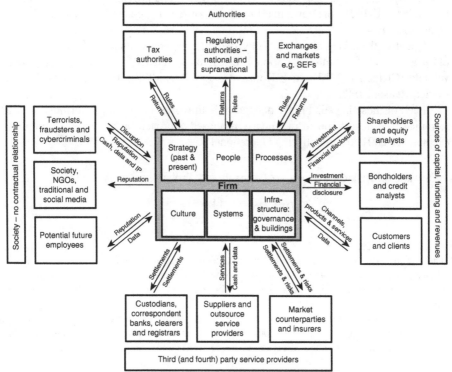

or external causes (6th and 7th Laws respectively), and the occurrence of Systemic Operational Risk Events (SOREs).[4] It identifies that internal causes primarily drive the occurrence of Operational Risk events, whilst the most important external cause, economic change, increases the occurrence and detection of Operational Risk events, and also their velocity, duration and lags. The ubiquitous role of causes in many of these laws is reflected in a revised version of the profession's butterfly diagram, which is included later in this Introduction.

Chapter 4 explores the extent to which Operational Risk losses reflect the dynamic interaction between firms and their risk profiles (8th Law: Risk Homeostasis). Firms will naturally respond to losses outside of their appetite, by enhancing controls.[5] As a consequence, the 8th Law implies that past losses may not always be a good guide to the future loss experiences of a firm. Additionally, as firms also respond to anticipated risks, then Chapter 4 provides an overview of the various behavioural biases that may influence humans in assessing remote risks. The 9th Law deals with the ability of firms to transfer risks to other entities. It describes how Market and Credit Risks can be transformed into Operational Risk, through the "granting" of Real Options, and that the absolute quantum of risk is conserved through this process. This chapter also notes the ability of firms to transfer actively Operational Risk through insurance, which is explored further in Chapter 12. Finally, the 10th Law explains how firms can proactively take Operational Risk by selling products and providing services, in return for fee income. It demonstrates that this source of revenue generates disproportionate Operational Risks.

Not all of these laws are original observations, and I have referenced the originators of ideas such as, Systemic Operational Risk Events, SOREs (McConnell, 2015); risk velocity (Chaparro, 2013); Risk Homeostasis (Wilde, 1998); and the Swiss Cheese Model (Reason, 1990).

Each of these laws is briefly defined in both words and a simple formula. These formulae take inspiration from an early proposed approach by the Basel Committee (September 2001) for quantifying Operational Risk:

$$\text{Operational Risk capital} = \gamma_{i,j} \times \text{Exposure}_{i,j} \times \text{Probability}_{i,j} \times \text{Average impacts}_{i,j}$$

$$= \gamma_{i,j} \times \text{Expected Loss}$$

---

[4]There seem to be two types of SOREs: instances where a number of banks independently act inappropriately, e.g. by mis-selling PPI; as well as, instances where a number of firms are impacted by the same external event, e.g. WorldCom litigation (2002) or Hurricane Sandy (2012).

[5]This is consistent with the 1960s Japanese manufacturing concept of poka-yoke or "mistake-proofing", which involves both the prevention of defects from occurring, and the amendment of processes, when defects do occur, to avoid their recurrence.

TABLE I.1 The coverage of the Ten Laws of Operational Risk and their units

Describe individual events	Describe patterns in events and interrelationships
1. Occurrence of events (events)	6. Concentration due to internal drivers (ratio of losses for different banks)
2. Detection of events (events over time)	7. Concentration due to external drivers (ratio of losses pre & post the GFC)
3. Velocity of losses (incurred losses ($) over time)	8. Risk Homeostasis (losses ($) over time)
4. Duration and severity of events (incurred losses ($))	9. Risk transference, transformation and conservation (events over time) and (losses ($) over time)
5. Lags in settlement (settled losses ($) over time)	10. Proactive taking of Operational Risk (losses ($) over time)

This formula assumes a defined relationship between expected losses and the tail of the loss distribution,[6] i.e. a factor $\gamma_{i,j}$ would have translated an estimate of expected losses for a Basel business line i and a Basel event type j into a capital charge.[7]

Whilst some of the formulae set out in this book are designed to illustrate the various interrelationships between different factors,[8] i.e. they are functions of these factors, others can actually be either calculated or measured. Each of these formulae are illustrated through the use of empirical data, primarily based upon an analysis of 443 large Operational Risk losses (defined as losses that are ≥$0.1 billion) suffered by 31 current and former Global Systemically Important Banks (G-SIBs) between 1989 and 2020. This data is sourced from the **IBM FIRST Risk Case Studies** of loss events that are in the public domain. IBM retains copyright to the materials in this database.

Chapter 5 focuses upon three taxonomies that underpin these Ten Laws, i.e. inadequacies or failures; impacts and causes. The taxonomy for inadequacies or failures describes the natures of both events and also control failures. The causal taxonomy is based upon a review of the causes explicitly (rather than implicitly) described in a number of very well-documented events. The correlations between these different causal

---

[6]The equation that Operational Risk capital requirement = Expected Operational Risk losses x a factor was later incorporated as one of the three approaches (C1) adopted by the Prudential Regulation Authority (PRA) to validate Pillar 2A assessments for Operational Risk, excluding Conduct Risk (PRA, April 2018).

[7]Analysing for ORX members the ratio of low value losses (€20k to €100k) : high value losses (≥€10 million) suggests that the average value of γ across all business lines and risk types ranges from 4x to 16x, in stressful economic conditions (Chapter 1).

[8]Operational Risk is rarely deterministic, like Newtonian mechanics, but is instead more akin to the statistical world of quantum mechanics, where almost everything is possible although not probable!

factors are calculated, with the strongest correlations relating to strategy; culture; governance; people; and processes. These taxonomies are used in subsequent chapters to support the estimation of remote events (Chapter 9); to identify both sensitivities to the impacts of economic change (Chapter 11) and predictive metrics (Chapter 13); and to explain the coverage of insurance policies (Chapter 12).

Part Two of the book concludes (Chapter 6) by analysing how well these Ten Laws actually explain the behaviours described in Chapter 1. It also assesses the existence of order within the laws, for example, a review of the formulae reveals, unexpectedly, that they imply that there are units attributable to different categories of controls, i.e. preventive, detective and corrective/resilience controls, respectively, have units of: events, time and impacts, e.g. USD. Consideration of the units within these formulae also demonstrates the importance of time, in particular relating to the duration of events; the velocity of losses; and the lags between the discovery and the settlement of losses. Additionally, a number of the laws highlight the importance to Operational Risk of changes in the behaviour of key stakeholders. Finally, the formulae also show that causes are central to the understanding and the management of Operational Risk, as they can variously influence the occurrence of events; the effectiveness of controls; and the scale of impacts.

These observations are reflected in a very different-looking butterfly diagram, in which internal and external causes span events/risks, controls and impacts. The most important causes, and the existence of correlations between different causal factors, are also highlighted. The primary nature of the inadequacies or failures that constitute Basel II's events/risks are included and are additionally linked to control failures. Impacts are also ordered by their velocity. Whilst the passage of time is represented across the bottom of the diagram, regarding both the duration of events, i.e. between the failure of preventive controls and the success of detective controls; and the lags in settlement, i.e. between the successful discovery of an event by detective controls and its eventual settlement.

The dotted lines reflect the causes; control failures and impacts of a well-publicised mis-marking incident in 2008.

Chapter 6 concludes by observing that there are three underlying pillars that drive these Ten Laws, which are recurrently referenced throughout the book:

1. *Business profile:* Both internal factors, such as strategy; culture; processes; people; systems; and infrastructure, including governance; and external factors, such as authorities, e.g. regulators; sources of capital, funding and revenues; third (and fourth) party service providers; and society.
2. *Three taxonomies:*
    i. *Causes:* Internal causes drive the concentration of events in individual firms, whilst external causes can drive industry-wide increases in occurrence/detection; duration; velocity; and lags.
    ii. *Inadequacies or failures* constitute both events and control failures, and are primarily driven by human failings.

FIGURE I.2   The revised butterfly/bow-tie diagram (Grimwade, 2020)

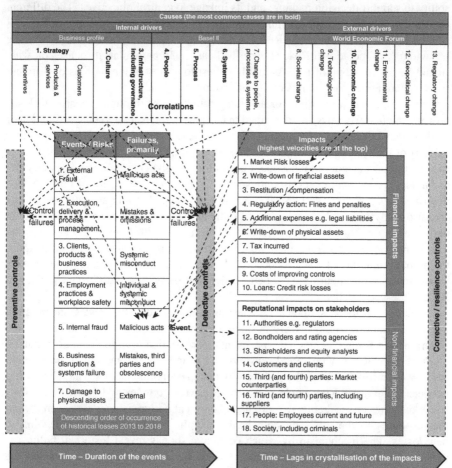

iii. *Impacts:* The nature of the different impacts is a key determinant of the velocity and the scale of losses.

3. *Behaviours/responses* of humans and institutions to different situations, i.e. both changes in existing behaviours and new behaviours. Within firms this includes responses to the detection of issues; near misses; and risks outside of appetite. It also includes the impacts of biases on their assessments of remote and emerging risks, and changes in the behaviours of various stakeholders, e.g. authorities (regulators); providers of capital, funding and revenues; and criminals.

Part Two of this book describes how the tools used by the Operational Risk profession should be redesigned for success by considering these Ten Laws. The first chapter (Chapter 7) considers the impact of the various laws on defining risk appetite both quantitatively and qualitatively; the relevance of appetite to different risk categories; its ability to support decision making; and its linkage to control objectives. The different articulations of risk appetite are linked back to the revised butterfly diagram. Chapter 8 addresses how best to undertake Risk & Control Self-Assessments (RCSAs), given the behaviours of Operational Risk as described earlier. In particular, it focuses on what should be out of scope of RCSAs and how best to represent the profiles of different risks that are either continuums or discontinuums.

More rigorous techniques for assessing remote risks through scenario analysis, utilising the first five laws, are described in Chapter 9, focusing upon the estimation of likelihood and the severity for the most important categories of impacts (based on either velocity or scale). The key insights are that the techniques for estimating likelihood are specific to each category of inadequacy or failure described in Chapter 5. Similarly, the techniques for estimating severity are specific to the main categories of impacts, also described in Chapter 5. Various quantitative approaches for validating the outputs of scenario analysis are also explained, to mitigate behavioural biases. The impacts in particular of the 5th Law on lags in settlement and the 7th Law: Concentration due to external factors on capital modelling are considered in Chapter 10. This includes the proposal that the relative proportions of Pillars 1, 2A and 2B capital requirements should resemble an "hourglass", to better reflect the behaviours of different Operational Risks, observed in Chapter 1.

Chapter 11 focuses upon stress testing utilising the 7th Law: Concentration due to external drivers, primarily business cycles. In particular, it identifies that the occurrence of some Operational Risk events increase due to both changes in human and institutional behaviours, and sensitivity to economic factors, whilst increases in severity are primarily driven by just sensitivities to economic factors. The relationship between Operational Risk and business cycles is very complex and variously involves some existing losses being exacerbated; historical failures being uncovered; and the responses to the crisis by both banks and their stakeholders alike leading to new losses. The mechanism by which economic shocks reveal historical failures is explained through a Real Option Model (Grimwade, 2016). Chapter 12 considers the circumstances in which Operational Risk can be transferred via insurance (9th Law) and its coverage in terms of both the nature of events and its impacts. This chapter also sets out more systematic approaches for the assessment, through reverse stress testing, of events that may damage a firm's viability in terms of its Operational Resilience, regulatory licenses, and business plans.

Whilst the tools described above are utilised periodically, Chapter 13 details how the day-to-day activities of Operational Risk managers can be enhanced through the consideration of these Ten Laws. Specifically, this chapter covers:

- Incident management and root cause analysis.
- Control assurance and the nature of control failures, which are the same as the nature of events.
- Predictive metrics: both the challenges and successes.

- Change management, including implementing new technology; new product and transaction approval and product stress testing.
- Reputational Risk quantification, for different categories of stakeholders, and its management.

Chapter 14 provides a summary as to how the various laws have been applied to the profession's tools.

Part Three of the book focuses on emerging Operational Risks, as it is these risks that are habitually cited as keeping executives awake at night. Chapter 15 sets out techniques for more systematically identifying emerging risks, and understanding the timescales over which they will influence Operational Risk. These techniques are then illustrated in Chapter 16, which considers four current internal and external threats and utilises the Ten Laws to predict how Operational Risk will respond. The four current internal and external threats are:

1. Pandemics.
2. Climate Change.
3. Cybercrime.
4. Technological advances, including algorithms (algos), artificial intelligence (AI) and machine learning.

The book concludes (Chapter 17) by reprising its key themes: summarising the behaviours of Operational Risk and providing an overview of the Ten Laws of Operational Risk and their underlying drivers. Chapter 17 also provides an overview of the proposed key enhancements to the Operational Risk management profession's tools and how they should be integrated into a strategy for achieving the objectives of Operational Risk management, i.e.:

1. Maximising returns, whilst staying within appetite now, and also in the future.
2. Growing their businesses both quickly and safely.
3. Meeting their stakeholders' expectations.

Although I wrote my first draft of these laws during a very short visit to Vienna in May 2019, they are built upon many years of both thinking about and managing Operational Risk. I have since spent the last two years testing these laws with empirical data, and studying both their structure and their implications. These Ten Laws were first published in the *Journal of Operational Risk* (Grimwade, 2020), and Chapters 2 to 4 borrow heavily from this paper. Whilst I find the overarching formula pleasingly elegant, ultimately, the value of these laws to me is that they both explain concepts that, as a practitioner, I have long felt to be true and that they have provided me with fresh insights and understanding of the behaviours of Operational Risk. I can think of no better reasons for reading this book.

Michael Grimwade
May 2021

FIGURE I.3 An overarching formula for Operational Risk

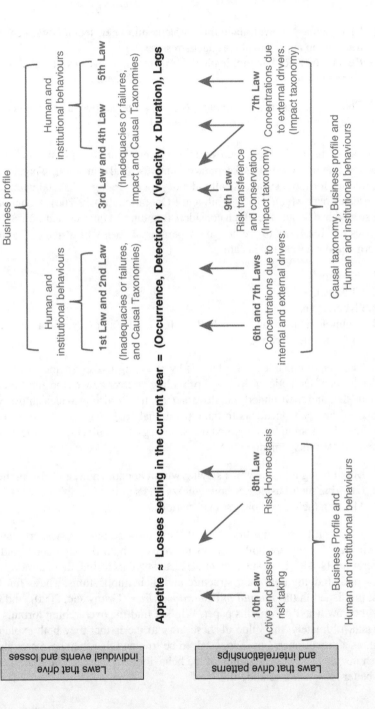

Appetite ≈ Losses settling in the current year = (Occurrence, Detection) x (Velocity x Duration), Lags

Laws that drive individual events and losses

Laws that drive patterns and interrelationships

Business profile

Human and institutional behaviours

1st Law and 2nd Law
(Inadequacies or failures, and Causal Taxonomies)

3rd Law and 4th Law
(Inadequacies or failures, Impact and Causal Taxonomies)

Human and institutional behaviours   5th Law

6th and 7th Laws
Concentrations due to internal and external drivers.

9th Law
Risk transference and conservation
(Impact taxonomy)

7th Law
Concentrations due to external drivers.
(Impact taxonomy)

Causal taxonomy, Business profile and Human and institutional behaviours

10th Law
Active and passive risk taking

8th Law
Risk Homeostasis

Business Profile and Human and institutional behaviours

Ten Laws of Operational Risk (Grimwade, 2020)

Part One of the book describes the extent to which Operational Risk has displayed observable patterns of behaviour over the last two decades (Chapter 1). The existence of patterns, whether trends over time or sustained stability, suggests that there may be laws that govern Operational Risk. If this was not the case, then the behaviour of Operational Risk over time would be random. Chapters 2 to 4 then set out Ten Laws that govern different aspects of the behaviour of Operational Risk.[1] Each law is explained with specific examples, and Chapter 2 concludes with an extended case study using data from one of the largest ever Operational Risk loss events to illustrate the first five laws. Chapter 5 focuses upon three taxonomies that underpin these Ten Laws, i.e. inadequacies or failures (both events and control failures); causes; and impacts. These taxonomies are subsequently used extensively in Part Two to support the estimation of remote events (scenario analysis); the identification of sensitivities to the impacts of business cycles and predictive metrics; and to explain the coverage of insurance policies. Finally, Chapter 6 considers how and why these Ten Laws help to explain the behaviours that were described in Chapter 1.

---

[1]As noted in the Introduction, these Ten Laws were first published in December 2020 in the *Journal of Operational Risk* (Grimwade, 2020). Consequently Chapters 2 to 4 borrow heavily from this paper.

TEN LAWS OF OPERATIONAL RISK

1. *Occurrence:* "Operational Risk events primarily arise from human failings, either directly or indirectly, ranging from mistakes to systemic misconduct to malicious acts. The types of events suffered by firms are driven by their business profiles and are exacerbated by internal and external causes, primarily culture, governance, resourcing and process definition. They are restricted by preventive controls, which may also be weakened by these causes."

2. *Detection:* "The frequency of *reported* Operational Risk events reflects detection rates of both currently occurring losses and historical undiscovered failures. Strengthening detective controls increases the frequencies of reported events, whilst weakening them may lower their observed frequency, in the short term." Detection success determines the duration of incidents, see 4th Law.

3. *Velocity:* "The rapidity (velocity) with which firms suffer losses (or gains) between an event occurring and ceasing is driven by the quantum of inadequacies or failures; causes; and the nature of the impacts generated by the event", i.e. fines and penalties are low-velocity, whilst Market Risk boundary losses have the highest velocities, up to a 1,000 times greater than regulatory fines.

4. *Duration and severity:* "The severity of an incident reflects a risk's velocity and the length of time to detection (for large losses the average is ~4 years). Average velocity declines with increased duration (average loss peaks between years 3 and 5). The severity of a loss may be limited by detective controls which accelerate discovery and corrective/resilience controls, e.g. insurance, that reduce the consequences of an event. Both may be weakened by internal causes."

5. *Lags in settlement:* "The length of time between detection and settlement is linked to systemic misconduct; regulatory involvement; litigation; sensitivity to economic cycles; and the distribution of compensation to customers." Almost three quarters of large losses crystallise over a year after detection.

6. *Concentration due to internal drivers:* "Different risks are concentrated because they are sensitive to the same internal causal factors that primarily drive occurrence. These factors lead to concentrations of events within banks." Pre-crisis ~80% of large losses were suffered by one third of the G-SIBs. During the crisis these banks particularly suffered Systemic Operational Risk Events.

7. *Concentration due to external drivers:* "The primary external driver of Operational Risk are business cycles, due to a mixture of economics and human behaviour. After an economic shock, some Operational Risk losses rise: existing losses are exacerbated, historical failures uncovered and responses to a crisis may lead to new losses. Occurrence, velocity, duration and lags all increase. After a severe downturn losses come in waves: first Market, then Credit, and finally Operational Risk."

8. *Risk Homeostasis:* "Over time a firm's expenditure on controls will increase in order to keep its expected Operational Risks in equilibrium with its risk appetite.

Whilst for emerging risks, control expenditure will rise in anticipation of increased future losses", e.g. the mitigation of Y2K.

9. *Risk transference, transformation and conservation:* "When Market and Credit Risks are sold to investors, e.g. through securitisations, they are transformed into Operational Risk that is retained by the arranger/distributor. The quantum of Operational Risk retained is equivalent of the Market and Credit Risks transferred, whilst the likelihood of this Operational Risk becoming a loss is diminished."

10. *Active and passive risk taking:* "Firms take Operational Risks both proactively through the provision of services in return for fee and commission income and passively, as a by-product of either the generation of trading and interest income or a firm's infrastructure and its corporate governance. Proactively taking Operational Risk is disproportionately risky."

CHAPTER 1

Patterns in the Behaviour of Operational Risk

At the beginning of the century the Quantitative Impact Studies (QIS) conducted by the Basel Committee provided the first systematic insights into the characteristics of Operational Risk across a population of different banks and business lines for impacts above €10k. Since these initial studies, the ORX loss data sharing consortium has picked up the baton and has continued to collate and publish summary Operational Risk loss data relating to its membership.

For a risk which was initially incorporated by the Basel Committee (Basel Committee, June 1999) into "Other risks", i.e. " . . . risks other than credit and market risks", these data collection exercises have revealed that Operational Risk displays both persistent patterns of behaviour and trends over time. This first chapter analyses the available industry data over two decades, focusing upon:

- The frequency and severity of Operational Risk losses;
- The relative significance of different risks for different business lines; and
- The concentration of losses within individual firms.

PATTERNS IN THE FREQUENCY AND SEVERITY OF OPERATIONAL RISK LOSSES

The first observation to make about the profile of Operational Risk losses is that individual large losses contribute a disproportionately large amount to the total value of losses suffered across the industry in any one year. In its report on the results of the first tranche of QIS-2 (Basel Committee, 2002), the Basel Committee noted that whilst "Just over 1 percent of the sample have gross loss amounts above €1 million...[they] . . . account for nearly three-quarters of the aggregate value of losses." Whilst demonstrably true, why this is the case is less obvious.

FIGURE 1.1   Distribution of total value of gross losses by size of individual losses

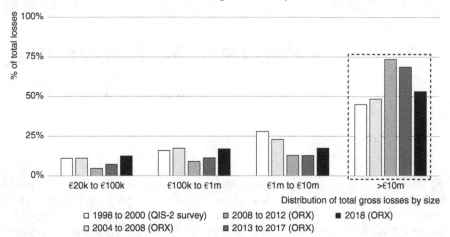

Distribution of total gross losses by size

☐ 1998 to 2000 (QIS-2 survey)   ▨ 2008 to 2012 (ORX)   ■ 2018 (ORX)
☐ 2004 to 2008 (ORX)   ■ 2013 to 2017 (ORX)

Comparing this QIS-2 data with data subsequently collected by ORX[1] in Figure 1.1 demonstrates that this first observation has not only remained true over time, but during the period 2008 to 2012 became even more extreme. This change, which occurred in the aftermath of the Global Financial Crisis (GFC), may have subsequently prompted the PRA to observe that Operational Risk's "... loss distribution is unusually fat-tailed, with infrequent but very large losses ..." (PRA 2018).

The flip side of this first observation is that the vast majority of Operational Risk loss events are of low value and contribute a disproportionately small amount to the total value of losses suffered across the industry in any one year. Whilst the number of losses with a value of €20k to €100k typically represents over 75% of the total number of losses suffered by banks (Figure 1.2), their financial contribution averages less than 10% of the total value of losses in any particular year (Figure 1.1).

A second observation on Figures 1.1 and 1.2 is that there appears to be a pattern in the Operational Risk losses over time, which coincides with the Global Financial Crisis. In Figure 1.2 the proportion of loss events with values of ≥€100k increases across all of the buckets for the period 2008 to 2012, before declining, whilst in Figure 1.1 the contribution of losses ≥€10 million to the total value of losses suffered by the contributing banks increases for the period 2008 to 2012, before again declining.

---

[1]QIS-2 was a survey of 30 banks with data collected for the period 1998 to 2000, whilst ORX's membership has steadily increased from 53 banks in 2008 to 83 banks at the end of 2018.

FIGURE 1.2 Distribution of total number of losses by size of individual losses[2]

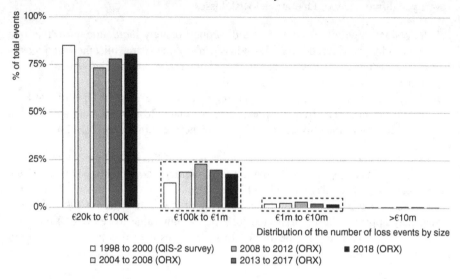

Distribution of the number of loss events by size

□ 1998 to 2000 (QIS-2 survey)   ▣ 2008 to 2012 (ORX)   ■ 2018 (ORX)
□ 2004 to 2008 (ORX)   ▣ 2013 to 2017 (ORX)

TABLE 1.1 Changes in average frequency and severity of losses ≥€10 million

	QIS-2 30 participating banks (1998 to 2000)	ORX membership An average of 58 banks (2008 to 2012)	ORX membership 83 banks (2018)
Frequency of losses ≥€10m per bank p.a.	Once every 2 years and 4 months	Once every 4 months	Once every 10 months
Average value of losses ≥€10m	€30m	€90m	€69m
Increase in losses ≥€10m relative to QIS-2	1	21×	6.5×

Analysing the average frequencies and the average severities of Operational Risk losses before, during and after the Global Financial Crisis (Table 1.1) demonstrates that the increase in the relative significance of losses ≥€10 million observed in Figure 1.1, is due to increases in both the frequency and the severity of these losses.

---

[2]The Basel Committee's 2001 QIS 2 exercise utilised a loss data collection threshold of ≥€10k, whilst ORX's members report losses ≥€20k.

In summary, two observations can be made from this survey data regarding the severity and frequency of Operational Risk losses:

1. Individual large losses contribute a disproportionately large amount to the total value of losses suffered across the industry in any one year, whilst the vast majority of loss events are of low value and contribute a disproportionately small amount to the total value of losses suffered; and
2. There appears to be a pattern in the frequency and severity of Operational Risk losses over time. The frequency and severity of large loss events both increased in the aftermath of the Global Financial Crisis, before subsequently declining.

A consequence of this second observation is that if this data is used to estimate γ for all risks and business lines from the Basel Committee's equation (Basel Committee, September 2001) that was included within the Introduction to this book, then the value of γ would vary significantly over time. The ratio of low value losses (€20k to €100k), which may approximate to "expected losses", to high value losses (≥€10 million), which may approximate to "unexpected losses", varies over this two-decade period between 4× and 16×.

PATTERNS IN THE RELATIVE SIGNIFICANCE OF DIFFERENT RISKS FOR DIFFERENT BUSINESS LINES

In 2001 the Basel Committee divided Operational Risk into seven subcategories of events,[3] which were used for collecting QIS-2 loss data (Basel Committee, May 2001). When the Basel Committee published the results (Basel Committee, 2002) it observed that "Over 40% of the individual loss events were categorised in the Execution, Delivery and Process Management [EDPM] event type, with another 35% categorised as External Fraud [EF]".

The data from QIS-2 and three ORX annual reports (2010, 2012 and 2014) can be used to calculate the average frequencies with which these different subcategories of Operational Risk occur. Despite the populations of these four data collection exercises/processes differing, i.e. the number of contributing banks ranges between 57 and 89, the analysis (Figure 1.3) reveals three interesting features:

1. *Frequency:* Some of these risks are more frequent than others. Even though both External and Internal Fraud involve malicious acts carried out by people, External Fraud is consistently 20× more frequent than Internal Fraud (IF);
2. *Stability:* The frequency of some of these risks also appear to be stable, e.g. EDPM, IF, Business Disruption & Systems Failure (BDSF) and Damage to Physical

---

[3]The definitions and composition of these seven subcategories will be considered in Chapter 5.

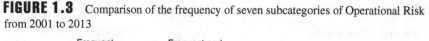

FIGURE 1.3 Comparison of the frequency of seven subcategories of Operational Risk from 2001 to 2013

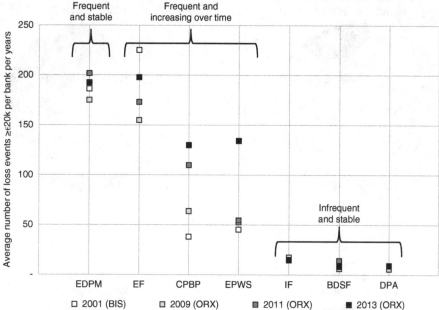

Assets (DPA). This stability is unusual. The second law of thermodynamics states that nothing in nature stays the same unless energy is being expended to keep it so, suggesting that a process may be at work here; and

3. *Dynamism:* The frequency of Clients, Products & Business Practices (CPBP) and Employment Practices & Workplace Safety (EPWS) loss events show the greatest change over this 12-year period. This suggests that these are the subcategories of Operational Risk responsible for the changing trends observed in Figures 1.1 and 1.2.

Comparing this QIS-2 data again to more recent data for the ORX membership (Figure 1.4) reveals that the relative composition of the number of losses per event type by business line is quite consistent:

Business lines: There are clear differences between the relative compositions of the number of events between Trading & Investment and Banking business lines,[4] i.e. for Trading & Investment businesses the number of loss events

---

[4]The Trading & Investment business line comprises Corporate Finance and Trading & Sales; whilst the Banking business line comprises Retail, Commercial and Private Banking.

FIGURE 1.4   Comparison of the number and value of events 1998 to 2018

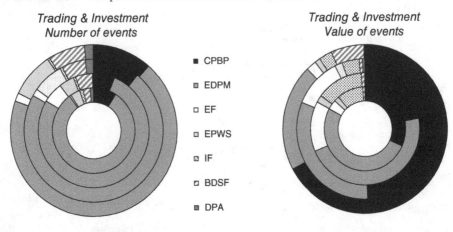

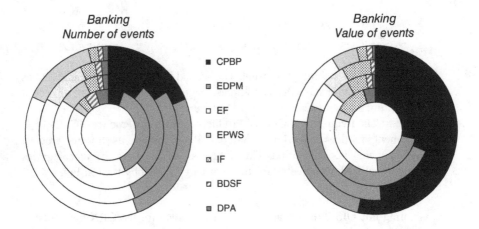

Key: The rings are in chronological order:
- The innermost ring: Loss data for 1998 to 2000 (Basel Committee, 2002);
- Then loss data for 2004 to 2008 (ORX, 2010);
- Then loss data for 2008 to 2012 (ORX, 2014); and
- The outermost ring: Loss data for 2013 to 2018 (ORX, 2019).

is dominated by EDPM; whilst for Banking businesses the number of loss events are more evenly split between External Fraud and EDPM. The relative values of losses between these two groups of business lines are also quite comparable, with the exception again of the relatively higher value of External Fraud experienced by the Banking businesses.

Number of loss events: There are increases in the relative number of CPBP and EPWS events over time across both Trading & Investment and Banking business lines. (This is consistent with Figure 1.3). There is also a steady increase in the relative number of BDSF loss events in the Trading & Investment business line, but this does not feature in Figure 1.3, potentially because it is missing data for the 2014 to 2018 period.

Value of losses: The key feature is clearly the marked increase in the relative value of CPBP losses for the period 2013 to 2018 across both Trading & Investment and Banking business lines. There is also a much less material increase in the relative contribution of the value of EPWS losses. The average values of the CPBP loss events must also be disproportionately large based upon a comparison of the pie charts on the left- and right-hand sides of Figure 1.4.

In commenting on the results of the second tranche of QIS-2, the Basel Committee noted that the "... gross loss amounts are concentrated in three event types: Execution, Delivery and Process Management (35%); Clients, Products and Business Practices (28%) and External Fraud (20%)." and that the value of EDPM losses were "smaller-than-average" whilst the value of CPBP losses were "larger-than-average". The disproportionate significance of CPBP has clearly become more marked over time.

Finally, whilst the contribution of DPA in these surveys is very small, when the QIS-2 analysis was extended to include more firms in 2001, the value of losses allocated to the DPA event type increased from 3% to 29% of total losses (Basel Committee, March 2003). This increase was attributed to the inclusion of " ... some large individual loss events associated with September 11 ... ".

In summary, despite Figures 1.1 and 1.2 showing some consistent patterns of behaviour and trends for Operational Risk, the underlying seven risk subcategories are distinctly different.

PATTERNS IN THE CONCENTRATION OF LOSSES WITHIN INDIVIDUAL FIRMS

The number of Operational Risk loss events suffered by the participants in QIS-2 varied quite significantly (Figure 1.5). Suggesting that some banks are riskier than others, assuming comparable loss data collection processes. The extent to which this is due to the composition of their business lines or the various internal causes contained within

FIGURE 1.5   Number of individual loss events reported by banks (Basel Committee, March 2002)

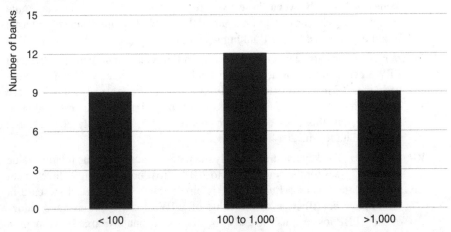

Ranges of the number of individual loss events ≥€10k per bank, log scale

the definition of Operational Risk is unclear based upon data published by the Basel Committee.

Analysis of the large losses (≥$0.1 billion) suffered by the G-SIBs pre and post the Global Financial Crisis suggests that this disparity in the losses suffered by different comparably large banks persists (Table 3.1, Chapter 3).

CONCLUSIONS

The analysis of various industry loss data collection exercises in this chapter highlights that Operational Risk displays a range of behaviours at differing levels, i.e. the overall Operational Risk level; the seven risk subcategories; business lines; and individual banks.

1. *Profile of Operational Risk losses:* The largest number of Operational Risk loss events have relatively low impacts; whilst a small number of loss events have disproportionately high impacts (Figures 1.1 and 1.2).
2. *Trends and dynamism:* There is a spike in number and value of Operational Risk loss events ≥€10 million that coincides with the aftermath of the Global Financial Crisis (Table 1.1 and Figures 1.1 and 1.2). The main driver of this is CPBP (Figures 1.3 and 1.4).

3. *Frequency and stability:* Some of the seven subcategories of Operational Risk are consistently more frequent than others, in particular EDPM and EF. The frequencies of some of these subcategories also appear to be quite stable over time e.g. EDPM, IF, BDSF and DPA (Figure 1.3).
4. *CPBP's disproportionate impacts:* The losses generated by this risk subcategory are disproportionately large (Figure 1.4) and, as noted above, it is more dynamic than many of the other subcategories of Operational Risk (Figures 1.3 and 1.4).
5. *Profile of different business lines:* The risk profiles of Trading & Investment and Banking business lines are actually quite similar with the exception that the Banking business line is more exposed to External Fraud loss events (Figure 1.4).
6. *Profile of individual banks:* The risk profiles of banks seem to differ quite markedly in terms of the volume of Operational Risk loss events that they suffer (Figure 1.5).

Observing these behaviours is interesting, but understanding them is even better, as this will allow the Operational Risk profession to develop more effective risk management tools and make better predictions. Consequently, Chapters 2 to 4 of this Part One of this book set out Ten Laws that govern these behaviours. Chapter 5 focuses upon three taxonomies that underpin these Ten Laws covering inadequacies or failures (both events and control failures); causes and impacts. Whilst Chapter 6 then considers the extent to which these laws can explain the observed behaviours of Operational Risk that were described in this first chapter.

CHAPTER 2

The Occurrence and Severity of Loss Events

This chapter sets out the first five Laws that describe for Operational Risk events: their occurrence (1st Law); their detection (2nd Law); the rapidity with which losses are incurred (velocity, 3rd Law); their duration and severity (4th Law); and the lags between detection and settlement (5th Law). This chapter concludes with an extended case study on one of the largest ever Operational Risk events, relating to Mortgage-Backed Security (MBS) litigation, which is used to illustrate these first five laws.

1ST LAW OF OPERATIONAL RISK: OCCURRENCE

The 1st Law addresses the occurrence of Operational Risk events. It states that "Operational Risk events primarily arise from human failings, either directly or indirectly, ranging from mistakes to systemic misconduct to malicious acts. The types of events suffered by firms are driven by their business profiles and are exacerbated by internal and external causes, primarily culture, governance, resourcing and process definition. They are restricted by preventive controls, which may also be weakened by these causes." This is summarised in Formula 2.1.

Formula 2.1   Occurrence of Operational Risk events

Occurrence of Operational Risk events, number of events	$\approx f$	(Business profile, Internal & external causes, Inadequacies or failures) − (Preventive controls, Inadequacies or failures, Internal causes)

Units	(Factor, Factor, Events)[1]	− (Events, Factor, Factor)
Residual propensity of occurrence in RCSAs	Inherent propensity of occurrence in RCSAs	Reduction in occurrence of events due to preventive controls

---

[1] "Business Profile" and "Causes" are numerical factors, i.e. they have no units.

EXPLANATION OF THE COMPONENTS OF THIS FORMULA

Whilst regulators define Market[2] and Credit Risks[3] in terms of external events, the Basel Committee (September 2001) knowingly defined Operational Risk in terms of the underlying causes, i.e. it is "...the risk of loss resulting from *inadequate or failed* internal processes, people and systems or from external events." This definition was intended to support the management of Operational Risk; however, the Basel Committee defined neither the nature of these inadequacies or failures, nor provided a detailed definition of the term "cause"[4], nor how these causes may relate to its event taxonomy (Annex 1 of Basel Committee, May 2001), which was intended to support quantification.

Formula 2.1 addresses these issues by representing a firm's inherent propensity for suffering an Operational Risk event as being a function of its business profile, internal and external causes and the nature of inadequacies or failures. The residual propensity for an event occurring is reduced by the firm's preventive controls, which may themselves be weakened by causes. This is summarised in Reason's Swiss Cheese Model, i.e. a loss may result when an event occurs and there are "holes" in the controls (Reason, 1990). Set out below are definitions for the key factors incorporated into this formula:

Events[5] are tangible occurrences that may (or may not) result in measurable, unintended effects (4th Law), which might include gains[6] as well as losses (Cech, 2009).

Business profile: This reflects a range of attributes of a firm, e.g. its products and services, associated customers and jurisdictions. It influences both the types of risks to which a firm is exposed and also their potential scale.[7]

---

[2]"...the risk of losses in on and off-balance sheet positions arising from adverse movements in market prices." EBA's website.

[3]"...the potential that a bank borrower or counterparty will fail to meet its obligations in accordance with agreed terms." (Basel Committee September 2000).

[4]The Basel Committee (May 2001) simply describes a cause narrowly as "...why a loss happened..."

[5]Alternatively "...an event leading to the actual outcome(s) of a business process to differ from the expected outcome(s), due to inadequate or failed processes, people and systems, or due to external facts or circumstances" (ORX, March 2018).

[6]Gains can be generated from Market Risk : Operational Risk boundary events.

[7]This is equivalent of Exposure in the XOI (Exposure, Occurrence, Impact) method (Naim and Condamin, 2019) or EI (Exposure Indicator) in the Basel Committee's (September 2001) Internal Measurement Approaches.

Causes: Whilst there are a variety of definitions of causes,[8] this book extends their scope to: "Factors that may increase either the actual or observed frequency of Operational Risk events (1st and 2nd Laws); their velocity and/or duration (3rd and 4th Laws). They may be either internal or external to a firm."

Inadequacies or failures: These constitute events, e.g. a mistake; an omission; misconduct; malicious acts; or an act of God. They also constitute control failures. Hence inadequacies or failures appears twice in Formula 2.1.

Preventive controls: These controls[9] reduce the likelihood of an incident occurring, and hence the number of events, e.g. a four eyes control prior to the release of payments. They may fail due to inadequacies or failures which may be exacerbated by internal causes, e.g. a regulator observed for one bank that "A heavy reliance on manual processes and the workload . . . meant that certain of the existing controls in place were not operating effectively." (Appendices I.3 and III).

ILLUSTRATIONS & OBSERVATIONS

Business profile

Describing business profile is challenging, it can readily become a random list of characteristics, making it difficult to determine completeness. Figure 2.1 represents the key interactions of a firm with different categories of third parties. All of these relationships collectively constitute the business profile of a firm. The nature and scale of these interactions differ depending upon the business line. The third parties listed in Figure 2.1 also represents the stakeholders with which a firm has a reputation, even criminals, i.e. banks have reputations with criminals for having strong or weak anti-fraud controls. The behaviour of these third parties may change due to either the actions of a firm or external factors (e.g. a pandemic).

---

[8] Alternatively "'Causes' typically refers only to those drivers and circumstances that lead to unintended or undesired outcomes, or operational risk events" (Cech, 2009). Whilst ORX and Oliver Wyman define causes as "the underlying environment that allows risk events to develop. These causes go beyond immediate triggers of an event such as a control failure" (ORX & Oliver Wyman, 2019). These definitions narrowly see causes as influencing only the frequency of events, but not their severity.

[9] The Basel Committee defined controls as ". . . activities designed and implemented to address risks" (Basel Committee, 1998).

The key interactions listed in Figure 2.1 may have varying significance in different jurisdictions, for example, the Basel Committee (Basel Committee, July 2009a) observed a number of regional differences in the Operational Risk profiles of banks:

- EDPM losses constitute the highest percentage of the total loss amounts in Australia and Japan;
- CPBP losses account for the majority of the total losses in Europe and North America; and
- EPWS losses represented the largest percentage of losses for Brazilian banks.

FIGURE 2.1   The business profile of a firm (Grimwade, 2020)

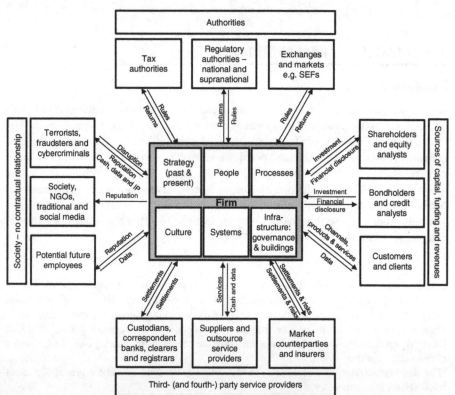

Events

"...inadequate or failed internal processes, people and system and external events", are each considered in turn:

1. *"People":* Humans are prone to make mistakes and can also be guilty of misconduct and malicious acts:
   - *Mistakes and omissions:* These commonly include "...slips, lapses, fumbles, mistakes, and procedural violations" (Reason 2000). Mistakes and omissions primarily relate to information (both physical and electronic) and its capture; storage; communication; and interpretation. Specific examples include failures to act; inaccuracies; duplications; transposition errors; replication of errors (McConnell, 2017); lost data (and assets); and miscommunication between stakeholders.
   - *Individual and systemic misconduct:* Individuals and groups of staff members can act inappropriately because it is the practice of either their firm or their industry in general.[10] For example, in the aftermath of Wells Fargo's unauthorised account opening scandal in 2016, the Bank dismissed 5,300 staff members. The culture of the firm, however, may have been a causal factor, as it was reported that former employees said that "if staff members cheated to hit targets, they did so because they feared they would lose their jobs if they did not."[11]
   - *Malicious acts:* Staff members may commit criminal acts, e.g. theft, fraud, forgery and acting dishonestly. An analysis of court cases in the UK (BDO, 2018) into the motivations, where known, of staff members who have been convicted of fraud highlights greed as the primary motivation, followed by need, e.g. the financing of addictions (drugs, alcohol and gambling) and financial need (debt and divorce).
2. *"Processes":* A poorly designed process may lead to systemic failures. It also may result in a loss event in its own right, for example, fines in the UK for poor "systems & controls". Otherwise, processes that are manual, ill-defined and ill-designed may simply facilitate mistakes and omissions; misconduct; and malicious acts.
3. *"Systems":* Outages and malfunctions are relatively common events, but with a few exceptions (e.g. physical degradation of hardware) they arise from human failings:
   - *Disruption of software:* Systems may fail, although usually when something changes, e.g. the extended outage suffered by RBS in 2012, which was caused

---

[10]The tendency for multiple firms to be simultaneously undertaking the same misconduct has led to the coining of the term Systemic Operational Risk Events, or SOREs (McConnell, 2015).
[11]*The Financial Times*, (28th September 2016) *"Wells Fargo chief faces mounting pressure"*.

by "a software compatibility issue between the upgraded software and the previous version . . . ".

- *Applications malfunctions:* Systems may continue to operate but inappropriately, e.g. in 2012 Knight Capital's order routing algo issued large numbers of erroneous sales and purchase orders.[12]
- *Hardware failures:* All physical objects degrade over time (2nd law of thermodynamics, again) and may suffer catastrophic failures, e.g. a disk failure caused data corruption, leading to an exchange halting trading in 2018.
- *Disruption of data and storage*, for example, due to quality or capacity.
- *Disruption of own infrastructure:* The connectivity within a system's architecture may be disrupted by upgrades to individual components, e.g. a bank suffered a 7-hour systems outage due to the incorrect replacement of a cable connecting its data storage to its mainframe in 2010.[13]

4. *"External"*

There are a range of external events including:

- *Third (and fourth) party failures:* These may include disruption to essential services, e.g. the UK's electricity outage in 2019 or the loss of customer data held by a third-party, e.g. the data hack of Equifax in 2017.
- *Malicious acts:* These are acts conducted by humans outside of a firm,[14] e.g. theft (Bangladesh Bank in 2015); fraud; business disruption caused by viruses; extortion and physical terrorist attacks, etc.
- *Acts of God:* Hurricane Sandy in 2012 and pandemics, e.g. the Spanish flu pandemic in 1918/19 (NB this text was written in the South of France during the pre-COVID-19 summer of 2019). The physical risks of Climate Change are considered in Chapter 16.

Table 2.1 represents the Author's view as to how these different inadequacies or failures may map to the Basel II event categories (Appendix I.1 contains examples for each shaded box). Supplementing this analysis, with the volume data from Figure 1.3, suggests that the most common loss events arise from human mistakes and omissions. Systemic misconduct by groups of staff members/firms seems to be less common, whilst malicious acts by staff members are orders of magnitude rarer still. This seems intuitively correct, i.e. people are generally honest but do make mistakes.

---

[12]Software malfunctions may arise from human failings, e.g. programming errors. Undesirable outcomes may also result from the operation of AI and machine learning (Chapter 16).

[13]These are consistent with an Financial Conduct Authority (FCA survey, November 2018) which captured both the nature and causes of IT incidents.

[14]Chapter 16 explores the use of Optimal Foraging Theory to explain/predict the behaviours of criminals.

TABLE 2.1 Author's view of the mapping of inadequacies or failures to the Basel II event taxonomy and their relative significance, based upon ORX incident data (Grimwade, 2020)

Nature of the events	Basel II event taxonomy	EDPM	CPBP	EPWS	EF	IF	BDSF	DPA
People	Mistakes and omissions	▓		▓			▓	
	Systemic misconduct		▓	▓				
	Misconduct by individuals		▓					
	Malicious acts						▓	
Systems[15]	Disruption of software							
	Application malfunctions		▓				▓	
	Hardware failures						▓	
	Disruption of data & storage						▓	
	Disruption of own Infrastructure						▓	
Process	Design/systemic failure	▓	▓	▓				
External	Third (and fourth) party failures	▓					▓	
	Malicious acts			▓			▓	
	Acts of God[16]			▓				
Significance	Average number of events ≥€20k[17] (Figure 1.3)	175 to 202	38 to 130	45 to 134	155 to 225	15 to 18	6 to 14	6 to 9

[15] System and process failures often also arise from human failures in designing these systems and processes. System failures may also arise from failures of operation.

[16] Including the impacts of Climate Change, e.g. storms/extreme rainfall; floods; rising sea levels; and storm surges (UNEP 2020).

[17] Several of these data points arise from the Basel Committee's QIS-2 data collection exercise, which used a threshold of ≥€10k.

Comparing the relative financial impacts of these event categories for 2013 to 2018, published by ORX, however, reveals that the absolute and average losses, for the same period, primarily arising from systemic misconduct (i.e. CPBP), are around 2½ times (i.e. €87 billion/€33 billion) and 3½ times (€1,121k/€321k)[18] larger respectively than the losses relating to mistakes (i.e. EDPM). This probably reflects the increased quantum of failure and duration for systemic events (3rd and 4th Laws).

Internal & external causes

Large Operational Risk loss events most often have multiple causes, hence some banks employ the "5 Whys" technique to establish the root cause (Chapter 13). Data on the multiple causes of Operational Risk losses is not systematically reported publicly. In order to understand the significance of the different causes, the Author has reviewed the cited causes in 16 well-documented[19] events which have also been collated into a causal taxonomy (Chapter 5 and Appendix III). The extent to which there are multiple cited causes of these events (the shaded squares) is demonstrated in Table 2.2. This analysis reveals a number of patterns in the explicit causes.

For large losses there are typically more than one cause, with the average for this small but well-documented sample being 4½ causes. Rogue trading events seem to involve the highest number of contributing causes, although this may be an artefact of their level of investigation and disclosure. The most commonly cited internal causes[20] of Operational Risk losses are:

- **Strategy**, e.g. typically in the form of incentive schemes,[21] which probably links to systemic and individual misconduct, e.g. a regulator noted "... sales and rewards could have exacerbated the risk of poor sales practices". Incentives are specifically designed to alter the behaviours of staff. Issues often seem to arise when staff behaviours are altered by incentives in an unintended manner!

---

[18]"Annual Banking Loss Report Operational Risk loss data for banks submitted between 2013 and 2018", (ORX, December 2019).
[19]Described within regulatory notices, published reports, legal settlements and submissions to legislative bodies, although the level of description of the contributing causes to these events often appears to be more detailed within Europe than the US.
[20]These causes may not apply to the whole firm, which may explain why researchers have identified organisational complexity as a key causal factor which may underpin many of these commonly cited causes (Chernobai et al, 2018).
[21]Research has suggested a link for US banks between Operational Risk losses and CEO remuneration and corporate governance. (Chernobai et al, 2011).

- *Governance*, primarily clarity over responsibilities and reporting lines, e.g. in one notice a regulator referenced "... unclear accountabilities, starting with a lack of ownership of key risks at the Executive Committee level". This may clearly undermine the effectiveness of the key controls.
- *People*, e.g. expertise and resourcing levels. Another regulator noted "... the IT Risk team ... was understaffed and its level of skill and resource was insufficient." This probably links to the propensity for humans to make mistakes and for control functions to have the time to challenge.
- *Process*, e.g. the lack of documented procedures. Another regulator described a failure "... to establish adequate processes ..." This also probably links to the propensity for human errors.

This suggests that the UK's Senior Managers Regime framework is actually quite well judged as it is targeted upon two of the key causal factors highlighted above, i.e. the clarity of responsibilities and the ability to cancel and clawback past incentives.

Culture seems to be relevant to a range of risks and variously relates to the "tone from the top" and also the differing behaviours of the first and second lines. Although intuitively culture should be more relevant for Conduct Risks/CPBP, this was generally implicit rather than explicitly referenced. The Author expects internal causes, such as culture, to influence a bank's Operational Risk profile by both making events more likely to occur and also weakening its mitigating controls.

These internal causes may be both correlated and also reinforce each other, producing feedback loops and domino effects, driving the concentration of loss events in individual banks (6th Law). Analysis of the overlaps between the causes in Table 2.2 reveals that the strongest correlations seem to be between strategy, culture, governance, people and process.[22] Whilst the most important external cause for CPBP, IF and EDPM is *currently* economic cycles, which can lead to industry-wide losses, and will be considered further in the 7th Law. In the coming years, however, COVID-19 and Climate Change may lead to the environmental change becoming the most important external cause (Chapter 16).

---

[22]Research published by the Federal Reserve, Richmond found for US banks "statistically significant correlations between macroeconomic growth and losses in CPBP and EDPM" (Abdymomunov, 2014).

TABLE 2.2 Identification of the explicit causes of 16 well-documented Operational Risk events (Grimwade, 2020)

Basel taxonomy and events → / Business profile and causes ↓	CPBP (Conduct Risk)							IF				EDPM	EPWS	EF	BDSF	
	LIBOR rigging	Mis-sale of investments	Mis-sale of derivatives	Mis-sale of PPI	Various conduct issues	Unauthorised acc opening	Sanctions & AML breach	Rogue traders (2004)	Mis-marking (2008)	Rogue trader (2011)	"London Whale"[23]	Improper foreclosure	Sex discrimination	Data hack	Rogue algo	Extended IT outage
1. Strategy — Objectives, sales incentives				■	■	■	■	■	■	■	■					
1. Strategy — Products & services, e.g. complexity		■	■								■					
1. Strategy — Customers, e.g. sophistication				■												
2. Culture, e.g. "tone from the top"	■	■	■	■	■	■		■	■	■	■		■			
3. Governance, e.g. oversight, policies etc	■						■					■			■	■
4. People, e.g. expertise, resourcing levels etc		■	■		■			■	■	■	■	■	■	■	■	■
5. Processes, e.g. design	■						■					■				■
6. Systems, e.g. age, architecture														■	■	■
7. Change re: people, processes & systems								■								■

Business profile causal categories: 1. Strategy.
Basel II internal causal categories[24]: 2–7.

[23] This has not been categorised as Internal Fraud as in July 2017 the Department of Justice abandoned its criminal cases against two JPMorgan Chase traders.

[24] Research on US banks between 1980 and 2005 found that the most commonly cited primary causes of loss events were "management action/inaction; employee action/inaction; lack of control; and omission" (Chernobai et al, 2011).

TABLE 2.2 (*Continued*)

Basel taxonomy and events → / Business profile and causes ↓ (External causal categories[25])	CPBP (Conduct Risk)							IF			EDPM		EPWS	EF		BDSF
	LIBOR rigging	Mis-sale of investments	Mis-sale of derivatives	Mis-sale of PPI	Various conduct issue	Unauthorised acc opening	Sanctions & AML breach	Rogue traders (2004)	Mis-marking (2008)	Rogue trader (2011)	"London Whale"	Improper foreclosure	Sex discrimination	Data hack	Rogue algo	Extended IT outage
8. Societal change, e.g. compensation culture				■												
9. Technological change, e.g. big data, AI & robotics																
10. Economic cycles, e.g. falls in asset prices	■	■	■					■	■		■	■				
11. Environmental change, e.g. extreme weather																
12. Geopolitical change, e.g. new trade sanctions							■									
13. Regulatory change, e.g. new requirements																

[25]The first five of these external causes are the five categories of threats considered by the World Economic Forum (2021).

IMPLICATIONS

Understanding why inadequacies or failures lead to events is central to the management of Operational Risk. This 1st Law explains a number of behaviours of Operational Risk that have previously been observed and understood by experienced risk managers.

Whilst the importance of a firm's business profile in determining its Operational Risk profile is unambiguous, Figure 2.1 provides a more systematic approach to capturing a firm's relationships with its stakeholders. This can assist a risk manager in identifying material omissions in a firm's risk assessments and scenario analysis. It also defines the broad set of stakeholders with which a firm has a reputation (Chapter 13).

Understanding the different types of inadequacies or failures (Table 2.1) that result in Operational Risk events should help risk managers to better assess the likelihood of these occurrences, i.e. human errors leading to mistakes and omissions are much more likely than systemic misconduct, which in turn is much more likely than malicious acts by individuals. Acts of God, by definition, are even rarer still.[26] In Banking businesses, human errors are as commonplace as the malicious acts of external criminals, which are an ever-present threat. The observation that the majority of Operational Risk events "... arise from human failings" may explain why just a single distribution (Poisson) is typically used to model the frequency of occurrence of events (Chapter 10).

Formula 2.1 highlights that causes can make Operational Risk events more likely to occur by either making inadequacies or failures more likely and/or by weakening the effectiveness of the mitigating preventive controls. Hence metrics which gauge the status of a cause may be predictive of the occurrence of future events. The predictive power of a metric will depend upon whether it is informative as to the likelihood of the occurrence of inadequacies or failures (a Key Risk Indicator or KRI) and/or the effectiveness of a preventive control (a Key Control Indicator, a KCI). Consequently the dashboards of "predictive KRIs" used by firms should combine both:

- *Predictive KRIs:* metrics which are informative of causes that make inadequacies or failures more likely; and
- *Predictive KCIs:* metrics which are informative as to the operational effectiveness of controls that prevent persistent threats, e.g. patching backlogs may be predictive of successful cyberattacks.

Clearly demonstrating that either KRIs or KCIs are truly predictive of future Operational Risk events is more likely to be possible for risks involving human mistakes and omissions or malicious acts of external criminals, which lead to a higher volume of events, than for acts of God, like a pandemic.

---

[26]Events may be rare either because they are intrinsically remote, or because the preventive controls are generally effective.

Finally, when firms are conducting *Risk & Control* Self-Assessments they should additionally focus on assessing the existence of the most commonly cited causes of large loss events (Table 2.2), e.g. strategy, including incentive schemes; governance; people (e.g. resourcing and expertise); and processes. These are especially important due to the observation that there appear to be correlations and feedback loops between these causal factors. This will be explored further in Chapter 5.

2ND LAW OF OPERATIONAL RISK: DETECTION

The 2nd Law considers the detection of events. It states that "The frequency of *reported* Operational Risk events reflects detection rates of both currently occurring losses and historical undiscovered failures. Strengthening detective controls increases the frequencies of reported events, whilst weakening them may lower the observed frequency, in the short term." Detection success determines the duration of incidents, see 4th Law. This 2nd Law is summarised in Formula 2.2:

Formula 2.2   The frequency of reported events

$$
\text{Frequency of reported events, events per period,}^{27,28} \approx \frac{(\text{Currently occurring events} + \text{Historical undetected events})}{\text{Reference period}} \times \text{\% Detection rate}
$$

Units:
$$
\frac{(\text{ Events } + \text{ Events })}{\text{Time}} \times \text{\%}
$$

EXPLANATION OF THE COMPONENTS OF THIS FORMULA

This formula explains that the volume of reported Operational Risk events is a function of the number of the events that have occurred historically, but are undetected, as well as those that are currently occurring and a firm's current detection rate of events. The detection rates, in the short term, are driven by the effectiveness of a firm's detective controls, which can themselves be weakened by internal causes. Additionally, internal and external causes may also act as catalysts for detection. Set out below are definitions for the key factors incorporated into this second formula:

---

[27]This is equivalent of occurrence in the XOI (Exposure, Occurrence, Impact) method (Naim and Condamin, 2019) or PE (Probability) in the Basel Committee's (September 2001) Internal Measurement Approaches.

[28]This implies that there is a second derivative of Frequency, i.e. Events/Time^2, the rate of change of frequency (Chapter 7).

Currently occurring losses: Loss events that are occurring during the current reference period.

Historical undiscovered losses: Loss events that have occurred in prior periods but have not been detected until the current period, i.e. end date may not equal detection date.[29]

Detection rate: Detective controls are designed to detect events that have occurred, and hence may reduce the duration of an ongoing event, rather than prevent them from occurring. The detection rate is the percentage of events detected. Consequently, a weakening of detective controls by internal and external causes may reduce the frequency of reported losses, in the short term. Additionally, undiscovered losses may also be identified through serendipity or discovery triggered by another event, e.g. past issues with loan documentation may only come to light as a result of a decision to sell the loans. External causes may also impact detection rates, for example, an economic shock may reveal historical cases of mis-sales, e.g. interest rate swaps mis-sold to Small & Medium Enterprises (SMEs) in the UK prior to the Global Financial Crisis.[30]

ILLUSTRATIONS & OBSERVATIONS

Average lags between occurrence and detection, for losses >€20k, vary by event types (Table 2.3), ranging from two months to almost two years, with CPBP-related losses having the longest lags.

TABLE 2.3   Average lags (days) by event types for losses >€20k for ORX members (BIS, 2020)

3 months		3 to 6 months		6 to 12 months		>1 year	
DPA	66	EF	117	EDPM	254	CPBP	566
BDSF	77	EPWS	165	IF	299		

---

[29] JK Galbraith coined the word "bezzle" for undiscovered embezzlement that builds up during a boom and may then come to light during a subsequent crash (Galbraith, 1955).

[30] "... the crisis forced a massive review of collateralised lending ... This undoubtedly identified a number of sleeping issues, and as a result detection of cases of External Fraud was brought forward, thereby increasing losses" (Cope and Carrivick, 2013).

Analysing the reporting of large loss events (≥$0.1 billion) for 31 G-SIBs over more than two decades reveals some further key differences:

1. The frequency of these large losses increased following the Global Financial Crisis, i.e. from once every 4 years (1996 to 2006) to once every 1 ¼ years (2007 to 2017), a factor of 3.2×;
2. The number of years when a G-SIB did not suffer a large loss reduced following the Global Financial Crisis, i.e. from 80% of the years to 65% of the years for 1996 to 2006 and 2007 to 2017 respectively; and
3. The highest number of occurrences of large losses for a single bank in the same year increased from three to ten, pre and post the Global Financial Crisis.

Consequently, in addition to changes in occurrence (1st Law), and the effectiveness of detective controls (2nd Law), as mentioned above, there can be other catalysts for discovery of historical incidents, for example:

1. *Firm-level changes*, such as the integration of a new acquisition, e.g. the migration of live products/trades onto a new platform may identify historical mis-bookings. The discovery of one event may also lead to the identification of others, for example, at UBS, following the detection of $2.3 billion of unauthorised trading losses in 2011, the Bank uncovered, during its subsequent reviews of controls, three unrelated unauthorised trading incidents, leading to the dismissal of two staff members.[31]
2. *Industry-wide incidents (e.g. SOREs)* that highlight past, industry-wide misconduct or errors and may lead to either internal or regulatory reviews, e.g. the initial discovery of benchmark manipulation led to the subsequent discovery of many more instances across multiple firms and markets, i.e. interest rates, FX and commodities.
3. *Economic shocks* can highlight past failures. For example, the introduction of negative interest rates, after the Global Financial Crisis, led to Operational Risk losses being suffered by the arrangers of some asset-backed securities (ABS), if they unknowingly failed to include floors within their structures. ABS tend to pay noteholders a floating rate coupon, and hence the structure includes interest rate swaps to hedge the underlying fixed-rate securities or loans. In the aftermath of the Global Financial Crisis swap reference rates became negative in the eurozone and Japan, causing some special purpose vehicles (SPV) that issued ABS to have to pay on both the fixed and the floating legs of their swaps (Risk.net, September 2016). This cost could not be passed onto the investors in the ABS, leaving it to be borne by the arrangers (Figure 4.3).

---

[31] *Reuters* (18th October 2012) "UBS found three other unauthorised trading incidents, court told".

FIGURE 2.2   The duration of large losses (≥$0.1 billion) by time bucket as a % of total number of loss events, pre and post the Global Financial Crisis (Grimwade, 2020)

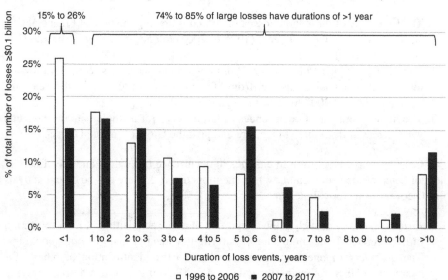

Analysing the duration of large losses (≥$0.1 billion) suffered by 31 current and former G-SIBs reveals even longer lags, with only 18% of incidents identified within 12 months, i.e. on average 82% of large losses identified in a year have had a duration of more than one year. Figure 2.2 compares the duration of these large losses pre and post the Global Financial Crisis, and highlights that average durations were 1.3× higher after the Global Financial Crisis (i.e. 3.4 years vs 4.2 years). As described above, this may reflect that the Global Financial Crisis was a catalyst for the discovery of historical Operational Risk incidents.

NB These large losses are dominated by CPBP events.

IMPLICATIONS

When undertaking RCSAs it is important for firms to understand that the current year's losses may be driven by weaknesses in both a firm's current and historical preventive controls and also its current detective controls, in particular relating to CPBP. Consequently, past loss events may indeed be a good predictor of losses in the near future. This is explored further in Chapter 8.

Finally, the variable nature of detection rates also means that banks that reduce their expenditure on controls may, rather counter-intuitively, observe a short-term reduction in reported Operational Risk loss events, if their detective controls are weakened.

3RD LAW OF OPERATIONAL RISK: VELOCITY[32]

The 3rd Law considers the rapidity with which losses (or gains) are suffered. It states that "The rapidity (velocity) with which firms suffer losses (or gains) between an event occurring and ceasing is driven by the quantum of inadequacies or failures; causes and the nature of the impacts generated by the event", i.e. fines and penalties are low velocity, whilst Market Risk boundary losses have the highest velocities, up to 1,000 times greater than regulatory fines. This is summarised in Formula 2.3.

Formula 2.3 Velocity – the rapidity with which losses or gains are suffered

Velocity, \$ of loss per period $\approx f$ of time[33]

$$\frac{\text{(Quantum of inadequacies or failures, Internal causes)} \times \text{(Nature of the impacts, External causes)} - \text{(Corrective controls, Inadequacies or failures, Causes)}}{\text{Time period between commencement and cessation}}$$

Units:

$$\frac{(\text{ Events, Factor }) \times (\text{ \$, Factor }) - (\text{ \$, Factor, Factor })}{\text{Time}}$$

EXPLANATION OF THE COMPONENTS OF THIS FORMULA

Formula 2.3 articulates the factors which determine the rapidity with which banks suffer losses or gains. Set out below are definitions for the key factors incorporated into this third formula:

> *Quantum of inadequacies or failures:* The magnitude of errors,[34,35] e.g. the number of mis-sales or erroneous trades. It reflects the scale of a firm's business

---

[32]There are a number of different definitions of risk velocity. In "A new dimension to Risk Assessment" Marta Ruiz Chaparro, (Chaparro, 2013) defines two terms covering: (a) Following the risk event, how long will it take for the impact to unfold; and (b) From the known position today, how long will it take for the risk to materialise? The definition of (a) is similar to the 5th Law: Lags in settlement.

[33]This implies that there is a second derivative of Velocity, i.e. Losses/Time^2, the rate of change of Risk Velocity, which is Risk Acceleration or Deceleration (Chapter 7).

[34]This is equivalent of Exposure in the XOI (Exposure, Occurrence, Impact) method (Naim and Condamin, 2019) or EI (Exposure Indicator) in the Basel Committee's (September 2001) Internal Measurement Approaches.

[35]McConnell states that "...the size/severity of any losses incurred relate to the estimated amount of information that has been corrupted and the length of time that corruption can be observed..." (McConnell, 2017).

profile and also the nature of the event, i.e. systemic or one-off. It may be exacerbated by internal causes. For example, a regulator observed for one bank that "Thousands of employees engaged in improper sales practices to satisfy goals and earn financial rewards under the Respondent's incentive program".

Nature of the impacts: Basel III (Basel Committee 2017a) defines impacts as:

- Direct charges, *including impairments and settlements, to the bank's P&L accounts and write-downs due to the operational risk event; and*
- Costs incurred *as a consequence of the event including external expenses with a direct link to the operational risk event (e.g. legal expenses directly related to the event and fees paid to advisors, attorneys or suppliers) and costs of repair or replacement, incurred to restore the position that was prevailing before the operational risk event.*

     The combination of the quantum of failure and the nature of impacts are a key component of any assessment of inherent severity/impact.

     A more detailed taxonomy of impacts is incorporated into Chapter 5 and Appendix II.

Corrective/resilience controls: These neither prevent events from occurring nor detect when an event has occurred, but instead they limit the impacts of an event, e.g. a throttle control that limits the volume of trades that an algo can generate in a defined period of time (Chapter 16).

ILLUSTRATIONS & OBSERVATIONS – THE NATURE OF IMPACTS

There are relatively few examples for which the total cost of a large loss event is fully disclosed. Examples of fuller disclosure include the data breach at Equifax in 2017; the extended systems outage at TSB in 2018; Danske Bank's AML issues at its Estonian branch (ongoing); and Payment Protection Insurance (PPI) settlements for some banks (Table 2.4). Reviewing these events and others with more limited disclosure illustrates the relative significance of the nature of the different impacts resulting from these events, i.e. the largest component of losses are variously compensation to customers; Market Risk losses; fines and penalties; and loss of assets (e.g. theft of cash)/write-downs of banking book assets (e.g. loans).

TABLE 2.4 The relative significance of different categories of financial[36] impact (Grimwade, 2020)

Events			Direct charges				Costs incurred		
	Impacts		Compensation	Market Risk	Fines & penalties	Loss/write-down of assets/P&L	Incremental costs	Third-party costs	Improving controls[37]
Fuller disclosure	Mis-sale of PPI	£19bn							Unknown
	AML breach[38]	Kr55bn			Potential settlement				
	Data hack[39]	$1.7bn							40
	Extended IT outage	<£½bn			Yet to be imposed				Unknown
Partial disclosure	Improper foreclosure	$25bn						Unknown	
	Mis-sale of MBS	$16bn						Unknown	
	London Whale[41]	$7bn						Unknown	
	Rogue trader	$6bn						Unknown	
	Rogue algo	$½bn						Unknown	

Key: % of total losses

≥76%   51% to 75%   25% to 50%   <25%

[36] Some of these incidents may also impact a firm's business, its customers and its markets, i.e. its Operational Resilience.

[37] Enhancement and remediation are excluded from the new Standardised Approach (Basel Committee 2017a).

[38] Danske Bank's 2018 financial statements disclosed Kr1.5bn of income attributable to its Estonian non-resident portfolio which may be confiscated and a Kr2bn 3-year AML investment programme. In Q1 2019 it disclosed Kr3.5bn of class action lawsuits. Analysts believe that global fines may be ~Kr50bn ("What's next in Danske Bank scandal", *The Financial Times*, 17 October, 2018).

[39] Equifax's Q1 2019 Financial Statements list the costs as: legal matters ($690 million); technology and data security ($390 million); legal and investigative fees ($185.5 million); and product liability ($86.5 million).

[40] Equifax's 2018 Annual Report states "In 2018, we added nearly 1,000 IT and security professionals to our workforce. We sought highly specialized, technical and diverse talent that will help Equifax develop a world-class security organization."

[41] Market Risk losses of $6.2 billion (2012), regulatory penalties of $920 million (2013) and an investor settlement of $150 million (2015).

The relative scale of fines and penalties may reflect whether they arise from systems and control failures as opposed to deliberate breaches. These direct charges are significantly larger than the other costs incurred (e.g. third-party costs and the costs of improving controls), where known. The nature of these different costs and their distributions can influence the shape of a bank's loss distribution. The size of losses are driven by the scale of a bank's operations, the quantum of failure (see below) and the distributions of the underlying losses, e.g. Market Risk, can be very fat-tailed.

ILLUSTRATIONS & OBSERVATIONS – THE QUANTUM OF FAILURES

It is quite intuitive that the quantum of error should be a contributing factor to the scale of loss, and equally that systemic errors will be more significant than individual mistakes and omissions. Examples include the mis-sale of PPI: LBG sold ~16 million PPI policies between 2000 and 2011, whilst HSBC sold only 5.4 million policies between 2000 and 2007/8, when it ceased selling the product. Losses are driven by differing volumes of policies mis-sold; customer claims rates and average settlements (Table 2.5).

ILLUSTRATIONS & OBSERVATIONS – VELOCITIES

An analysis of different impacts (Figure 2.3) reveals that there is a very significant range of typical velocities, i.e. up to 1,000×:

- Fines and penalties, e.g. AML breaches, have velocities of approximately <$10 million per day;
- Compensation, (e.g. PPI) and stolen assets (e.g. SWIFT cyber frauds) both have velocities ranging between $10 million to $100 million per day;
- Damage to physical assets, e.g. due to extreme weather. These are *currently* quite rare, but intuitively they will be very high velocity events; and
- Market Risk, e.g. rogue algos and traders have the highest velocities >$100 million per day.

TABLE 2.5 Analysis of PPI settlements as at 31st December, 2018

Banks	Duration	Policies sold	Claims rates	Average settlements	Cost
LBG	2000 to 2011	16.0 million	53%	£2,300[42]	£19.5 billion
HSBC	2000 to 2007/8	5.4 million	43%	$2,200	$5.1 billion

[42]LBG's average settlement charge includes admin costs.

Despite fines, penalties and compensation impacts having lower velocities than Market Risk, they can still generate comparable or larger absolute impacts, through the steady accretion of losses over many years. In addition to the quantum of failure, the range of velocities variously reflects the extent to which:

- Mitigating controls evolve between events over a period of time, e.g. SWIFT cyber-payment frauds (Figure 4.1). This is considered further in the 8th Law;
- Rogue algos may distort the market place in which they are operating, creating a tipping point that disproportionately exacerbates a firm's losses (Grimwade, 2019). This is discussed further in Chapter 16; and
- Certain impacts are sensitive to external causes, primarily economic downturns in the form of deteriorating credit worthiness; increased market volatility; and directional market moves, such as the appearance of negative interest rates and negative commodity prices.

Finally, Figure 2.3 also implies that generally events can either have high velocities or lead to high absolute losses but not both. Losses arising from acquisitions, however, are an exception. Through the acquisition of other firms, the acquiring firm can potentially become a successor-in-interest in litigation involving its newly acquired

FIGURE 2.3   Differing rates of velocity of five significant Operational Risks with differing types of underlying losses (Grimwade, 2020)

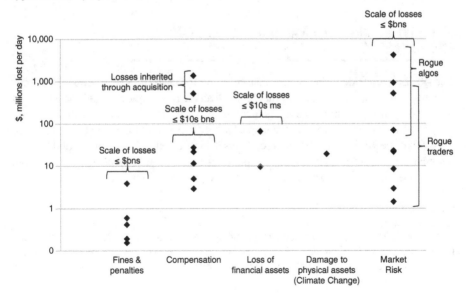

subsidiary. If the duration of due diligence is short, then the resulting legal settlements can have both high absolute values and velocities, i.e. on a par with a malfunctioning algo. This suggests that due diligence relating to acquisitions may actually be one of the most important occasional controls for mitigating Operational Risk.[43]

Analysing losses $\geq$\$0.1 billion pre and post the Global Financial Crisis (i.e. 1996 to 2006 vs 2007 to 2017) reveals that velocity increased 2.3×, i.e. from \$2.1 million per day to \$4.7 million per day. The apparent sensitivity of velocities to an economic shock will be explored further in Chapter 3.

IMPLICATIONS

As a consequence of the range in velocities (i.e. up to 1,000×), banks need to implement controls aligned to the velocity of their risks. Whilst Formula 2.3 includes corrective/resilience controls there are generally few controls to mitigate velocity, for all but the highest velocity risks. Examples include throttle controls that limit the volume of trades that an algo can generate during a defined period of time, and maybe also pre-acquisition due diligence. For most risks, with lower velocities, the mitigating controls instead relate to restricting the duration of an event, e.g. controls for ensuring regulatory compliance can be end of day/end of month. Finally, the wide variations in the scale of different impacts of events may explain why a variety of distributions are typically used to model severity (Chapter 10).

4TH LAW OF OPERATIONAL RISK: DURATION AND SEVERITY

The 4th Law considers the factors that combine to drive the severity of loss events. It states that "The severity of an incident reflects a risk's velocity and the length of time to detection (for large losses the average is ~4 years). Average velocity declines with increased duration (average loss peaks between years 3 and 5). The severity of a loss may be limited by detective controls which accelerate discovery and corrective/resilience controls, e.g. insurance, that reduce the consequences of an event. Both may be weakened by internal causes." This is summarised in Formula 2.4.

---

[43]The significance of Operational Risk losses arising from acquisitions is consistent with a meeting the Author had in the mid-1990s with the Head of Strategy of a major international bank, who claimed (correctly) that he had the greatest ability to destroy value for his bank through an ill-judged acquisition.

Formula 2.4 Drivers of the severity of Operational Risk losses or gains

Severity[44] of losses, ^{45} $\approx f$ (Velocity $\times$ (Duration $-$ (Detective controls, Inadequacies or failures, Internal causes)))
$-$ (Corrective controls, Inadequacies or failures, Internal causes)

Units: ($ / Time $\times$ (Time $-$ (Time, Factor, Factor))) $-$ ($, Factor, Factor)

"Length of time to detection"

| Residual severity in RCSAs | Inherent severity in RCSAs |

EXPLANATION OF THE COMPONENTS OF THIS FORMULA

Formula 2.4 articulates that the severity of losses is driven by duration or "length of time to detection" multiplied by velocity less the effects of detective and corrective/resilience controls. Set out below are definitions for the key factors incorporated into this fourth formula:

Duration: The length of time between an event commencing and ceasing, i.e. the failure of a preventive control before the success of a detective control. Duration and velocity are most relevant for losses that accrete over time rather than events where losses are almost instantaneous, e.g. a terrorist attack. Other events may involve a single failure at a point in time, generating an exposure that deteriorates over time, e.g. a mis-hedged structured product.

Corrective/resilience controls: As per the 3rd Law, although the corrective/resilience controls in this formula would also include controls such as risk transference via insurance policies and recovery sites to enhance Operational Resilience. For example, whilst the total cost of Equifax's 2017 data hack is currently estimated at $1.7 billion, the firm has made a successful $125 million insurance claim.[46] These controls may be weakened

---

[44]This is equivalent of impact in the XOI (Exposure, Occurrence, Impact) method (Naim and Condamin, 2019) or LGE (Loss Given Event) in the Basel Committee's (September 2001) Internal Measurement Approaches.

[45]From an Operational Resilience perspective severity may be measured in time (i.e. the duration of disruption), rather than $.

[46]Equifax's Q1 2019 Financial Statements "... we have received the maximum reimbursement under the insurance policy of $125.0 million..."

by internal causes leading, for example, to a failure to comply with the requirements of a firm's insurers. (Chapter 12 considers the extent to which the impacts of Operational Risks can be transferred via insurance policies). Corrective/resilience controls may also be involved in obtaining recoveries.

An assessment of duration, in the absence of detective controls is a key contributor to any assessment of inherent severity/impact.

ILLUSTRATIONS & OBSERVATIONS

The average duration of losses ≥\$0.1 billion is ~4 years[47] both pre and post the Global Financial Crisis (i.e. 3.4 years for 1996 to 2006 and 4.2 years for 2007 to 2017). This small increase in duration post the Global Financial Crisis (1.3×) may reflect an increase in the detection of historical loss events as described by the 2nd Law. Additionally, Figure 2.4 highlights that there is a spike in losses with durations of >10 years during the period of 2007 to 2017. This primarily consists of the payment of compensation regarding PPI in the UK covering 2000 to 2011 and the settlement of prolonged breaches of US sanctions that, in some cases, dated back to the 1990s. The scale of compensation in the UK may have been exacerbated by the development of both a claims culture and industry. Removing these two categories of events from the data set leads to comparable duration periods pre and post-crisis.

Analysis of loss data both pre and post the Global Financial Crisis (Figure 2.4) reveals that the average velocity reduces with increased duration of loss events, however, average losses peaked between years 3 to 5. (If the average values of losses were normally distributed then the post-crisis losses in years 3 to 4 represent an almost 3 STD event or 0.4% probability.) Average velocity is clearly higher for the period 2007 to 2017 than 1996 to 2006 (Figure 2.4). This is discussed further in the 7th Law.

IMPLICATIONS

When conducting RCSAs, Operational Risk managers should avoid *just* undertaking trigger-based RCSAs, as is the current fashion amongst some firms, as the largest average loss events will typically arise from incidents with an average duration of between 3 and 5 years, that may be occurring in plain sight, and involve systemic misconduct. This is considered further in Chapter 8.

---

[47] Study conducted using IBM FIRST Risk Case Studies loss data from 1980 to 2005 has previously observed that "¾ of all events last no more than 48 months" (Chernobai et al, 2011).

FIGURE 2.4 Duration and average value of losses and velocity, pre & post crisis (Grimwade, 2020)

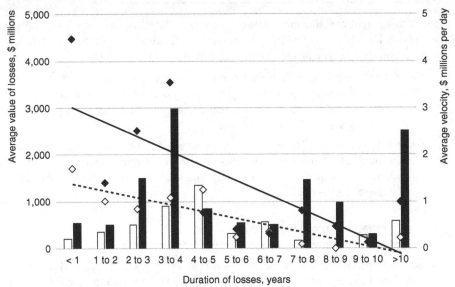

□ Average value of losses – 1996 to 2006   ■ Average value of losses – 2007 to 2017

◇ Average velocities – 1996 to 2006   ◆ Average velocities – 2007 to 2017

5TH LAW OF OPERATIONAL RISK: LAGS IN SETTLEMENT

The 5th Law considers the lags that occur between the detection of an event and the settlement of losses. It states that "The length of time between detection and settlement is linked to systemic misconduct; regulatory involvement; litigation; sensitivity to economic cycles; and the distribution of compensation to customers. Almost three quarters of large losses crystallise over a year after detection." This is summarised in Formula 2.5.

Formula 2.5   Total losses equals current and prior year events

Net losses crystallising in the current year	≈	Incidents detected and losses and recoveries crystallise in the current year	+	Incidents that were detected in prior years but losses and recoveries crystallise in the current year
Units: %, by value for large losses (≥$0.1bn): 1989 to 2007		$ 28% by value	+	$ 72% by value

EXPLANATION OF THE COMPONENTS OF THIS FORMULA

This formula highlights that almost three quarters of the value of losses ≥$0.1 billion that the G-SIBs suffer in any particular year actually relate to prior years. Set out below are definitions for the key factors incorporated into this fifth formula:

> *Current year net losses:* These incidents are detected and losses and recoveries crystallise within 12 months, i.e. the majority of the direct charges are incurred in that year, although costs of enhancing controls and any subsequent fines may be incurred in subsequent years, e.g. the London Whale.

> *Prior year net losses:* These incidents are detected in prior years, but for which the majority of the losses are incurred and recoveries made in subsequent years, e.g. compensation paid to customers relating to the mis-sale of PPI or insurance recoveries.

ILLUSTRATIONS & OBSERVATIONS

The lags between detection and recognition also vary by event types (BIS, 2020), i.e. the shortest average lags are EF and EDPM (<100 days) and the longest are for CPBP and EPWS (261 and 448 days respectively). Whilst analysing large loss events (≥$0.1 billion) suffered by 31 current and former G-SIBs between 1989 and 2017 reveals larger lags between detection and recognition of Operational Risk events (Figure 2.5), i.e.:

1. *Sudden losses (18% by value of large losses):* Most categories of Operational Risks crystallise almost immediately upon detection, e.g. internal and external frauds, systems' failures and processing errors. Some of these events may have some exposure to economic cycles, e.g. mis-marking of MBS in response to market falls (Table 2.6); improper foreclosure; and staff litigation following headcount reductions; and

2. *Clients, Products & Business Practices (82% by value of large losses).* These losses have average lags of 3 to 4 years, involve systemic misconduct and can be split between:
   - Losses involving systemic misconduct, but which are *insensitive* to economic cycles (36% of large losses by value), e.g. AML fines, benchmark manipulation and the mis-sale of PPI.[48] These losses are not directly linked to economic

---

[48]It is arguable whether some PPI losses were actually linked to economic cycle as some claims of mis-sale may have been fuelled by purchasers who became unemployed during the Global Financial Crisis, and were unsuccessful claiming on their policies (Grimwade, 2016). Similarly the Global Financial Crisis highlighted the vulnerability of benchmark to manipulation.

FIGURE 2.5 Historical lags between detection and settlement for losses ≥$0.1 billion for 31 current and former G-SIBs (Grimwade, 2018)

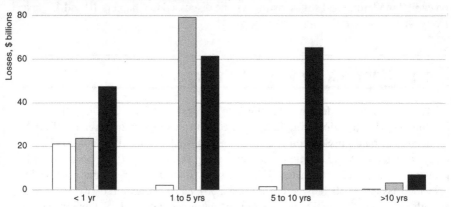

□ Sudden & insensitive to economic cycles (IF, EF, EDPM, BDSF, DPA & EPWS)   ■ Lagging & sensitive to economic cycles (CPBP)
□ Lagging & insensitive to economic cycles (CPBP)

cycles. The extended settlement period reflects a combination of the duration of both regulatory investigations and civil litigation, and, in the case of PPI, the process of receiving and handling individual customer claims; and

■ Losses involving systemic misconduct, which are *sensitive* to economic cycles (46% of large losses by value). Examples include MBS and collateralised debt obligation (CDO) litigation and the mis-sale of swaps. These exhibit the longest lags, maybe reflecting that in addition to the duration of regulatory reviews and civil litigation there are also lags in an economic slowdown leading to investors suffering losses (the 7th Law) and the uncovering of historical misconduct.

Banks establish provisions for these events over a number of years and often, when they finally settle, there is limited impact on their current year's P&L, e.g. in May 2018 RBS reached a $4.9 billion MBS settlement in the US, and announced that it had already established a $3.46 billion provision. This will be explored further in the 7th Law.

IMPLICATIONS

These lags, relating primarily to CPBP, should be reflected in firms' approaches to capital modelling and stress testing, i.e. stressed business plans should reflect not only when loss events are likely to settle but also the likely intentions of firms to establish provisions over a number of years in advance of any final settlement. The timing of banks establishing provisions will be explored further in Chapter 3, whilst the impacts on capital modelling and stress testing will be discussed in Chapters 10 and 11, respectively.

CASE STUDY FOR THE FIRST FIVE LAWS

This case study is designed to illustrate the first five laws. It utilises information from the litigation brought by the Federal Housing Finance Agency (FHFA) against 17 banks in September 2011. The FHFA alleged that the banks had made false statements and omitted material facts in selling ~$200 billion of MBS to Fannie Mae and Freddie Mac. The case study focuses on one of these 17 banks, which issued MBS between 2005 and 2007 and also acquired two issuers of MBS in 2008 ("... at the request and encouragement of the U.S. Government"), through which the parent bank became a successor-in-interest in the subsequent litigation.

1st Law: Occurrence of Operational Risk events

The US Department of Justice concluded that *all* of the 103 MBS issuances, arranged by the parent bank between Q4 2005 and Q3 2007 and by the subsidiaries that it acquired in 2008, had misleading prospectuses.

Occurrence of Operational $\approx f$ Risk events, number of events	(Business profile, Internal causes, Inadequacies or failures) – (Preventive controls, Inadequacies or failures, Internal causes)

103 Misleading MBS prospectuses	$\approx$	103 Misleading MBS prospectuses from Q4 2005 to Q3 2007 and via two acquisitions in 2008	–	0 Third-party due diligence was overridden by management

Business profile: The parent bank was one of the largest issuers of private MBS in 2007 with a 5.7% market share. Its two acquisitions in 2008 made it a successor-in-interest in an additional 12.5% share (i.e. 6.8% and also 5.7%) of the US MBS issuances in 2007.

Inadequacies & failures: The inaccuracies included loan-to-value (LTV) for properties and also the percentage of properties not owner occupied in these misleading prospectuses and are illustrated in Table 2.6 along with the outcomes:

TABLE 2.6 An extract from an US Securities & Exchange Commission (SEC) lawsuit

Example tranches of MBS	Inaccuracies				Outcomes		
	% with LTV ≤ 80%		% non-owner occupied		Credit ratings: Moody's, S&P, Fitch		% delinquent/ defaulted/ foreclosed
	Prospectus	Data review	Prospectus	Data review	When issued	At July 2011	
2005-A2	95%	56%	16%	27%	Aaa/ AAA/–	Caa3/ CCC/–	24%
2006-RM1	57%	35%	4%	12%	Aaa/ AAA/ AAA	Caa2/ CCC/ CC	50%
2007-CH2	57%	41%	5%	15%	Aaa/ AAA/ AAA	B3/B/ CCC	45%

Preventive controls: Banks used third-party due diligence vendors which graded the loans that they reviewed. Loans would be rejected, for example, for high loan-to-values; or unreasonably high income or property valuations; or inadequate or missing documentation, etc. In some instances the banks overrode the due diligence ratings either through case-by-case review of the rejected loans or through "bulk" waivers.

Internal causes: Competition both to provide mortgages to customers and to sell MBS to investors "led to a reduction in diligence and oversight" on the part of the bank, and from 2005 to 2007, the bank's underwriting guidelines and origination standards were "deteriorating." (FHFA, 2011). In addition, during this period mortgage loan originators throughout the industry pressured appraisers to issue inflated property valuations that met or exceeded the amount needed for the subject loans to be approved, regardless of the accuracy of such appraisals.

(Continued)

2nd Law: The frequency of reported events

The misleading nature of the prospectuses was only identified when the FHFA undertook a review of a sample of loans. Hence the detection rate of the inadequacies or failures for the MBS issuances arranged by the parent bank by the end of 2007, was zero.

Frequency of reported events, events per period	$\approx$	(Currently occurring events + Historical undetected events)	$\times$	(Detective controls, Inadequacies or failures, Causes)
		Reference period		

0 events	$\approx$	6	+	24	$\times$	0%
		Misleading MBS prospectuses (2007)	+	Misleading MBS prospectuses (2005 & 06)		
		1 year (2007)				

The parent bank understood when it acquired two banks in 2008 that it would be the successor-in-interest to any litigation arising from their activities prior to their acquisition. The profile of how the parent bank became exposed to litigation on these MBS issuances is set out in Figure 2.6.

FIGURE 2.6   Profile of the accretion of the parent bank's exposure to litigation on these MBS issuances (Grimwade, 2020)

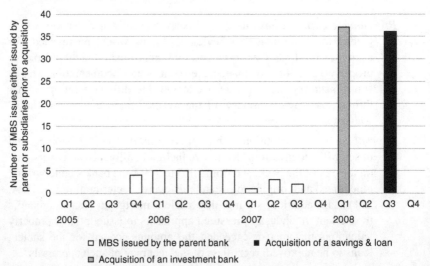

In summary, approximately two-thirds of the parent bank's MBS litigation exposure resulted from its two acquisitions in 2008.

3rd Law: Velocity – the rapidity with which losses are suffered

There are two velocities for this loss, i.e. one for the accretion of exposure by the parent bank of MBS issues that it arranged (see below) and another relating to the two acquisitions that it made in 2008.

Velocity, $ of loss per period of time for the parent bank	$\approx f$	(Quantum of inadequacies or failures, Internal causes) $\times$ (Nature of the impacts, External causes) $\times$ (Corrective controls, Inadequacies or failures, Causes)
		Time period between commencement and cessation
$2.26bn p.a.	$\approx$	$4.7bn of MBS issued per year by the parent bank $\times$ 48% average settlement rate[49]

As highlighted in Figure 2.3, the velocities on the two acquisitions are approximately two orders of magnitude higher, due to the short duration of the due diligence.

> *Quantum of inadequacies or failures:* All of the 30 prospectuses produced by the parent bank contained inaccuracies, as described previously. The total value of these issues was $9.4 billion.

> *External causes:* The economic slowdown led to foreclosure rates peaking in Q4 2009 at 16% for Alt-A and 29% for subprime loans.

> *Nature of the impacts:* The[49] loans underpinning the MBS issued by the parent bank had levels of delinquency, default, and foreclosure of between 15% and 63%. This deterioration in the performance of the underlying loans led to the credit ratings on the MBS falling from AAA to sub-investment grades. Subsequent legal settlements comprised claims by investors, consumer relief and regulatory penalties against the banks, with an average value of 48% of the value of securities underwritten (Figure 2.7).

(Continued)

---

[49]The ABX AAA index dropped ~40% between July 2007 and March 2008.

FIGURE 2.7   Relationship between value of MBS issued and penalties and settlements (Grimwade, 2020)

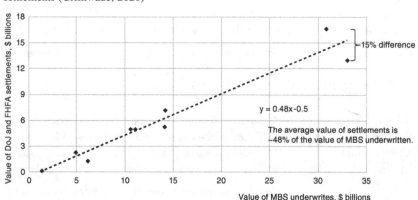

4th Law: Drivers of the severity of Operational Risk losses

The scale of the loss suffered by the parent bank was driven by the velocity of losses (i.e. the volume of MBS that was issued with misleading prospectuses and by the value of poor quality underlying loans, leading to investor losses) and the duration of their issuance (i.e. 2 years).

Severity ≈ (Velocity × (Duration − (Detective controls, Inadequacies or of failures, Internal causes))) − (Corrective controls, Inadequacies losses, $ or failures, Internal causes)

$4.5bn   ≈   ($2.26n pa × (2 years − 0 reduction by detective controls))
                        − (13.5% reduction in rejected loans)

> *Corrective controls:* The third-party due diligence vendors did reject some inappropriate loans, e.g. one of the parent bank's vendors observed, that between Q1 2006 and Q2 2007, 27% of loans reviewed by them were initially rejected, of which around half remained rejected whilst the other half of these "rejected" loans were subsequently accepted. This may have contributed to a reduced settlement, as a percentage of issued MBS, which is ~15% lower than that for another major issuer (Figure 2.7).

5th Law: Total losses equals current and prior year events

This litigation for MBS is clearly an event which occurred prior to 2013, i.e. between 2005 and 2008.

Losses crystallising in the current year	$\approx$	Losses discovered and crystallised in the current year	$+$	Events that were discovered in prior years but crystallise/settle in the current year
%, by value for large losses ($\geq$\$0.1bn): Charge for MBS litigation to litigation provision		0		\$13bn

Although the settlement was reached in Q4 2013, provisions for this litigation were established in prior quarters (Figure 2.8), including \$9.15 billion in Q3 2013.

FIGURE 2.8 Charges (and releases) from the parent bank's litigation provision (Grimwade, 2020)

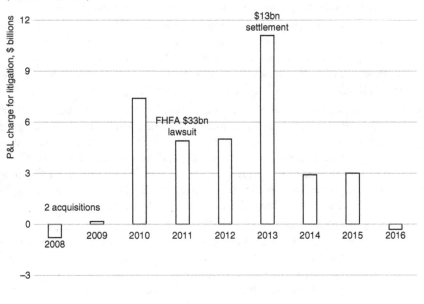

CONCLUSIONS

The first five laws detail the factors involved in:

1. The occurrence of events (1st Law);
2. The detection of events (2nd Law);
3. The rapidity with which firms suffer losses, i.e. velocity (3rd Law);
4. The duration of events and the severity of losses (4th Law); and
5. The varying lags between detection and settlement (5th Law).

Understanding these factors is clearly central to the management of Operational Risk. Key observations made in this chapter include:

Inadequacies or failures: Different inadequacies or failures, which constitute Operational Risk events, are to varying degrees responsible for the seven risk subcategories (Table 2.1). Understanding that EDPM is driven by human error – whilst CPBP is driven by systemic misconduct, Internal Fraud by individual malicious acts and DPA by acts of God – helps to explain the differing frequencies of these risks. This is considered further in Part Two. Inadequacies or failures also constitute control failures.

Business profile: Whilst the importance of a firm's business profile in determining its Operational Risk profile is unambiguous, Figure 2.1 provides a more systematic approach to capturing a firm's relationships with its stakeholders and their quantum. It also defines the broad set of stakeholders with which a firm has a reputation. This is considered further in Chapter 13.

Causes and predictive metrics: Formula 2.1 highlights that causes can make Operational Risk events more likely to occur by either making inadequacies or failures more likely and/or by weakening the effectiveness of preventive controls. The predictive power of a metric will depend upon whether it is informative as to the likelihood of the occurrence of inadequacies or failures (a KRI) and/or the effectiveness of a preventive control (a KCI). This is also considered further in Chapter 13, which includes a section on predictive metrics.

Causes and RCSAs: Causes are central to the first four laws. Consequently, when firms are conducting RCSAs they should additionally focus on assessing the existence of the most commonly cited causes of large loss events (Table 2.2), i.e. strategy, including incentive schemes; governance; people (e.g. resourcing and expertise); and processes. These are especially important due to the observation that there appear to be correlations and feedback loops between these causal factors (Chapter 5). The implications are considered further in Chapter 8 on RCSAs.

Detection of events and RCSAs: When undertaking RCSAs it is also important for firms to understand that the current year's losses may be driven by weaknesses in both a firm's current and historical preventive controls and also its current detective controls. Consequently, Operational Risk managers should avoid *just* undertaking trigger-based RCSAs, as is the current fashion amongst some firms, as the largest average loss events will typically arise from incidents with average durations of between 3 and 5 years, and which may well be occurring in plain sight. This will also be considered further in Chapter 8.

Velocity of losses: Whilst Formula 2.3 includes corrective/resilience controls, there are generally few controls to mitigate velocity, for all but the highest velocity risks. Examples include a real-time throttle control that limits the volume of trades that an algo can generate during a defined period of time. For most risks, with lower velocities, the mitigating controls instead relate to restricting the duration of an event, e.g. controls for ensuring regulatory compliance can be end of day/end of month. This will be considered further regarding both RCSAs and scenario analysis in Chapters 8 and 9, respectively.

Lags between detection and settlement: These lags, relating primarily to CPBP, should be reflected in firms' approaches to capital modelling and stress testing, i.e. stressed business plans should reflect not only when loss events are likely to settle but also the likely intentions of firms to establish provisions over a number of years in advance of any final settlement. The timing of banks establishing provisions will be explored further in Chapter 3, whilst the impacts on capital modelling and stress testing will be discussed in Chapters 10 and 11, respectively.

Sensitivity to economic cycles: Analysis of losses $\geq\$0.1$ billion suffered by the G-SIBs pre and post the Global Financial Crisis indicates that an economic slowdown adversely influences occurrence/detection (1st and 2nd Laws); velocity (3rd Law), duration and severity (4th Law), and lags (5th Law). This will be investigated further in Chapter 3, and subsequently again in Chapters 10 and 11 on capital modelling and stress testing, respectively.

Concentration and Systemic Operational Risk Events (SOREs)

This chapter considers the extent to which internal (6th Law) and external drivers (7th Law) lead to the concentration of losses within firms and across the industry. This is important for regulators setting minimum capital requirements (Pillar 1 & 2A) and buffers (Pillar 2B) to absorb losses in periods of stress.

6TH LAW OF OPERATIONAL RISK: CONCENTRATION DUE TO INTERNAL DRIVERS

The 6th Law considers the internal factors influencing the concentration of losses within banks. It states that "Different risks are concentrated because they are sensitive to the same internal causal factors that primarily drive occurrence. These factors lead to concentrations of events within banks." This is summarised in Formula 3.1.

Formula 3.1   Drivers of concentration of Operational Risk losses in banks

		Average frequency of events			Average severity per event	
Average losses	≈	(Occurrence	+ Detection)	×	(Velocity ×	Duration)
Units:		(Events / time)		×	($ / time ×	Time)
Comparison of different firms		1st and 2nd Laws Driven by internal causes			3rd Law Driven by internal causes[1]	4th Law

---

[1]"Some causes immediately precede an event (triggers), others are facilitative, occurring in the background (environmental conditions), still others magnify the impact of an event once it is already in progress (exacerbators)" (Cech, 2009).

EXPLANATION OF FORMULA

Two or more risks may display signs of correlation if they respond in the same internal causal factors by either increasing or decreasing their frequency of occurrence/detection; and/or their velocity; and/or their duration.

ILLUSTRATIONS & OBSERVATIONS

In terms of large losses suffered between 1996 and 2006, Table 3.1 highlights that the most significant differentiator between three quantiles of G-SIBs is the frequency of loss occurrence/detection.

The top tercile of G-SIBs suffered 79% of the large loss events during this 11-year period. In contrast, velocity and duration are smaller differentiators of concentration. Analysing the composition of large loss events ($\geq$$0.1 billion) suffered by the 11 current and former G-SIBs with the highest number of large losses from 1996 to 2006 reveals that over 90% of these events, by number, relate to losses involving primarily either systemic or individual misconduct (Figure 3.1). These are linked to causes (Table 2.1) such as strategy, including incentives; people (e.g. expertise and resourcing), and to a lesser extent governance and culture. This is higher than for the middle tercile of 10 banks, for which misconduct driven risks were only 78%.

In terms of the composition of these three quantiles of G-SIBs analysed earlier:

- The bottom tercile: the largest constituent group are Asian banks;
- The middle tercile: the largest constituent group are European banks; and

TABLE 3.1   Differing Operational Risk profiles of 31 G-SIBs for 1996 to 2006 (Grimwade, 2020)

3 quantiles of 31 G-SIBs for 1996 to 2006	Average frequency of losses ≥$100 million	Average velocity per event of losses ≥$100 million	Average duration per event of losses ≥$100 million
Bottom tercile of 31 G-SIBs	An event every 110 years[2]	$92m p.a.	3.5 years
Middle tercile of 31 G-SIBs	An event every 6.1 years	$134m p.a.	2.9 years
Top tercile of 31 G-SIBs	An event every 1.8 years	$160m p.a.	3.5 years

---

[2]This tercile suffered just one event during this period.

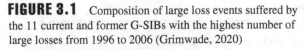

FIGURE 3.1　Composition of large loss events suffered by the 11 current and former G-SIBs with the highest number of large losses from 1996 to 2006 (Grimwade, 2020)

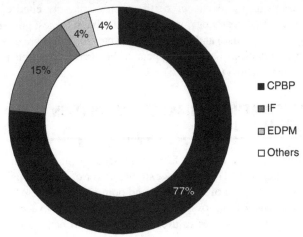

- The top tercile: the largest group are American banks. (NB All of the banks that are in this top tercile, remain in this group when the same analysis is performed for the period 2007 to 2017).

This geographical bias may reflect a combination of both differing business profiles, e.g. the greater contribution of trading and fee income to the revenues (10th Law) of the US and European banks, as well as the differing regulatory regimes in their home jurisdictions, and incentive schemes.

Post-crisis, across the industry, there was a wave of discoveries of Systemic Operational Risk Events (McConnell, 2015), such as mis-sale of MBS, CDOs and derivatives and regulatory breaches, e.g. benchmark manipulation. These SOREs were concentrated primarily amongst the US and European banks. There is no one reason for this concentration but instead it is probably the combination of the business profiles, cultures and control frameworks of these banks, and management's and staff members' responses to the same internal and external pressures, as well as a degree of cross-pollination of practices between banks through staff moves and third parties, such as brokers. The discovery of malpractice in one firm often led the management of other banks and regulators to discover similar malpractice elsewhere (2nd Law).

IMPLICATIONS

When firms are conducting *Risk & Control* Self-Assessments they should additionally focus on assessing the existence of the most commonly cited causes of large loss events (Table 2.2), e.g. strategy, including incentive schemes; governance; people (e.g. resourcing and expertise) and processes (Chapter 8). These are especially important due to the observation that there appear to be correlations and feedback loops between these causal factors (Chapter 5).

7TH LAW OF OPERATIONAL RISK: CONCENTRATION DUE TO EXTERNAL DRIVERS

The 7th Law considers the external factors influencing the concentration of losses within banks. It states that "The primary external driver of Operational Risk are business cycles, due to a mixture of economics and human behaviour. After an economic shock, some Operational Risk losses rise: existing losses are exacerbated, historical failures uncovered and responses to a crisis may lead to new losses.[3] Occurrence, velocity, duration and lags all increase. [This is summarised in Formula 3.2.] After a severe downturn losses come in waves: first Market, then Credit, and finally Operational Risk."

Formula 3.2 Ratio of Operational Risk losses pre & post an economic shock

Ratio of losses pre & post an economic shock	Ratio of average frequencies pre & post an economic shock	Ratio of average severities pre & post an economic shock		Ratio of lags in settlement for CPBP losses sensitive : insensitive
≈	(Occurrence + Detection)	× (Velocity	× Duration)	, Lags
Units:	(Ratio + Ratio)	× (Ratio	× Ratio)	Ratio
	1st and 2nd Laws	3rd Law	4th Law	5th Law
Comparison of pre & post-crisis, i.e. 2007 to 2017 vs 1996 to 2006	3.2× Driven by the interaction between internal & external causes	2.3×	1.3×	1.6×
		2.9× Driven by the interaction between internal & external causes[4]		

---

[3]The Basel Committee describes these as "Feedback (second round) effects" (Basel Committee 2017b).

[4]"Some causes immediately precede an event (triggers), others are facilitative, occurring in the background (environmental conditions), still others magnify the impact of an event once it is already in progress (exacerbators)" (Cech, 2009).

This is essentially the same formula as Formula 3.1, with the addition of lags in settlement, but the ratios in this example are being calculated pre and post an economic shock, i.e. the Global Financial Crisis.

ILLUSTRATION & OBSERVATIONS

Although the definition of Operational Risk makes no reference to any causes of losses that can be readily linked to economic cycles, losses rose after the Global Financial Crisis. It is difficult to obtain a consistent data set of Operational Risk losses over time; consequently, Figure 3.1 contains a plot of Operational Risk losses as a % of revenues for ORX members since 2004 – both consolidated loss data and also split between two business lines, i.e. Trading & Investment and Banking. This metric has been selected because it is in the public domain and, as a ratio rather than absolute losses, it should be less impacted by the expansion of ORX's membership over time.[5] Whilst the average ratio of losses to revenues across the ORX members is 2.3%, the peak, in the aftermath of the Global Financial Crisis in 2011 is 6.2%. This represents an approximate three STDs increase, making 2011 a 1-in-300-year event, which seems broadly appropriate, for the worst economic slowdown since the Great Depression. (This is consistent with the trends observed earlier in Figures 1.1 and 1.2 and also Table 1.1). Figure 3.2 also

FIGURE 3.2　Operational Risk losses as a % of annual revenues for 2004 to 2019 (sources: ORX's Annual Loss Reports for 2010, 2012, 2014, 2017, 2018, 2019 and 2020)[6]

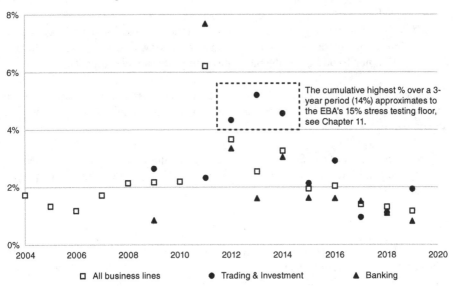

The cumulative highest % over a 3-year period (14%) approximates to the EBA's 15% stress testing floor, see Chapter 11.

□ All business lines　　● Trading & Investment　　▲ Banking

---

[5]The Basel III requirement for banks with revenues of >€1 billion to disclose their annual loss data for each of the years of their ILM calculations (Basel Committee, 2017) will significantly aid this type of analysis in future.

[6]The data point for 2006 is actually the average ratio of Operational Risk losses to revenues for the period 2004 to 2008.

shows that whilst both Trading & Investment and Banking business lines experienced increases in losses after the Financial Crisis, the peak years differ, i.e. 2013 and 2011 respectively.

Analysing large loss events (≥$0.1 billion), suffered by banks in the aftermath of the Global Financial Crisis, reveals that on average they occurred more frequently, and had both higher velocities and longer durations than in the proceeding 11 years. Overall this led to an increase in the total value of large losses of ~9×. (This is similar to the ratio of peak to trough ratios of losses as a % of revenues.)

The correlations are, however, complex, as illustrated by considering the occurrence and detection of fraud in the aftermath of the Global Financial Crisis:

> *First-party fraud*, e.g. application fraud declined,[7] maybe because as banks retrenched their lending activities, both fraudsters and customers alike found it harder to obtain loans (Figure 11.3). Anecdotally, desperation frauds associated with secured lending increased in response to the Global Financial Crisis, e.g. car dealerships that had obtained loans secured on their forecourts of cars, may sell these cars out of trust, i.e. without repaying their loans to their bank, in order to pay other creditors, such as their payroll.

> *Second-party fraud*, i.e. fraudulent payments initiated by client staff ("bookkeeper frauds"). Anecdotally,[8] discovery of these frauds increased. These frauds often come to light when a company suffers financial pressures. The owners or administrators may then sue their banks for any losses arising from the banks allowing these fraudulent payments to be made outside of an account's mandate.

> *Third-party fraud*, e.g. account takeover frauds. These increased, as maybe professional fraudsters redirected their efforts away from first-party frauds. (Chapter 16 addresses the motivations of professional criminals.)

The Global Financial Crisis also resulted in new loss events arising from the responses of banks and also sometimes individual staff members to the economic shock. Examples include:

- *Systemic misconduct:* Settlements by banks for improper foreclosure; misleading financial information on their proprietary ABS exposures and also employee litigation;[9]

---

[7]Data sourced from Cifas.

[8]Additionally " ... the crisis forced a massive review of collateralised lending ... This undoubtedly identified a number of sleeping issues, and as a result detection of cases of External Fraud was brought forward ... increasing losses" (Cope and Carrivick, 2013).

[9]For US banks research suggests that EPWS losses are negatively correlated with GDP (Abdymomunov, 2014); similarly, in the UK employment tribunal cases for unfair dismissal and discrimination seem to lag rising unemployment (Grimwade, 2016).

TABLE 3.2 Drivers for Operational Risks events rising during an economic slowdown

Drivers of these Operational Risk losses	Examples of losses
1. Existing losses are exacerbated, whilst others decline, e.g. due to reduced business volumes. (1st and 3rd Laws)[10]	*Occurrence and velocity:* ■ Payment errors, e.g. accidental payments to Lehman. ■ A rise in account takeover frauds (third-party frauds). ■ But a decline in application frauds (first-party frauds). ■ Fat-finger typing losses are larger in volatile markets.
2. Historical failures uncovered via Real Options (2nd and 4th Laws)	*Detection/duration and velocity:* ■ Mis-sale MBS, CDOs and interest rate derivatives. ■ Negative rates and prices revealed asymmetries in structured notes and log normal functions in models. ■ "Bookkeeper frauds" (second-party frauds). ■ Benchmark manipulation came to light in the crisis.
3. Responses to an economic shock may lead to new losses, e.g.: ■ Firms' responses; or ■ Individuals' responses; or ■ Customers' responses. (1st Law)	*Occurrence and velocity:* ■ Failure to treat customers fairly in financial difficulties, e.g. inappropriate foreclosure in the US. ■ Misleading disclosures on proprietary ABS exposures. ■ Mis-marking of proprietary ABS books by staff. ■ Staff litigation regarding bonuses and dismissals. ■ Frauds of "need" conducted by customers.

■ *Individual misconduct:* E.g. A trader who manipulated the price of a gilt in a QE auction in 2011; and

■ *Malicious acts:* Traders who mis-marked their ABS books in 2007/08 in response to falling prices.

These different drivers of these are summarised in Table 3.2.

---

[10]Research indicates a pattern "... where the frequency of losses in the early-crisis period (H2 2006 to H2 2007) was similar or slightly lower than pre-crisis losses, then increased above pre-crisis levels in the peak-crisis period (H1 2008 to H1 2009), and finally fell off to lower levels in the late crisis period (H2 2009 to H2 2011)." This pattern was clearest for External Fraud and EDPM (Cope and Carrivick, 2013).

Historically, large Operational Risk losses have spiked to varying degrees at least three times over the last three decades. Each spike is associated with either the bursting of an economic bubble or the impact of a monetary policy response to an economic shock, i.e. the six unexpected US dollar interest rate hikes in 1994; the bursting of the dot.com bubble in 2001; and the Global Financial Crisis that resulted from the bursting of the US residential property bubble.

Analysing the occurrence of large losses suffered by 31 current and former G-SIBs shows that pre-crisis single large loss events were rare (1 in 7 years), and multiple large losses occurring in the same year at the same bank were rarer still (1 in 20 years). Whilst post-crisis the occurrence of single large events was unaltered, the occurrence of multiple events increased to 1 in 5 years (Figure 3.3). These multiple, same-year loss events were concentrated in the same 11 G-SIBs both pre- and post-crisis. This seems to be consistent with the Basel Committee's observations in Chapter 1 on differences between firms as to the occurrence of Operational Risk losses (Figure 1.5).

Analysing the nature of the impacts of these large loss events (i.e. ≥$0.1 billion) reveals that ~60% by value are linked to either deteriorating Credit Risk (53%), e.g. MBS and CDO litigation; post-underwriting litigation and improper foreclosure;

FIGURE 3.3   The occurrence of large losses (≥$0.1 billion) discovered at the same bank in the same year

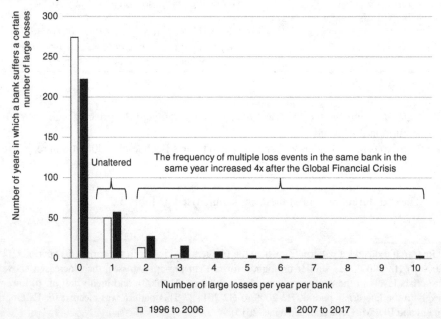

and directional market movements (7%), e.g. the mis-sale of interest rate derivatives and fixed income products and unauthorised trading (Figure 11.1).

Real Options can provide an explanation for this observation, i.e. when firms have mis-sold or misrepresented investment products or hedges, they effectively grant their customers and investors a Real Option – the right (but not the obligation) to claim redress if they suffer losses. These Real Options can be triggered by economic shocks that cause customers and investors either to suffer losses or lost opportunities, and consequently to sue their banks, due to their misconduct, i.e. these Real Options are de facto American options. In practice, this can turn the Market and Credit Risk losses of customers and investors into Operational Risk losses for their banks (9th and 10th Laws). Re-analysing the data from the case study allows the nature of a Real Option to be revealed. Plotting estimated fee income from MBS arranged by one US bank (and its subsidiaries) between 2005 and 2007 that were subject to litigation, and the resulting settlement, produces a graph that clearly resembles the pay-off for a short call option (Grimwade, 2019). Overlaying delinquency rates of the underlying mortgages indicates both how this Real Option was triggered (Figure 3.4) and the drivers of severity.

Just like with a financial option, Figure 3.4, implies that an economic shock of sufficient scale will trigger litigation relating to instances of past misconduct. An even more severe economic shock, however, may not necessarily trigger any more litigation, but the resulting settlements/Operational Risk losses, may be even more severe, as the scale of settlements will be proportionate to the level of economic loss suffered by the litigants. This may prove to be very important regarding any such Real Options that are triggered through the economic consequences of the COVID-19 pandemic.

FIGURE 3.4 Triggering an Operational Risk Real Option: US MBS litigation and mortgage delinquency rates (Grimwade, 2020)

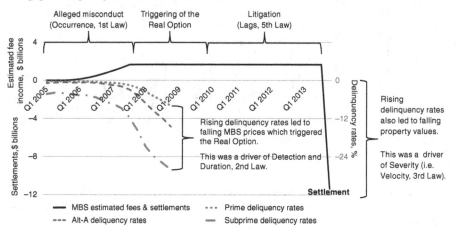

Correlations with Market & Credit Risks

The 5th Law describes the occurrence of lags between detection and settlement, which vary, depending upon the nature of the Operational Risk events. Whilst most banks do not disclose their total Operational Risk losses, some banks do publish their annual charges for litigation and regulatory settlements, which represent a significant proportion of their total Operational Risk losses. Analysing these charges for 13 large banks (a subset of the 31 current and former G-SIBs)[11] reveals that after the Global Financial Crisis, losses from different risk types came in sequential and overlapping waves (Figure 3.5), i.e.:

- 2008: Market Risk losses peaked, as measured by negative trading revenues;
- 2009: Credit Risk losses peaked, as measured by impairment charges; and
- 2013: Operational Risk losses peaked, as measured by charges for litigation and regulatory settlements. (Grimwade, 2018).

This profile of charges for litigation and regulatory settlements looks different from the profiles of Operational Risk losses in Figure 3.2. This reflects that in ORX's

FIGURE 3.5   Profile of trading losses (Market Risk), impairments (Credit Risk) and litigation and regulatory settlements (Operational Risk) for 13 banks (Grimwade, 2020)

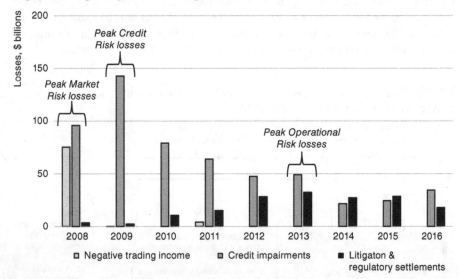

[11]The data is sourced from the financial statements of 13 current and former G-SIBs. The financial statements of the other G-SIBs did not provide sufficient disclosure to include in this analysis.

annual reports, all subsequent losses relating to a single event, such as PPI, are recorded in the year that a provision was initially established, i.e. 2011 for PPI. In contrast, Figure 3.5 shows the actual years in which all subsequent charges were reported by banks in their financial statements. Analysing further the lags in settlements of CPBP losses represented in Figure 2.5 indicates that the lags for CPBP losses that are sensitive to economic cycles are ~1.6× longer than for CPBP losses that are insensitive to economic cycles.

External events

An external event can also lead to industry-wide loss events/SOREs. In Chapter 1 it was noted that whilst the contribution of Damage to Physical Assets in the initial QIS-2 surveys was very small (3% of total losses), when the QIS-2 analysis was extended to include more firms in 2001, the value of losses allocated to DPA increased to 29% of the total losses (Basel Committee, March 2003). This increase was attributed to the inclusion of "... some large individual loss events associated with September 11 ...". A consequence of Climate Change may be an increase in these non-economic external drivers of industry-wide losses (Chapter 16).

IMPLICATIONS

The 7th Law implies that economic shocks lead to increases in both the average frequency and severity of large losses. The more severe the economic shock, the greater the severity of the Operational Risk losses suffered by banks. Whilst the 5th Law described the observed lags between detection and settlement, Figure 3.5, shows the relative timing as to when Market, Credit and Operational Risk losses peak after an economic shock. The 5th Law also indicates that lags increase for CPBP losses after an economic shock.

As Operational Risk displays cyclicality, the methodology for calculating capital requirements should be based upon a "through the cycle" approach for cyclical Operational Risks, reflecting both their sensitivities and lags, that avoids increasing a bank's capital requirements at a point in the cycle when it is least able to raise new capital (Grimwade, 2018). This will be explored further in Chapters 10 and 11 on capital modelling and stress testing respectively.

CONCLUSIONS

Operational Risk managers often focus upon the enhancement of specific controls to mitigate either the potential occurrence of a specific risk or the recurrence of an actual loss event. Instead, the 6th and 7th Laws suggest that Operational Risk managers would be better advised to focus upon the following situations:

- The underlying causes that may lead to a concentration of Operational Risk losses within their own bank. The most commonly cited causes of large loss events (Table 2.2) are strategy, including incentive schemes; governance; people (e.g. resourcing and expertise); and processes. As noted earlier, these are especially important due to the observation that there appear to be correlations and feedback loops between these causal factors.
- Controls relating to specific products and services that may generate Operational Risk losses in the event of an economic shock. This is considered further under the 9th and 10th Laws.

CHAPTER 4

Homeostasis, Risk Transference, Transformation and Conservation, and Active Risk Taking

This chapter explores the extent to which Operational Risk losses reflect the responses of firms and their stakeholders (8th Law); the transference, transformation and conservation of risk (9th Law), and the proactive taking of Operational Risk in return for income (10th Law).

8TH LAW OF OPERATIONAL RISK: RISK HOMEOSTASIS

The 8th Law considers how banks respond to loss events by investing in their controls. It states that "Over time a firm's expenditure on controls will increase in order to keep its expected Operational Risks in equilibrium with its risk appetite. Whilst for emerging risks, control expenditure will rise in anticipation of increased future losses, e.g. the mitigation of Y2K." This is summarised in Formula 4.1.

Formula 4.1 The equilibrium between risk and control

Appetite for $\approx$ expected losses over time, \$ / time	(Δ Occurrence $-$ Δ Preventive Controls) $\times$ (Δ Duration $-$ Δ Detective Controls) $\times$ (Δ Velocity $-$ Δ Corrective / Resilience Controls)
Units:	(Events / Time)　$\times$ (Time)　$\times$ (\$ / Time)

EXPLANATION OF THE COMPONENTS OF THIS FORMULA

Risk Homeostasis suggests that humans maximise their benefit by comparing the expected costs and benefits of safer and riskier behaviours to achieve a "target level of risk" (Wilde, 1998). Applying this theory to Operational Risk suggests that risk and control should equilibrate to keep firms within appetite.

ILLUSTRATION & OBSERVATIONS

The observation in Chapter 1 that the occurrence of some risks is quite stable (Figure 1.3), may imply the existence of Risk Homeostasis. The observable responses of the industry to new risks provide more tangible evidence of its existence. For example, the first publicly disclosed SWIFT cyber-payment fraud occurred in 2015. Analysing SWIFT cyber-payment frauds, in the public domain (Bouveret, 2018), supplemented with recent losses, reveals the trend in the success of these frauds appears to be downwards[1] (Figure 4.1), possibly reflecting the significant industry-wide responses to the first frauds.

Risk Homeostasis is also driven by the tendency of professional criminals to optimise their strategies, akin to the concept of Optimal Foraging Theory observed by zoologists (this is discussed further in Chapter 16). Evidence of this can be seen in the opportunistic responses of criminals to advantageous situations, involving both customer confusion and disruption of banks. For example, the extended TSB systems outage in April 2018 resulted in £49 million of fraud and operational losses.

FIGURE 4.1   Gross and net losses from public SWIFT cyber-payments frauds over the last decade

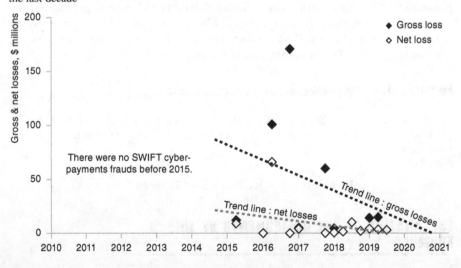

---

[1]The correlation coefficient of the net losses is negative 0.41.

Similarly, it is likely that the COVID-19 pandemic will generate customer uncertainty and disruption to banks, e.g. staffing shortages may reduce customer access to both branches and call centres and also weaken the responsiveness of IT departments. These circumstances will probably lead to cybercriminals increasing their attempts at a range of frauds including account takeover fraud.[2]

Risk Homeostasis can also be observed in the interactions between regulators and banks. Over the last two decades the scale of regulatory fines in the UK has clearly increased. At the end of 2002, the largest fine ever imposed by the Financial Services Authority (FSA) was £4.0 million for Credit Suisse First Boston International for attempting to mislead the Japanese regulatory and tax authorities. The record for the largest fine imposed by the FSA and its successor, the FCA, has changed hands seven times since then. Six times since 2009, after the FSA proposed in March 2010 bigger fines to achieve credible deterrence, i.e. up to 20% of a firm's income linked to the regulatory breach. For example, £157.5 million (post 30% discount) of UBS's £233.8 million fine for FX failings was driven by the FCA's desire to impose a penalty that would deter other firms from committing further or similar breaches (Figure 4.2).

Since Barclays' record fine of £284.4 million (including £100 million of deterrence, post discount) in May 2015 there have been no fines imposed by the FCA that are even close to this amount. This may be evidence that these fines are having their desired effect of changing bank behaviours.[3] Evidence of Risk Homeostasis may also

FIGURE 4.2 Value of new record FSA & FCA fines over the last 19 years

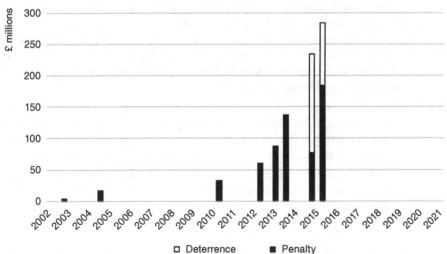

---

[2]ORX'S Annual Banking Loss Report (ORX, 2021) reveals a €2 billion increase in External Fraud in 2020 when compared to average External Fraud losses over the previous five years (€2.1 billion).

[3]Calculating the correlation of FCA fines against time since five banks were fined for failings regarding FX markets results in a correlation coefficient (r) of −0.53.

be seen in Figure 1.1, with a peak of the proportion by value of total losses comprising events ≥€10 million being followed by a subsequent decline.

Banks will also increase control expenditure to address emerging threats, as illustrated by Y2K. Until the 1990s, the dates in many computer programs used a two-digit abbreviation for the year. Companies collectively spent USD billions in the run-up to the new millennium mitigating the risk that their programmes might malfunction, and as a consequence, 1st January 2000 was largely uneventful.

Biases and language (Grimwade, 2016)

As a species humans are not very good at estimating the occurrence of remote events, because people are all impacted by a series of natural biases that influence the way they assess risks. Unfortunately, to make matters worse, psychologists have also identified that whilst individuals accept that other people are biased; they generally resist the view that they themselves are biased![4] There are many of these biases but the ones which are most relevant to Operational Risk managers include:

Anchoring/Proximity Bias: When people form subjective estimates, they start with a point of reference, a possibly arbitrary value, and then adjust away from it. In one experiment subjects were divided into two populations. Each population was asked two questions: The first was asked "Was Gandhi older or *younger than 140* when he died?" and "How old was he when he died?" The second population was asked "Was Gandhi older or *younger than 9* when he died?" and "How old was he when he died?" The average of the answers from the first population was 67 years and 50 years from the second population.[5] So by asking a clearly erroneous question, the psychologists influenced the answers that their subjects provided, by lodging either a high or a low number in their subjects' subconscious minds.

Example Bias: The more easily people can recall examples, the more common they judge a thing to be. This means that Operational Risk managers, insurance brokers, consultants and even regulators may be susceptible to overestimating Operational Risk, as they are constantly exposed to these events.

Imagination Inflation: Before the 1976 US Presidential election, subjects were asked to imagine either Jimmy Carter or Gerald Ford winning the election and giving their inauguration address. Subjects who imagined that Carter had

---

[4]For example, a survey of doctors found that 61% said that they were not personally influenced by gifts from drugs companies; but only 16% thought that the same was true for other doctors (Gardner, 2009).

[5]Gandhi was actually 78 years old when he was assassinated in 1948 (Gardner, 2009).

won were more certain that he eventually would. Whilst, similarly, those who imagined Ford had won were more certain that he would later win. The very act of contemplating a risk/an event occurring, may lead to the overestimation of the likelihood of the event actually occurring (Gardner, 2009).

Group Polarisation Bias: When people who share beliefs get together in groups, they become more convinced that their beliefs are correct, and they also become more extreme in their views. People will also conform to the group's view and express opinions which are clearly incorrect. In one experiment, groups of subjects sat in a room and answered questions that supposedly tested their visual perception. Only one person in the group was a genuine subject; the others were "stooges" who, as the experiment progresses, gave clearly wrong answers. The only genuine subjects in the groups conformed to the obviously wrong group consensus one third of the time (Gardner, 2009).

Additionally, people can be prone to optimism and wishful thinking, for example, either overestimating the robustness of the firm's control environment or being unduly optimistic over the effectiveness of their response to an event. Incentive conflicts that arise when staff members have a vested personal interest in the outcome of an assessment (Motivation Bias) may also distort their assessments.[6]

Finally, once a belief is in place, Confirmation Bias may mean that humans screen what they see and hear, in a biased manner, to ensure that their beliefs are proven correct.

In addition to the challenges provided by these biases, commonly used terms to describe probability are not consistently understood by people. Research conducted in 2004 illustrates this challenge (Hillson, 2005). The researchers sent emails to over 5,000 people interested in risk management seeking their perceived definitions, ranging from 0% to 100%, for 15 probability-related terms. Approximately 10% of recipients replied. Their responses grouped words into two broad categories:

% to 20%	Six terms, i.e. "seldom", "unlikely", "improbable", "rare", "highly unlikely" and "impossible".
25% to 50%	One term: "possible".
55% to 80%	Eight terms, i.e. "almost certain", "highly probable", "good chance", "likely", "quite likely", "probable", "better than even" and "definite".

Two of the terms used above were intended to be unambiguous, i.e. "definite" and "impossible" and should probably have elicited responses on 100% and 0%

---

[6]The Author once worked for a bank for which "mis-statement of the financial accounts" was surprisingly its most significant Operational Risk. This coincided with the Group Finance function compiling a business case for a new general ledger system. The Author suspected that the scenario was an example of Motivation Bias, i.e. an attempt to justify an already planned project.

respectively. Instead the responses were 80% and 8% respectively. "Rare" was actually considered slightly less likely than "impossible"!

The researchers observed that the occurrence of just one term ("possible") in the 25% to 50% band, suggesting that the English language, despite all its complexity, is lacking in this mid-range.

The challenges posed by these biases and the language for describing risks may, however, distort the effectiveness of the 8th Law due to limitations on the abilities of Operational Risk managers to assess and articulate risks (Chapters 8, 9 and 11).

IMPLICATIONS

A consequence of the 8th Law is the implication that risks that lead to high volume: low impact losses and short lags should be excluded from RCSAs because firms will naturally respond to these risks through Risk Homeostasis. The increasing use of AI and machine learning by firms to provide new analysis to identify frauds and money laundering more quickly may also accelerate the rapidity of Risk Homeostasis.

This law also predicts that any potential spike in Conduct Risk losses as a result of the COVID-19 pandemic may be smaller than otherwise for banks due to the control enhancements, to address misconduct, implemented in the aftermath of the Global Financial Crisis over a decade earlier. This may not be the case across all branches of financial services, e.g. fund management suffered less during the Global Financial Crisis and may be more adversely impacted by the COVID-19 pandemic.

Finally, when conducting scenario analysis for emerging risks banks, more recent external events should be weighted more heavily to better reflect the control enhancements implemented by the banking industry in response to a new risk.

9TH LAW OF OPERATIONAL RISK: RISK TRANSFERENCE, TRANSFORMATION AND CONSERVATION

The 9th Law considers how risk is both transformed and conserved when it is transferred from banks to their customers. It states that "When Market and Credit Risks are sold to investors, e.g. through securitisations, they are transformed into Operational Risk that is retained by the arranger/distributor. The quantum of Operational Risk retained is equivalent of the Market and Credit Risks transferred, whilst the likelihood of this Operational Risk becoming a loss is diminished." This is summarised in Formulae 4.2a and 4.2b.

Formula 4.2a Risk Transference, Transformation and Conservation – the quantum of risk

	Securitisation	
Quantum of Operational Risks	$\approx$	Quantum of Market + Credit Risks
(Retained by the arranger/distributor in the case of misconduct)		(Transferred to customers/investors)
$ / time		$ / time

Formula 4.2b The reduction in the frequency of events

Frequency of Operational Risk events suffered by the arranger/distributor	$\approx$	Frequency of material Market & Credit Risk losses suffered by customers/investors	$\times$	% services provided involving misconduct by the arranger/distributor
Events/time		Events/time Driven by external causes		A factor Driven by internal causes

EXPLANATION OF THE COMPONENTS OF THESE FORMULAE

When a customer/investor buys a product that exposes them to Market and Credit Risks, and subsequently suffers a loss, leading to a claim of misconduct (a Real Option, see the 7th Law), then the potential Operational Risk loss that may be suffered by the arranger/distributor approximates to their customers' Market and Credit Risk losses (Figure 4.3). The likelihood of such a claim arising is driven by the combined likelihoods of both the customer/investor suffering a loss and the arranger/distributor being guilty of misconduct, and hence it is more remote than simply the customer/investor suffering a loss.

ILLUSTRATIONS & OBSERVATIONS

Examples of the conservation of risk include post-crisis litigation settlements on CDOs, e.g. in June 2011, JPMorgan reached a settlement with the SEC (without admitting or denying the allegations) in which 15 investors that had purchased $145.8 million of mezzanine notes in a CDO squared, which "became nearly worthless..." (SEC, 2011) months after issue received $125.9 million in compensation, ~86% of the notional value of the notes.

   Transference of Operational Risk can also occur contractually via insurance policies. These contracts define both the nature of events (1st Law) and of impacts

FIGURE 4.3   The differing risk profiles and income streams of originators, arrangers/distributors and investors (Grimwade, 2020)

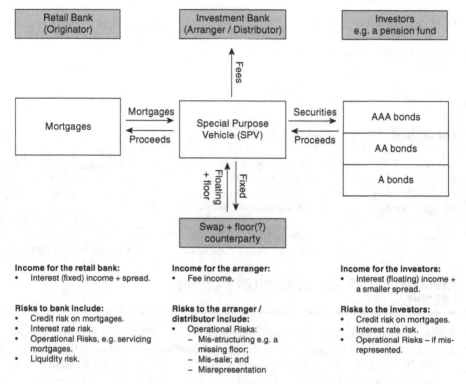

Income for the retail bank:
• Interest (fixed) income + spread.

Income for the arranger:
• Fee income.

Income for the investors:
• Interest (floating) income + a smaller spread.

Risks to bank include:
• Credit risk on mortgages.
• Interest rate risk.
• Operational Risks, e.g. servicing mortgages.
• Liquidity risk.

Risks to the arranger / distributor include:
• Operational Risks:
    – Mis-structuring e.g. a missing floor;
    – Mis-sale; and
    – Misrepresentation

Risks to the investors:
• Credit risk on mortgages.
• Interest rate risk.
• Operational Risks – if mis-represented.

(3rd Law) which are transferred to the insurer above an excess and up to an agreed amount, for a set period of time (2nd and 4th Laws). They also specify events that are excluded (e.g. industry-wide events, which would lead multiple correlated claims are often excluded, e.g. pandemics), and impose obligations on the purchasers, e.g. in terms of specific preventive controls and responses to an event that has occurred. The premium paid to the insurance company and any associated investment income has to cover not only customer claims, but also the insurer's administration costs and costs of capital. Insurance as a mitigant for Operational Risk is discussed in Chapter 12.

IMPLICATIONS

When considering a firm's risk profile Operational Risk managers need to focus more upon the historical sales of products to customers that involve risk transference than current processes for recording transactions and making payments. Equally when conducting stress testing, the focus should not only be on changes in the value of assets on a bank's balance sheet but also the value of assets (and risks) transferred to their customers (Chapters 11 and 13).

10TH LAW OF OPERATIONAL RISK: ACTIVE AND PASSIVE RISK TAKING

The 10th Law observes that exposure to Operational Risk can be active, as well as passive. It states that "Firms take Operational Risks both proactively through the provision of services in return for fee and commission income and passively, as a by-product of either the generation of trading and interest income or a firm's infrastructure and its corporate governance. Proactively taking Operational Risk is disproportionately risky." This is summarised in Formula 4.3.

Formula 4.3   Proactive and passively taken Operational Risks

Operational Risk losses generated by a firm's business profile, p.a.	≈	Fee & commission income p.a	+	Trading & interest Income p.a.	+	A firm's infrastructure and corporate governance p.a.
		Proactively taken Operational Risks		**Passively** taken Operational Risks		**Passively** taken Operational Risks
$ / time		$ / time		$ / time		$ / time

EXPLANATION OF THE FORMULA

Firms expose themselves to differing risks in order to generate three types of income:

1. *Fee and commission income* is obtained for charging customers for the services that they receive, e.g. fees for soft underwriting; providing advice; fund management; and selling insurance policies. Providing these services typically involves the taking of just Operational Risk. Examples of resulting losses include the misrepresentation of MBS; the mis-sale of PPI; post-underwriting litigation (e.g. WorldCom); the deliberate breaching of US sanctions; breach of a fund's investment mandate; and the overcharging of fees and commissions to customers.
2. *Trading income* primarily involves the proactive taking of Market Risk, whilst also generating Credit, Liquidity and Operational Risks as by-products. Examples of resulting losses include benchmark manipulation; the mis-sale of derivatives; and unauthorised trading, by both rogue algos and traders.

3. *Interest income* primarily involves the proactive taking of Credit Risk by banks advancing loans to customers which are funded through deposit taking, whilst also generating Market, Liquidity and Operational Risks as by-products. Examples of resulting losses include compensation for improper foreclosures; and the levying of incorrect interest rates on loans.

Operational Risk losses can also sometimes arise from a bank's infrastructure and its corporate governance, for example, employee-related litigation; weak KYC controls; extended systems outages; litigation relating to allegedly misleading shareholders and investors; and physical damage, e.g. due to Climate Change.

ILLUSTRATION & OBSERVATIONS

Analysis of large Operational Risk losses (≥$0.1 billion) suffered between 2007 to 2017 by 31 current and former G-SIBs reveals that 68% of losses, by value over this period, arose from the provision of fee- and commission-generating services (Figure 4.4). The relationship between the income streams that generate Operational Risks appears not to be constant, i.e. losses relating to fees and commissions for the period 1996 to 2006 only made up 46% of these losses by value. One interpretation of this data is that Operational Risk losses linked to income streams that generate fees

FIGURE 4.4   The relationship between large losses and income streams (Grimwade, 2020)

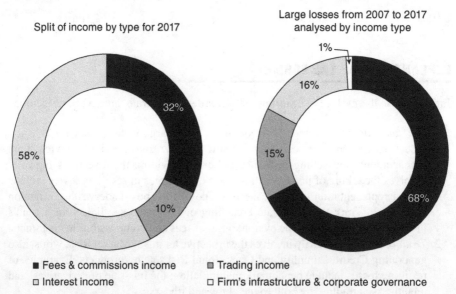

Split of income by type for 2017

Large losses from 2007 to 2017 analysed by income type

■ Fees & commissions income   ▨ Trading income
□ Interest income   □ Firm's infrastructure & corporate governance

and commissions are more strongly procyclical, maybe as a consequence of the Real Option Model described in the 7th Law.

Comparing the values of large Operational Risk losses from 2007 to 2017, split by the types of income stream that generated these losses, and the composition of revenues of the 31 current and former G-SIBs for 2017[7] (Figure 4.4), highlights a number of features.

Operational Risk losses arising from interest income were disproportionately low in comparison to their percentage of total income. This may reflect that under Basel II Operational Risk losses exclude boundary losses for Credit Risk but not Market Risk. These losses did, however, increase during the Global Financial Crisis, primarily due to the improper foreclosure settlement in the US in 2012.

In contrast, Operational Risk losses after the Global Financial Crisis linked to trading income were more in line with their share of income. Operational Risk losses arising from fees and commission income were disproportionately high after the Global Financial Crisis, primarily due to the MBS and PPI settlements in the US and UK respectively.[8]

In the 11-year period from 2007 to 2017, the ratio of average large losses ($\geq$\$0.1 billion) to 2017 revenues, split by income type for the 31 current and former G-SIBs in this sample (Table 4.1), gives the following ratios:

TABLE 4.1 Ratio of average large losses ($\geq$\$0.1 billion) for 2007 to 2017 revenues split by income stream for 31 current and former G-SIBs

▪ Losses linked to fee & commission income	4.6%
▪ Losses linked to trading income	3.1%
▪ Losses linked to interest income	0.6%

The importance of income streams may be driven by a combination of the sophistication of customers and the rigour of different legal and regulatory jurisdictions. The "home" jurisdiction of a bank may be less relevant for international businesses, e.g. trading & sales and payments, but more relevant for retail and SME banking, which are typically more domestic. For example, PPI settlements are primarily a UK occurrence, whilst many of the benchmark rigging settlements were international.

---

[7]2017 revenues are used as the loss data includes losses suffered by all of the predecessor banks of the 31 current and former G-SIBs, e.g. it includes losses suffered by Merrill Lynch before the completion of Bank of America's acquisition in January 2009.
[8]This is a concern, as after the Global Financial Crisis low interest rates (Brei et al., 2019), investor demand for yield, and higher capital requirements for Market and Credit Risks, led banks to expand their fee- and commission-generating businesses (Grimwade, 2016).

IMPLICATIONS

As a consequence of this 10th Law firms' RCSAs should target fee-generating businesses and consider the effectiveness of both current and historical controls. This is especially relevant for banks, given that they have been expanding these businesses in the aftermath of the Global Financial Crisis (Brei et al., 2019).

CONCLUSIONS

These final three laws describe some of the most interesting concepts associated with Operational Risk.

Risk Homeostasis describes how the controls of banks are dynamic and respond to changing risk profiles. As a consequence, for risks that lead to high volume:low impact losses, with short lags, controls should be naturally enhanced through the incident management processes of banks (Chapter 13), and hence they should be excluded from RCSAs (Chapter 8). Additionally the combination of Risk Homeostasis and Proximity Bias (Chapter 9) may cause Operational Risk managers to overestimate the consequences of emerging risks.

Risk transference, transformation and conservation describes how in the process of transferring Market and/or Credit Risks to another entity, the risks can be transformed into Operational Risk and retained by the transferring entity in the eventuality of misconduct. Managing these risks requires Operational Risk managers to have a much broader/Enterprise Risk understanding of risk management.

That firms proactively take Operational Risk in order to generate fee and commission income places a much greater burden on the profession to quantify much more dynamically these risks (Chapters 9 and 10), to help firms maximise returns, whilst staying within appetite. The post-crisis Basel reforms and ultra-low/negative interest rates have combined to encourage (inadvertently) firms to take proactively more Operational Risk through the expansion of their fee and commission income-generating businesses (Brei et al., 2019).

CHAPTER 5

Three Taxonomies: Inadequacies or Failures, Impacts and Causes

This chapter considers in more detail the three taxonomies referenced extensively in the Ten Laws, i.e. inadequacies or failures, which describe both events and control failures; impacts and internal and external causes. Whilst taxonomies are often largely of interest to Operational Risk management professionals and academics, they can also provide commercial value. For example, they can facilitate the aggregation of consistent data across both individual firms and the industry to support RCSAs (e.g. the completeness of risks considered), trend analysis, capital modelling and stress testing. Additionally these three taxonomies form one of three pillars that underpin the Ten Laws and which drive the behaviours of Operational Risk.

Approaches to classification

The key challenges when designing any taxonomy are ensuring that it is complete; has an appropriate level of granularity/reflects significance; and that the definitions are mutually exclusive. Whilst the Ten Laws indicate that taxonomies are required for inadequacies or failures (i.e. both events and control failures), impacts and causes they do not provide any guidance on their content. Consequently, the Author has leveraged, where possible, the approaches of biology, his first profession, which has been systematically ordering the natural world for several centuries. In order to produce taxonomies that are compete and mutually exclusive, biologists primarily document the unique characteristics of organisms and use this as a basis for their groupings.

Operational Risk managers can ensure completeness by producing taxonomies in a similar bottom-up way to biologists by categorising observed events, control failures, causes and impacts. Alternatively, Operational Risk managers can adopt more top-down approaches, either harnessing the wisdom of crowds or by identifying some fundamental boundaries that naturally limit the real world. This last approach is most relevant for the impact taxonomy.

1. TAXONOMIES OF INADEQUACIES OR FAILURES COVERING BOTH EVENTS AND CONTROL FAILURES

The Basel Committee (May 2001) defined seven subcategories of Operational Risk that were subsequently incorporated into Basel II (June 2004). Crudely, these seven subcategories capture Operational Risk losses that relate to a firm's business profile, as described in Figure 2.1:

1. Processes (EDPM);
2. Products and fiduciary duties of care to customers and other stakeholders (CPBP);
3. Systems (BDSF);
4. People (EPWS);
5. Infrastructure – physical assets (DPA);
6. Fraud – involving staff members (IF); and
7. Fraud – not involving staff members (EF).

Although the Basel Committee's taxonomy has been periodically criticised (e.g. ORX's and Oliver Wyman's proposed alternative taxonomy for Operational and Non-Financial Risk (ORX & Oliver Wyman, 2019)) at the highest level, it seems complete, when compared to the business profiles of banks. When these seven subcategories are split into the nature of their events (Table 5.1), however, then four categories of issues become apparent:

1. *Inconsistencies:* There are inconsistencies between the definitions and the examples provided within Basel II. For example, the definition of CPBP references "unintentional or negligent failure" whilst the examples include "market manipulation". Fines and settlements arising from the manipulation of benchmarks (e.g. LIBOR and FX) were typically categorised as CPBP, despite the actions of the staff members involved being clearly intentional.
2. *Significance:* The number of Level 2 Operational Risk categories seems to bear little relationship to the significance of the individual risks. For example, External Fraud is one of the most important categories of Operational Risk in terms of the number of events and the value of losses suffered by banks (Figure 1.1) but still has only two Level 2 categories. Since the Basel II taxonomy has been developed, the nature of frauds has also changed significantly with the demise of cash and cheques and the rise of online banking; contactless payments; digitisation and cybercrime.

TABLE 5.1 Basel definitions of the subcategories of Operational Risk and the nature of the events

Definitions of the event types (Level 1)	Nature of the events (Table 2.1, 1st Law)	Number of Level 2 risks	% of value of Banking losses[1]
1. CPBP – Products and fiduciary duties: Losses arising from: ■ *An unintentional or negligent* failure to meet a professional obligation to specific clients (including fiduciary and suitability requirements), or ■ The nature or design of a product.	■ *Internal:* Mainly systemic or individual misconduct with some design/systemic process failures; application malfunctions. ■ *External:* Outsourcing of processes and systems can lead to events arising from third-party failures, e.g. data leakage.	5	54%
2. EDPM – Processes: Losses from failed: ■ Transaction processing or process management; or ■ Relations with trade counterparties and vendors.	■ *Internal:* Mainly mistakes and omissions by people, with some process design/systemic failures. ■ *External:* Outsourcing of processes can lead to events arising from third-party failures.	6	23%
3. External fraud – Malicious acts: Losses due to acts of a type intended to defraud, misappropriate property or circumvent the law, by a third-party.	■ *External:* Malicious acts carried out by a third-party, with no help from any staff members.	2	14%

4. EPWS – People:
 	
Losses arising from:
■ Acts inconsistent with employment, health or safety laws or agreements; or
■ Diversity/discrimination events; or
■ Payment of personal injury claims.
	■ *Internal:* Mixture of:
	  ■ Individual misconduct by employees; and
	  ■ Systemic misconduct by employers.
	■ *Internal or external:* A physical accident (slips, trips & falls); or a malicious act; or an act of God.
		3	5%

(Continued)

---

[1]ORX Annual Report, 2018.

TABLE 5.1 (*Continued*)

Definitions of the event types (Level 1)	Nature of the events (Table 2.1, 1st Law)	Number of Level 2 risks	% of value of Banking losses[1]
5. Internal fraud – Malicious acts: Losses due to acts of a type intended to defraud, misappropriate property or *circumvent regulations*, the law or company policy, excluding diversity/discrimination events, which involves at least one internal party.	▪ *Internal:* All involve malicious acts by a staff member, but potentially may also involve help or coercion from a third-party.	2	2%
6. BDSF – Systems: Losses arising from disruption of business or system failures.	▪ *Internal:* Mainly mistakes and omissions; disruption of software; application malfunctions; and infrastructure failures, with some physical deterioration of hardware. ▪ *External:* Outsourcing of processes and systems can lead to events arising from third-party failures.	1	1%
7. DPA – Physical assets: Losses arising from loss or damage to physical assets from natural disaster or other events.	▪ *Internal or external:* Ranging from: ▪ Small-scale accidents (mistakes and omissions) and malicious acts of vandalism; to ▪ Malicious acts carried out by terrorists and natural disasters (acts of God).	1	1%

3. *Themes:* There are groups of Operational Risks loss events that have common causes, but which are allocated to a number of the seven subcategories, for example, failures by third (and fourth) parties cut across EDPM, CPBP and BDSF, and equally cybercrime primarily cuts across both EF and BDSF (This is illustrated in Appendix IV.1 which is a taxonomy for cybercrime risks based upon a review of 800 actual external events sourced from the IBM FIRST Risk Case Studies).

FIGURE 5.1 Representation of the discontinuous risk profile of Damage to Physical Assets

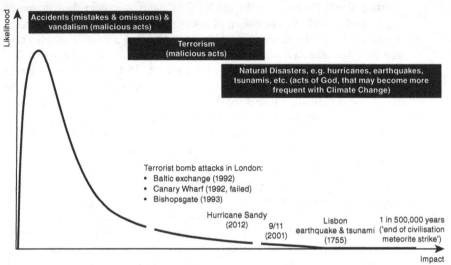

4. *Inadequacies or failures:* The nature of the inadequacies or failures is quite variable in these subcategories of Operational Risk, i.e. with the exception of fraud, they combine both internal and external events, as well as systemic misconduct with one-off mistakes and omissions (Table 2.1, 1st Law). This diversity may make both understanding and modelling these risks more challenging, as there may be no relationship between day-to-day losses and tail events (Figure 5.1).[2]

Unfortunately, it is not practical to change the overall structure of the Basel II event taxonomy because it is enshrined in regulation and has been used for collecting and reporting loss data for almost two decades. These issues can be addressed whilst maintaining the mapping to the Basel II taxonomy:

Inconsistencies: The Basel II taxonomy should be amended to reflect industry practice, i.e. that CPBP encompasses both intentional and unintentional misconduct.

---

[2]The challenges of how to represent continuous and dis-continuous risks are considered further in Chapter 8.

Significance: Risks can be promoted that currently appear at lower levels within the existing Basel II taxonomy to reflect their increased significance. Equally existing Basel II Level 1 risks can be split, again to reflect their increased significance. Both the promotion of lower risks and the splitting of existing Level 1 risks allows the mapping of data to Basel II to remain in place. These are the approaches adopted by the ORX and Oliver Wyman taxonomy (ORX & Oliver Wyman, 2019), which has 16 Level 1 and 59 Level 2 risks. Like all taxonomies, however, it has a few issues. For example, the granularity of the taxonomy is variable, e.g. technology does not currently reflect the expansion of digitisation and the development of algos, AI and machine learning.[3] (This is illustrated in Appendix IV.2, which contains a taxonomy for IT risks based upon a review of 800 actual external events sourced from the IBM FIRST Risk Case Studies.)

Themes: These allow related events or risks to be grouped, whilst still maintaining the mapping to the Basel II taxonomy, as it is a rearrangement of lower-level risks. The definitions of the other risks need to be amended to exclude explicitly risks that have been included in these new groups, e.g. if cyber is a separate group then cyber-related frauds, business disruption and data leakages need to excluded from External Fraud, BDSF and CPBP. Alternatively, they can also be reflected by adding into a firm's loss event database an additional data field to flag Operational Risk events associated with themes such as, cyber, third- (and fourth-) party failures, change, and COVID-19.

Inadequacies or failures: In Chapter 2, the inadequacies or failures incorporated within Basel II's definition of Operational Risk describe both the nature of events and control failures. Table 5.2 provides a taxonomy of inadequacies or failures for events. Whilst, as noted previously, the overall structure of the Basel II event taxonomy cannot be amended, it would be possible for firms to capture the nature of these inadequacies or failures as an additional data field for each event.

---

[3] A few failed controls and causes also seem to have crept into the ORX & Oliver Wyman taxonomy. For example "Inadequate business continuity planning" is a failed control, rather than an event, and whilst poor Operational Resilience may lead to a regulatory fine, so could many other failed controls, e.g. inadequate surveillance. Consequently, this particular risk may fit better under "Regulatory Compliance". Equally, "Inadequate data architecture/IT infrastructure" feels like a cause, i.e. it increases the likelihood of an event occurring, rather than being an event/risk in its own right.

TABLE 5.2 Taxonomy of inadequacies or failures – the nature of the events

The nature of events			Definitions or examples from various public sources
Internal	People	Mistakes and omissions primarily relate to data, both physical and electronic, and its ■ Communication; ■ Capture; ■ Storage; ■ Interpretation. as well as the loss of assets.	■ Miscommunication (e.g. Completeness, Accuracy, Cut-off) of information. ■ Omissions (Completeness) e.g.: Failure to populate all required data fields in a payment system (2020) or to include floors in structured products. ■ Failure to meet a deadline (Cut-off) e.g.: Settlements, corporate actions or submissions. ■ Inaccuracies (Accuracy) e.g.: 　■ *Drafting* e.g.: An incorrect waterfall incorporated in a CDO's documentation (1999). 　■ *Selection* e.g.: Payment to the wrong legal entity in a group in Chapter 11 (2008). 　■ *Transposition* e.g.: Ordering 610k shares at ¥16 instead of 16 shares at ¥610k (2001). 　■ *Replication* e.g.: Data "corruption that is copied from elsewhere" (McConnell, 2017). 　■ *Duplication* e.g.: Trader submitted an order 145 times by leaning on his F12 key (1998). ■ *Misinterpretation (Rights & Obligations)* e.g.: Authorities' statutes, rules and regulations. ■ *Loss (Existence)* e.g.: Foreclosure processes were undermined by missing physical documents (2010) or a bank lost five tapes containing electronic customer data (2004). ■ *Accidents* e.g.: "Slips, trips & falls".
		Misconduct by individuals	■ Individual staff members can act inappropriately, e.g. The FCA "…concluded that [the trader's] trading…was designed to move the price of the Bond, in an attempt to sell it to the Bank of England at an abnormal and artificial level" (2014).
		Systemic misconduct	■ Groups of staff members can act inappropriately because it is the practice of either their firm or their industry in general, for example, mis-sale of PPI; the systemic breaching of sanctions; and the facilitation of tax evasion.
		Malicious acts	■ *Staff members may commit a criminal act* e.g.: Theft, fraud, forgery and acting dishonestly.
	Process	Design/systematic failure	■ *Systemic failures* due to a poorly designed process. ■ *Regulatory penalties* for poorly designed processes, e.g. a fine in the UK for poor "systems & controls".

(Continued)

TABLE 5.2   (*Continued*)

The nature of events		Definitions or examples from various public sources
Systems* (Appendix IV.2)	Disruption of software	■ *Disruption of software* e.g.: Disruption of internet banking for >1 week, including slow performance, crashes, inability to log on and access to other customers' data! (2018).
	Application malfunctions	■ *System miscalculations* e.g.: Error calculating end-capital for personal insurance policies over a 10-year period (2005). ■ *Incorrect decisions* e.g.: The calculator used to assess the affordability of overdrafts from 2011 to 2015 failed to consider some housing and living expenses. ■ *System generated duplicated or erroneous transactions* e.g.: Erroneous orders generated by order router leading to a $460 million trading loss (2012). ■ *System mispricing* e.g.: Malfunction of an investment bank's electronic trading system led to ~16,000 erroneous, mispriced orders being placed on major exchanges (2013).
	Hardware failures	■ *Printer failure* e.g.: Multiple statements in the same envelope (2010). ■ *Disk failure* e.g.: Trading halted on an exchange by data corruption caused by destroyed server disk drives (2018).
	Disruption of data & storage	■ *Quality* e.g.: Failings in a bank's prudential reporting, included "credit ratings data was not feeding correctly into the LRR system..." (2019). ■ *Storage* e.g.: A bank's currency system failed to settle roughly 22,000 FX trades due to insufficient disk space (2003).
	Disruption of own infrastructure	■ *Batch-scheduler failures* e.g.: Delays for ~1 week to processing debit cards transactions, ATM withdrawals and other electronic banking services due to disruption of the batch-scheduling software (2010). ■ *Networks & middleware failures* e.g.: A 7-hour systems-wide outage due to the incorrect replacement of a cable connecting the data-storage system to the mainframe (2010).

TABLE 5.2 *(Continued)*

The nature of events		Definitions or examples from various public sources
External	Third- (and fourth-) party failures	▪ *Telecoms & internet* e.g.: A 12-hour outage of mobile devices (2007). ▪ *Utilities e.g. power outages & surges* e.g.: A data-storage disk system experienced an electrical outage, which corrupted its data. Wholesale payment and securities transactions were disrupted for ~1 week (2003).
	Malicious acts	▪ *Third-party may commit a criminal act* e.g.: Theft, fraud, forgery, extortion and acting dishonestly. (See Appendix IV.1 for a more detailed cybercrime taxonomy.)
	Acts of God	▪ Isolated natural disasters e.g. a fire. ▪ Systemic events, with multiple impacts, e.g. an earthquake, a hurricane or a pandemic.

*System and process failures often also arise from design failures. System failures may also arise from failures of operation.

There are two aspects of this taxonomy that link to other professions:

1. *Auditors:* Mistakes and omissions can be linked to the control testing objectives of auditors;[4] and
2. *Insurers:* The nature of the inadequacies or failures that constitute events is similar to how insurance companies categorise incidents. This is explored further in Chapter 12.

As noted in Chapter 2, the taxonomy of inadequacies or failures for events also describes the nature of controls failures. Table 5.3 has been amended to provide specific examples of control failures.

Conclusions

For better or for worse all Operational Risk event/risk taxonomies for evermore will need to map to the Basel II event taxonomy, because of the desire to continue to utilise

---

[4]When the Author trained as an accountant in the late 1980s/early 1990s, his firm had seven defined objectives for audit tests, i.e., Completeness; Accuracy; Existence; Valuation; Cut-Off; Rights & Obligations; and Presentation & Disclosure.

TABLE 5.3   Taxonomy of inadequacies or failures – the nature of the control failures (Appendix I.3)

The nature of control failures			Definitions or examples from various public sources
Internal control failures	People – Operating effectiveness	Mistakes and omissions	*Controls not performed* e.g.: ▪ "...the managers responsible ... were unaware that their staff had stopped following agreed procedures [checks on internal trades]." *Control incorrectly or partially performed* e.g.: ▪ "...in a number of instances, maker/checker controls were not properly evidenced and did not identify errors". ▪ "Multiple limit breaches were routinely signed-off without rigorous investigation or actions taken to reduce positions". *Failure to act* e.g.: on exceptions: ▪ "Operations did not have the reflex to inform their ... supervisors or Front Office supervisors of ... anomalies". ▪ "Certain control functions failed to escalate in a timely manner price testing variances that were identified ..."
		Misconduct and malicious acts	The mistakes and omissions described above can also occur deliberately. In addition: *Circumvention of controls – falsification* e.g.: ▪ The FSA received complaint files which had been "altered improperly" in "the form of amendments to existing documents". ▪ "To hide his losses and the size of his positions, he created fictitious options." ▪ *Circumvention of controls – breach of segregation of duties* e.g.: A bank clerk made two fraudulent transfers with a total value of €90 million. "Two of [his] colleagues, whose passwords were used to carry out and approve the transactions, were initially questioned but soon declared innocent." ▪ *Circumvention of controls – collusion* e.g.: A trader "... sent a list of four AAA bonds to his bond salesman contact [at another bank] ... and requested month-end prices for the bonds. At approximately the same time, [he also] communicated to his contact the desired prices on the bonds".

TABLE 5.3 (*Continued*)

The nature of control failures		Definitions or examples from various public sources
Internal control failures	Process – Design effectiveness	*Poorly designed controls* for achieving Completeness; Accuracy; Existence; Valuation; Cut-Off; Rights & Obligations; and Presentation & Disclosure e.g.: ■ "The identification of suspicious trading patterns had to be performed manually. However, it was not generally feasible for . . . desk supervisors to perform this task for high volume trading desks . . ." ■ The bank "extracted the relevant trading data for reconciliation purposes from its systems at different points in time which created timing gaps". *Missing controls* e.g.: ■ The bank " . . . had no specific systems and controls relating to its LIBOR or EURIBOR submissions processes until December 2009". ■ The firm " . . . did not have . . . a control to compare orders leaving SMARS with those that entered it."
	Systems – variously design or operating effectiveness	■ Disruption of software e.g.: " . . . while [the firm] had installed a tool to inspect network traffic for evidence of malicious activity, an expired certificate prevented that tool from performing its intended function of detecting malicious traffic." ■ Application malfunctions e.g.: " . . . due to the concerns over the reliability of the VaR calculation, the VaR limit breaches in currency options was removed from the front page of the report . . .". ■ Disruption of data & storage e.g.: controls fail due to being fed incomplete, or inaccurate data, or data in the wrong format, or untimely data.
External control failures	Third- (and fourth-) party failures	■ Any of the above e.g.: Non-Functional Testing " . . . had been constrained by the test environments . . . and . . . had been conducted at lower volumes than originally planned".
	Malicious acts	■ *External circumvention of controls* e.g.: " . . . the attackers removed the data in small increments, using standard encrypted web protocols to disguise the exchanges as normal network traffic."

historical loss data. Consequently, enhancements are restricted to: adding more granularity at lower levels (see Appendices IV.1 and IV.2); promoting groups of risks to higher levels in the taxonomy; and tagging events with additional data fields relating to the nature of the events (i.e. inadequacies or failures) and key themes. The two taxonomies for inadequacies or failures are clearly useful inputs into both RCSA assessments and controls testing.

2. IMPACT TAXONOMY

The Basel Committee initially defined six "loss effect types"[5] in its guidance for QIS-2 (Basel Committee (Annex 5), 2001). Subsequently, Basel III (Basel Committee, 2017) defined the impacts of Operational Risk events in a hybrid manner, i.e. both on a principles basis, splitting them between Direct Charges and Costs Incurred, and also reflecting potential accounting treatments, i.e. the inclusion of provisions, reserves, pending losses and timing differences. This does not, however, lead to a self-evidently complete taxonomy. In the absence of good-quality data on the composition of impacts of actual losses suffered by firms (Table 2.4), an alternative approach is to take an accounting perspective,[6] i.e. the financial impacts of a loss event comprise either:

- *Lost revenues* (lost credits to the P&L and debits to cash), e.g. due to the failure of a firm to claim monies to which it was entitled; or
- *Charges* (debits to the P&L, and credits to provisions and ultimately cash) to settle new expense items, such as regulatory action/fines; restitution/compensation; legal liabilities and other third-party costs; or
- *Write-down* of the value of balance sheet items (i.e. crediting the balance sheet and debiting the P&L). This does not involve the payment of cash, e.g. loss or damage to physical assets; or electronic assets, such as cash that is stolen; or
- *Damage to the reputation* of a firm with its key stakeholders, listed in Figure 2.1.

Chapter 12 subsequently analyses which of the inadequacies or failures that constitute events (Table 5.2) and impacts (Table 5.4) are insurable.

Although Basel III provides some high-level criteria of what impacts should and should not be included within the value of Operational Risk losses, much more detailed industry standards are provided by ORX (ORX, 2017). Whilst ORX is currently in the process of collating a taxonomy of Operational Risk impacts, Table 5.4 provides a reasonable listing in the meantime, split between impacts driven by the P&L and those

---

[5]These six "loss effect types" were: Legal Liability; Regulatory Action; Loss or Damage to Assets; Restitution; Loss of Resource; and Write-downs (Basel Committee, May 2001).
[6]Accounting was the Author's second profession.

TABLE 5.4 The nature of impacts and their relative velocity (Appendix II)

P&L & balance sheet		Level 2 – examples	Scale $	Velocity $/day
Lost revenues or charges (P&L)	Uncollected revenues due to an Operational Risk event.	■ Uncollected revenues, e.g. failure to claim revenues to which a firm is entitled and loss of entitlement to revenues.		
	Impairments and settlements, to the bank's P&L accounts due to an Operational Risk event.	■ Restitution/compensation payments linked to a firm's business profile and third-party relationships (Figure 2.1), e.g.: ■ *Customers & investors:* e.g.: ■ Credit and Market Risk losses suffered; ■ Frauds suffered by customers; and ■ Loss of client assets in safe custody. ■ *Counterparties, customers and suppliers:* Interest on monies owed. ■ *Suppliers:* Breach of contract or licencing agreements, e.g. data. ■ *Employees (current & potential)* e.g.: ■ Lost historical earnings, e.g. due to payroll errors; and ■ Lost future earnings for an inappropriate dismissal. ■ *Visitors (e.g. customers, suppliers etc.):* third-party liability.		
		■ Regulatory action: Fines and penalties.		
		■ Tax incurred e.g.: ■ On behalf of others, e.g. clients or employees; and ■ Loss of treatment, e.g. failed tax arbitrage/avoidance schemes.		
	Additional expenses or foregone expenditure[7] with a direct link to the Operational Risk event.	■ Legal liabilities: ORX include legal expenses that relate to Operational Risk events both for when firms act as the plaintiff as well as the defendant.		Not enough data

(Continued)

---

[7] An unexpected impact of COVID-19 was a reduction in budgeted travel & entertainment expenditure for international banks.

TABLE 5.4   *(Continued)*

P&L & balance sheet		Level 2 – examples	Scale $	Velocity $/day
		▪ Other third-party expenses, e.g. accountants, office cleaners (COVID-19) etc.		
		▪ Additional staff costs, e.g.: ▪ Incentives and overtime payments for employees; and ▪ Third-party contractor costs.		
		▪ Additional costs, e.g. temporary offices and recovery sites.		
	Costs of repair or replacement, incurred to restore the position that was prevailing before the Operational Risk event.	▪ Physical assets: ▪ Buildings; ▪ IT equipment; and ▪ Fixtures & fittings, but avoid double counting with write-downs.		
		▪ Costs of improving controls*		
Write-off of assets (balance sheet)	Write-downs of assets due to an Operational Risk event, e.g.: ▪ Theft: asset stolen ▪ Fraud: asset never existed; ▪ Extortion; ▪ Accidental asset transfers ▪ Damage; and ▪ Loss of recourse.	▪ Market Risk losses or gains (mark-to-market) for the Bank, arising from an Operational Risk event, e.g. rogue trading or fat-fingered typing.		

TABLE 5.4 *(Continued)*

P&L & balance sheet		Level 2 – examples	Scale $	Velocity $/day

		■ Financial and physical assets:
		  ■ Cash and bearer bonds;
		  ■ Securities;
		  ■ Physical commodities;
		  ■ Buildings;
		  ■ IT equipment; and
		  ■ Fixtures & fittings.		

		■ Loans: Credit Risk losses, exacerbated by operational failures, e.g. failure to perfect security; put in place netting agreements or to call margin.*		
Reputational impacts (Stakeholders listed on Figure 2.1)	Authorities	■ Higher fines, if a repeat offender (Table 9.1). ■ Additional capital requirements, lowering return on equity. ■ Licence restrictions on ability to conduct new activities. ■ *Operational Resilience:* Threat to the financial system, requiring risk mitigation plans.	Not enough data	Not enough data
	Investors: Bondholders	■ Higher funding costs if a firm's credit rating is downgraded (Figure 13.11).		
	Investors: Shareholders	■ Higher costs of capital if existing investors sell shares and the price falls (Figure 13.9).		
	Infrastructure and counterparties	■ *Operational Resilience:* Disorderly operation of markets. ■ *Operational Resilience:* Threaten a firm's safety and soundness, e.g. through loss of revenues and/or liquidity.		
	Suppliers and outsourcers	■ Adverse reaction.		
	Customers	■ *Operational Resilience:* Intolerable levels of harm to a firm's clients. ■ Loss of future customer and client revenues (Figure 13.10) – EBA stress testing only. Not an Operational Risk loss for capital calculations (EBA, July 2018).		

TABLE 5.4   *(Continued)*

P&L & balance sheet		Level 2 – examples	Scale $	Velocity $/day
	Employees: current & future	▪ Impact on staff morale and inability to retain existing employees. ▪ Inability to recruit new employees.		
	Criminals	▪ Higher levels of fraud if a firm has a poor reputation for fraud prevention.		

* These are not included in gross losses (Basel Committee, 2017).

Key: Scale and velocity of losses (based on Figure 2.3)

Not enough data ☐   £10ms ☐ $100ms ▨ $1bns ▨ $10bns ■

driven by the write-down of the balance sheet. The completeness of the third parties with whom banks may agree settlements is described in Figure 2.1. In contrast, costs incurred are rather more diverse and diffuse, whilst the completeness of the list of assets that firms may have to write down is determined by the composition of their balance sheets. Where available, scales and velocities associated with these impacts have been included, based on Figure 2.3. Table 5.4 also implies that high-value impacts either can be high velocity or can accrete slowly over time, but not both.

Reputational impacts are often referred to as being non-financial. This may reflect that their impacts are harder to quantify as they arise from changes in the behaviours of a firm's stakeholders. The list of stakeholders with which a firm has a reputation is again derived from Figure 2.1. Quantification often involves comparing an outcome to an expectation as to what would have happened . . . but didn't! As will be seen in Chapters 11, 12 and 13, changes in the behaviours of stakeholders and the reputational impacts can, however, potentially be very significant.

3. CAUSAL TAXONOMY

Despite the Basel Committee basing its definition for Operational Risk "on the underlying causes" (Basel Committee, September 2001) it neither collected data on causes through the QIS exercises nor developed a more detailed taxonomy of causes. In contrast ORX incorporated a simple causal taxonomy into its Operational Risk loss reporting standards (ORX, 2017), and has recently published a more sophisticated causal taxonomy through a process of collating its members' existing taxonomies (ORX, November 2020).

In the meantime, whilst the Laws of Operational Risk demonstrate the central importance of causes they provide no insight into the structure of a causal taxonomy. In order to develop a more complete taxonomy the Author has emulated biologists by identifying the range of causes for 16 well-documented events (Chapter 2). In Table 5.5,

TABLE 5.5 Causal taxonomy based upon a review of large, well-documented events (Appendix III)

	Level 1	Level 2	Examples from various public sources
Business profile causal categories	**1. Strategy** — Past & present	Sales incentives	■ "Thousands of employees engaged in improper sales practices to satisfy goals and earn financial rewards under the Respondent's incentive program."
		Business objectives	■ "Senior management's emphasis on increasing efficiency compromised the effectiveness of certain controls."
	Products & services	Income streams	■ "Total net PPI income as a percentage of overall profit before . . . tax was on average 14% for 2003 to 2006."
		Complexity	■ "Inappropriate sales of more complex varieties of interest rate hedging products."
	Customers	Sophistication	■ ". . . when sold to customers who are likely to lack expertise (i.e. non-sophisticated customers) . . . some interest rate hedging products may be inappropriate."
	2. Culture	Tone from the top	■ ". . . a widespread sense of complacency, a reactive stance in dealing with risks . . . . This complacent attitude was seen at the top of the institution."
		Risk takers	■ "Some of the Traders treated aggressively anyone who questioned their activities . . ."
		Control functions	■ "Certain personnel within control functions . . . were overly deferential in challenging certain traders."
	3. Infrastructure, including governance	Oversight	■ "Inadequate oversight and challenge by the Board and its committees of emerging non-financial risks."
		Appetite & policy frameworks	■ "A lack of clear articulation of minimum standards in the form of Group-wide policies . . ."
		Reporting lines	■ ". . . there were no clear lines of responsibility . . ."
	4. People	Expertise	■ "Too much reliance [was] placed on inexperienced and/or junior staff."
		Resourcing levels	■ "A heavy reliance on manual processes and the workload . . . meant that certain of the existing controls in place were not operating effectively."

(Continued)

TABLE 5.5 (*Continued*)

	Level 1	Level 2	Examples from various public sources
Basel II internal causal categories		Training	■ "... advisers were not provided with adequate training ..."
		Mis-understanding	■ "For reasons that are not clear ... the junior staff in Operations interpreted ... [the] email to mean that they were no longer required to carry out any checks ..."
		Supervision	■ "... management and supervision of traders ... were not effective ..."
	5. Processes[8]	Manual processes	■ "The booking structure ... was complex and overly reliant on large spreadsheets ..."
		Definition of processes	■ "Failing to establish adequate processes for loan modifications."
	6. Systems[9]	Systems' age	■ "... an expired digital certificate contributed to the attackers' ability to communicate with compromised servers and steal data without detection ..."
		Systems' architecture	■ "Risk ... relied upon a number of disparate systems to calculate VaR ..."
	7. Change to the above, i.e.:	People	■ "Reassignments and reorganisations within certain control functions ... exacerbated the situation."
		Processes	■ None in the public domain.
		Systems	■ IT "upgraded the batch scheduler software ... because this software could no longer be sufficiently supported ..."
	8. Societal change	Compensation culture	■ "...claims management companies also ramped up their efforts to cash in before August 2019."
	9. Technological change	Big data, AI and robotics	■ None in the public domain.

---

[8]*Processes:* This includes deficiencies in the design of processes, but excludes human errors, which are covered within People.

[9]*Systems:* This includes outages arising from aging systems and poor architectures but, as above, it also excludes human errors.

TABLE 5.5 (*Continued*)

<table>
<tr><th></th><th>Level 1</th><th>Level 2</th><th>Examples from various public sources</th></tr>
<tr><td rowspan="14">External change causal categories</td><td rowspan="3">10. Economic cycle</td><td>Market moves</td><td>▪ "...the greatest volumes [of interest rate hedges] were sold in the period 2005–2008, before the base rate fell sharply to its current, sustained historic low."</td></tr>
<tr><td>Fall in asset values</td><td>▪ "...changing market conditions in late 2007 and during 2008 ..."</td></tr>
<tr><td>Increase in defaults</td><td>▪ "Under the settlement, roughly 750,000 borrowers who lost their homes to foreclosure between 2008 and 2011 can expect to receive a...cash payment."</td></tr>
<tr><td rowspan="3">11. Environmental change</td><td>De-carbonisation</td><td>▪ None in the public domain.</td></tr>
<tr><td>Extreme weather</td><td>▪ Closure of NYSE due to Hurricane Sandy "...to ensure safety of our people and communities."</td></tr>
<tr><td>Pandemics</td><td>▪ The COVID-19 pandemic coincided with operational disruption; market dislocation (e.g. negative future oil prices); an economic slowdown and a spike in cybercrime.</td></tr>
<tr><td>12. Geopolitical change</td><td>New trade sanctions</td><td>▪ "When the US imposed heightened sanctions against Iran in mid-1995, the bank developed a practice to manipulate and delete information ..."</td></tr>
<tr><td>13. Regulatory/ statutory change</td><td>New requirements</td><td>▪ "...the Judicial Review ... against, what the industry believed was the creation, and the retrospective application of new requirements by the FSA."
▪ The UK Supreme Court "...considered that the Orient-Express decision... was wrongly decided... and conclude that it should be overruled."</td></tr>
</table>

each Level 2 cause is illustrated by a quote from either external reports, or settlements or regulatory notices (the sources are detailed in Appendix III). The causes of these actual events were supplemented with six external causes, five of which were taken from the World Economic Forum's annual global risks reports (World Economic Forum, 2021). The relative significance of these different causes can be visualised using a technique borrowed from lean six sigma (Figure 5.2). As noted in Chapter 2, the strongest correlations seem to be between strategy, culture, governance, people and

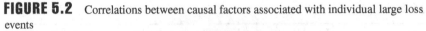

FIGURE 5.2   Correlations between causal factors associated with individual large loss events

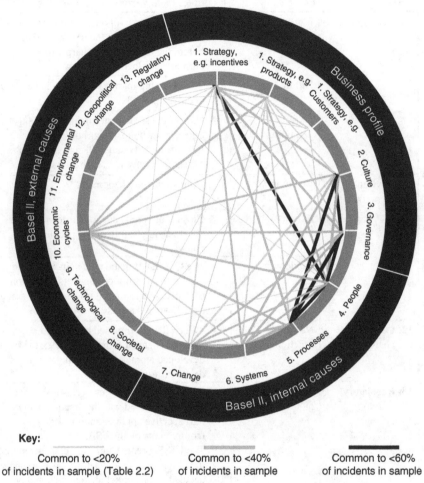

Key:

| Common to <20% of incidents in sample (Table 2.2) | Common to <40% of incidents in sample | Common to <60% of incidents in sample |

processes, which have P values of between 2.2 to 2.6, i.e. the probability of these higher values is between 1% and 2%.

The internal causes may be both correlated and also reinforce each other, producing feedback loops and domino effects, driving the concentration of loss events in individual firms (6th Law). Figure 5.2 demonstrates that the most important external cause is currently economic cycles,[10] and Formula 3.2 (7th Law) shows that

---

[10]Research published by the Federal Reserve, Richmond found for US banks "statistically significant correlations between macroeconomic growth and losses in CPBP and EDPM" (Abdymomunov, 2014).

this causal factor appears to drive increases in occurrence and detection, velocity, duration and lags of Operational Risk losses.

In the coming years, however, COVID-19 and Climate Change may lead to environmental change becoming the most important external cause, and consequently, this cause may need to be split further between pandemics and Climate Change.

CONCLUSIONS

Whilst no taxonomy is ever perfect they should always be elegant, i.e. they should have a clear and defined structure which is self-evidently complete and meaningful; for example, the range of impacts from Operational Risk events should be based upon the structure of a firm's P&L and balance sheet and its various stakeholders.

Taxonomies should also always be back-tested to establish their completeness and whether the most significant groups are being appropriately prioritised. No matter how elegant they are, if they do not adequately categorise a significant portion of real-world data, then they are incorrect.[11]

Additionally, taxonomies should be value-adding, whether that is by helping Operational Risk managers to ensure completeness; to aggregate consistently data; or to understand their risks. For example, the taxonomy of inadequacies or failures is subsequently used in this book to identify the impacts of behavioural changes in stakeholders caused by an economic shock (Table 11.3); the ability to utilise insurance policies to offset specific events (Table 12.2); and the identification of predictive metrics (Table 13.4). Similarly, the impact taxonomy is utilised in scenario analysis (Chapter 9); stressing impacts for economic shocks (Table 11.2); and the ability to utilise insurance policies to offset specific impacts (Table 12.2). Finally, the taxonomies in this chapter provide three potentially interesting insights pertaining to modelling:

1. The observation that the majority of Operational Risk events "...arise from human failings" (Tables 2.1 and 5.3) may explain why just a single distribution (Poisson) is typically used to model the frequency of occurrence of events.
2. The wide variations in the scale of different impacts of events (Table 5.4) may explain why a variety of different distributions are typically used to model severity.
3. The existence of correlations for very large loss events between different underlying causal factors (Figure 5.2) may contribute to why some banks suffer more very large losses than others. As inadequacies or failures that constitute events also describe control failures, then causal factors that are linked to mistakes and omissions may increase both the occurrence of events and control failures.

---

[11] The great evolutionary biologist Thomas Huxley famously said, "The great tragedy of science is the slaying of a beautiful hypothesis by an ugly fact."

In contrast, the limitations of the Basel II event taxonomy, and the absence of established industry standard taxonomies for control failures, causes and impacts, may have contributed to some of the various framework challenges faced by the Operational Risk profession.

Finally, the nature of these taxonomies is one of the three underlying pillars that drive these Ten Laws, i.e. that explain why Operational Risk displays patterns of behaviour. The other two pillars are the business profiles of firms and human and institutional behaviours and biases. This will be explored further in the concluding chapter of Part One.

CHAPTER 6

Conclusions – How and Why

This final chapter of Part One considers the collective nature of these Ten Laws that govern Operational Risk (summarised in Table 6.1). The chapter also assesses how well these Ten Laws explain the patterns of behaviour of Operational Risk observed in Chapter 1, and why this may be.

THE NATURE OF THE TEN LAWS

Pleasingly, there is a structure to the Ten Laws: the left-hand side of Table 6.1 describes the occurrence and the financial significance of individual loss events, whilst the right-hand side describes how Operational Risk interacts with other factors, such as internal and external causes and also the behaviours of firms and their stakeholders, e.g. firms both proactively take Operational Risk (10th Law) and react to actual or potential exposures that are outside of their appetites (8th Law).

The criticality of time

It is noteworthy that time plays an important role in many of these formulae, in terms of the duration of events; the rapidity with which losses are suffered; and the lags between occurrence and detection and between detection and settlement. As a consequence, time should probably feature much more significantly within the appetite statements (Chapter 7), capital models (Chapter 10), stress testing of firms (Chapter 11) and emerging risks (Part Three). The focus of Basel II on a one-year time horizon may well have reduced the attention paid historically by the industry to the importance of time. For example, rather than just stating that systemic misconduct is outside of appetite, banks could articulate an expectation as to how promptly systemic misconduct should be identified. Equally, stress tests could more consistently reflect the time horizons over which Conduct Risks, which are sensitive to business cycles, may crystallise (5th and 7th Laws). Meanwhile the emergence of Climate Change risks requires the consideration of even longer time horizons.

TABLE 6.1   Coverage of the Ten Laws and their units

Describe individual events	Describe patterns in events and interrelationships
1. Occurrence of events (events)	6. Concentration due to internal drivers (ratio of losses for different banks)
2. Detection of events (events over time)	7. Concentration due to external drivers (ratio of losses pre & post the GFC)
3. Velocity of losses (incurred losses ($) over time)	8. Risk Homeostasis (losses ($) over time)
4. Duration and severity of events (incurred losses ($))	9. Risk transference, transformation and conservation (events over time) and (losses ($) over time)
5. Lags in settlement (settled losses ($) over time)	10. Proactive taking of Operational Risk (losses ($) over time)

The objectives of controls

There is some debate within the profession as to the categorisation and nomenclature of different controls. An implication of the laws on the left-hand side of Table 6.1 is that different controls either reduce the occurrence or the duration or the consequences of Operational Risk events.[1] If classified in this way, then the effectiveness of these different categories of controls can be assessed, as follows:

- *Preventive controls:* As these limit the occurrence of Operational Risk events, their effectiveness could be assessed in terms of events prevented, i.e. negative events;
- *Detective controls:* Whilst not preventing the occurrence of Operational Risk events, these controls detect when an event has occurred. Weak detective controls delay discovery, leading to longer durations. Consequently, their effectiveness could be assessed in terms of the shortening of the duration of events that are continuing to occur, i.e. reduced duration or negative time;[2] and

---

[1] In addition to preventive, detective and corrective/resilience controls the Chartered Institute of Internal Audit also defines directive controls, e.g. accounting manuals, documented procedures and training. Directive controls do not seem to have unique objectives, but instead seem to span the other three categories of controls (Chartered Institute of Internal Audit, 2020).

[2] The effectiveness of detective controls could also be measured as events identified, but ultimately as all events will be identified eventually the measure of success is length of time to discover (i.e. time). Depending on the velocity of the impacts this may variously be measured in seconds/minutes (e.g. for a rogue algo) or weeks and months (e.g. fines and penalties).

■ *Corrective/resilience controls:* Whilst these neither prevent nor detect the occurrence of Operational Risk events, they can limit the impacts, including the financial and operational consequences. As a result, their effectiveness could be measured in the limitation of losses incurred after an event has occurred, i.e. negative losses ($), such as recoveries of stolen assets; insurance claims; and the restriction of the scale with which a rogue algo can malfunction, through throttle controls. The effectiveness of controls intended to enhance Operational Resilience can also be assessed in terms of time, i.e. the shortening of recovery times.

These relationships are consolidated into the 8th Law, which describes the equilibrium, over time, between risk in the form of occurrence, duration and the velocity of losses with preventive, detective and corrective/resilience controls. This equilibrium should align to a firm's appetite (Chapter 7).

An overarching formula

The Ten Laws can also be represented as a single overarching formula (Formula 6.1). There are a number of interesting aspects of Operational Risk highlighted in this formula. It describes losses suffered by a firm in a particular year, which is influenced not just by occurrence (1st Law), but also by the detection of events (2nd Law) and the lags in settlement (5th Law). The formula also makes clear that the Operational Risk losses suffered by a firm will arise from a combination of proactively taken Operational Risks, as well as other risks to which the firm is passively exposed (10th Law). As noted above, the level of losses suffered by firms should equilibrate over time to their risk appetite through the 8th Law: Risk Homeostasis. The taxonomies described in Chapter 5 are very influential. Causal factors are all-pervasive. Internal causes drive the occurrence of Operational Risk events (1st Law), whilst external causes can drive occurrence, detection/duration, velocity and lags (7th Law). The taxonomy of inadequacies or failures describes both the nature of events and control failures and as a result influences occurrence, duration and velocity, whilst the nature of different consequences described in the impact taxonomy also influences the velocity of losses. Finally, the 9th Law (Risk Transference, Transformation and Conservation), is an important factor in both the velocity of some losses, and also recoveries through insurance.

The spans of influence of both human and institutional behaviours and biases, and business profile are also highlighted.

HOW DO THE TEN LAWS EXPLAIN THE PATTERNS IN THE BEHAVIOUR OF OPERATIONAL RISK

The analysis of various industry loss data collection exercises in Chapter 1 highlighted that Operational Risk displays a range of patterns of behaviour at differing levels, i.e.

Formula 6.1 An overarching formula for Operational Risk

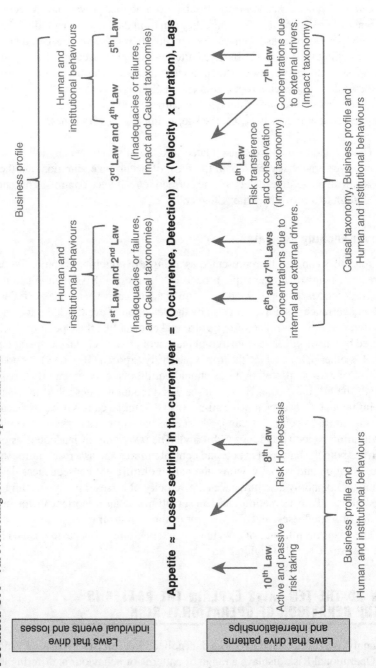

$$\textbf{Appetite} \approx \textbf{Losses settling in the current year} = \textbf{(Occurrence, Detection)} \times \textbf{(Velocity} \times \textbf{Duration), Lags}$$

at Level 1: Operational Risk; at the seven Basel II risk subcategories; for different business lines and individual banks:

1. *Profile of Operational Risk losses:* The largest number of Operational Risk loss events have relatively low impacts; whilst a small number of loss events have disproportionately high impacts (Figures 1.1 and 1.2).
2. *Trends and dynamism:* There is a spike in the number and value of Operational Risk loss events $\geq$€10 million that coincides with the aftermath of the Global Financial Crisis (Table 1.1 and Figures 1.1 and 1.2). The main driver of this is CPBP (Figures 1.3 and 1.4).
3. *Frequency and stability:* Some of the seven subcategories of Operational Risk are consistently more frequent than others, in particular EDPM and EF. The frequencies of some of these subcategories also appear to be quite stable over time, e.g. EDPM, IF, BDSF and DPA (Figure 1.3).
4. *CPBP's disproportionate impacts:* The losses generated by this risk subcategory are disproportionately large (Figure 1.4) and, as noted earlier, it is more dynamic than many of the other subcategories of Operational Risk (Figure 1.3).
5. *Profile of different business lines:* The risk profiles of Trading & Investment and Banking business lines are actually quite similar with the exception that the Banking business line is more exposed to External Fraud loss events (Figure 1.4).
6. *Profile of individual banks:* The risk profiles of banks seem to differ quite markedly in terms of the volume of Operational Risk loss events that they suffer (Figure 1.5).

How these six observations are explained by the Ten Laws is described below:

1. *Profile of Operational Risk losses:* The largest number of loss events have relatively low impacts; whilst a small number of loss events have disproportionately high impacts.

The 1st Law states that the occurrence of Operational Risk events is driven by: business profile; internal and external causes; and inadequacies or failures; and is limited by preventive controls. Whilst the 3rd and 4th Laws state that the value of individual loss events are driven by the quantum of inadequacies or failures; the nature of the impacts, and hence velocity; internal and external causes; and the duration of the incident; and are limited by both detective and corrective/resilience controls.

Consequently, the left-hand side of Figure 1.1 must be driven by incidents with a high volume of inadequacies or failures but with low values for the quantum of inadequacies or failures; the nature of impacts; and the duration of the incidents.

Whilst the 3rd and 4th Laws indicate that the right-hand side of the Figure 1.1 must be driven by events for which one or more of the following are unusually large: the quantum of these inadequacies or failures; the nature of the impacts; and the duration (Table 2.3), whilst the associated detective and corrective/resilience controls must also have been ineffective.

The left-hand side of Figure 1.1

Analysing the revenues of the 83 banking members of ORX in 2018 reveals that they generate $3\frac{1}{2}$ times as much revenues from Banking as from Trading & Investment business lines (ORX report, 2019). Banking business lines typically have higher volumes of lower value transactions than Trading & Investment business lines, i.e. the differences are three or four orders of magnitude (Figure 6.2). Consequently, it is not surprising that the Banking business line generates the majority of the volume of Operational Risk losses reported by ORX, i.e. 11 times more loss events for the period 2013 to 2018 than the Trading & Investment business lines.

Table 2.1 illustrates the Author's view that mistakes and omissions – and malicious acts perpetrated by criminals against the Banking business line – are much more common than incidents involving systemic misconduct. The nature of impacts caused by mistakes and omissions is typically compensation to customers, but the higher volume and lower value of Banking business line transactions means that losses caused by one-off errors are typically of short duration (Table 2.3) and low value. Equally, external frauds committed by criminals are also typically individually lower-value events.

In conclusion, the left-hand side of Figure 1.1 is driven by the business profile of the Banking business line (i.e. high volume:low value transactions) and the nature of the events, i.e. mistakes and omissions of staff members and malicious acts carried out by external criminals.

Right-hand side of Figure 1.1

Reviewing the total value of losses suffered by ORX members from 2010 to 2018 (€264 billion) and overlaying the very large losses ($\geq$$1 billion) suffered by nine individual members[3] that are in the public domain,[4] reveals that just over 50% of the losses by value actually comprised just 0.01% of the total number of loss events (38 events with an average value of €3.7 billion). These very large loss events are the main driver of the profile of the right-hand side of Figure 1.1, and are primarily Systemic Operational Risk Events, i.e. MBS litigation (20% of the total value of losses); PPI (14%); inappropriate foreclosure (5%); benchmark manipulation (3%); and AML and sanction breaches (3%).

Figure 6.1 represents the contribution of these 38 very large losses to the total value of losses suffered by ORX members for each of the years from 2010 to 2018. In this graph the losses from events, such as PPI, are reflected in the year in which they were first recorded, i.e. 2011, even though the majority of the provisions and payments to customers occurred in subsequent years.

---

[3]These nine ORX members were members throughout this period.
[4]Obtained from either IBM FIRST Risk Case Studies or from the financial statements of the banks, e.g. for PPI losses.

FIGURE 6.1　The contribution of 38 very large loss events to the total losses suffered by ORX's membership

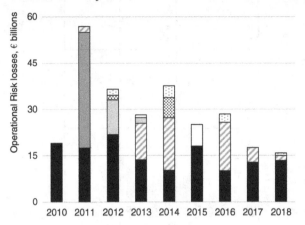

Selecting a sample of five of these 38 events, which represent alone 19% of the total value of ORX losses across this nine-year period, demonstrates that these losses were so extreme because they involve systemic misconduct that resulted in excessive levels of failures over extended periods, i.e. the duration of these events range from 1 year to more than a decade; and the value of transactions involved ranges from $8.7 billion of foreclosures to ~$50 billion of PPI policies sold.

None of these five losses involve high velocity events, with the exception of the acquisitions which contributed to the $13 billion misrepresentation of MBS settlement (see the case study in Chapter 2). In addition, four out of the five examples are linked to an external cause, i.e. the Global Financial Crisis,[5] either as a trigger to varying degrees for an event being detected (e.g. benchmark manipulation; mis-sale of PPI and misrepresentation of MBS) and/or exacerbating the resulting levels of loss (e.g. misrepresentation of MBS and inappropriate foreclosure). Finally, corrective/resilience controls played no role at all in mitigating any of these losses.

The extreme combination of these factors from the 3rd and 4th Laws (Table 6.2) helps to explain the disproportionately large contribution of these few Operational Risk loss events.

2. *Trends and dynamism:* There is a spike in the number and value of Operational Risk loss events ≥€10 million that coincides with the aftermath of the Global Financial Crisis.

---

[5]The fifth event is linked to the Geopolitics external cause.

TABLE 6.2 Key drivers of the scale of five very large loss events up to December 2018

Individual loss bank loss events	1. Quantum of failures	2. The nature of impacts	3. External causes	4. Duration	5. Corrective controls
Clients, Products & Business Practices PPI mis-sale – £19.5bn	**Systemic** mis-sale of policies: 16 million policies	Compensation, average claim: £2.3k Claim rate: ~50%	■ Change in regulatory view. ■ Social media. ■ Financial Crisis led to claims.	>10 years	N/A
Misrepresentation of MBS – $13bn	**Systemic** misrepresentation of 103 MBS issues with a value of $33bn	Compensation & penalties: 39% of value	■ Financial Crisis e.g. led to a rise in delinquency and investor losses.	2½ years	N/A
Inappropriate foreclosure[6] – $6.8bn	**Systemic** inappropriate foreclosure. In 2010 loans transferred to foreclosure: $8.7bn	■ Settlement. ■ Compensation to foreclosed borrowers. ■ Consumer relief.	■ Financial Crisis: a dramatic rise in foreclosures revealed inadequate processes.	1 year	N/A
Benchmark manipulation – $2.5bn	**"Culture of misconduct"** P&L benefit unknown	■ Penalty for misconduct. ■ Penalty for not co-operating.	■ Financial Crisis: revealed vulnerabilities of benchmarks.	>5 years	N/A
AML & sanction breaches – $8.9bn	**Systematic** payments for sanctioned countries: $8.8bn	■ Penalty ~value of payments. ■ Criminal conviction.	■ Geopolitics re: sanctions.	8 years	N/A

[6] It is debatable whether inappropriate foreclosure should be classified as CPBP or EDPM.

The 7th Law explains how external causes can result in industry-wide increases in the occurrence and the detection/duration; and the velocity of Operational Risk incidents. A material enough change in an external cause (e.g. a severe economic shock) will consequently result in a significant spike in Operational Risk losses.

Analysing large loss events ($\geq$$0.1 billion) suffered by banks before and after the Global Financial Crisis (1996 to 2006 vs 2007 to 2017) reveals that post-crisis on average they occurred more frequently (3.2$\times$), had higher velocities (2.3$\times$) and had marginally longer durations (1.3$\times$) than in the proceeding 11 years. Overall this led to an increase in the total value of these large losses of ~9$\times$. The mechanism for this observation is that a severe enough external event, such as an economic shock, can result in:

- Existing losses being exacerbated (i.e. both increased occurrence and higher velocities), whilst the occurrence of other categories of losses may decline, e.g. due to reduced business volumes (Chapter 11);
- Historical failures being uncovered, increasing both detection rates and duration. The value of these loss events may also be exacerbated by increased velocity. This can be understood in terms of a Real Option Model (Chapter 3); and
- Inappropriate responses to an economic shock may lead to new losses, which may also be exacerbated by increased velocity.

Both the historical failures (e.g. benchmark manipulation) and inappropriate responses (e.g. inappropriate foreclosure) may be industry-wide, leading to Systemic Operational Risk Events.

The profile of Operational Risk events may also be influenced by changes in the behaviours of various stakeholders (Figure 2.1 and Chapter 11) including criminals (Chapter 16).

3. *Frequency and stability:* Some of the seven subcategories of Operational Risk are consistently more frequent than others, in particular EDPM and EF. The frequencies of some of these risks also appear to be stable over time, e.g. EDPM, IF, BDSF and DPA.

The 1st Law states that occurrence is driven by business profile; internal and external causes and inadequacies or failures; and is limited by preventive controls. Consequently:

- The most frequent incidents are due to the most commonly occurring inadequacies or failures; and
- The most stable risks are due to either an insensitivity to external causes or as a consequence of the 8th Law: Risk Homeostasis, i.e. risks and controls remain in equilibrium over time.

The mapping of the nature of different inadequacies or failures to the seven subcategories of Operational Risk (Table 2.1) shows that the majority of incidents are due to human errors and the malicious acts of external criminals. Other events involving systemic misconduct, or misconduct by individuals are rarer. The frequencies of most of the different categories of Operational Risk are underpinned by the nature of humans to make mistakes and to do wrong (Chapter 17). Whilst DPA is driven by a combination of very rare malicious acts carried out by, for example, terrorists or natural disasters (acts of God).

The stability of some of the categories of Operational Risk over time suggests that the occurrence of incidents associated with these risks are not as susceptible to industry-wide external causes, such as a severe economic slowdown. For example, whilst EDPM losses may decline after a severe downturn as business volumes typically also decline (Figure 11.8), DPA is primarily driven by acts of God, and is insensitive to severe economic slowdowns[7] but may eventually increase due to the impacts of Climate Change (Chapter 16). Risk Homeostasis (8th Law) may also have a role in this stability for risks that generate losses that have short durations and lags (Figure 11.9).

4. *CPBP results in disproportionately large losses, and are more dynamic*

The 3rd and 4th Laws state that the value of individual loss events are driven by the quantum of inadequacies or failures; the nature of impacts; internal and external causes; and the duration of the incident; and is limited by both detective and corrective/resilience controls.

As Table 6.2 illustrates, some of the largest ever Operational Risk losses are CPBP, due to these events often being systemic in nature rather than one-off mistakes and omissions (1st Law: Occurrence), increasing the quantum of failures. Additionally, very large CPBP losses often involve both the provision of services (10th Law: Active and passive risk taking); risk transference (9th Law: Risk Transference, Transformation and Conservation) and hence sensitivity to economic shocks (7th Law: Concentration due to external causes). All exacerbate the scale of the resulting losses, whilst the sensitivity to economic cycles may naturally result in peaks and troughs in CPBP losses over time. Finally, the duration of these events and the subsequent lags in settlement may mean that the effects of Risk Homeostasis (8th Law) are only observable over much longer time periods (Figure 4.2).

5. *The risk profiles of Trading & Investment and Banking business lines differ*

Again the 1st Law states that the occurrence of Operational Risk events is driven by: business profile; internal and external causes; and inadequacies or failures; and is limited by preventive controls. There are clear differences in business profiles of

---

[7]There is evidence both for and against a link between economic recessions and a rise in building fires.

the Trading & Investment and Banking business lines, i.e. for Trading & Investment the number of loss events is dominated by EDPM; whilst for Banking business lines the number of loss events are more evenly split between External Fraud and EDPM (Figure 1.4). The relative contribution to the total value of losses between these two groups of business lines are also quite comparable, with the exception again of the relatively higher occurrence of External Fraud experienced by the Banking business lines.

The drivers for these observations relate to specific aspects of the profiles of these different business lines. The original version of Figure 2.1 has been annotated to highlight key differences, such as the numbers of customers the value of transactions and the nature and variety of customer channels (Figure 6.2).

> **6.** *Profile of individual banks: The risk profiles of banks seem to differ quite markedly in terms of the volume of Operational Risk loss events that they suffer.*

The 6th Law predicts that losses may be higher in certain groups due to increased occurrence, velocity and duration of incidents. Analysing the G-SIBs reveals that the primary driver of the concentration of losses within certain banks is occurrence (Table 3.1). Consequently, per the 1st Law, this must be due to a combination of: business profile; internal causes; the nature of the inadequacies or failures; and the associated preventive controls.

Analysing the G-SIBs into three equal cohorts based upon the number of large losses ($\geq\$0.1$ billion) that they suffered from 1996 to 2006 reveals that the final cohort contains almost 80% of the loss events. Over 90% of these events, by number, relate to losses involving primarily either systemic or individual misconduct (Figure 3.1). These are linked to causes (Table 2.1), such as: strategy, including incentives; people (e.g. expertise and resourcing); and to a lesser extent governance and culture. The largest national group represented within this cohort are American banks.

All of the banks that are in this final cohort remain in this group when the same analysis is performed for the period 2007 to 2017.

WHY DO THESE LAWS EXPLAIN PATTERNS IN THE BEHAVIOUR OF OPERATIONAL RISK?

Whilst these laws clearly can explain the observed patterns of the behaviours of Operational Risk that were described in Chapter 1, this does not address why these patterns exist. The Author believes that there are three underlying pillars that drive these patterns:

1. *The business profiles of firms* determine both the profile of their risks and the potential quantum of failure (Table 2.5 and Figure 2.1);
2. *The nature of the three taxonomies* described in Chapter 5, i.e. inadequacies or failures (both events and control failures) causes and impacts; and

FIGURE 6.2 The business profile of a firm annotated for factors driving the differences between Banking and Trading & Investment business lines (Revision of Figure 2.1)

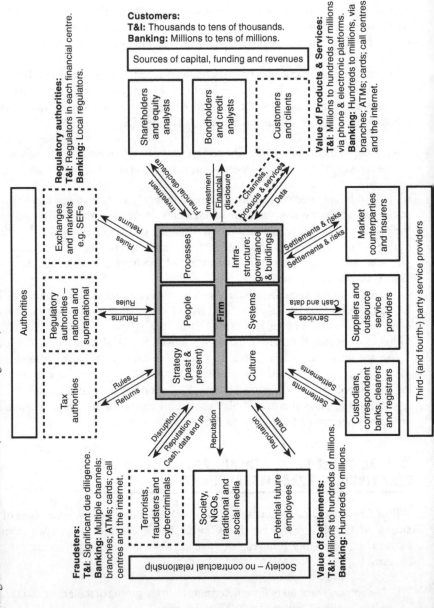

3. *Human and institutional behaviours and biases* influence the activities of a firm's stakeholders altering the occurrence of inadequacies or failures, such as misconduct and malicious acts, by both changing existing behaviours and also leading to new behaviours. They can also alter the assessment of remote risks and the extent to which firms learn lessons and consequently suffer fewer Operational Risk loss events over time.

The influence of each of these three pillars are considered in turn.

Business profiles

This is summarised in Figure 2.1, which sets out the range of sources of internally generated risks to which firms are exposed arising from processes, people, systems (as defined by Basel II), as well as a firm's strategy, infrastructure, including governance, and culture. Figure 2.1 also defines the range of sources of externally generated risks relating to authorities; sources of capital, funding and revenues; third (and fourth) parties; and society as a whole. A firm's business profile is driven by its present strategy, as well as the ghosts of past strategies. The influence of strategy can be seen in Figure 6.2 which compares some of these factors for Banking and Trading & Investment businesses in terms of the number of customers; the value and volume of transactions; customer channels and geographical/regulatory footprints. As discussed previously, it is the business profiles of ORX members (predominantly Banking) that is a key contributing factor to the shapes of both Figures 1.1 and 1.2, by influencing, in particular, the occurrence and scale of losses through several of the Ten Laws, i.e. 1st Law: Occurrence; 3rd Law: Velocity; 6th and 7th Laws: Concentration due to internal and external causes; 9th Law: Risk Transference, Transformation and Conservation; and 10th Law: Active and passive risk taking. Finally, aspects of a firm's business profile can also drive both causal factors and staff behaviours. This will be discussed further later in this chapter.

Three taxonomies

These three taxonomies define the nature of Operational Risk.

Taxonomy of causal factors The scope of causal factors is much broader than implied by the definition of Operational Risk provided by Basel II. The taxonomy of causal factors provided by Table 5.5 extends the range of causal factors beyond "processes, people and systems" to include causes linked to a firm's business profile. For example, as noted above, the strategy of a firm, and the associated incentives, can alter the behaviours of staff members in undesirable ways, e.g. in a mis-marking incident the authorities highlighted that "As a result of his manipulation [the trader] was able to secure significant year-end bonuses..." (SEC, February 2012).

It is clear from Formula 6.1 that the first seven laws and the 9th Law all include either internal or external causes, which can influence the occurrence of events; the effectiveness of preventive, detective and corrective/resilience controls; the scale of any consequential financial impacts; and the duration of lags in settlements. This is reflected in Figure 6.3, a revised butterfly/bow-tie diagram, which illustrates the all-pervasive nature of causes by listing them across the top of the diagram, rather than on the left-hand side, as is traditional. The dotted lines in Figure 6.3 reflect the influences of causes on occurrence, control failures and impacts based upon a well-publicised mis-marking incident from 2008.

Whilst the 6th Law highlights the importance of internal causes to the occurrence of loss events, it is external causes, currently in the form of business cycles, which recently have been most influential (Figures 3.2 and 11.1).

Additionally, the various causal factors are not all independent of each other, instead some of them appear to be correlated exacerbating their influence (Figure 5.2). Finally, as highlighted in Figure 6.3, the same causal factors may have multiple influences, i.e. on occurrence, the effectiveness of controls and the scale of impacts. These causal factors contribute to both the observed concentrations of Operational Risk losses in individual firms and also industry-wide trends.

Taxonomy of inadequacies or failures Inadequacies or failures constitute the nature of both events and control failures. A review of the volume of incidents recorded against the seven Basel II subcategories suggests that the most common loss events arise from human mistakes and omissions. Systemic misconduct by groups of staff members/firms seems to be less common, whilst malicious acts by staff members are orders of magnitude rarer still. The BDO FraudTrack report (BDO, 2018) highlights the importance of alternatively "Greed" and "Need" in motivating staff members to commit malicious acts. This seems intuitively correct, i.e. people are generally honest but do make mistakes. The exception is obviously professional criminals (Chapter 16).

In the revised butterfly diagram the seven Basel II subcategories of Operational Risk are ordered based upon their frequency in Figure 1.4. In addition the primary nature of the associated inadequacies or failures has been added to each risk based on Table 2.1. Finally, as inadequacies or failures are not only the nature of events (1st Law), but also the nature of control failures, then their influence also spans the first seven laws and the 9th Law. This has been reflected in the butterfly diagram by indicating the existence of more than one inadequacy or failure relating to a single event, i.e. whilst there can only be one inadequacy or failure that constitutes the event itself, other inadequacies or failures have been included that relate to the failure of the mitigating controls. This reflects the Reason's Swiss Cheese Model (Figure 13.2).

Taxonomy of the nature of impacts The nature of the impacts arising from an Operational Risk event are clearly also critical to understanding the behaviours of Operational Risk (Figure 2.3 and Table 5.4). The largest losses that firms suffer are in the

FIGURE 6.3   A revised butterfly/bow-tie diagram (Grimwade, 2020)

The dotted lines reflect the causes; control failures and impacts of a well-publicised mis-marking incident in 2008.

* The costs of improving controls, Reputational Risk and Credit Boundary losses fall outside of the definition of Operational Risk loss events for Basel II.

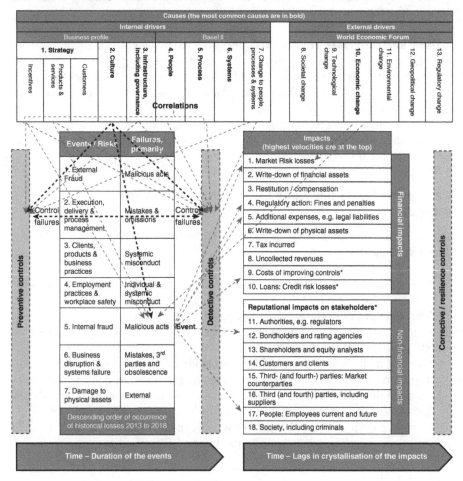

form of restitution and compensation. The scale of the largest of these impacts is frequently driven by the 9th Law: Risk Transference, Transformation and Conservation, i.e. when Market and Credit Risks are transferred to customers and clients, they are both transformed into Operational Risk for the arranging firm, and their scale is con-served.[8] This relationship between Operational Risk and Market and Credit Risks is also one driver for the sensitivity of Operational Risk to economic cycles, as explained through the 7th Law: Concentration due to external causes and the Real Option Model (Figure 3.4). The existence of Market Risk : Operational Risk boundary losses also leads to the existence of potentially very high velocity losses.

Revised butterfly/bow-tie diagram These three taxonomies do not exist in isolation of each other. Whilst Figure 6.3 is much more complex than a traditional butterfly/bow-tie diagram, it more clearly highlights the interactions between these three taxonomies and how inadequacies or failures constitute both the occurrence of events and also the failure of controls.

Additionally, across the bottom of this revised butterfly/bow-tie diagram is time, reflecting the earlier comments on the criticality of both the duration of events[9] and the lags that can occur in settlement (Figures 2.4 and 2.5, and also Figure 11.9).

The importance of human and institutional behaviours and biases

Human and institutional behaviours and biases influence a number of aspects of Oper-ational Risk, including:

- The occurrence of internal and external inadequacies or failures, which spans the first seven laws plus the 9th Law.
- The responses of staff members and firms to the detection of issues; near misses; and risks outside of appetite, which influence the 2nd and 4th Laws and also the 8th Law: Risk Homeostasis.
- Changes in the behaviours of a firms stakeholders and also new behaviours.
- The impacts of various biases, on the assessments of remote and emerging risks both within firms and also by their various stakeholders, including regulatory authorities. This influences the responses of firms and their various stakeholders (Figure 2.1) to external changes, such as economic shocks (Chapter 11); the evolving cybercrime threat; and Climate Change (Chapter 16).

---

[8]Figure 11.1, highlights the relative significance of Market and Credit Risks on Operational Risk.
[9]The time elapsed between the failure of preventive controls and the success of detective controls.

All of the Ten Laws are in some way influenced by human and institutional behaviours and biases, for example:

- *1st Law: Occurrence:* The propensity for humans to make mistakes, and also to be motivated by both "Greed" and "Need" (BDO, 2018).
- *2nd Law: Detection and 4th Law: Duration and severity:* The effectiveness of detective controls in identifying events can be influenced by the responses of staff e.g. the failure to act on exceptions (Table 5.3).
- *5th Law: Lags in settlement:* Extended periods of time between detection and settlement of loss events is linked to a number of factors, including the nature of the event, e.g. systemic misconduct; regulatory involvement; litigation; and the distribution of compensation to customers. Institutions can clearly often influence the precise timing of regulatory and legal settlements.
- *7th Law: Concentration due to external drivers:* This explicitly recognises that an economic shock can act as a catalyst for changes in the behaviours of a variety of stakeholders, including, banks, customers (Figure 11.8), criminals (Figure 11.3 and Chapter 16), and regulators (Figure 4.2). This is discussed further in Chapter 11.
- *8th Law: Risk Homeostasis:* This law predicts that the management of firms will increase expenditure on controls in order to keep expected Operational Risks in equilibrium with risk appetite (Figure 4.1). In assessing a firm's current and future risk exposures, however, staff members and authorities alike are prone to a series of behavioural biases that may distort their conclusions and behaviours. This relates to both individuals (Anchoring/Proximity Bias; Example Bias; Imagination Inflation and Confirmation Bias) and groups (Group Polarisation Bias). The combination of these biases and the limitations of language in describing risks (Chapter 4) may, however, restrict the effectiveness of the 8th Law.
- *10th Law: Active and passive risk taking:* An institution's perception of risk will influence its appetite for risk taking.

Different aspects of the nature of human and institutional behaviours and responses, including biases, appear throughout Parts Two and Three, and these various influences are summarised in Chapter 17.

Finally, it is important to note that these three pillars that underpin the Ten Laws of Operational Risk should not be viewed in isolation. Instead they dynamically interact with each other as illustrated in Figure 6.4. For example, strategy/incentives can inappropriately influence staff behaviours, whilst a firm's culture may also influence how it responds to incidents that have occurred, control weaknesses, and emerging threats through the 8th Law: Risk Homeostasis.

FIGURE 6.4　Illustration of the interactions between the three pillars driving the Ten Laws

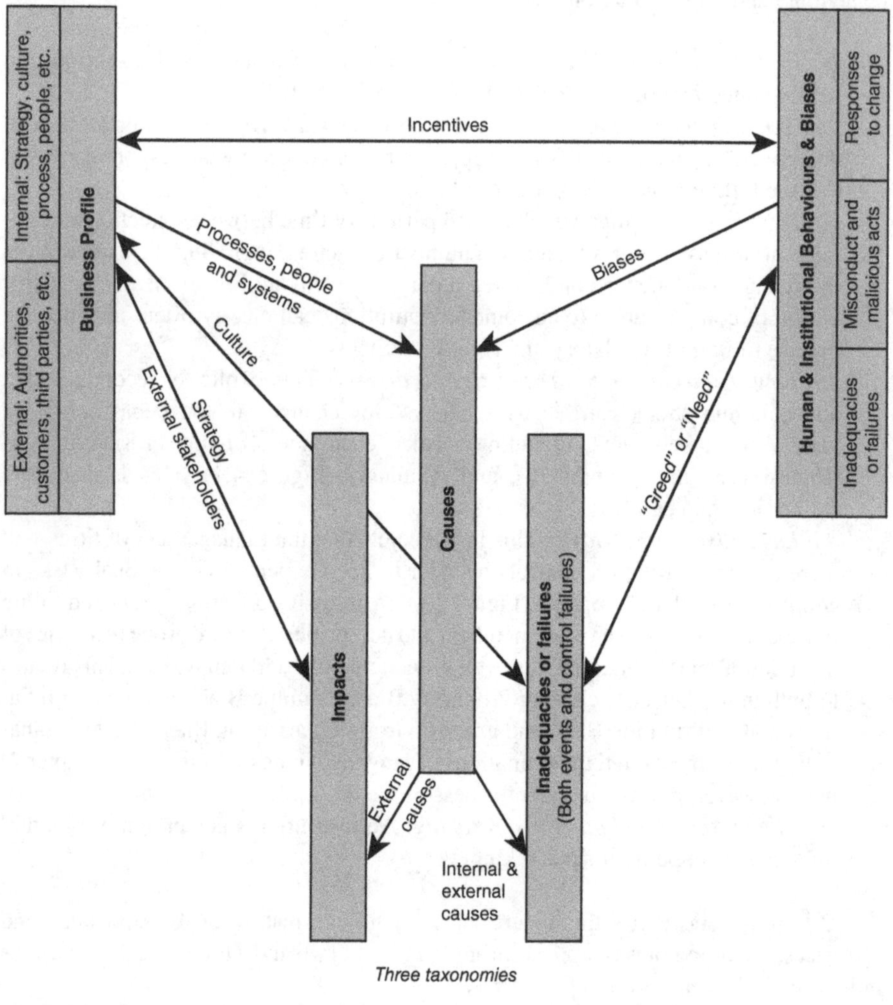

Three taxonomies

APPLICATION OF THESE TEN LAWS OF OPERATIONAL RISK

Interesting though these Ten Laws are, they serve no purpose unless they both guide Operational Risk managers in the present and also help them to predict the future. Consequently, Part Two is entitled "Operational Risk management tools designed for success", whilst Part Three focuses on predicting how Operational Risk may behave in different circumstances.

Two

Operational Risk Management Tools Designed for Success

Given the number of Systemic Operational Risk Events (Figure P2.1) before, during and after the Global Financial Crisis there have clearly been periods of failure in the management of Operational Risk. This is despite the run-up to the crisis coinciding with the enhancement of risk management practices, i.e. the Basel Committee published its draft proposals for the new Basel capital accord (Basel II) in January 2001; its sound practices for managing Operational Risk in February 2003; before the final version of the text of Basel II was approved in June 2004. The causes of the failure of the industry's Operational Risk tools is inevitably a combination of both design and operation.

One of the challenges facing the profession remains that there are no universally recognised standards for the different components of an Operational Risk management framework. Differing attempts since the Global Financial Crisis include the Basel Committee's *Review of the Principles for the Sound Management of Operational Risk* (Basel Committee, 2014); various surveys conducted by ORX into scenario analysis; RCSAs; emerging risks and taxonomies; and the Institute of Operational Risk's (IOR) Sound Practices Guides.[1] Maybe as a result of a lack of industry standards, the profession's tools are subject to ongoing discussion and debate, and whilst there are many views as to how to make them more value adding, ultimately there is no consensus.

---

[1] Whilst summaries of ORX's surveys are published, the detailed documents are available for members only or by subscription, similarly with the IOR's Sound Practices Guides.

FIGURE P2.1   SOREs that coincided with the implementation of Basel II (Grimwade, 2016)

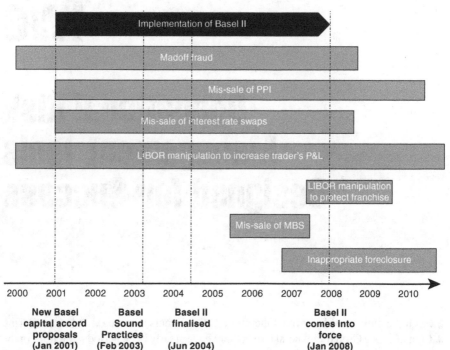

Consequently, the second part of this book describes how the tools used by the Operational Risk profession should be redesigned for these Ten Laws. The first chapter (Chapter 7) considers the impact of the various laws on defining risk appetite both quantitatively and qualitatively, their relevance for different categories of Operational Risks and their ability to support decision making. The different articulations of risk appetite are linked back the revised butterfly diagram (Figure 6.3). Chapter 8 addresses how best to undertake Risk & Control Self-Assessments, given the observed behaviours of Operational Risk. In particular, it focuses on what should be in and out of scope of RCSAs and how best to represent the profiles of different risks that are either continuums or discontinuums.

More rigorous techniques for assessing remote risks through scenario analysis, utilising the first five laws, are described in Chapter 9, focusing upon the estimation of the likelihood and the severity for the most important categories of inadequacies or failure and impacts respectively. Various quantitative approaches for validating the outputs of scenario analysis are also explained to mitigate the behavioural biases described in Chapter 4. The impacts in particular of the 5th Law: Lags in settlement and the

7th Law: Concentrations due to external factors on capital modelling are considered in Chapter 10. This includes the proposal that the relative proportions of capital between Pillars 1, 2A and 2B capital requirements should resemble an "hourglass", to better reflect the behaviours of different Operational Risks, observed in Chapter 1, primarily sensitivity to business cycles.

Chapter 11 focuses upon stress testing utilising the 7th Law: Concentrations due to external drivers. In particular, it identifies that the occurrence of some Operational Risk events increase due to both changes in human and institutional behaviours, and sensitivity to economic factors, whilst increases in severity are primarily driven by economic factors. The relationship between Operational Risk and business cycles is very complex and variously involves existing losses being exacerbated, historical failures being uncovered and the responses to the crisis by both banks and their stakeholders leading to new losses. The mechanism by which economic shocks reveal historical failures can be explained through a Real Option Model. Chapter 12 considers the circumstances in which Operational Risk can be transferred via insurance (4th and 9th Laws) and the assessment, through reverse stress testing, of events that may damage the viability of the business model of a firm. Whilst the tools described above are utilised periodically, Chapter 13 sets out how the day-to-day activities of Operational Risk managers can also be enhanced through the consideration of these Ten Laws. Specifically, this chapter covers:

- Incident management and root cause analysis.
- Control assurance and the nature of control failures.
- Predictive metrics.
- Change management, including implementing new technology, New Product & Transaction Approval and product stress testing.
- Reputational risk: Quantification and management.

Finally, Chapter 14 provides a summary as to how the various laws have been applied to the profession's tools.

CHAPTER 7

Defining and Cascading Operational Risk Appetites

This chapter considers the extent to which the Ten Laws described in Chapters 2 to 4 can help explain why developing risk appetite statements for Operational Risk is challenging and the range of potential solutions.

In its "Principles for An Effective Risk Appetite Framework", the Financial Stability Board (FSB) defined risk appetite succinctly as an articulation of "the aggregate level and types of risk that a financial institution is willing to accept, or to avoid, in order to achieve its business objectives . . . It should also address more difficult to quantify risks such as reputation and conduct risks as well as money laundering and unethical practices" (FSB, 2013).

Within these principles, the FSB allocates responsibility to the Board for approving a firm's risk appetite statement, which should include both quantitative and qualitative measures. These quantitative measures should be translated into risk limits that are cascaded to business lines and legal entities, and which can be both aggregated and disaggregated to enable measurement of risk against appetite. For Market Risk this is relatively straightforward,[1] as firm-level limits for Value at Risk (VaR) can be sub-allocated to businesses, and ultimately cascade down to the limits and mandates of individual desks and traders. Meanwhile the qualitative statements should articulate clearly the motivations for taking on or avoiding certain types of risk and establish some form of boundaries or indicators to enable the monitoring of these risks.

In a 2014 survey of the practices of banks, however, the Basel Committee noted that "Many banks indicated that establishing a risk appetite and tolerance[2] statement was more challenging for Operational Risk than for other risk categories such as Credit Risk and Market Risk, and attributed this to the nature and pervasiveness of Operational Risk." (Basel Committee, 2014).

---

[1] Although the treatment of diversification benefits can be problematic, as the sum of individual VaR limits will be greater than a firm's Group-level VaR limit.

[2] The FSB notes that the terms "risk appetite" and "risk tolerance" are used by authors with slightly different meanings; however, the FSB just uses the term "risk appetite" (FSB, 2013).

This is problematic, as an effective risk appetite statement, should help Operational Risk managers to "evaluate opportunities for appropriate risk taking and act as a defence against excessive risk-taking" (FSB, 2013). Fortunately, the Ten Laws both indicate why risk appetite is so difficult to articulate, and also provide some insights into how this can be more successfully achieved.

THE CHALLENGES OF DEVELOPING AN OPERATIONAL RISK APPETITE STATEMENT

The 10th Law articulates that Operational Risk is both actively and passively taken, just like Market and Credit Risk, so any risk appetite statement should articulate how much Operational Risk a firm is prepared to take actively in return for fee income; and passively, as a by-product of the generation of trading and interest income.

As the definition of Operational Risk encompasses "inadequacies or failures" it literally touches all staff members within a firm, in a way that Market and Credit Risk do not. This means that any risk appetite statement somehow needs to cascade down an organisation to its lowest levels.

An effective risk appetite statement also needs to address the diversity arising from a firm's business profile (1st Law, Figure 2.1); the varying frequencies of different events (1st Law, Figure 1.3); the all-pervasive influence of causes (1st to 4th Laws, Figure 6.3); and finally the range of velocities with which different events generate losses (3rd Law, Figure 2.3).

Additionally, there are significant lags between the occurrences of events and the settlement of losses (5th Law, Figure 2.5). As a consequence, a firm's largest current year losses are most likely to be driven by its historical, rather than current, risk appetite, business strategy and control framework. This is also the case for Credit Risk. Finally, Operational Risk is cyclical (7th Law), again like Credit Risk, so any risk appetite has to be "through the cycle", i.e. define the amount of Operational Risk that a firm wants to take in terms of both the peaks and troughs in economic cycles.

As a consequence, articulating Operational Risk appetite requires a portfolio of approaches.

POTENTIAL SOLUTIONS

The first four Laws of Operational Risk respectively described the occurrence and detection of events; and the velocity and duration of their impacts, and hence their severity. They also describe the nature of preventive, detective and corrective/resilience controls, and the all-pervasive influence of causes. This is summarised in a butterfly diagram (Figure 7.1) which has been annotated for potential quantitative approaches for defining appetite.

FIGURE 7.1 Potential approaches for defining Operational Risk appetite (Revision of Figure 6.3)

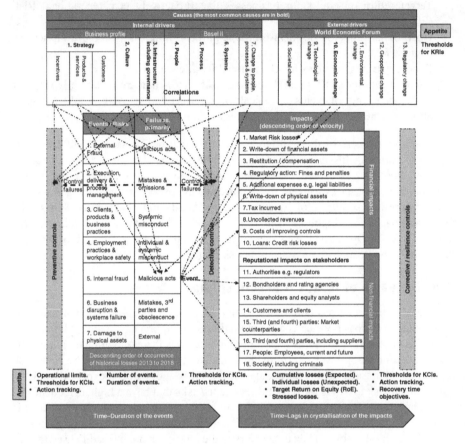

Quantitative measures

Existing quantitative measures for setting Operational Risk appetite include:

- Cumulative number of Operational Risk loss events against a threshold. In practice, this can be either the total number of events or events above a certain materiality (Figure 1.2).
- Cumulative value of Operational Risk losses (expected) against a threshold. In practice, this can be either an absolute amount or as a % of revenues (left-hand side of Figure 1.1). This can also be stressed for economic shocks (Figure 3.2).
- Value of an individual large event with a particular likelihood (unexpected). This can also be either an absolute amount or as a % of revenues. This can also be

stressed for economic shocks (right-hand side of Figure 1.1). The duration of a large event may also form part of an appetite statement.

- Target return on equity for businesses that proactively take Operational Risk (Figure 4.4).
- Operational limits on business profile, e.g. the volume and value of transactions (Figure 7.1).
- Recovery time objectives for Operational Resilience.
- Value of metrics (KRIs) that describe causal factors that are particularly relevant to the occurrence of events or the scale of impacts relative to a threshold, the operation of controls (KCIs) and the progress with remedial actions (Figure 7.1).

The effectiveness of these different measures can be assessed for different categories of events against criteria, based on FSB (2013), such as ability to: be cascaded/disaggregated; be aggregated; be scaled; support the evaluation of new risk-taking opportunities; and act as triggers for action "against excessive risk-taking"[3] when a firm's risk profile is outside of appetite. The key merits and weaknesses of these different approaches are highlighted in Table 7.1. This illustrates why, unlike VaR for Market Risk, for Operational Risk there is no one metric that can be used for setting a firm's risk appetite and for measuring its risk profile.

Expected value of losses – practicalities

The Basel Committee has noted that setting appetite by using operational losses as a percentage of gross revenue is a "commonly observed practice" (Basel Committee, 2014). The common use of this metric probably reflects the ease with which it can be cascaded from group-level into individual businesses and also be split by event/risk type. It also naturally scales for changes in business activity. The expected value of Operational Risk losses is most useful for events/risks that have a higher frequency of occurrence, rather than for risks that infrequently crystallise into losses. In practice, this means it is most relevant for EDPM and External Fraud, in retail banks (Figure 1.4). Table 7.1 highlights several key issues. Firstly the metric cannot be readily used to support the evaluation of new opportunities. Secondly, it is generally a backward-looking metric, i.e. it is the Operational Risk equivalent of a trader's stop-loss limit – a trigger for action, after the event. The metric can be forward-looking, however, if firms consider the trend/the acceleration[4] of losses and respond prior to the appetite being breached. Firms implicitly balance control expenditure and losses for passively taken risks. Economists would describe this as an efficient frontier. In response to an increase in Operational Risk losses, firms may choose to enhance control or curtail business activity to reduce their exposures, in line with the 8th Law: Risk Homeostasis. This is illustrated in Figure 7.2 – the graph line is exponential, reflecting the impact of the law of diminishing returns.

---

[3]Per the FSB this includes "... to accept, or to avoid ...".
[4]Risk Acceleration (or Deceleration) was defined in Chapter 2 as the second derivative of Velocity, i.e. either Events or Losses/Time^2, i.e. it is the rate of change of Risk Frequency or Velocity.

TABLE 7.1   Assessment of potential quantitative Operational Risk appetite measures

	Potential risk appetite measures	Assessment of measures	Relevant event types
Proactive and passive Operational Risk exposures	▪ Cumulative number of loss events (1st and 2nd Laws). ▪ Cumulative value of losses (3rd and 4th Laws), e.g. absolute level of appetite for losses.	▪ Difficult to cascade. ▪ Straightforward to aggregate. ▪ Scaling requires judgement. ▪ Backward-looking – difficult to evaluate new opportunities.	▪ These are issues for all event types.
		▪ Trigger for action, if either a threshold is breached or a metric is trending upwards.	▪ *High volume:low value* events, e.g. mistakes and omissions and external frauds for retail banking[5] (Table 2.1).
	▪ Cumulative value of losses (3rd and 4th Laws), e.g. expected losses as a % of revenues.[6]	▪ Straightforward both to cascade and aggregate. ▪ Automatically scales. ▪ But also backward-looking.	▪ All event types.
		▪ Trigger for action, as above.	▪ *High volume:low value* events also (Table 2.1).
	▪ Individual loss events (1st to 4th Laws), e.g. an unexpected loss as a % of revenues with a likelihood or a Recovery Time Objective.	▪ Straightforward to cascade. ▪ Diversification hinders aggregation. ▪ Scalable for % revenues. *▪ Forward-looking,* can be used to evaluate new opportunities. *▪ Trigger for action,* by comparison to scenarios.	▪ *Low volume:high value* events. Supports decision making for new business opportunities that generate remote but very high value events e.g. systemic misconduct (Table 2.1).
	▪ Value of metrics (KRIs) that describe causal factors (1st to 4th Laws).	▪ Cascade requires judgement. ▪ Difficult to aggregate. ▪ Scaling requires judgement. *▪ Trigger for action,* forward-looking, but often imprecise. ▪ Cannot be used to evaluate new opportunities.	▪ *High volume:low value* events. KRIs indicating stretch may presage mistakes and omissions. ▪ *Low volume:high value* events. KRIs for economic slowdown may presage investor losses & litigation from *historical* sales.

(Continued)

---

[5] A motor finance division of a UK bank, for which the Author used to work, set a threshold for the value of successful application frauds at 0.1% of monthly car loan advances.

[6] This can be either actual or budgeted, to reduce volatility in Trading & Investment business lines.

TABLE 7.1   (*Continued*)

	Potential risk appetite measures	Assessment of measures	Relevant event types
Proactive Operational Risk exposures	■ Value of metrics (KCIs) indicating the effectiveness of controls (1st to 4th Laws).	■ Straightforward to cascade. ■ Difficult to aggregate. ■ Scaling is not relevant. ■ *Trigger for action*, forward-looking, but maybe imprecise. ■ Cannot be used to evaluate new opportunities. ■ Relates to the current rather than the historical control environment.	■ *Persistent threats:* KCIs are highly predictive if the controls are preventing persistent threats e.g. cybercrime. ■ *Inherently remote:* KCIs are much less predictive of losses if the controls are mitigating inherently remote risks, e.g. a pandemic.

	■ Target Return on Equity for businesses proactively taking Operational Risk (10th Law).	■ Straightforward to cascade, for material businesses.
		■ Diversification hinders aggregation.
		■ Scalable.
		■ *Forward-looking*, can be used to evaluate new opportunities.
		■ *Trigger for action*, if revenues fall and risks rise.
			■ Effective for:
			  ■ *Low volume:high value* events; and
			  ■ Material businesses.
			■ But can only be run infrequently and is insensitive to lower value risks.

	■ Operational limits on business profile, e.g. the volume and value of transactions.	■ Cascade requires judgement. ■ Difficult to aggregate. ■ Scaling is not relevant. ■ *Trigger for action* when breached. ■ *Forward-looking*, can form part of the evaluation of new opportunities.	■ *High volume:low value* events. Volume limits may restrict stretch, and hence mistakes and omissions. ■ *Low volume:high value* events. Value limits may restrict the scale of remote losses.

	■ Recovery time objectives/impact tolerances	■ Bottom-up approach, so does not require cascade, or aggregation or scaling.
		■ *Trigger for action* if a "severe but plausible" scenario would breach for tolerance.
		■ *Forward-looking*, can support investment decisions.
			■ *Business disruption that:*
			  ■ Causes intolerable levels of harm to clients;
			  ■ Poses a risk to a firm's safety and soundness;
			  ■ Threatens the UK's financial system; and
			  ■ Threatens the orderly operation of markets.

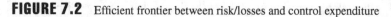

FIGURE 7.2 Efficient frontier between risk/losses and control expenditure

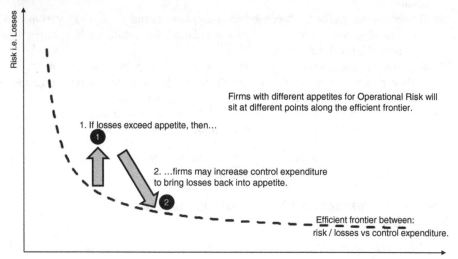

This is an effective process for the higher frequency risks described earlier, because for these risks there are relatively short lags between detection and settlement (Figure 2.5, 5th Law), and hence current losses reflect the current control environment. In contrast, this process is ineffective for managing risks that have long lags between detection and settlement, i.e. CPBP.

Although Figure 7.2 may look very theoretical, it illustrates what firms often do in practice, for example, many years ago, when the Author was working for a High Street bank, it suffered visible systems disruption. This acted as a trigger for criminals to launch a surge of fraudulent payments, presumably because they assumed the bank was ill-positioned to respond. The bank's response, however, was rapid – it lowered the floor limit for manual checks on client payments and redirected staff to carry out these checks. The surge in attacks dissipated within a couple of days, as the success rate of the criminals plummeted, and the bank was then able to return its floor limits to their original levels.

As noted earlier (Chapter 4), firms will also increase their control expenditure in anticipation of their risk profile exceeding appetite, e.g. Y2K at the beginning of the millennium.

Whilst setting a firm's appetite for expected Operational Risk losses is an art, which should reflect its business profile (Figure 2.1), there are at least four potential inputs for arriving at an actual number:[7]

(i) *Historical internal data:* The patterns and trends of a firm's historical Operational Risk losses (excluding unexpected losses, see later) can be readily

---

[7]The PRA requires firms to provide "clear and coherent explanations for forecasts" of Operational Risk losses (PRA, 2018).

analysed, after taking account of any key business changes, e.g. disposals of businesses;

(ii) *Peer comparison:* The ORX consortium publishes summary loss data for its members annually, which can be used as a benchmark to back-test a firm's appetite statement (Figure 3.2);

(iii) *Staff expectations:* Department Heads can make estimates of what they might typically expect to lose in the next 12 months from day-to-day losses, reflecting both a firm's business plan and base case economic scenarios; and

(iv) *Modelling:* Operational Risk capital models can produce a value for expected Operational Risk losses by setting the confidence interval to 50%.[8]

These four inputs can help ensure that a firm's Operational Risk appetite for expected losses is of the right order of magnitude.

Appetite for unexpected Operational Risk losses (Grimwade, 2016)

As indicated above, an appetite statement for expected Operational Risk losses, should exclude unexpected losses, as an individual event can lead to a breach of appetite and may also be unrelated to a firm's current business footprint and risk profile, e.g. the loss may relate to historical/legacy activities (5th Law: Lags in settlement).

In order to address this issue, firms should also define appetite statements for unexpected Operational Risk losses, which is analogous to other risk types. The key benefits of this approach is that it articulates appetite for low volume:high value risks, which can be used for assessing whether the outputs of scenario analysis are either inside or outside of appetite, prior to losses being suffered. They can also be used to appraise new business opportunities (e.g. a new business line or a particularly large transaction) if the Operational Risk profile is sufficiently different and material. These appetites can also be articulated as a percentage of revenues but are additionally associated with a likelihood, i.e. a firm may lose:

X% of budgeted revenues from an Operational Risk loss event once every Y years

The likelihoods used, i.e. once every Y years, should be the same as the likelihoods that are often used for either a firm's RCSAs or scenario analysis (e.g. 1 in 25 years and 1 in 50 years, equivalent of once or twice in a working lifetime). A firm's appetite for unexpected loss may also influence its decisions regarding the excesses and caps on its own insurance policies (Chapter 12).

A weakness of this approach, however, is that appetites for unexpected Operational Risk losses cannot be simply cascaded and aggregated in the same way as for expected

---

[8]This may approximate to Decision Theory's expected utility, i.e. it is the sum of the various outcomes × probability for a 12-month time horizon.

Operational Risk. For example, imagine a firm has an appetite for a $100 million loss once every 50 years and a business line runs 10 scenarios, each with an impact of $25 million and likelihoods of once every 50 years. Has the business breached the firm's appetite, as over a 50-year period, it could be expected to lose $250 million?

In practice, this question can only be answered by inputting the data into a capital model and analysing the outputs. The limitations on scenario analysis, the estimation of correlation and Operational Risk modelling (Chapters 9 and 10), can place restrictions, however, on the precision of management decisions that can be made from these techniques, particularly when used at lower levels within firms.

Finally, having both expected and unexpected appetites requires a basis for making the rather esoteric decision as to whether a large event that has occurred was either expected or unexpected! The approaches that can be adopted for making these "judgements of Solomon" include combinations of:

1. Setting an arbitrary monetary cut-off e.g. losses over €0.5 million could be treated as unexpected;
2. Treating all losses that arise from legacy or non-core businesses as unexpected; or
3. Making case-by-case decisions, which are reviewed and approved by an appropriate governance committee; or
4. Calculating the probability of occurrence by fitting a distribution a firm's historical loss data; or
5. Capturing all events that arise from mistakes and omissions and external fraud as expected, and everything else (e.g. individual and systemic misconduct) is unexpected.

Target return on equity For businesses which proactively take Operational Risk (10th Law) through activities such as soft underwriting; provision of correspondent banking; M&A advisory; and fund management, then risk appetite can also be defined in terms of a target return on equity/economic capital (RoE). This is, however, only effective for businesses that are large enough to have sufficient internal loss data and scenarios to enable their Operational Risk economic capital to be meaningfully modelled.

"Through the cycle"

The cyclical nature of the Operational Risk (7th Law) means that expected and unexpected appetites should also be set at higher levels for stressed economic conditions (Figure 3.2, and also Chapter 11). Firms can use similar data points for developing an appetite for stressed losses as for expected losses, i.e. historical internal data, peer comparison, staff expectations and capital modelling. In addition, firms can stress certain parameters within their scenarios, e.g. for scenarios linked to Market Risk boundary losses, firms can make the market movements more extreme.

The all-pervasive nature of Operational Risk and the limitations of appetites primarily articulated as expected and unexpected losses requires additional approaches for articulating and cascading Operational Risk appetite.

Cascading Board-level risk appetite statements into day-to-day processes & controls

Operational Risk limits and thresholds Whilst Operational Risk management does not have the same universal concept of limits as Market and Credit Risk management, there are instances in which firms can set limits that restrict their business profile,[9] and hence their potential to suffer Operational Risk losses. These limits are typically restrictions on business profile (Figure 2.1), e.g. the volume and value of transactions, that are intended to truncate a firm's exposure to tail losses (i.e. they are examples of corrective/resilience controls, 3rd Law). Examples of Operational Risk limits that operate by restricting exposure/the quantum of inadequacies or failures include: fat-finger typing limits (EDPM); limits for authorisation of manual payments and floor limits for reviewing client payments (Internal and External Fraud); maximum value of soft underwrites (CPBP); and maximum open position limits for algos (BDSF). Two of these examples are explored in more detail.

Fat-finger limits can take a variety of forms, depending on the trading platform and market (e.g. notional limit or a DV01 limit or the number of lots). They are designed to restrict the losses that a firm may suffer as a result of a trader keying in multiple extra zeros on the end of a trade or just executing a buy rather than a sell. Figure 7.3 illustrates how these limits can be seen as corrective/resilience controls, by truncating a firm's exposure to tail events.

Fat-finger limits can be set with consideration of a firm's appetite for unexpected Operational Risk losses and the scale of losses that may be suffered based upon the value of the limit; the likelihood of a large error; the length of time to detection (e.g. 1 day); and the likelihood of an extreme market movement.

Another example of limits are caps on the maximum value of soft underwrites undertaken by investment banks. In the eventuality of investors suffering losses and the registration documents being misleading, then the investors have a "right of recovery" from the underwriters under the US Securities Act[10] of 1933 (e.g. investors successfully sued the underwriters following the collapses of both WorldCom and REFCO). The exposure of individual underwriters can be restricted by firms limiting the maximum value of each underwrite (Formula 9.3).

---

[9]This is equivalent of Exposure in the XOI (Exposure, Occurrence, Impact) method (Naim and Condamin, 2019) or EI (Exposure Indicator) in the Basel Committee's (September 2001) Internal Measurement Approaches.

[10]Section 11, however, does provide the underwriters with a defence if, at the time of the issue, they had "reasonable ground to believe and did believe . . ." the misleading registration statement.

FIGURE 7.3 Representation of the impact of fat-finger limits and the link to appetite (Grimwade, 2016)

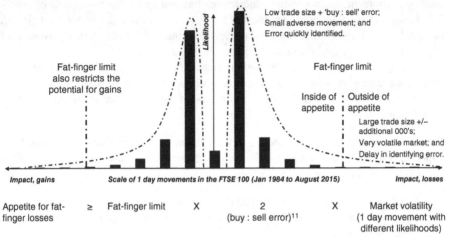

Appetite for fat-finger losses	≥	Fat-finger limit	X	2 (buy : sell error)[11]	X	Market volatility (1 day movement with different likelihoods)

As will be seen in Chapters 9 and 10, there is a linkage between the levels at which these limits are set and a firm's Operational Risk capital requirement, when calculated using a scenario-based model.[12]

Firms can also set Operational Risk limits in the form of volume caps, for example, the maximum number of structured trades that can be booked in a period, reflecting resourcing constraints within support functions; and throttle limits, restricting the number of trades executed per second by an algo. For limits relating to the volume and value of transactions there is a clear link to the scale of any potential losses (Quantum of inadequacies or failures, 3rd Law).

KRIs and KCIs

Firms can also set thresholds for a series of KRIs which provide approximate measures of the state of different causal factors that can increase the likelihood of events occurring, weaken the relevant mitigating controls and exacerbate the potential impacts of events when they do occur (1st to 4th Laws). Examples of KRIs include increases in customer driven transaction volumes, staff turnover and staff shortages,

---

[11]Buy-sell errors effectively double the size of a position, i.e. whilst the scale of the trade is correct because its sign is incorrect, e.g. a 100 lot sell rather than a 100 lot purchase creates a 200 lot position.

[12]A case study in Chapter 9 will describe how the very remote risk of underwriter litigation can be quantified using Fault Tree Analysis.

which influence the likelihood that humans may make mistakes and omissions. KRIs linked to market volatility; large, directional market movements; and a deteriorating credit environment, pertain to the occurrence, duration and value of impacts of events (7th Law). Setting thresholds for these KRIs can alert firms to a change in their risk profile, but, as Figure 5.2 illustrates, without too much precision, given a average of 4 ½ causes per large loss event analysed in Chapter 2.

Setting both limits for operational metrics that firms can control, such as the volume of structured products, and thresholds for external metrics that are less easily controlled (i.e. KRIs) is based very much on experience and judgement of management rather than science.

Qualitative statements In response to the challenge of cascading Operational Risk appetite, firms have supplemented their quantitative appetite statements with qualitative statements, in the form of a combination of:

- *Avoidance:* Details of activities and risks that a firm wishes to avoid; and
- *Outcomes:* Descriptions of desired and undesired outcomes for activities a firm wishes to undertake.

Activities that firms may wish to avoid are primarily associated with customers, products and services that are detailed in Figure 2.1. For example, firms may wish to avoid doing business with customers that present a higher risk of AML issues (e.g. bureau de change due to their handling of cash); higher risk products (e.g. leveraged investment products, Figure 13.6) and services (e.g. provision of correspondent banking services), as well as proprietary and algo trading. A real-world example of this is the following statement by HSBC's CEO in 2015: "We have absolutely no appetite to do business with clients who are evading their taxes or who fail to meet our financial crime compliance standards".[13]

These outcome statements can be organised under the seven Basel II subcategories of Operational Risk. For example, the High Street banks do not want to mis-sell products, such as PPI to customers, but it is unlikely that they could put in place controls to prevent this from ever occurring again (Figure 7.2), other than ceasing from selling the products altogether. Consequently, a more realistic generic appetite statement might be to:

- "Seek to avoid the mis-sale of products [this drives a firm's preventive controls, 1st Law]; and to
- Identify promptly any systemic mis-sale [this drives a firm's detective controls, 2nd Law]; and to

---

[13] An extract from an open letter published in some UK Sunday newspapers on 15th February, 2015, from HSBC's then CEO, Stuart Gulliver, and addressed to HSBC customers and staff, and relating to the bank's Swiss Private Banking business.

- Compensate any disadvantaged customers appropriately". [this drives a firm's corrective/resilience controls, in this case limiting reputational damage, 4th Law][14]

These types of high-level statements can be used to help guide managers in evaluating new opportunities. They can also be embedded within a firm's policies. This can be done by setting out in each policy the risks covered, the firm's appetite for those risks and the key controls that mitigate them, keeping the firm within appetite (Figure 7.4). There are three benefits of this approach, i.e.:

1. Determining whether a firm's controls for mitigating key risks are aligned to its stated appetite for Operational Risk. Gaps and inadequacies can then be addressed through remedial actions;

FIGURE 7.4 Cascade of Board-level Operational Risk appetite statements into individual policies

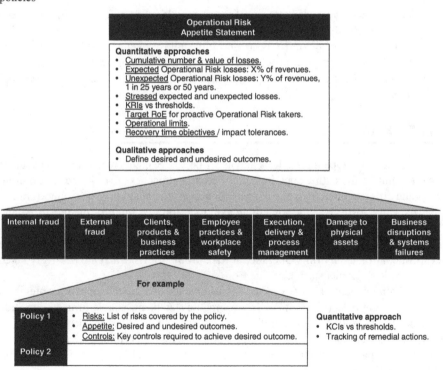

---

[14]Incorporating into appetite statements an articulation of how firms wish to respond to events is consistent with the UK regulators' Policy Statements on Operational Resilience, e.g. PRA (2021).

2. Linking policies to specific Operational Risks, and mapping those risks back to a taxonomy, provides assurance as to the completeness of a firm's policy framework; and

3. Requiring policy owners to consider proactively the risks that their policies are designed to mitigate, and the potential impacts of those policies.

While determining the appropriate controls to keep the firm within appetite clearly still requires judgement and experience on the part of the owners of the policies, the nature of the impacts/relative velocity can be a key guide. For example, risks that generate Market Risk boundary losses require a higher frequency of detective controls because of their higher velocity than Conduct Risks. Hence algos require real-time monitoring, whilst sale reviews are only conducted periodically and ex post. Policies can, however, be dynamic, for example, the COVID-19 pandemic has required a relaxation of the "Off-Premises Trading" policies of firms due to the need for remote working (Chapter 16).

Once the population of key controls has been identified that are required to keep a firm within appetite then they can be subject to additional first- and second-line oversight, e.g. reporting of KCIs against thresholds; regular first-line attestations and second-line control testing (Chapter 13). Remedial actions relating to these key controls should be tracked to completion, and delays outside of an agreed threshold escalated.

CONCLUSIONS

The complexity of Operational Risk and its all-pervasive nature means that there can be no one solution for setting appetite, i.e. different approaches are required for different risks and different objectives e.g. triggers for action vs evaluation of new opportunities.

Expected losses provide something akin to a stop-loss limit for the most frequent loss events, i.e. EDPM (primarily mistakes and omissions) and External Fraud losses in Banking. There is clearly a dynamic balance (an efficient frontier) between the costs of control and a firm's Operational Risk profile for risks that are passively taken (8th Law: Risk Homeostasis).

Defining appetite for unexpected losses extends quantitative appetite statements to less frequent risks (Figure 1.3). These appetite statements enable firms to conclude whether the outputs of their regular scenario analysis is either inside or outside of appetite. They can also be used to evaluate new business opportunities (e.g. a new business line or a particularly large transaction) if the Operational Risk profile is sufficiently different and material.

For businesses which proactively take Operational Risk (10th Law), then risk appetite can also be defined in terms of a target return on equity, but only if the businesses are large enough to model meaningfully economic capital.

These measures can all be stressed for economic shocks.

In addition, setting limits for operational metrics, i.e. the volume and value of transactions can reduce both the likelihood of Operational Risk events and their impacts. Monitoring KRIs for internal causes (e.g. staff turnover) can also give an indication of whether a business's risk profile is deteriorating, but again there is limited precision in the relationship with losses. Setting thresholds for external metrics that are less easily controlled can give an indication of whether a firm's Operational Risk profile is deteriorating, but these metrics again lack precision. In both cases the setting of these limits and thresholds is generally (but not always, e.g. fat-finger limits) a matter of experience and judgement rather than science.

Qualitative statements on desirable and undesirable outcomes can help Operational Risk managers to evaluate less material new opportunities. Additionally, embedding these qualitative statements into policies can help to drive the implementation of appropriate mitigating key controls at all levels within a firm.

Finally, a firm's appetite statement should drive all of the other aspects of its Operational Risk management framework. Tailoring the Operational Risk management tools in line with a firm's appetite is very challenging as it is also based upon experience and judgement, and requires Board-level engagement and approval of an Operational Risk strategy (Chapter 17).

CHAPTER 8

Risk & Control Self-Assessments

This chapter considers the ongoing challenges faced by the industry in embedding RCSA processes and the extent to which more commercial value can be obtained by firms by utilising the Ten Laws described in Chapters 2 to 4.

One of the Basel Committee's Sound Practices principles (Number 4) states that "Banks should identify and assess the operational risk inherent in all material products, activities, processes and systems..." (Basel Committee, February 2003). For banks a key tool for meeting this principle are their RCSAs. In their 2014 review of progress implementing their Sound Practices principles, the Basel Committee observed quite a range of practices including top-down, or bottom-up or multi-tiered approaches; assessments of some or all of the inherent risks, controls and residual risks; with their scope being either just businesses or all functions (Basel Committee, 2014).

A more recent survey of RCSA practices conducted by ORX, in 2019, identified a number of continuing challenges, i.e. RCSAs are often out of date and not informative enough, and the RCSA process can be inefficient[1] (ORX, 2020). These challenges reflect that the RCSAs are often a periodic activity (typically annual) and that much time and resources are invested in running these processes, which can be perceived as being tick-box exercises. This is unfortunate as RCSAs should provide tangible commercial value to firms by identifying:

- High inherent risks, which can be used to select scenarios; tailor insurance policies and support the ICAAP;
- Key controls, which mitigate these high inherent risks, which can then be subjected to attestation and additional assurance; and
- Residual risks that are outside of appetite, which can then be subjected to remediation.[2]

---

[1]RCSAs may overlap with other specialist risk assessments, e.g. for Conduct Risk; COBIT (Control Objectives for Information and Related Technologies); Third-Party Risk Management (TPRM); National Institute of Standards and Technology (NIST); and BCM and Operational Resilience assessments (Figure 14.1).

[2]RCSAs are reminiscent of the Japanese manufacturing concept of poka-yoke for "mistake-proofing" processes, i.e. both trying to avoid errors from occurring and amending processes, when errors do occur to prevent their recurrence.

In addition, requiring departments to review their Operational Risks and controls is probably more effective at increasing their awareness of risk than online or classroom-based training.

Despite RCSAs having been undertaken by some banks for almost 30 years in some shape or form, clearly this tool has still not yet become either standardised or established as a value added activity.

REDESIGNING RCSAs BASED UPON THE TEN LAWS

The RCSA process primarily consists of three distinct activities, as defined by ORX (ORX, 2020): scoping and inherent risk assessment; control assessment; and residual risk management (i.e. assessment and remediation). The impacts of the relevant Ten Laws are considered in turn.

Scoping and inherent risk assessment

The first challenge of an RCSA process is defining the scope, in order for the assessment to be as complete as an individual firm requires. The scope should reflect both the range of risks to which the firm is exposed and also their magnitude, i.e. firms are exposed to a near infinite number of risks, not all of which can be included in a RCSA, hence firms require criteria for excluding both the trivial and the excessively remote, e.g. a humanity-ending meteorite strike!

Understanding business profile: The 1st Law states that the "... types of events suffered by firms are driven by their business profiles ... ", hence the starting point for an RCSA should be an articulation of a business's or support function's profile, as illustrated in Figure 8.1.

In practice this means understanding the department's revenues streams and product mix (e.g. desk mandates); volumes and values of transactions; sales channels (face-to-face, telephone, and internet); systems architecture; the key manual processes and resourcing; and organisation structures. Understanding a business's revenue streams is particularly important as the 10th Law states that "Firms take Operational Risks both proactively through the provision of services in return for fee and commission income and passively, as a by-product of either the generation of trading and interest income or a firm's infrastructure and its corporate governance. Proactively taking Operational Risk is disproportionately risky." Additionally, the 2nd Law on Detection indicates that "the frequency of *reported* Operational Risk events reflects detection rates of *both* currently occurring losses and historical undiscovered failures." Consequently, an understanding of a business's risk profile needs to also reflect its past strategies back-books and a recognition that future

FIGURE 8.1 The drivers of the occurrence of Operational Risk events (Repeat of Figure 6.2)

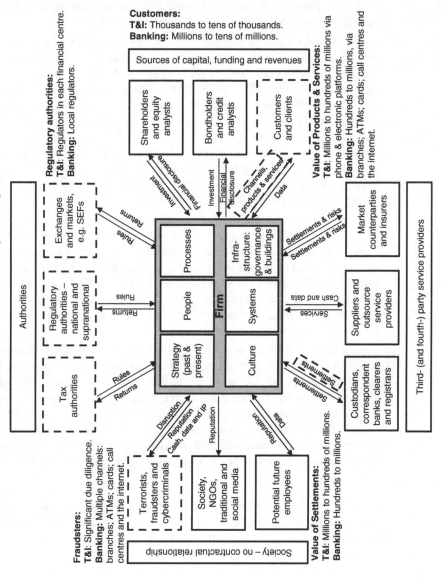

137

losses may be driven by past control frameworks. Finally, Operational Risk managers should also aim to identify any concentrations of risk/single points of failure associated with important business services, e.g. dependence upon common technology, Strategic Information Technology Enterprises (SITEs), third- (and fourth-) parties and outsource service providers.[3]

Identifying causes: Causes are defined in this book as "Factors that may increase either the actual or observed frequency of Operational Risk events (1st and 2nd Laws); their velocity and/or duration (3rd and 4th Laws). They may be either internal or external to a firm". Consequently, as part of the scoping process, Operational Risk managers should identify relevant causes at different levels in the organisation. The causal taxonomy set out in Appendix III can be used to facilitate these discussions, and there should be particular focus upon strategy, culture, governance, people and processes, which show stronger correlations (Figure 5.2). The 6th Law (Table 3.1) indicates that whilst internal causes increase the occurrence of Operational Risk events, they have less impact on the velocity and duration of events.

Identifying inherent risks: The 1st Law states that Operational Risk loss events "... primarily arise from human failings, either directly or indirectly, ranging from mistakes to systemic misconduct to malicious acts ... " Operational Risk managers should facilitate the first line identifying how their business profile, causal factors and human failings combine to generate loss events. Other tools that can be used to support this process include taxonomies for inadequacies or failures (e.g. Tables 5.2 and 5.3), and details of both relevant internal and external Operational Risk events.

Assessing inherent risks involves estimating the likelihood and impacts of an event if a firm's controls fail. When considering likelihood, firms must consider the nature of the event. As noted in Chapter 2, human errors leading to mistakes and omissions are much more likely than systemic misconduct, which in turn is much more likely than malicious acts by employees, whilst acts of God, by definition, are even rarer still (Table 2.1). In Banking businesses, human errors are as commonplace as the malicious acts of external criminals, which are an ever-present threat. Consequently, if a firm has weak controls mitigating:

- Cybercrime, then the likelihood of it suffering a major loss is higher, as cyber-criminals are continually looking for weaknesses in firms' controls; whilst for
- A pandemic, then the likelihood remains remote because acts of God are rare, although not zero.

---

[3] SITEs that are necessary for a firm's systems to operate. Other single points of failure include the undersea cables that support the internet and communications between countries and continents.

Humans are prone to a range of biases which makes it difficult for them to estimate accurately the likelihood of rare events (Chapter 4). Consequently, to make this task easier, firms should use a Likelihood Matrix (Table 8.1), which employs an approximate log scale representing humans' struggle to differentiate meaningfully between risks that are varying degrees of "really quite likely".

A similar matrix can be produced for assessing impacts (Table 8.2), reflecting the scale and velocity of loss events (3rd and 4th Laws and Figure 2.3) and the associated reputational impacts (Table 5.4), with Operational Resilience as a separate column, for impacts cutting across all of these stakeholders.

The assessment of inherent (and also residual) risk is simplistically attempting to represent an entire risk distribution with just two data points. The spectrum diagrams (Figure 8.2) illustrate this challenge for two risks which both generate Market Risk : Operational Risk boundary losses. (The severity of the risks is indicated using the colours from the Impact Matrix, Table 8.2). Fat-fingered typing generates a continuum of risk that includes lower value expected losses to higher value unexpected losses, making determining residual risk very difficult. Impact limiting fat-finger limits (Figure 7.3) restrict the losses arising from the most extreme events. In contrast, the risks associated with an algo turning rogue is more of a discontinuum ranging from zero for higher likelihoods to being exceedingly fat-tailed, for very rare events (Figure 16.9). These spectrum diagrams give a sense of the range/volatility of potential outcomes.

An approach to addressing this issue involves articulating estimated impacts for two fixed likelihoods based upon a firm's current control environment, e.g. expected losses, i.e. "Almost certain" or "Possible" and unexpected losses, i.e. "Unlikely", or "Highly Unlikely" or "Rare".

TABLE 8.1 Likelihood Matrix

Likelihoods[4]		Description – events will happen	Nature of events, i.e. inadequacies or failures
Almost certain	100%	■ In the next year	Mistakes and omissions Malicious acts by criminals
Possible	20% to 30%	■ During the planning cycle, i.e. 3 to 5 years	
Unlikely	10%	■ Once during your career with a firm	Individual and systemic misconduct by staff members Malicious acts by employees
Highly unlikely	2%	■ Once in a working lifetime	
Rare	<1%	■ Once in a hundred years and beyond	Acts of God

[4]Dr David Hillson has tested the probabilities that people associate with these words (Chapter 4).

TABLE 8.2   Impact Matrix

Importance	Financial impacts[5]		Reputational impacts		
	Scale of losses (log scale)	Velocity (log scale)	Operational Resilience	Authorities	Other stakeholders[6]
Critical	>$100m	>$100m per day	Extended and visible failure outside of tolerance	Cease & desist orders/penalties and enforcement actions	Damage to a firm's reputation for competence or integrity
Severe	>$10m	>$10m per day	Intermediate incidents: Numbers and nature of stakeholders impacted. Duration of impact.	S166 reviews	Intermediate incidents: Traditional & social media coverage.
Significant	>$1m	>$1m per day		Risk Mitigation Programme actions	
Limited	>$100k	>$100k per day		Inform regulator, but no formal action taken	
Minimal	>$10k	>$10k per day	Short invisible failure	No need to inform regulator	Passing reference in traditional & social media

As noted above the majority of risks to which firms are exposed are high volume: low value events. The 8th Law: Risk Homeostasis, states that "Over time a firm's expenditure on controls will increase in order to keep its expected Operational Risks in equilibrium with its risk appetite". Consequently, firms should focus upon the identification and mitigation of lower volume : higher value Operational Risks, for which Risk Homeostasis is less effective, and de-scope higher frequency losses (primarily EDPM). Adopting this approach significantly reduces the effort required to conduct RCSAs and hence increases the net commercial value[7] derived by firms.

---

[5]The 3rd Law states that the factors driving Velocity include: the quantum of inadequacies or failures, the nature of impacts (Figure 2.3), and internal and external causes.
[6]Stakeholders are defined in Figure 2.1, i.e. working clockwise current & future: shareholders and equity analysts; bondholders and credit analysts; customers and clients; market counter-parties and insurers; suppliers; custodians, correspondent banks, etc.; staff members; NGOs; traditional and social media; and criminals.
[7]Net commercial value is defined by the Author as the value obtained by a firm less the effort required to obtain that value. It is a concept that links to the Efficient Frontier included in Figure 7.2, in Chapter 7.

FIGURE 8.2 Spectrum diagrams can represent different Operational Risk distributions (log scale)

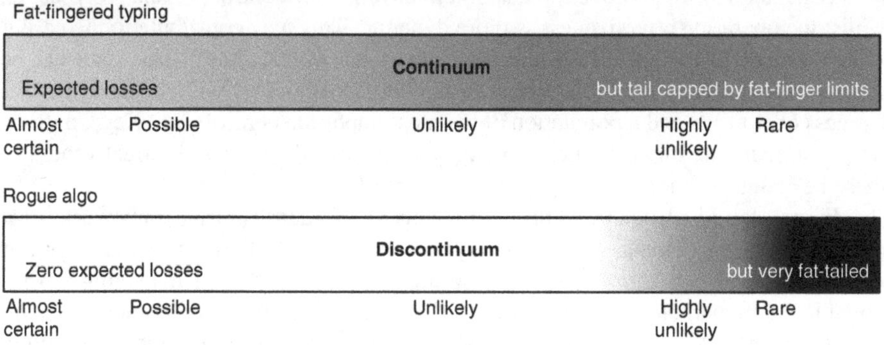

Fat-fingered typing

Continuum				
Expected losses			but tail capped by fat-finger limits	
Almost certain	Possible	Unlikely	Highly unlikely	Rare

Rogue algo

Discontinuum				
Zero expected losses			but very fat-tailed	
Almost certain	Possible	Unlikely	Highly unlikely	Rare

Control assessment

As part of their RCSA processes firms should identify the three categories of controls defined by the Ten Laws (Figure 6.3), i.e.:

1. *Preventive controls:* These can stop the occurrence of Operational Risk events;
2. *Detective controls:* These controls can detect when an event has occurred; and
3. *Corrective/resilience controls:* These controls can limit the impacts, including the financial consequences, when an Operational Risk event occurs, e.g. through recoveries of stolen assets; insurance claims; restriction of the scale with which a rogue algo can malfunction.

Traditionally, each control should be individually assessed for both their design[8] and operating[9] effectiveness at reducing risk. The different ways in which these categories of controls reduce risk is a consideration for the assessment of residual risk. In making these assessments, firms should consider the extent to which controls are automated vs manual; and also any evidence of performance, e.g. the results of first-line KCIs and attestations; first or second control testing (e.g. SOx, Volcker, Operational Risk and Compliance monitoring); second-line assurance reviews; third-line internal audits; and open remedial actions. As noted previously, firms should also consider the

---

[8]PCAOB defines a control as being *designed effectively* when if "...operated as prescribed...[it] satisfies the company's control objectives and can effectively prevent or detect errors..." (PCAOB, Auditing Standard No 5).

[9]PCAOB defines a control as *operating effectively* when it is "operating as designed and...the person performing the control possesses the necessary authority and competence to perform the control effectively" (PCAOB, Auditing Standard No 5).

impacts of different causal factors on the effectiveness of their controls, e.g. people causes such as expertise and resourcing levels, which may impact operational effectiveness (Chapter 13). In practice the design effectiveness of controls is relatively stable, whilst the operating effectiveness is more dynamic. This may contribute to the earlier observation by ORX that RCSAs are often out of date (ORX, 2020). This issue can be addressed by utilising the RCSA process to identify both issues with the design effectiveness of controls and a population of the most important controls (i.e. Key Controls, which mitigate the highest inherent risks) and monitor the operating effectiveness of these key controls on an ongoing basis (Chapter 13).

Firms should also assess the completeness of their control frameworks, for example, through comparison to industry standards (e.g. COBIT for technology); or regulations (e.g. regulatory guidelines on algos (FCA, 2018) and managing Operational Risks in market-related activities (CEBS, October 2010)); taxonomies based on industry events (Appendix IV); or the same departments in different locations within large banks.

Residual risk management (assessment & remediation)

In assessing its residual risk, firms need to conclude whether the cluster of controls mitigating a risk has an appropriate mix of preventive, detective and corrective/resilience controls. As noted above, preventive controls stop the occurrence of events, and hence reduce a firm's assessment of the likelihood of the risk crystallising (1st Law). For some risks, however, there may be no effective preventive controls, e.g. fat-finger typing. Detective controls limit the duration of events, and hence may reduce a firm's assessment of the impact of a risk when it crystallises (2nd and 4th Laws). Finally, corrective/resilience controls can restrict the financial consequences of events, and hence also reduce a firm's assessment of the impact of a risk when it crystallises (3rd and 4th Laws).

The frequency of these mitigating controls should be aligned to the velocity of the risks (3rd Law), e.g. high velocity risks, such as those associated with a malfunctioning algo, require real-time monitoring controls, whilst controls for ensuring regulatory compliance can be end of day or even end of month (Figure 2.3).

The Operational Risk function should also aim to identify any controls in place that are excessive or duplicative. The fact that anecdotally this rarely occurs may be indicative of the level of confidence many Operational Risk managers have in these assessments.

Risks that are outside of appetite need to be resolved through either treatment (i.e. remedial actions); tolerance (i.e. risk acceptance); transference (e.g. via insurance, if possible); or termination of the activity. Typically firms respond to residual risks that are outside of appetite by either enhancing controls or risk accepting. Remedial actions for risks that are outside of appetite due to ineffective design of their mitigating controls are often more substantial than issues with operating effectiveness.

Linkage to appetite The granularity and frequency of a firm's RCSA processes should reflect its risk appetite. Firms that have very low appetites for expected Operational Risk should be conducting process driven RCSAs at a granular level, whilst firms with higher appetites for expected Operational Risk should be conducting top-down risk assessments focused on identifying higher inherent risks (Chapter 17).

Second line The results of RCSA exercises need to be validated by the second line. Validation can include review of the process followed by the first line, e.g. appropriate stakeholder involvement; documentation; and formal approval. Back-testing can be undertaken against internal and external loss events. Analysis of RCSA data can also be used to ascertain the reasonableness of the mix of preventive; detective and corrective/resilience controls, e.g. highlighting any Critical and Severe risks with only small numbers of associated mitigating controls. Comparison between the current and previous RCSAs can highlight the number of ratings that have changed and new risks, controls and remedial actions added. Low levels of change suggest either a very stable risk and control environment or a tick-box exercise. Peer reviews can involve either the second line comparing the risks and controls of similar departments in different locations or first-line departments reviewing and challenging each other's RCSAs. All of these techniques help to compensate for the various biases described in Chapter 4.

Direction of industry travel

In their summary report ORX identified three directions of travel for the industry (ORX, 2020). Each are commented upon in turn below:

1. Move towards a process-orientated RCSA rather than a purely risk-based orientation. Process-orientated RCSAs resonate more with the 1st line and thereby drive more buy-in. The major challenge was how to identify processes at the right level to ensure it adds value and aggregation, and the potential cost and time in moving towards this approach.

The more granular the assessments the more likely the net commercial value of the RCSA process will be negative, i.e. costs will outweigh the commercial benefits. Events associated with processes (EDPM) are typically high volume:low value arising from mistakes and omissions, which lend themselves to dynamic remediation through Risk Homeostasis, i.e. issues are fixed as they are identified. If risks are to be assessed at a process level then the focus should be upon activities that can lead to either systemic failure and/or high velocity loss events (Figure 2.3). Although some risks (e.g. unauthorised trading) are best assessed on a firm-wide basis as the controls reside in a variety of different support functions.

2. Move towards a hybrid of regular RCSAs and trigger-based RCSAs to provide a more dynamic view of current and emerging risks, and thereby manage accordingly.

When undertaking RCSAs it is also important for firms to understand that the current year's losses may be driven by weaknesses in both a firm's current and historical preventive controls and also its current detective controls (2nd Law). Consequently, Operational Risk managers should avoid *just* undertaking trigger-based RCSAs, as the largest average loss events will typically arise from incidents with an average duration of between 3 and 5 years, and may be occurring in plain sight. Additionally, Table 2.2 and Figure 5.2 indicate that change is not the most important internal cause of Operational Risk loss events.

3. Some institutions are moving away from assessing inherent risk and moving straight to looking at "residual" risk and control effectiveness. This is very much an emerging practice in the absence of clear definitions of residual risk.

The identification of inherent or rare risks (Figure 8.2) is important for supporting the selection of scenarios, tailoring insurance policies and supporting the ICAAP; and can also narrow the focus of the firm's control testing. The concept of inherent risk needs to be extended to better reflect risks that can generate high impacts at either high velocity or through the steady accretion over time through systemic failure (Table 6.2).

CONCLUSIONS

Apocryphally, Einstein defined insanity as doing the same thing over and over again and expecting a different result. After almost 30 years of conducting RCSAs the Operational Risk profession is still struggling to obtain commercial value from this activity, i.e. Operational Risk managers are expending too much effort to obtain too little reward. The Ten Laws of Operational Risk suggest that the keys to balancing effort and reward must be based upon:

- *Scope – business profile:* RCSAs should be driven from the business profiles of firms (Figure 2.1, 1st Law) to ensure the completeness of the scope of the exercise. Operational Risk managers should in particular focus on businesses that provide services, as proactively taking Operational Risk is "disproportionately risky" (10th Law).
- *Scope – causes:* RCSAs should include the identification of the most important internal causes, as these both increase the occurrence of inadequacies or failures that constitute both events and control failures (Figure 6.3, 1st to 5th Laws).
- *Scope – prioritise* risks that lead to either high velocity losses (3rd Law) or the slow accretion of larger losses over time (4th Law), through systemic failure (Table 5.4). Ensure that the regularity of the mitigating controls are aligned to the velocity of the risks (Figure 2.3). The extended duration of very large losses means that firms

should avoid just conducting trigger-based RCSAs. Also prioritise products and services that transfer Market and Credit Risk to customers or investors (9th Law) and that may be sensitive to economic shocks (7th Law).

- *Scope – deprioritise* risks that generate high volume:low value losses arising from mistakes and omissions that will naturally be remediated through the day-to-day Operational Risk management practices (8th Law).
- *Inadequacies or failures (events):* The nature of an event needs to be identified as this indicates the relative likelihood of occurrence, for example, mistakes and omissions are commonplace; systematic misconduct are rarer; and acts of God are even more remote (Table 2.1, 1st Law).
- *Duration of events:* A firm's current year's losses may be driven by weaknesses in both its current and historical preventive controls and also its current detective controls (2nd Law). Consequently, Operational Risk managers should avoid *just* undertaking trigger-based RCSAs.
- *Design effectiveness:* The focus should be on the design effectiveness of controls, which is relatively stable and drives remedial actions. Whilst operating effectiveness should be assessed through the day-to-day KCI monitoring and the control assurance activities described in Chapter 13.
- *Risk profile:* Representing complex risks as just two data points for inherent and residual risks is overly simplistic. The use of spectrum diagrams may better capture the continuous or dis-continuous nature of some key Operational Risks.

Ultimately, the acid test of whether RCSAs add commercial value is whether they support a firm's decision making, both to maximise returns and to grow quickly and safely.

CHAPTER 9

Scenario Analysis

This chapter considers the ongoing challenges faced by the industry in undertaking scenario analysis due to both behavioural biases and language, and the extent to which more commercial value can be obtained by firms by utilising the Ten Laws described in Chapters 2 to 4 to make scenario analysis more systematic.

Basel II (Basel Committee, 2004) mandated that banks must conduct scenario analysis "...to evaluate its exposure to high-severity events" by assessing the likelihood and impacts of specific Operational Risk events across a one-year time horizon. The value of conducting scenario analysis is demonstrated by the observations in Figure 1.1 that individual large losses contribute a disproportionately large amount to the total value of losses suffered across the industry. Additionally, Figure 6.1 illustrates how extreme Operational Risk losses can be, with just 38 very large losses constituting just over 50% of the total value of all losses suffered by ORX members between 2010 and 2018.

CHALLENGES – BIASES AND LANGUAGE

Scenario analysis combines both "...expert opinion in conjunction with external data..." (Basel Committee, 2004). As a species, however, humans are not very good at estimating the occurrence of remote events, because people are all impacted by a series of natural biases that influence the way they assess risks[1] (Chapter 4). Unfortunately, to make matters worse, psychologists have also identified that whilst individuals accept that other people are biased; they generally resist the view that they themselves are biased![2] There are many of these biases but the ones which are most relevant to Operational Risk managers for scenario analysis include:

> *Anchoring/Proximity Bias*: When people form subjective estimates, they start with a point of reference, a possibly arbitrary value, and then adjust away from it.

---

[1] These biases are adaptive as they enable humans to make quick decisions, which are generally appropriate, in response to common threats.
[2] For example, a survey of doctors found that 61% said that they were not personally influenced by gifts from drugs companies; but only 16% thought that the same was true for other doctors (Gardner, 2009).

Group Polarisation Bias: When people who share beliefs get together in groups, they become more convinced that their beliefs are correct, and they also become more extreme in their views. People will also conform to the Group's view and express opinions which are clearly incorrect.

Example Bias: The more easily people can recall examples, the more common they judge a thing to be.

Imagination Inflation: The act of imagining an outcome for an event occurring may lead to the overestimation of the likelihood of that event actually occurring.

Confirmation Bias: Once a belief is in place, humans will screen what they see and hear, in a biased manner, to ensure that their beliefs are proven correct.

Optimism and Wishful Thinking: Participants overestimate the robustness of the firm's control environment and are unduly optimistic over the effectiveness of their response.

Motivation Bias: Incentive conflicts may arise when participants have a vested personal interest in making either themselves or the results of the scenario analysis programme more advantageous.

Additionally, commonly used terms to describe probability are not consistently understood by people.

Finally, some risks are just unknowable, i.e. either despite being real they are just too remote to estimate effectively, or they are so dynamic that past experience is irrelevant to the future due to the 8th Law: Risk Homeostasis. For example, it is almost inevitable that cybercriminals/nation states will develop technology that will circumvent almost any of a firm's countermeasures, for a short period of time, prior to firms responding (Chapter 16).

There are a number of steps that firms should follow to undertake scenario analysis, and this chapter primarily focuses upon utilising the Ten Laws to facilitate: identifying a portfolio of scenarios; estimating impacts and likelihoods; and validating the outputs of scenario analysis to mitigate these biases.

IDENTIFYING A PORTFOLIO OF SCENARIOS

A firm's portfolio of scenarios should reflect both its business and risk profiles. In practice this involves considering both the risks posed by the components of Figure 2.1 and a firm's historical experience of losses and near misses and high inherent risk/unexpected exposures, as identified through the RCSAs. In prioritising scenarios, firms should take into account the nature of the impacts and hence the scale and velocity of any resulting losses (Table 5.4). Firms should also consider the design and operating effectiveness of the associated preventive, detective and corrective/resilience controls, based on a combination of the RCSAs (Chapter 8) and ongoing monitoring of key controls (Chapter 13). Finally, firms should assess relevant external events (in the public domain) and emerging threats, as set out in Figure 15.1 (Chapter 15).

Firms may also identify potential scenarios through workshops; questionnaires; and interviews and meetings to gauge the opinions of first, second and third lines of defence. In large firms, scenarios can be identified both through bottom-up and top-down processes. A bottom-up process involves businesses, divisions, countries and regions formulating their own lists of scenarios. Whilst a top-down process involves the Group function defining a set of common scenarios that all must undertake either individually (e.g. a local rogue trader event) or collectively (e.g. a pandemic or a Group-wide systems outage).[3]

Scenarios run by firms are often a combination of both of these approaches, i.e. scenarios specifically relevant to their businesses, as well as a smaller number of Group-wide scenarios. The number of scenarios identified will vary depending on the size of the firm. For UK banks the PRA has set the minimum number of scenarios at 13.[4]

In order to obtain assurance as to the completeness of the portfolio of scenarios, they should be mapped to the level 3 Basel II event subcategories. The portfolio of scenarios in each business should also be compared to both peer businesses within the firm and external loss events suffered by business peers to identify any gaps.

These lists of scenarios should be approved via a formal governance processes, i.e. the governance bodies which receive reports on the outputs of scenario analysis should also be responsible for their approval. The PRA indicates that this should include "the firm's Board, Executive Committee or Risk Committee" (PRA, 2018).

Firms may run multiple scenarios relating to the more significant Basel II event categories (e.g. a bank may run a range of rogue trader scenarios, i.e. an intra-day unauthorised position, fictitious trades, mis-marking, etc.). Additionally, firms should also run scenarios that may just generate credit boundary losses (e.g. deficiencies in a firm's security documentation relating to supposedly secured property loans); Operational Resilience; and reputational damage, as a consequence of an Operational Risk failure. Whilst the outputs of these scenarios do not feed into any capital models, they can be very informative regarding the firm's risk profile.

ESTIMATING THE IMPACTS OF RARE EVENTS

The scale of individual Operational Risk losses are defined by the 3rd and 4th Laws, i.e. by the velocity and the duration of loss events.

---

[3]One firm referred to its Group-wide scenarios as the "Dirty Thirty"!

[4]"The PRA's methodologies for setting Pillar 2 capital" (PRA, 2018) states that the regulator expects to see "at least 10 scenarios not related to conduct/legal events and additionally the top 3 conduct/legal scenarios."

Formula 9.1 and 9.2 Drivers of velocity and duration, and hence severity

Velocity,
$ of loss
per $\approx f$
period of
time

$$\frac{(\text{Quantum of inadequacies or failures, Internal causes}) \times (\text{Nature of the impacts, External causes}) - (\text{Corrective controls, Inadequacies or failures, Causes})}{\text{Time period between commencement and cessation}}$$

Severity[5]
of $\approx f$
losses, $

$$\begin{array}{c}(\textbf{Velocity} \times (\text{Duration} - (\text{Detective controls, Inadequacies or failures, Internal causes}))) \\ - (\text{Corrective controls, inadequacies or failures, Internal causes})\end{array}$$

The 3rd and 4th Laws suggest that when estimating the losses associated with remote events, Operational Risk managers should consider:

- The quantum of failure, and how this may be restricted by corrective/resilience controls;
- The nature of the impacts, and how these may be influenced by external causes;
- The effectiveness of detective controls, and hence the duration of an event;
- The restriction of losses through further corrective/resilience controls; and
- The operational effectiveness of a firm's various detective and corrective/resilience controls, as a consequence of internal causes.

In order to illustrate how the 3rd and 4th Laws may be applied, a series of examples are set out, focused upon the impacts in Table 5.4 that have either the largest scale or highest velocities, i.e. Market Risk; restitution/compensation payments; write-off of cash; and regulatory fines and penalties.

Market Risk losses

Market Risk : Operational Risk boundary losses display some of the highest velocities of any risks. Figure 9.1 illustrates some of the factors that drive the scale of losses for three actual rogue trader events that occurred within a three month period of each other. (The size of the outer circles reflect the scale of the unauthorised positions and the inner circles reflect the scale of losses suffered.)

Consequently, during a Scenarios Analysis workshop, the facilitator may pose the following questions to attendees:

---

[5]This is equivalent of impact in the XOI (Exposure, Occurrence, Impact) method (Naim and Condamin, 2019) or LGE (Loss Given Event) in the Basel Committee's (September 2001) Internal Measurement Approaches.

FIGURE 9.1 Three rogue trader events that occurred over a three-month period (Grimwade, 2016)

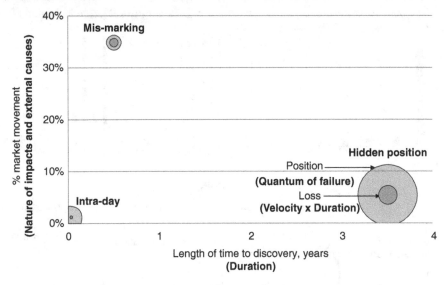

1. "How big an unauthorised position could one of our traders build up?"
2. "How long would it take for us to identify this position?"/"How effective are our detective controls?"
3. "How much might the market have moved before we identified this unauthorised position?"

For Operational Risks that generate Market Risk boundary losses through mistakes and omissions, e.g. fat-fingered typing, then the impacts and likelihoods are intrinsically linked (Figure 9.2) as the distribution of losses is a continuum.[6] The scale of losses are driven by the scale of the typing error (the quantum of failure); market volatility (an external cause) and the length of time to detection (duration). The quantum of failure is restricted by corrective/resilience controls, i.e. fat-finger typing limits; and the duration is limited by a firm's trade affirmation processes.

Each of these factors can be assessed individually. Disaggregating these drivers makes their estimation easier. Additionally, this estimation technique for this scenario is naturally dynamic, i.e. the outcome of the scenario will automatically fluctuate with actual error rates; market volatility; the range to trade sizes executed and the scale of fat-finger limits.

---

[6]Although this is not the case for losses arising from a malfunctioning trading algorithm (Figure 2.3).

FIGURE 9.2   Estimating the impacts and likelihoods for fat-fingered typing using Market Risk techniques (Grimwade, 2016)

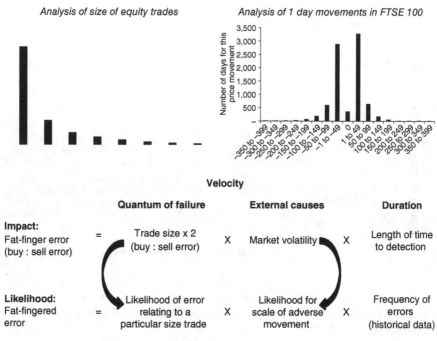

	Quantum of failure		External causes		Duration
Impact: Fat-finger error (buy : sell error)	=	Trade size x 2 (buy : sell error)	X Market volatility	X	Length of time to detection
Likelihood: Fat-fingered error	=	Likelihood of error relating to a particular size trade	X Likelihood for scale of adverse movement	X	Frequency of errors (historical data)

Restitution/compensation payments, e.g. misrepresentation of securities

In addition to the 3rd and 4th Laws, the 9th Law: Risk Transference, Transformation and Conservation, can also be used to quantify remote losses in instances "When Market and Credit Risks are sold to investors, e.g. through securitisations, they are transformed into Operational Risk that is retained by the arranger/distributor. The quantum of Operational Risk retained is equivalent of the Market and Credit Risks transferred, whilst the likelihood of this Operational Risk becoming a loss is diminished."

The Global Financial Crisis highlighted that some of the most significant Operational Risk losses involved the restitution due to misrepresentation to investors of MBS, CDOs and corporate bonds. As a consequence of the 9th Law the impacts of these events can be quantified using Credit Risk techniques. For example, the impacts of litigation by investors in bonds, issued by corporates that subsequently defaulted, against the underwriters, can be estimated by adapting Credit Risk's concepts of Exposure At Default (EAD) and Loss Given Default (LGD). This is summarised in Formula 9.3.

Formula 9.3 Estimating the impacts of underwriter litigation by adapting Credit Risk techniques

Exposure at issuer's default	×	Loss given issuer's default	=	Scenario impact
Akin to Credit Risk's Exposure At Default		*Akin of Credit Risk's Loss Given Default*		

- Largest single underwrites;
- Cumulative underwrites for single names in a ~2-year period; and
- Average underwrites, etc.

Settlement %s:[7]
- WorldCom ~30%;
- Lehman ~12%
- MF Global ~9%; and
- REFCO ~8%.

This estimation technique for this scenario is also naturally dynamic, i.e. the outcome of the scenario will automatically fluctuate with changes in the volume and the value of a firm's underwriting (EAD), its underwriting limits and also trends in legal settlements (LGD). Consistent with this, Figure 2.7 illustrated the relationship between the value of MBS issued by banks prior to the Global Financial Crisis and the settlements and penalties subsequently agreed.

Loss of financial assets, e.g. SWIFT cyber-payment fraud

The first publicly disclosed SWIFT cyber-payment fraud seems to have taken place in 2015. Analysing SWIFT cyber-payment frauds, in the public domain, reveals that the thefts generally relate to emerging market banks and are quite infrequent given the number of SWIFT users. Recovery rates range between 20% and 100%, reflecting a combination of the sophistication of criminals in laundering the money and the varying speeds of response from the banks. In one fraud, $9 million that was successfully stolen was laundered through 23 Hong Kong companies. The discovery of a theft was delayed, at another bank, by the attack coinciding with a local festival. Finally, whilst the trend in the success of these frauds appears to be downwards (Figure 4.1), possibly reflecting industry-wide responses to the first frauds (8th Law: Risk Homeostasis), the data set is only losses in the public domain, "known knowns", and is currently too small to be statistically significant.

---

[7]Underwriting litigation settlement rates/Loss Given Default can obviously be stressed to reflect an economic shock (Chapter 11).

Formula 9.4 Estimation of SWIFT cyber-payment frauds

$$
\text{Gross theft} \;=\; \frac{\overbrace{\underset{\text{payments}}{\text{Typical value of}}}^{\text{Quantum of failure}} \times \overbrace{\underset{\text{payments}}{\text{Number of}}}^{\text{Velocity}}}{\text{Time}} \times \overbrace{\underset{\text{to detection}}{\text{Length of time}}}^{\text{Duration}}
$$

Analysis of industry data reveals that thefts generally consist of multiple smaller/typical-sized payments, which will again vary between banks, initially ranged between USD millions and USD tens of millions[8] (the average gross loss is ~\$48 million whilst the median value is \$15 million). In estimating the potential scale of these frauds firms need to identify the key drivers, i.e. typical volume and values of payment (Formula 9.4).

The length of time to detection reflects the effectiveness of a firm's detective controls, e.g. intrusion detection software and whether cash management processes are real-time. Whilst the % recovery rates is driven by both the ability of the targeted bank to recover its funds from the recipient banks, before it can be laundered by the criminals, and also the ability to submit a successful claim under a Crime/Computer Crime Policy. The effectiveness of some policies, may also be influenced by the extent to which the criminals have exploited a systemic/industry-wide weakness (Chapter 12).

Regulatory actions – fines and penalties

Regulatory fines and penalties do not adhere as neatly to the 3rd, 4th and 9th Laws of Operational Risk, because of the involvement of, to varying degrees people and formulae in determining the scale of fines.

For example, the FCA has published its five step methodology for determining the scale of fines (Table 9.1). Steps 1 and 2 capture the "Quantum of inadequacies or failures" from the 3rd Law. The incorporation of deterrence into steps 3 and 4 reflects the 8th Law: Risk Homeostasis, i.e. "... control expenditure will rise in anticipation of increased future losses." After the Global Financial Crisis regulators increased the scale of fines in order to encourage banks to change their behaviours and enhance their controls (Figure 4.2).

Clearly, each of the items in this calculation is either known or can be estimated within a scenario analysis workshop, and Formula 9.5 contains a worked example for failures of AML controls.

---

[8]SWIFT believe that the cybercriminals evolved their techniques in response to control enhancements, and that after early 2018, the average fraudulent transaction amounts reduced to between \$0.25 million to \$2 million (SWIFT, 2019).

TABLE 9.1 FCA's methodology for setting fines

FCA's methodology			Laws of Operational Risk
Step 1:	Disgorgement	▪ The FCA will deprive a firm of the financial benefit derived from the breach.	
Step 2:	Seriousness of failings	▪ The FCA assesses the revenue arising from the relevant activity – this can obviously be scaled; and ▪ The FCA assesses the seriousness of the breach. There are five levels ranging from 0% to 20%, increasing in 5% increments. The FCA describes the basis of its decision, so this can then be applied to the firm undertaking scenario analysis.	This is akin to "Quantum of inadequacies or failures" (3rd Law).
Step 3:	Mitigating and aggravating factors	▪ Aggravating factors might include responsiveness to warnings, and fines imposed on other institutions, as well as previous final notices; whilst ▪ Mitigating factors will reflect the level of co-operation during any subsequent investigation. These factors can again be assessed for the firm undertaking the scenario analysis using other Final Notices as guides.	This reflects Risk Homeostasis, i.e. "… control expenditure will rise in anticipation of increased future losses" (8th Law).
Step 4:	Adjustments for deterrence	▪ The FCA may increase the penalty if it believes the penalty is insufficient to deter either the firm who committed the breach, or others, from committing further or similar breaches. This tends to be employed for more serious breaches.	
Step 5:	Settlement discount	▪ The penalty can be reduced depending upon at what stage at which the FCA and the firm reached agreement. The discount given may be up to 30%.	Co-operation with a regulator can be seen as a corrective control (4th Law).

Formula 9.5 An example of the composition of an FCA fine for failures of AML controls

£Ym	×	50%	×	(15%	+	5%)	×	−30%	= 7% of £Ym
Total Revenues		% of customers with incomplete AML		Seriousness of breach		Mitigating & aggravating factors		Co-operation: discount or penalty	Final penalty, after discount

Reputational impacts Reputational impacts are often referred to as being non-financial. This may reflect that their impacts are harder to quantify as they arise from changes in the behaviours of a firm's stakeholders. The list of stakeholders with which a firm has a reputation is again derived from Figure 2.1. As part of a scenario analysis workshop participants can also identify which stakeholders are potentially impacted by a specific scenario. Quantification is often focused upon impacts on shareholders/share prices; bondholders/credit ratings and customers/revenues, see Chapter 12 (reverse stress testing) and Chapter 13 (Reputational Risk quantification and management).

ESTIMATING THE LIKELIHOODS OF RARE EVENTS – TOP-DOWN AND BOTTOM-UP

The occurrence of individual Operational Risk losses are defined by the 1st Law (Formula 9.6).

Estimating the likelihood of the occurrence of rare Operational Risk events is inherently even more challenging than estimating impacts. Techniques range from top-down to bottom-up approaches:

Formula 9.6 Occurrence of Operational Risk events (Repeat of Formula 2.1)

Occurrence of Operational Risk events, number of events $\approx f$ (Business profile, Internal & external causes, Inadequacies or failures)

    – (Preventive controls, Inadequacies or failures, Internal causes)

Calculation of industry frequencies – top-down

A top-down technique for helping with the estimation of likelihoods is to calculate an historical frequency of similar events occurring. For events in the public domain Operational Risk managers can select a group of peer firms and observe the frequency of occurrence over several years. Equally, for events unlikely to be in the public domain

Operational Risk managers can utilise the working life experiences of their own senior staff members (Formula 9.7).

Formula 9.7 Calculation of industry frequencies, utilising either public or private loss data

$$\frac{\text{Public: Number of public domain losses; or Private: Number of losses experienced by staff}}{\text{Public: Number of peer firms} \times \text{years of data; or Private: Sum of years of working in different firms}} = \frac{\text{Historical frequency of either public or private losses}}{} \approx \frac{\text{Estimate of likelihood}}{}$$

Utilising the private experiences of senior staff may be the only option available for rare risks which lead to losses which do not reach the public domain, e.g. missed corporate actions or the failed execution of trigger events on a structured product. Using public data in this way is particularly useful for observing frequencies of events that are independent of an individual firm's processes and systems, i.e. those that are caused by "inadequate or failed . . . people" and "from external events". For example, it is difficult for even experienced managers to judge the likelihood of a staff member acting irrationally (e.g. by taking an unauthorised position). It is possible, however, to observe the frequency with which losses classified as Internal Fraud have occurred within Trading & Sales environments across a sample of banks, or by utilising data from industry loss databases, such as ORX.[9] Equally, firms may observe the frequencies of external events across the globe impacting specific asset classes, such as damage to physical assets, e.g. ships or the occurrence of cyberattacks. Finally, expanding the group of firms and shortening the period over which data is collected can help identify and quantify very dynamic emerging risks. For emerging risks that peak and then decline, due to enhancements in industry infrastructure and controls over time (8th Law: Risk Homeostasis), then observing the trends and calculating frequencies for a series of time periods may help firms to avoid misestimating these risks.

Fault Tree Analysis – analysing the drivers of likelihood – bottom-up

Fault Tree Analysis is a bottom-up approach for estimating the likelihood of an event occurring by identifying a sequence of lower-level events which are then combined using terms such as AND and OR, if there are multiple pathways to loss. This technique was originally developed within engineering, and involves preparing more granular analysis of how losses can occur and the sequence of controls that need to fail and

---

[9]There were 90 Internal Frauds in Trading & Sales between 2012 and 2017 amongst the ~60 ORX members (average for this period). So the frequency of occurrence is 60 banks × 6 years/90 events, i.e. 1 in 4 years, with an average value of ~€8 million.

their effectiveness. Naturally with this approach each additional pathway makes an event more likely to occur; whilst the more effective the preventive controls that are in place the less likely it is to occur.

In a simplified version of Fault Tree Analysis the reliability of the controls that need to fail can be substituted with observed frequencies of failure. In the following example, again for the risk of post-underwriting securities litigation, the likelihood is driven by:

- The Probability of Default (PD) by an issuer (External Cause);
- The duration of exposure. This reflects the volume and credit ratings of a firm's underwriting (Business Profile). Whilst Section 13 of the US Securities Act of 1933 restricts the timescale for litigation to within three years after issuance, in practice within two years seems more common; and
- The likelihood of litigation arising and being successful. This reflects "inadequacies or failures" as Section 11 of the US Securities Act provides the underwriters with a defence if, at the time of the issue, they had "reasonable ground to believe and did believe..." the misleading registration statement.[10]

As Figure 9.3 demonstrates, each of these factors can be either measured internally or externally or derived or estimated. A number of firms use this technique for this

FIGURE 9.3   An example of using Fault Tree Analysis to estimate the likelihood of a post-underwriting securities litigation scenario

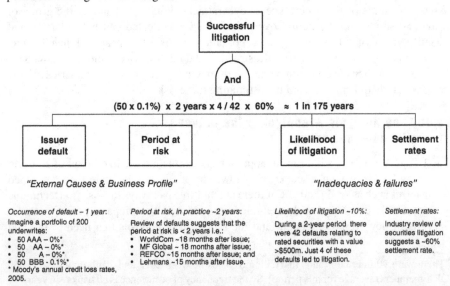

---

[10]This approach has similarities with the X and O (eXposure and Occurrence) of the XOI method (Naim and Condamin, 2019).

FIGURE 9.4 Estimating to likelihood of a successful cyberattack (Grimwade, 2019)

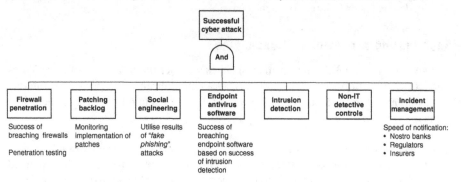

specific risk because the risk is both demonstrably real but too remote for staff members to estimate effectively. For a risk which is both rare and fat-tailed, this technique provides not only more accurate estimates of likelihood, but does so again dynamically so that the results change intuitively with business profile (i.e. the volume of underwrites and the riskiness of the issuers) and the external causes, i.e. the point within the credit cycle. This also allows banks to stress their exposures to this risk. This will be considered further in Chapter 11.

As noted in Chapter 2, the design and operational effectiveness of controls that prevent persistent threats such as cybercrime can be highly predictive of the occurrence Operational Risk loss events. Hence, the likelihood of a successful cyberattack could be estimated by assessing the effectiveness of the portfolio of controls ("defence in depth"), as illustrated in Figure 9.4.

VALIDATING THE OUTPUTS OF SCENARIO ANALYSIS

Maybe as a consequence of the inherent subjectivity of scenario analysis and the challenges presented by the various biases, Basel II (Basel Committee, 2004) mandated that the outputs of scenario analysis must "...be validated and reassessed through comparison to actual loss experience to ensure their reasonableness." Consequently, in addition to ensuring that the scenarios have been reviewed and challenged through formal governance processes (e.g. a "Wise-man" panel), the Ten Laws can be used for both individual scenarios and portfolios of scenarios to triangulate them against three sources of internal and external data:

1. Back-testing the *portfolio* of scenarios against internal and external loss data;
2. Back-testing *individual* scenarios against similar scenarios within the same firm, internal and external loss data, and insurance policies; and

3. Back-testing the *outputs of scenario-based models* against maximum quantum of inadequacies or failures for each scenario.

Back-testing a portfolio of scenarios

Utilising the 1st and 3rd Laws, firms can check whether the frequency of large losses implied by their portfolio of scenarios is reasonable through comparison to internal and external historical data, weighted for more recent data to reflect Risk Homeostasis (8th Law) for example:

- *Frequency of large losses (>€10 million):* Firms can use their scenarios to calculate the implied frequency of occurrence of large losses over, for example, a defined period. This can be compared to both their own internal loss experiences and also external data. In Table 1.1 the frequency losses ≥€10 million for 1998 to 2018 ranges between one event per bank every 4 months down to just one event per bank every 2 years 4 months.
- *Ratio of losses between €1 million and €9.9 million, with losses above €10 million:* The implied ratio for a portfolio of scenarios can be calculated and compared again with both a firm's internal loss experience and those of the ORX consortium members, e.g. based on Figure 1.2 this ratio has ranged between 5 and 8 (Figure 9.5) for different periods between 1998 to 2018.

This analysis may be used to highlight if the scenarios suggest a firm has a materially different Operational Risk profile from either its own past or its peers.

FIGURE 9.5   Back-testing a portfolio of scenarios against both historical internal & external losses

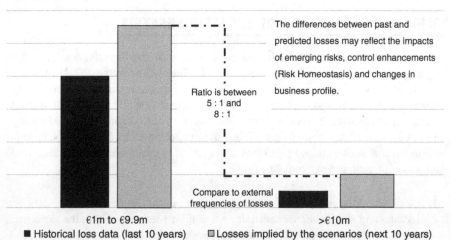

The differences between past and predicted losses may reflect the impacts of emerging risks, control enhancements (Risk Homeostasis) and changes in business profile.

Ratio is between 5 : 1 and 8 : 1

Compare to external frequencies of losses

€1m to €9.9m   >€10m

■ Historical loss data (last 10 years)   ☐ Losses implied by the scenarios (next 10 years)

Back-testing individual scenarios

Banks can also assess the reasonableness of their individual scenarios through comparison to the frequency of occurrence of large losses in the public domain for each risk (1st and 2nd Laws). The frequency of large losses can be derived, as shown earlier, by dividing the number of large loss events in the public domain suffered by peer firms by the number of peer firms × the number of years of loss data. The impact of the scenarios can also be compared to the maximum and average or median values of large loss events. This enables firms to identify scenarios which are potential outliers (i.e. either too large or too small; and/or too likely or too remote) for further review and challenge to determine the potential business or methodological causes. Figure 9.6 shows both the frequency of these events, and also the average value of the events and the largest losses suffered, which is reflected in the size of the bubbles. Whilst this analysis will not capture smaller loss events, it is reasonable for larger losses and enables firms to compare themselves against appropriate peers.

Additionally, in this analysis the frequency of losses arising from systemic events (SOREs) that impact a number of firms (e.g. the collapse of WorldCom) have been calculated as if these events were either a single occurrence, as well as a number of independent events impacting multiple banks across the industry. This clearly has a very significant impact on the observed frequency. This is also relevant regarding the occurrence of losses arising from particularly virulent industry-wide viruses, e.g. NotPetya.

For risks that can be transferred (9th Law) using insurance policies, e.g. a terrorist attack that might lead to both damage to physical assets and the death of staff, then the pricing of the relevant insurance policies can be used to deduce the insurance

FIGURE 9.6 Observed frequencies and ranges of impacts of common and/or industry-wide losses (Grimwade, 2016)

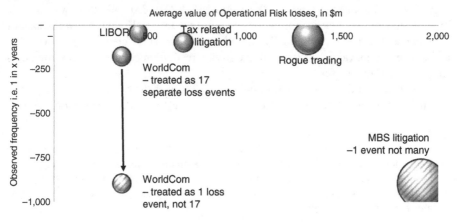

company's estimate of the frequency of occurrence. This can be calculated by dividing the level of cover for a 12-month period by the annual premium plus an assumed re-investment rate for the premium and also the insurer's cost of capital to give a crude estimate of the frequency of occurrence (Formula 9.8).

Formula 9.8 The estimation of the frequency of occurrence of an insurable event[11]

$$
\begin{array}{ccc}
\text{Frequency of} & < & \dfrac{\text{Insurance cover}}{(\text{Insurance premium} + \text{investment returns}) -} \\
\text{occurrence} & \begin{array}{c}(\text{i.e. more} \\ \text{remote})\end{array} & (\text{admin costs} + \text{cost of capital})
\end{array}
$$

Back-testing against the outputs of scenario-based models

The outputs of models (i.e. undiversified risk at 99.9%) for individual scenarios can also be checked against the maximum quantum of inadequacies or failures (3rd Law) that a firm may suffer, by considering its largest payments; or its largest underwrites; or its largest fat-finger limits, etc. This may help to answer the question "Is it really possible for us to lose that much?"

CONCLUSIONS

Estimating the impacts and likelihoods of rare Operational Risk events is inherently subjective. The biases, to which all humans are prone, and the vagaries of the precise meanings of words in the English language for describing the differing probabilities of events exacerbate these challenges still further.

In describing the drivers for both the occurrence of events and their impacts (velocity × duration) the Laws of Operational Risk (1st, 3rd and 4th Laws) provide more systematic approaches for estimation rather than simply running workshops of subject matter experts. Additionally, the 9th Law: Risk Transference, Transformation and Conservation, can be utilised for quantifying restitution/compensation settlements for some customer losses.

The nature of the different impacts (Table 5.4) drives the specific techniques used for their estimation, whether Market Risk losses, restitution/compensation, theft of

---

[11]This is effective if a firm has standard levels of cover. If a bank, however, seeks to obtain unusually high levels of cover, then the costs of the additional layers may become disproportionally expensive, despite the likelihood of claims against these additional layers being even more remote, because the insurers may reflect in their pricing their customer's desire for this additional cover.

assets, or regulatory fines. Similarly the techniques for estimating likelihood are specific to the particular nature of the events (Table 5.2, 1st Law) e.g. mistakes and omissions, systematic misconduct and acts of God. For the estimation of the likelihood of events that arise from *persistent* threats (e.g. cybercrime), then the design and operational effectiveness of the preventive controls can be assessed and the occurrence of failure estimated. As the threats are persistent then the occurrence of failure of the preventive controls equates to the likelihood of occurrence of a loss event. By deconstructing scenario analysis in these ways, the estimation of these risks can be facilitated. For impacts that are sensitive to business cycles, then the techniques in this chapter can support stress testing (Chapter 11) by identifying the factors to adjust to reflect an economic shock, such as market volatility and probabilities of defaults.

Finally, back-testing the outputs of scenario analysis can help to mitigate the impacts of the various biases.

CHAPTER 10

Operational Risk Capital Modelling

This chapter considers the ongoing challenges faced by firms and regulators alike in quantifying Operational Risk capital due to a combination of its extremely fat-tailed nature (Figure 6.1) and the inherent subjectivity of scenario analysis, as discussed in Chapter 9. Overlaying existing approaches for quantifying Operational Risk (both economic and regulatory capital) with the Ten Laws, described in Chapters 2 to 4, highlights some of the problems with the existing approaches. The chapter also considers the merits of the Basel Committee's new Standardised Approach (Basel Committee, 2017a). As a consequence of these challenges, validating the outputs of these models is even more critical, and hence this chapter includes a range of validation techniques. The chapter concludes by proposing a more tailored and holistic approach to quantification, reflecting in particular the 5th and 7th Laws and integrating different approaches for different risks.

The importance of quantifying Operational Risk is emphasised by the 10th Law, which states that "firms take Operational Risk both proactively through the provision of services in return for fee and commission income and passively, as by-product of either the generation of trading and interest income or a firm's infrastructure and its corporate governance". If firms are to compare objectively businesses that variously generate interest income, trading income and fee and commission income, then Operational Risk needs to be quantified in a comparable manner to Market and Credit Risks.

A brief history of modelling

Almost three decades ago[1] banks first began to model Operational Risk, as a component of their economic capital, utilising actuarial techniques borrowed from the general insurance industry.[2] Basel II (Basel Committee, 2004) incorporated these advanced approaches into regulatory capital, alongside two less sophisticated approaches.

---

[1] Probably the first Operational Risk capital model was developed by Bankers Trust and discussed at conferences in 1996 at which the Author was also speaking. ("*Operational Risks and Financial Institutions*", published by RiskBooks, 1998).

[2] The Bankers Trust model was run by an external firm of actuaries, Tillinghast.

The Basel Committee additionally both encouraged banks to move along the spectrum of available approaches over time, and expected internationally active banks to adopt the more sophisticated approaches, in line with their more significant Operational Risk profiles.

In 2017, however, as part of the Basel Committee's post-crisis reforms (Basel Committee, 2017a) it proposed the removal of the Advanced Measurement Approach (AMA) for calculating Pillar 1 capital requirements, but remained silent on the use of models for estimating Pillar 2A and 2B capital requirements. As noted above, banks originally developed these models because their Operational Risks were so significant, and also varied between their different business lines. The Operational Risk losses suffered during the Global Financial Crisis have only served to emphasise, still further, the importance of this risk category. Consequently, banks are likely to continue to use these models for both regulatory capital, although for Pillar 2A and 2B, rather than Pillar 1,[3] and also economic capital.

BASEL II'S ADVANCED MEASUREMENT APPROACH – ACTUARIAL MODEL

As previously mentioned, Operational Risk capital models are typically based upon actuarial modelling techniques borrowed from the general insurance industry (Figure 10.1).

Consequently, these models separately analyse the frequency of Operational Risk loss events, which are driven by the 1st and 2nd Laws, and the severity of events, which are driven by the 3rd and 4th Laws. As noted in Chapter 5, banks typically use a single distribution (Poisson) to model the frequency of their internal loss data,[4] maybe reflecting the 1st Law, i.e. that the majority of Operational Risk events "... arise from human failings" (Tables 2.1 and 5.2). In contrast, banks typically use multiple different distributions to model the severity of their losses. The loss data used by banks in these models ranges between just their own internal loss data (Loss Distribution Approach (LDA) models) to just scenarios, with combinations in between (hybrid models). As noted in Chapter 5, the wide variations in the scale of different impacts of events (Table 5.4) may explain why a variety of different distributions are typically used to model severity, including log normal and Weibull. Whilst the combination of different internal and external events in a single Basel category, as illustrated in Figure 5.1, may explain why many banks also utilise different distributions for the body (commonly log normal) and

---

[3]Regulatory capital requirements consist of: Pillar 1: Minimum capital requirements; Pillar 2A: Risks not adequately captured under Pillar 1; and Pillar 2B: Factors external to the bank e.g. business cycle effects (Basel Committee, 2004).

[4]The Basel Committee's 2008 Survey of AMA banks reported 93% usage of Poisson (Basel Committee, July 2009b).

FIGURE 10.1 Overview of Operational Risk capital models

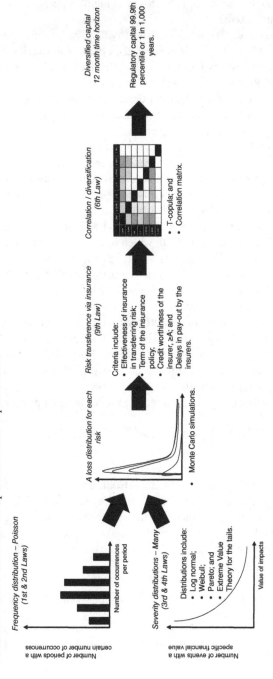

the tail (commonly generalised Pareto) of some of their severity distributions (Basel Committee, July 2009b).[5]

Once the separate frequency and severity distributions are combined into loss distributions via a Monte Carlo simulation, then banks can overlay risk mitigation from relevant insurance policies (9th Law). The effectiveness of insurance policies mitigating Operational Risk will be considered in Chapter 12.

Finally, the different loss distributions are combined to reflect the existence of correlations (6th Law). The existence of correlations for very large loss events may reflect the influence of different underlying causal factors (Table 5.5 and Figure 5.2), and also external drivers relating to detection and/or settlement.[6] Correlations, can be either calculated from internal data, if firms have sufficient number of loss events, or external data, e.g. ORX provide correlation matrices to their members. Additionally, firms can also calculate correlations of tail events by selecting a population of peer banks, and analysing tail losses, e.g. losses $\geq$\$0.1 billion, which can be sourced from providers of public domain loss data, e.g. ORX News and IBM FIRST Risk Case Studies. This can involve analysing the frequency with which individual banks suffer multiple large loss events in the same year (Figure 3.3). Alternatively, firms can estimate the correlations between different risk types by considering their sensitivities to the key causal factors (Table 2.2 and Figure 5.2), i.e. risks that are sensitive to the same causal factors should display higher degrees of correlation.

The loss distributions for the different risks are then aggregated using a non-Gaussian, non-normal distribution. The EBA suggests firms use T-copulas with low degrees of freedom, "... say 3 or 4 ... " (EBA, 2015). The regulatory capital requirement for AMA banks is the combination of expected and unexpected losses, unless banks can adequately demonstrate that their expected losses are captured in their internal business practices, e.g. their budgeting and/or product pricing (Basel Committee, 2004).

Challenges

Based upon the results of QIS-2, the Basel Committee concluded that Operational Risk capital should represent 12% of a bank's total capital requirement. The Basel Committee had previously believed that this figure should be 20%. Additionally, the Basel Committee stated "... that the level of capital required under the AMA will be lower than under simpler approaches ... ", and it set an initial floor of 75% of the Standardised

---

[5]This is noted in the EBA's Regulatory Technical Standards (2015) on the assessment AMA models.
[6]During the initial COVID-19 outbreak the number and value of regulatory settlements declined, maybe as a result of regulators redirecting their focus to supporting firms, rather than fining them for past misconduct. (Risk.net, July 2020).

Approach (TSA) requirement, i.e. 9% (Basel Committee, 2001). As a consequence, AMA banks may initially have calibrated the outputs of their AMA models against their TSA capital requirements. This was unfortunate because the periods covered by QIS-2, i.e. 1998 to 2001, were relatively benign for Operational Risk losses, leading to the miscalibration of TSA, and hence also of the AMA models.

An analysis of nine banks that were AMA in 2016 and that also disclosed annually their charges for litigation and regulatory settlements between 2008 and 2016[7] reveals that these charges represented on average 20% of their total losses (i.e. Market Risk, plus Credit Risk,[8] plus Operational Risk losses) and 22% of their total Risk Weighted Assets (RWAs) in 2016 (Figure 10.2), suggesting that the Basel Committee's initial estimate was closer to the correct value for Operational Risk losses during a period of economic stress. A review of the levels of Operational Risk capital for eight of

FIGURE 10.2 Analysis of losses and RWAs for nine AMA banks 2008 to 2016[9] (Grimwade, 2018)

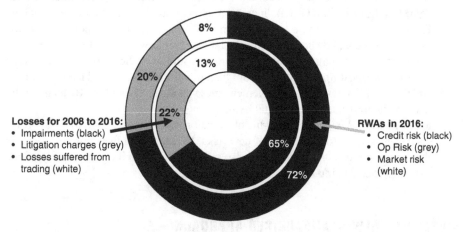

Losses for 2008 to 2016:
- Impairments (black)
- Litigation charges (grey)
- Losses suffered from trading (white)

RWAs in 2016:
- Credit risk (black)
- Op Risk (grey)
- Market risk (white)

---

[7]These charges primarily relate to CPBP. Figure 1.4 shows that CPBP represented the majority of losses during this period.

[8]Market Risk losses were measured as negative trading income, and Credit Risk losses are the banks' impairment charges. These nine banks are a subset of the 13 banks (both AMA and non-AMA) analysed in Figure 3.5.

[9]The split of losses in Figure 10.2 is similar to the results of both the EBA 2018 and the Federal Reserve 2020 stress tests:

- EBA 2018 stressed losses were: Credit Risk, 67%; Market Risk, 18%; and Operational Risk, 15% (EBA, November 2018); and
- Federal Reserve's 2020 stress test: Credit Risk, 68%; Market Risk, 12%; and Operational Risk, 20% (Federal Reserve, 2020).

these G-SIBs, which were consistently AMA between 2008 and 2016, reveals that their Operational Risk capital requirements on average rose by 66% during this period. The scale of these increases varied between banks, reflecting different loss experiences, acquisitions and modelling methodologies (Grimwade, 2018).

Figure 10.1 also highlights that a number of key Laws of Operational Risk are not reflected in typical AMA models, specifically:

- *5th Law: Lags in settlement.* The Basel capital requirements are based on a 12-month time horizon. Banks include all of their loss data, despite Figure 2.5 showing that 72% of the value of large losses ($\geq$$0.1 billion) for current and former G-SIBs crystallise more than a year after detection. Ignoring these lags will tend to lead to the overstatement of the Operational Risk capital requirements of banks.
- *7th Law: Concentration due to external drivers*, primarily the sensitivity of Operational Risk losses to economic cycles. The total value of large losses ($\geq$$0.1 billion) for the G-SIBs increased by ~9× in the aftermath of the Global Financial Crisis. In Figure 10.1, the correlation matrices focus upon changes in the occurrence and detection of losses (1st and 2nd Laws) rather than changes in the velocity and the duration of losses (3rd and 4th Laws). Sensitivity to economic cycles is the most important driver of Operational Risk losses, and hence without additional stress testing to supplement these models, via Pillar 2B, banks will tend to underestimate their capital requirements.
- *8th Law: Risk Homeostasis*, and the observation that banks respond to the appearance of new risks (or the threat of new risks) by enhancing their controls, means that banks using LDA models may also overstate their capital requirements, due to these models being backward-looking.

BASEL III'S NEW STANDARDISED APPROACH – A PROXY FOR RISK PROFILE, SCALED FOR ACTUAL LOSSES

These challenges with AMA, and the absence of a regulatory standard for Operational Risk capital models in Basel II, will have contributed to the Basel Committee's observation that "...the lack of comparability arising from a wide range of internal modelling practices have exacerbated variability in RWA calculations, and have eroded confidence in RWA capital ratios" (Basel Committee, 2016).

The Basel Committee's new Standardised Approach utilises revenues over the preceding three years as a proxy for a firm's current Operational Risk profile, scaled up or down for the historical loss experience of banks over the preceding ten years (Basel Committee, 2017a). This is summarised in Formula 10.1. The Basel Committee's stated objectives were "promoting comparability", "reducing model complexity", whilst providing a "sufficiently risk sensitive measure" (Basel Committee, 2016).

Formula 10.1 The new Standardised Approach

Business Indicator Component   **Internal Loss Multiplier**

$$
\begin{array}{c}
\text{Business} \\
\text{Indicator}
\end{array}
\times
\begin{array}{c}
\text{Business Indicator} \\
\text{Marginal} \\
\text{Coefficients}
\end{array}
\times \; \text{Ln}
\left[
\text{Exp}(1) - 1 +
\left[
\dfrac{
\begin{array}{c}
\text{Average annual} \\
\textit{net} \text{ losses over} \\
10 \text{ years} \times 15
\end{array}
}{
\begin{array}{c}
\text{Business} \\
\text{Indicator} \\
\text{Component}
\end{array}
}
\right]^{0.8}
\right]
$$

Business Indicator is derived from the average revenues of banks over the preceding three years. It consists of three components: interest income and dividends; net trading and bank book income; and other operating and fee income. The methodology for calculating these three components has been modified to remove some of the spurious behaviours of Basel II's TSA, e.g. trading P&L is an absolute number, so that if the investment banking arm of a universal makes a large trading loss then the Group will in future not benefit from a negative Operational Risk capital requirement for this business.[10]

Business Indicator Marginal Coefficients (α) vary depending upon size of a bank, i.e.: 12% for the Business Indicator values of ≤€1 billion; and 15% for Business Indicator values of €1 billion to €30 billion; and 18% for Business Indicator values of >€30 billion.

Internal Loss Multiplier (ILM) is calculated as a log function, allowing the Business Indicator Component to be either scaled up or down for the historical loss experiences of banks (for losses >€20k) over the preceding ten years. Local supervisors have discretion, however, to set the ILM to "1", removing this "risk sensitive" element of the new Standardised Approach.

Challenges

The Basel Committee is cognisant of the limitations of the new Standardised Approach. Its Business Indicator measure is very crude when compared to the complexity of the business profiles of banks, as summarised in Figure 2.1. The new Standardised Approach (unlike Basel II's TSA) treats all revenues as being equally risky, however, the 10th Law states that "Proactively taking Operational Risk is disproportionately risky" (Table 4.1).

---

[10]This issue was previously addressed by Basel II as follows: "If negative gross income distorts a bank's Pillar 1 capital charge, supervisors will consider appropriate supervisory action under Pillar 2" (Basel Committee, 2004).

FIGURE 10.3   Average losses ≥$0.1 billion over ten years vs average recent revenues for 31 large banks (Grimwade, 2018)

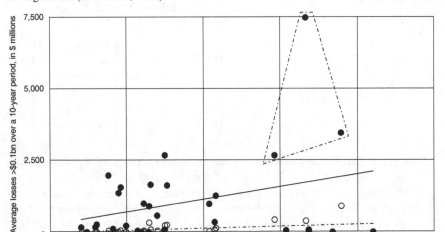

Additionally, the assumption of a relationship between the scale of revenues and Operational Risk losses also seems questionable. Figure 10.3 analyses the annual average large losses (≥$0.1 billion) for two 10-year periods (i.e. 1998 to 2007 and 2008 to 2017) before, and during and after the Global Financial Crisis and average recent revenues (2015 and 2016) for 31 current and former G-SIBs. The trend line for 1998 to 2007 is almost flat, showing little relationship between losses and revenues, whilst the trend line for 2008 to 2017 does rise with revenues, but only as a result of the losses suffered by the three largest US banks which are quite disproportionate in comparison to the largest Asian banks. The variations between banks from different regions and between decades suggests that the new Standardised Approach will need to be periodically recalibrated. The Basel Committee's track record on recalibration is limited, however, as no such recalibration ever occurred for Basel II's TSA. (Grimwade, 2018).

The incorporation of the historical loss experiences of banks over the previous ten years also makes stress testing a little more complicated (7th Law). When the new Standardised Approach goes live (currently planned for January 2023) the historical loss data will include both the tail end of losses arising from the Global Financial Crisis, as well as any new losses arising from the COVID-19 pandemic. Additionally, the Internal Loss Multiplier leads to a 10-year delay in banks subsequently obtaining credit for any enhancements to their controls following a large loss (8th Law: Risk Homeostasis).

Finally, the new Standardised Approach is backward-looking, and is consequently blind to emerging risks (e.g. Climate Change risks), and also changes in a bank's business model (e.g. increased usage of AI and machine learning).

Conclusions

In striving for a methodology that delivers both greater simplicity and consistency for Pillar 1 capital requirements, Basel III's new Standardised Approach clearly has reduced risk sensitivity. An unintended consequence may be the encouragement of banks to increase their proactive Operational Risk taking to boost their returns on regulatory capital (10th Law), as under the new Standardised Approach, all forms of revenue generation initially receive the same dollar for dollar Pillar 1 Operational Risk capital requirement, irrespective of their inherent riskiness. Ultimately, however, the new Standardised Approach sets consistent minimum capital requirements for Operational Risk for banks, which progressively increases with size. Consequently, banks that are systemically important will naturally hold more Operational Risk capital than smaller, less systemically important banks. The sensitivity of Operational Risk to emerging risks, changing business models, control enhancements (8th Law: Risk Homeostasis), and economic cycles (7th Law: Concentration due to external drivers) can all be addressed via Pillar 2 (2A and 2B), as Basel II originally intended.[11]

MODEL VALIDATION

Due to the challenges presented by the modelling of Operational Risk, capital models should be validated to determine if they "...are reliable and effective in...measuring operational risk..." (EBA, 2015). In addition to assessing the documentation, inputs and governance surrounding these models, firms can use various techniques to validate the reasonableness of their outputs.

Sensitivity analysis

Firms can adjust both the inputs into their actuarial models and parameters within the model to identify the scale of the impact on the model. For example, for models that make use of scenario analysis, the likelihoods and severities can be individually and collectively adjusted by +/−10%. Key correlation factors and modelling parameters (e.g. number of simulations or the degrees of freedom associated with the T-copula)

---

[11] As noted earlier, regulatory capital requirements comprise: Pillar 1: Minimum capital requirements; Pillar 2A: Risks not adequately captured under Pillar 1; and Pillar 2B: Factors external to the bank e.g. business cycle effects (Basel Committee, 2004).

can be similarly adjusted. Any factors which, when adjusted, create a cliff edge should be subject to further review and challenge. Equally, for the new Standardised Approach, firms can analyse the sensitivity of their Internal Loss Multiplier to individual very large loss events.

Benchmarking against internal data

The outputs of models (i.e. undiversified risk at 99.9%) for individual scenarios can also be checked against key business metrics (Figure 2.1) to determine the reasonableness of the outputs of the model as well as the outputs of scenario analysis, as discussed in Chapter 9. The metrics that might be considered could include the largest payments; or the largest underwrites; or the largest fat-finger limits, etc. This may help a firm to answer the question "Is it really possible for us to lose that much?"

Additionally, the PRA has published its own approaches for estimating Pillar 2A capital for Operational Risk (PRA, 2018), excluding Conduct Risk. These approaches can also be utilised by firms to back-test the outputs of their Operational Risk capital models. The three approaches are:

1. *Extrapolation of forecast losses* to 1 in 1,000 years. A review of the ratio of low value ORX losses (€20k to €100k) to higher value ORX losses (≥€10 million) suggests that the multiplier is up to 16× (Chapter 1).
2. *Extrapolation of the average of the five largest losses* (reported in COREP 17) for each of the last five years for each Basel event type out to 1 in 1,000 years using a Pareto distribution. A review of the ratio of annual charges for litigation and regulatory settlements to Pillar 1 capital for AMA banks suggests that these approximate to the total value of losses in any one year multiplied by between 1 ½ and 5, with an average of ~3 (Grimwade, 2018).
3. *Extrapolation of a firm's five largest scenarios* out to 1 in 1,000 years, using a fat-tailed distribution (presumably Pareto again), and a predefined diversification benefit. The PRA has not published the diversification benefit that they intend to use, however, anecdotally around 30% to 35% is reasonable.

Benchmarking against capital requirements

The outputs of AMA and Pillar 2A Operational Risk capital models can also be benchmarked against the outputs of those of other banks, as part of their Pillar 3 disclosures, especially if banks publish their AMA or economic capital requirements split by division. This supplemental disclosure enables other firms to benchmark their own capital models by using various business profile scaling factors/exposure indicators, such as gross revenues;[12] balance sheets; Market Risk capital; the notional value of derivatives;

---

[12]For investment banks gross revenues are a poor scaling factor due to their volatility.

the value of underwriting and staff numbers, etc.[13] These metrics can either be obtained from the bank's financial statements or industry league tables. Whilst this analysis will not inform a firm whether its Operational Risk capital requirement calculated by its model is correct, it will identify if it is disproportionately too big or too small relative to a peer, scaled for these exposure indicators.

In conclusion, by using these techniques, firms can establish the reasonableness and consistency of their Operational Risk capital requirements.

A MORE HOLISTIC APPROACH TO OPERATIONAL RISK CAPITAL MODELLING – AN "HOURGLASS"

As a consequence of the complexity of Operational Risk, the industry needs to move away from a one-size-fits-all approach, i.e. the different categories of risks require specific modelling techniques, which may respectively come from the insurance industry, or the accounting profession or regulators, reflecting the Ten Laws. Critically, the 5th Law identified that historical large losses (Figure 2.5) can be split into three broad categories that reflect a combination for the timing of losses crystallising and their sensitivity to economic cycles:

1. *Sudden and insensitive to economic cycles (8%):* Six of the Basel II categories of Operational Risks crystallise almost immediately, upon detection, i.e. all of them excluding CPBP[14] (Figure 11.9). But these risks represent a mere 8% by value of large losses ($\geq$\$0.1 billion) suffered by the 31 current and former G-SIBs, since 1989.
2. *Lagging and insensitive to economic cycles (36%):* These CPBP losses are **insensitive** to economic cycles and have average lags of 3 years between detection and settlement. They include settlements for the mis-sale of PPI in the UK; market manipulation (e.g. LIBOR and FX); AML/sanction breaches and the facilitation of tax evasion. They represent 36% by value of large losses ($\geq$\$0.1 billion) suffered by these 31 banks.
3. *Lagging and sensitive to economic cycles (56%):* These are CPBP losses that are **sensitive** to economic shocks, and they show the longest lags, an average of 4 years (7th Law). Examples include MBS and CDO litigation; compensation for both inappropriate foreclosure and the mis-sale of derivatives; and post-underwriting litigation. They represent 56% by value of large losses ($\geq$\$0.1 billion) suffered by these 31 banks.

The modelling of each is considered in turn.

---

[13]The Basel Committee considered similar metrics as potential Exposure Indicators (Basel Committee, May 2001).
[14]EPWS also has long lags but it makes only a relatively small contribution to large loss events.

Sudden and insensitive to economic cycles

Pillar 1 capital should be set aside for risks resulting in these sudden losses that are insensitive to economic cycles, which typically crystallise after detection within the 12-month time horizon defined by Basel II. This could be done by restricting the new Standardised Approach methodology to these six Basel categories. The percentages used would, however, need to be recalibrated periodically to reflect risks that have emerged and industry changes (8th Law). Alternatively, an AMA-style model could be used, as these loss events resemble losses that could be insured by a general insurer.

Pillar 2A capital would still have to be set aside for risks of which banks had no prior experience because either these risks are emerging threats or the firms have had the good fortune not to suffer such events. Pillar 2A capital can be assessed using a combination of scenario analysis and external data. Whilst scenario analysis can be quite subjective, hindering its usefulness as an input into capital, its objectivity can be improved by firms systematically identifying the drivers of impacts to aide quantification, as described in Chapter 9.

2. Lagging and insensitive to economic cycles

This category of losses involves regulatory settlements (i.e. restitution and compensation, and regulatory fines and penalties, per Table 9.1) relating to misconduct that is insensitive to economic cycles. Critically the value of any compensation and restitution is not linked (directly or indirectly) to Market and Credit Risks. The average lag between detection and settlement is 3 years, i.e. well beyond Basel II's 12-month time horizon. Consequently, for these risks, firms should not set aside Pillar 1 capital, but instead establish accounting provisions for losses crystallising in the next 12 months for these litigation and regulatory settlements. These provisions are in effect direct deductions from revenues and hence retained earnings and capital resources. The costs of these settlements also tend to be quite predictable, as there have often been similar settlements involving other firms, i.e. these events are often Systemic Operational Risk Events. This approach could only be used in circumstances when these provisions both comply with the relevant accounting standards and also avoid undermining a firm's negotiating position. The observation, however, that when a firm agrees a large settlement, there is often only a limited impact on its current quarter's results, suggests that firms are indeed establishing significant provisions for litigation and regulatory settlements in the years preceding resolution. As with Market Risk, regulators could impose back-testing penalties for any significant under-accruals.[15]

In addition, a multiplier for Pillar 2A capital may also be required to reflect coincidence/correlation with other risks, i.e. Market, Credit and other categories of Operational Risk, e.g. rising unemployment may have been a contributing factor to claims

---

[15]This was previously proposed in a paper by Marco Migueis (Migueis, 2018).

of mis-sale of PPI, whilst correlated causes (Figure 5.2) may lead to clusters[16] of Operational Risk losses (6th Law: Concentration due to internal drivers). This multiplier would also need to address the ~20% of these large loses that do settle within 12 months of detection.

In conclusion, as ~80% of these large CPBP losses that are lagging and insensitive to economic cycles settle more than one year after detection then firms can readily estimate the losses that they may suffer over a 12-month time horizon and establish appropriate accounting provisions, which are direct deductions from current year revenues and retained revenues and hence capital. This is a more real-world approach than assuming that all of these losses will settle within one year, when they clearly do not.

Lagging and sensitive to economic cycles

A more sophisticated approach is required for this category of losses, which also involves regulatory settlements (i.e. restitution and compensation, and regulatory fines and penalties, per Table 5.4) relating to misconduct but these losses are sensitive to economic cycles, i.e. the value of restitution and compensation is linked (directly or indirectly) to either Market or Credit Risk. The average lag between detection and settlement is 4 years, i.e. well beyond Basel II's 12-month time horizon. As these losses are correlated with Market and Credit Risk losses (Figure 3.5), then firms should establish Pillar 2B capital requirements, rather than simply establishing provisions on an annual basis, as Market and Credit Risk losses may already have eroded the profitability and capital bases of firms during an economic crisis.[17] The estimation of these exposures would utilise the scenario analysis techniques, described in Chapter 9 and stressed in Chapter 11, for impacts that are sensitive to economic cycles, and AMA-style models. The critical feature of a Pillar 2B capital requirement is that it is a countercyclical buffer, i.e. this capital can be utilised by firms during an economic shock, without the requirement to raise additional capital.

The "hourglass" solution

Considering these different categories of risk suggests that the composition of Operational Risk capital requirements should resemble an hourglass (Figure 10.4) with roughly comparable amounts of Pillar 1 and 2B capital.[18] This is consistent with

---

[16]For example, some banks have reached settlements regarding the rigging of benchmarks across multiple different and unrelated markets and jurisdictions, e.g. interest rates, FX, precious metals and electricity.

[17]The EBA 2018 stress test results for 48 EU and EEA banks showed that they would collectively suffer €138 billion of losses, after tax, in Year 1; followed by zero aggregate profit in Year 2, before becoming profitable again in Year 3. (EBA, November 2018).

[18]The percentages have been adjusted to reflect CPBP losses that crystallised within 12 months of the end date, and rounded to avoid spurious accuracy.

FIGURE 10.4 Operational Risk capital requirements should look like an hourglass (Grimwade, 2018)

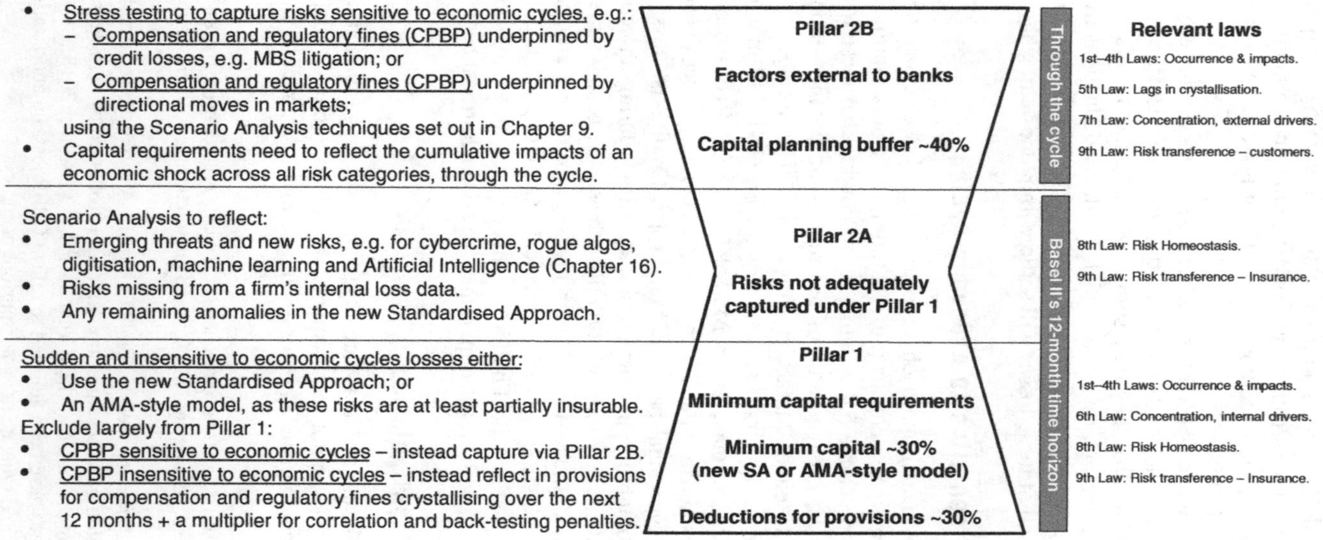

- Stress testing to capture risks sensitive to economic cycles, e.g.:
  - Compensation and regulatory fines (CPBP) underpinned by credit losses, e.g. MBS litigation; or
  - Compensation and regulatory fines (CPBP) underpinned by directional moves in markets;
  using the Scenario Analysis techniques set out in Chapter 9.
- Capital requirements need to reflect the cumulative impacts of an economic shock across all risk categories, through the cycle.

Scenario Analysis to reflect:
- Emerging threats and new risks, e.g. for cybercrime, rogue algos, digitisation, machine learning and Artificial Intelligence (Chapter 16).
- Risks missing from a firm's internal loss data.
- Any remaining anomalies in the new Standardised Approach.

Sudden and insensitive to economic cycles losses either:
- Use the new Standardised Approach; or
- An AMA-style model, as these risks are at least partially insurable.
Exclude largely from Pillar 1:
  - CPBP sensitive to economic cycles – instead capture via Pillar 2B.
  - CPBP insensitive to economic cycles – instead reflect in provisions for compensation and regulatory fines crystallising over the next 12 months + a multiplier for correlation and back-testing penalties.

Through the cycle

Pillar 2B

Factors external to banks

Capital planning buffer ~40%

Pillar 2A

Risks not adequately captured under Pillar 1

Basel II's 12-month time horizon

Pillar 1

Minimum capital requirements

Minimum capital ~30% (new SA or AMA-style model)

Deductions for provisions ~30%

Relevant laws

1st–4th Laws: Occurrence & impacts.
5th Law: Lags in crystallisation.
7th Law: Concentration, external drivers.
9th Law: Risk transference – customers.

8th Law: Risk Homeostasis.
9th Law: Risk transference – Insurance.

1st–4th Laws: Occurrence & impacts.
6th Law: Concentration, internal drivers.
8th Law: Risk Homeostasis.
9th Law: Risk transference – Insurance.

178

observed patterns in Operational Risk losses over the last three decades and through various economic cycles, i.e. there are significant spikes in Operational Risk losses associated with economic shocks (Figures 3.2 and 11.1, Grimwade, 2016). Between these shocks Operational Risk losses are more random.

CONCLUSIONS

Basel II envisaged a combination of minimum capital requirements (Pillar 1) with Pillar 2 capital covering risks not adequately captured under Pillar 1 and the impacts of external factors, such as business cycles.

Whilst this hourglass approach is consistent with Basel II, it differs by identifying that different risks primarily drive different pillars. In doing so, it more effectively reflects the characteristics of Operational Risk set out in Chapter 1, and described by the Ten Laws.

Specifically, it better reflects the lags between detection and settlement of events leading to the payment of compensation and regulatory fines (5th Law: Lags in settlement). It is also designed to avoid the double counting of risks sensitive to economic cycles (7th Law: Concentration due to external drivers) between Pillar 1 and 2B. Finally, the tendency for new risks to emerge (8th Law: Risk Homeostasis) is clearly reflected in Pillar 2A.

In this approach, scenario analysis and AMA-style models are not the basis for a reduction to Pillar 1 capital per se, as originally intended under Basel II, but instead the drivers for a better understanding of both Pillar 2A and 2B capital.

CHAPTER 11

Stress Testing

This chapter analyses the historical profile of Operational Risk losses; provides an overview of the different regulatory approaches to stress testing; and also assesses the results of recent industry exercises. It then considers how these approaches may be enhanced by utilising the Ten Laws and the taxonomies of inadequacies or failures (events) and impacts described in Tables 5.2 and 5.4.

Stress testing is a forward-looking risk management tool used to estimate the potential impacts, across all risks, of an adverse scenario on a firm, portfolio or product (NB Chapter 13 specifically considers the stress testing of individual products). The objectives of stress testing are to assess and quantify a firm's vulnerabilities and resiliency to stress events, and to enhance decision making in the management of these risks. For Operational Risk, its foundations should be an understanding of how a firm's business profile and its Operational Risk profile will dynamically interact with an external shock.

THE HISTORICAL PROFILE OF OPERATIONAL RISK LOSSES

Analysing large Operational Risk losses ($\geq$\$0.1 billion) by their end/detection dates, rather than their settlement dates (Figure 11.1), over the last three decades reveals spikes in Operational Risk losses that seem to coincide with changes in business cycle, i.e. there are distinct spikes in Operational Risk losses associated with both the bursting of the dot.com bubble and also the Global Financial Crisis.[1,2]

Investigating the nature of the impacts of these large losses reveals the contribution of primarily Credit Risk and to a lesser extent Market Risk (Figure 11.1). Approximately, 53% by value of these large Operational Risk losses are linked to Credit Risk.

---

[1]There is also a small spike associated with an unexpectedly rapid tightening of US interest rates in 1994.

[2]The observation that Operational Risk can be cyclical pre-dates the Global Financial Crisis e.g. (Cagan & Lantsman, 2007).

FIGURE 11.1 Analysis of large losses ≥$0.1 billion for 31 current and former G-SIBs, analysed by end date and split by risk drivers[3,4]

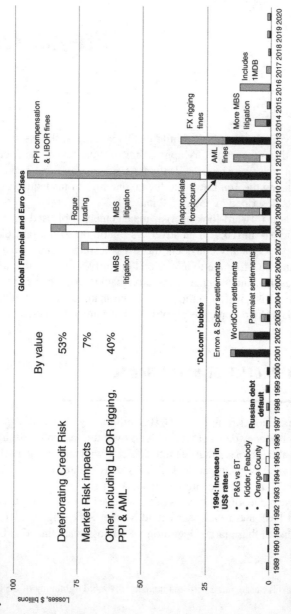

[3]Figure 11.1 illustrates the first two eras of Operational Risk, i.e. the first era (the 1990s) was a period of largely idiosyncratic losses, whilst the second era (2001 to 2015) was marked by misconduct losses linked to the bursting of asset bubbles (Grimwade, 2019).
[4]Figure 11.1 shows a more extreme spike than Figure 3.2 due to the removal of the smoothing effect of settlement lags.

For example, the compensation paid by banks to settle MBS litigation after the Global Financial Crisis was underpinned by losses suffered by the litigants due to a rise in delinquency rates and defaults of US residential mortgages (Chapter 2). In contrast, only around 7% by value of these large Operational Risk losses are linked to directional market movements. A relevant example is the compensation paid to settle claims of the mis-sale of GBP interest rate derivatives that locked customers into fixed rates (>5%) preventing them from benefiting from the sharp drop in floating rates in 2008/09, down to what was then the lowest ever rate of ½% (Figure 11.4).[5]

OVERVIEW OF THE REGULATORY APPROACHES TO STRESS TESTING

Stress testing of Operational Risk is typically undertaken as part of regular, industry-wide exercises, within specific regulatory jurisdictions. For Operational Risk the focus is on CPBP because of both its significance and apparent economic sensitivity (Figure 1.4). As projecting future Operational Risk losses is clearly subjective, as per scenario analysis described in Chapter 9, regulators provide varying degrees of guidance to banks to make their assessments both more systematic and consistent.

The occurrence of events and the nature of impacts

The focus for the Bank of England for Conduct Risk is *known* conduct-related issues. Banks have to include stressed projections of all potential costs relating to known misconduct risks, in excess of their existing accounting provisions (Bank of England, March 2019). The EBA is additionally more explicit in wanting banks to capture both "...historical material conduct risk events and new conduct risk events...", and the scope of the impacts is also broader than the Basel II criteria, including opportunity costs, internal costs and any potential loss of future earnings (see the impacts taxonomy, Table 5.4). For non-conduct-related Operational Risks, the EBA requires that the projections of banks, under their adverse scenario, should reach the 90th percentile of the historical yearly aggregate amount of losses, i.e. this represents a one in ten year stress (EBA, July 2018). Whilst in the US, the Federal Reserve's Comprehensive Capital Analysis and Review (CCAR) process broadly focuses upon the evaluation of the type of Operational Risk loss events to which the firm is exposed and the sensitivity of those events to internal and external operating environments (Federal Reserve S15-18 and S15-19).

---

[5]The EBA states in its guidelines that "Institutions should analyse carefully the possible interaction of operational risk losses with credit and market risks" (EBA, July 2018).

The different regulators naturally all focus on the most material risks. The Bank of England requires additional analysis of each risk that amounts to 10% or more of the total additional misconduct costs each year during the stress test time horizon. The EBA also highlights the importance of future costs linked to both *material* historical or new conduct events. An historical material Conduct Risk event is defined as any misconduct issue that has triggered aggregate gross losses during the preceding five-year period of greater than 10bps (0.1%) of the firm's current Common Equity Tier 1 (CET1).

The timing of losses/stress test horizon

The Bank of England requires firms to allocate their estimates of future Conduct Risk losses to individual years within the five-year time horizon of their stress tests on "a systematic basis". Similarly the EBA requires firms to "... report the projected loss in the year when the settlement of the misconduct issue will most likely occur", and if there is uncertainty, firms are simply to split the losses equally over the three years of their exercise. For CCAR, losses are allocated to one of the nine quarters of the US stress tests.

Loss estimation techniques

The Bank of England requires banks to provide both quantitative and qualitative information to support the material assumptions underlying their stressed projections. It specifically requires banks to provide stressed projections of future misconduct costs, irrespective of whether a provision has been recognised, by evaluating a range of settlement outcomes and assigning probabilities to each outcome. Whilst banks may ignore individual risks and outcomes where the likelihood of settlement is remote, they have to assess the need to include costs in the stressed projections to cover the possibility that, at the aggregate level, one or more remote settlement outcomes may crystallise. For instances of potential customer redress, banks need to provide "... details (by vintage) of the volume and value of past business written, the proportion of business that the bank expects to pay redress for, and the average expected value of redress". Sensibly, the Bank of England also highlights that the nature of some of the misconduct losses may themselves be sensitive to the scenario's macroeconomic factors, i.e. "... the prices of securities, interest rates or FX rates ..." (Figure 11.4).

The EBA also allows banks to adopt both qualitative and quantitative approaches for Conduct Risks. Factors to be considered include: historical internal loss data; scenario analysis; external loss data; levels of expected losses and judgement. In addition, the EBA sets floors for different categories of Operational Risk. For the 2020 exercise, material Conduct Risk losses were floored at average historical losses over five years × three × a stress factor (1.15). Whilst non-Conduct Risks were floored at average historical losses over five years × three × a stress factor (1.5). For banks that lack sufficient historical loss data to apply these floors, then the EBA has a fall-back solution of multiplying their gross earnings by 15% and then splitting these projected losses equally between each of the three years of their stress test (EBA, January 2018). This 15% floor is comparable to the highest cumulative average losses for ORX members, as a percentage of business line revenues, over a three-year period (14%), in Figure 3.2.

Changes in capital requirements

The Bank of England requires firms to predict their RWAs in line with their current Pillar 1 approach. The EBA floors the capital requirements of TSA banks at the level at the beginning of the exercise, i.e. firms do not receive a capital benefit from any reduction in their revenues due to an economic slowdown. AMA banks are required to rerun their models based upon their forecast Operational Risk losses.

The unique US approach

The Federal Reserve has developed a unique regulatory approach. In addition to the firms conducting their own stress tests they also provide detailed submissions (historical losses and total assets), which are input into a standard model, that then produces P&L and capital projections for individual firms, to which the management actions of individual firms are overlain.[6] Operational Risk loss estimates are derived as the average of projections from two modelling approaches: a linear regression model and an historical simulation. The regression model captures the sensitivity of Operational Risk losses to business cycles, via a number of key variables (Table 11.1). The model projects aggregate Operational Risk losses (excluding Damage to Physical Assets) for the industry over the nine quarters of the CCAR process, and then allocates these losses to firms based on their balance sheet assets.[7]

TABLE 11.1 Key variables used in the Federal Reserve's regression model

"Wall Street" variables	"Main Street" variables	Firm-specific variables
▪ Market volatility (VIX).	▪ House prices.	▪ Total assets.
▪ 10-year Treasury yield.	▪ Unemployment rates.	▪ Operational Risk losses.
▪ Corporate bond yields.		

---

[6]The Dodd–Frank Act Stress Test (DFAST) is "... a forward-looking quantitative evaluation of the impact of a stressful economic ... conditions on a firms capital". CCAR then incorporates the firms' "planned capital actions" (Federal Reserve, 2019).

[7]NB The largest industry-wide losses in the US arose from MBS related litigation (see the case study in Chapter 2). As these losses related to the arrangement of the issuance of securities, these banks no longer have any related balance sheets assets.

The historical simulation model projects Operational Risk losses for each firm for each of the seven Basel II event types using a LDA model (Chapter 10). The bodies of the frequency and severity distributions are based on data for an individual firm, whilst the tails are based on industry data, scaled for the assets of the individual firm.[8] The projected Operational Risk losses for each event type are summed to arrive at a total loss number, i.e. correlation in a stress scenario is assumed to be 100%.

ASSESSMENT OF THE RECENT RESULTS OF INDUSTRY EXERCISES

The level of disclosure of the results of these regulatory stress tests varies between these three regulators, with the EBA providing the most granularity regarding the impacts of different risk types on losses and capital. In the EBA's report on the results of the 2018 stress testing exercise for 48 banks (EBA, November 2018), it disclosed the split between Market (18%), Credit (67%), and Operational Risk (15%) losses over the three years of their stress test. These splits are broadly comparable to the data for the period of 2008 to 2016 for nine current and former G-SIBs that were all AMA and disclose their annual charges for litigation and regulatory settlements (Figure 10.2) , i.e. 13%, 65% and 22% respectively. The Federal Reserve's 2020 stress test, for 33 banks, produced very similar ratios, i.e. 12%, 68% and 20% respectively (Federal Reserve, 2020), suggesting both a significant influence of historical loss data, and also a compression of losses into just nine quarters that may actually crystallise over longer periods.

The resulting splits of these losses over the three years of the EBA stress test (Figure 11.2), however, differ from the distribution of losses for the period of 2008 to 2016 for the 13 current and former G-SIBs (a mixture of AMA and TSA firms) that disclose their annual charges for litigation and regulatory settlements (Figure 3.5 is repeated below for comparison). The historical data for 2008 to 2016 shows the value of losses for these different risk categories peaking in waves, i.e. Market Risk (2008, or Year 1), Credit Risk (2009, or Year 2), and Operational Risk (2013, or Year 6), rather than all in Year 1, as in the EBA exercise. It is intuitively correct that increased market volatility and directional moves in markets may have immediate impacts on firms, whilst the impacts of an economic shock may take time to ripple through the economy and to result in higher levels of corporate and personal defaults, whilst Operational Risk loss events arising from the Real Option Model (Figure 3.4) in the form of litigation and/or regulatory action clearly involve more extended timescales.

In the EBA's 2018 exercise, 12 of the 48 participating banks were current or former G-SIBs, and half of them used AMA models to calculate their Pillar 1 capital.

---

[8] Scaling of Operational Risk loss data is problematic, as evidenced by Figure 10.3.

FIGURE 11.2 Profile of Market, Credit and Operational Risk losses from the EBA 2018 stress test

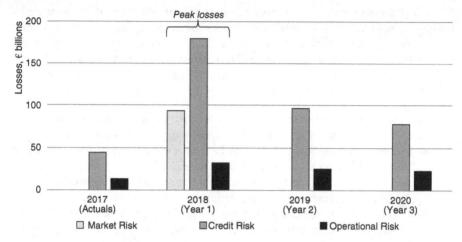

Profile of trading losses (Market Risk), impairments (Credit Risk) and litigation and regulatory settlements (Operational Risk) for 13 banks (Repeat of Figure 3.5)

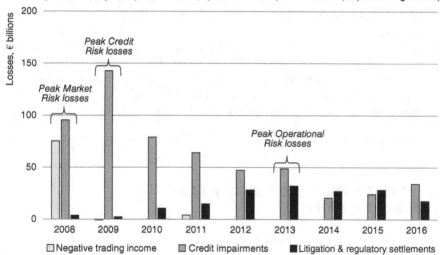

For these six AMA banks, the increase in their Operational Risk capital requirements was between only 2% and 16%, with both average and median values of 10%. This is significantly lower than the 75% overall projected increase in Operational Risk losses in 2018, suggesting that their Pillar 1 capital requirements are already significantly capturing losses associated with business cycle/economic shocks.

CONCLUSIONS

These regulatory approaches to stress testing are all quite silent on the mechanisms by which an economic shock actually results in increased Operational Risk losses. Whilst, just as with the identification of emerging risks (Chapter 15), there is no definitive answer, the process and the value obtained from stress testing can be enhanced through a better understanding of the behaviour of Operational Risk. There are three key areas for enhancement:

1. *Concentration due to external drivers (7th Law):* Ensuring that the assessments cover the full range of drivers. After an economic shock some existing losses are exacerbated; historical failures may be uncovered; and the responses of banks and stakeholders may lead to new losses. These changes in risk profile arise from changes in both economic factors, and also human and institutional behaviours e.g. by bankers, customers, investors, regulators and criminals alike.
2. *Risk Homeostasis (8th Law):* Using the previous five years of historical internal losses as a baseline for forecasting future losses ignores both the propensity for banks to enhance their controls in response to losses outside of appetite and also the infrequency of economic shocks. Consequently, when EU banks undertake stress testing for the COVID-19 pandemic their losses from the Global Financial Crisis will be largely outside of the five years of historical internal loss data used by the EBA.
3. *Lags in settlement of losses (5th Law):* During the Global Financial Crisis the lags in the crystallisation of Operational Risk losses linked to litigation and regulatory settlements resulted in Operational Risk losses peaking well beyond the time horizons of both the nine quarters of the Federal Reserve's CCAR process and the three years of the EBA's stress testing.

The next section will consider how the Ten Laws can be used to enhance stress testing.

AN APPROACH BASED UPON THE TEN LAWS OF OPERATIONAL RISK

The 7th Law considers the external factors influencing the concentration of losses within firms. It states that "The primary external driver of Operational Risk are business cycles, due to a mixture of economics and human behaviour. After an economic shock, some Operational Risk losses rise: existing losses are exacerbated, historical failures uncovered and responses to a crisis may lead to new losses. Occurrence, velocity, duration and lags all increase. [This is summarised in Formula 11.1.] After a severe downturn losses come in waves: first Market, then Credit, and finally Operational Risk."

Formula 11.1 Ratio of Operational Risk losses pre & post an economic shock

Ratio of losses pre & post an economic shock	Ratio of average frequencies pre & post an economic shock	Ratio of average severities pre & post an economic shock	Ratio of lags in settlement for CPBP losses sensitive : insensitive
≈	(Occurrence + Detection) ×	(Velocity × Duration)	, Lags
Units:	(Ratio + Ratio) ×	(Ratio × Ratio)	Ratio
	1st and 2nd Laws	3rd Law 4th Law	5th Law
Comparison of pre & post-crisis, i.e. 2007 to 2017 vs 1996 to 2006	3.2× Driven by the interaction between internal & external causes	2.3× 1.3× 2.9× Driven by the interaction between internal & external causes[9]	1.6×

Although the definition of Operational Risk makes no reference to any specific causes of losses that can be readily linked to economic shocks, as noted earlier, historically losses clearly fluctuate with business cycles (Figure 11.1). Comparison of large losses ($\geq$\$0.1 billion) suffered by 31 current and former G-SIBs before and after 2007 reveals that there are significant increases in both the occurrence and detection (3.2×), and also the velocity (2.3×) of Operational Risk events. Additionally, there is a much smaller increase in duration (1.3×).

More granular analysis of the ORX loss data set indicates that the Global Financial Crisis was marked by a series of distinct phases in Operational Risk losses, "... where the frequency of losses in the early-crisis period [H2 2006 to H2 2007] was similar or slightly lower than pre-crisis losses, then increased above pre-crisis levels in the peak-crisis period [H1 2008 to H1 2009], and finally fell off to lower levels in the late crisis period [H2 2009 to H2 2011]." This pattern was most pronounced for External Fraud and EDPM. Whilst CPBP in Retail Banking exhibited a significant after-peak spike in loss amounts, mainly due to mortgage related legal settlements (Cope and Carrivick, 2013).

These different items of research allude to both the significance and also the complexity of the sensitivity of Operational Risk to business cycles. The remainder of this

---

[9]"Some causes immediately precede an event (triggers), others are facilitative, occurring in the background (environmental conditions), still others magnify the impact of an event once it is already in progress (exacerbators)" (Cech, 2009).

chapter sets out an approach to stress testing reflecting both the 7th Law and also the areas previously listed for enhancement of the various regulatory approaches. The systematic nature of this approach should also help to mitigate the biases described in Chapter 4.

1. Identify behavioural changes

As noted previously, some of the sensitivity to business cycles arises from behavioural changes. Consequently, firms need to review and assess the propensity for business cycles to lead to changes in the behaviours of the stakeholders listed in Figure 2.1, i.e. staff members; authorities (e.g. regulators); sources of capital, funding and revenues (e.g. investors and customers); and society, including criminals. The COVID-19 pandemic highlights some of these different effects, for example, changes in investor sentiment drove dramatic changes in trade volumes in some markets during H1 2020, e.g. the volumes of UK equities traded on the London Stock Exchange increased 140% in March 2020 (44.8 million trades) in comparison to March 2019 (18.4 million trades). In contrast, retail customer demand for products and services suffered equally dramatic declines, changing both the business and risk profiles of firms, e.g. in May 2020 the monthly volume of new mortgages linked to house purchases fell 85% to just 9,273, in comparison to 65,181, a year earlier.[10] After the Global Financial Crisis, similar reductions in new business volumes led to criminals changing their attack vectors, i.e. away from application fraud and towards account takeover frauds (Figure 11.3).

FIGURE 11.3   Frauds reported to CIFAS before, during and after the Global Financial Crisis

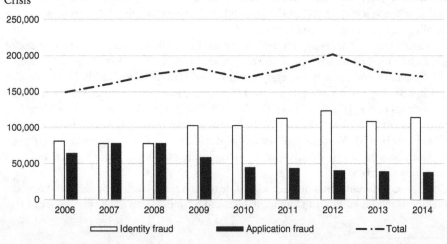

---

[10]This data is available on the Bank of England's website under Statistics: Household credit.

Whilst the outbreak of the COVID-19 pandemic has also been marked by a spike in account takeover frauds and ransomware attacks. Additionally, financial stress may also drive, previously law abiding customers to crimes of "need".[11] Finally, there is also some evidence of changes in the behaviours of regulators. During the first wave of the COVID-19 pandemic, the number and value of regulatory settlements declined, maybe as a result of regulators redirecting their focus to supporting firms, rather than fining them for past misconduct (Risk.net, July 2020). In contrast, in the aftermath of the Global Financial Crisis, the FCA imposed six record breaking fines, but only several years after the initial bank bailouts (Figure 4.2).

All of these changes in the behaviour can alter the occurrence of Operational Risk events.

2. Identify sensitivities to economic factors

As noted previously, some of the sensitivity to business cycles arises from specific economic factors. Consequently, firms need to review and assess the sensitivity of different impacts, listed in the impact taxonomy in Table 5.4, to the various economic factors, typically included in regulatory stress tests. For the Bank of England stress tests these factors include: directional moves in interest and exchange rates; increased market volatility (e.g. a rise in the VIX index); falling equity markets and residential property prices; rising unemployment and corporate defaults; and the widening of credit spreads:

> *Restitution and compensation – customers and investors:* The most significant Operational Risk impact is restitution and compensation (This is a major component of the CPBP losses that are sensitive to economic cycles, described in Chapter 10). The 9th Law: Risk Transference, Transformation and Conservation, states that "When Market and Credit Risks are sold to investors, e.g. through securitisations, they are transformed into Operational Risk that is retained by the arranger/distributor. The quantum of Operational Risk retained is equivalent of the Market and Credit Risks transferred, whilst the likelihood of this Operational Risk becoming a loss is diminished."
>
> Consequently, an economic shock that causes either investment or hedging products to suffer losses, may not only trigger claims for compensation (Figures 11.4), if there is evidence of either misconduct or deficiencies in the sales processes, but may also drive the scale of the resulting losses. As described in Chapter 3, these exposures can be seen as Real Options (Figure 3.4). Historical examples of these types of loss events include the

---

[11] As noted in Chapter 2, BDO's FraudTrack 2018 Survey broadly splits the motivations of criminals between "Greed" and "Need".

FIGURE 11.4   The triggering of claims of mis-sale of interest rate swaps and exacerbating compensation

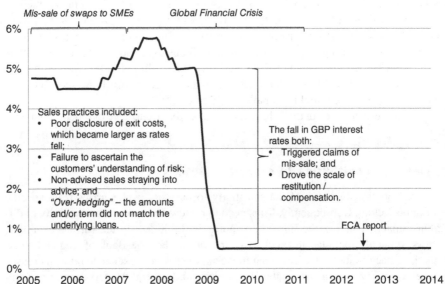

misrepresentation of MBS and CDOs, in the run-up to the Global Financial Crisis (Chapter 2); and also the mis-sale of interest swaps to UK SMEs. Figure 11.4 illustrates how a directional market move can both trigger claims of mis-sale and also drive the scale of losses.

Restitution and compensation may also need to be paid to customers who have not been treated fairly when in financial difficulties. For example, the $25 billion inappropriate foreclosure settlement in the US in 2012 and the more recent £64 million fine and £300 million compensation package agreed by Lloyds Banking Group with the FCA in 2020 (FCA, June 2020).

Restitution and compensation – Employees: UK employment tribunal cases rise[12] with rising unemployment, i.e. making employees redundant appears to be a catalyst for litigation (Figure 11.5).[13]

---

[12]The employment tribunal data reflects receipts of claims rather than settlements. The claims relate to dismissals, redundancy pay and discrimination. The data excludes disputes relating to equal pay, the working time directive and the minimum wage.

[13]Research published prior to the Global Financial Crisis identified a strong correlation between an increase in "People-related Risks" and the VIX index. This category of "People-related Risks" corresponded to two Basel II categories, i.e. Internal Fraud and Employment Practices & Workplace Safety (Cagan & Lantsman, 2007).

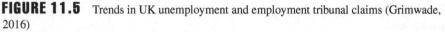

FIGURE 11.5 Trends in UK unemployment and employment tribunal claims (Grimwade, 2016)

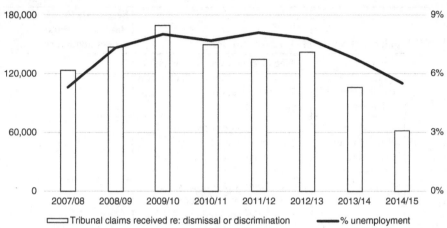

Write-down of balance sheet assets – trading positions: Increased market volatility results in any trade execution errors (e.g. fat-fingered typing) being exacerbated, i.e. the losses (or gains) may be larger (Figure 11.7). Increased trade volumes in volatile markets may also increase the volume of errors. Equally, directional moves in markets may exacerbate the losses (or gains) on any pre-existing unauthorised positions, as well as potentially encouraging previously honest traders to conceal their trading losses (Figure 9.1). For example between August 2007 and February 2008 a small group of ABS traders at Credit Suisse mis-marked their books, in response to falling markets and mounting losses.

Write-down of balance sheet assets – customer and counterparty receivables: Credit Risk losses arising from customer defaults can be exacerbated by Operational Risk e.g. due to loss of recourse from a lack of netting agreements, or the failure to perfect charges over security, or the failure to call margin. Corporate defaults may also be the catalyst for litigation by bondholders/ investors against the underwriters to recover their losses (Figure 11.6), as well as uncovering previously hidden second-party frauds (i.e. "bookkeeper" frauds).

Lost future earnings: Firms may lose revenues as a consequence of the default of suppliers and outsource service providers.

Table 11.2 maps economic factors to the impacts of events (Table 5.4). This underpins the 2.3× increase in the velocity of large losses (≥$0.1 billion), pre and post the Financial Crisis, and also contributes to a 3.2× increase in their occurrence, by triggering claims through the Real Options Model (Figure 3.4).

TABLE 11.2 Mapping of the impacts of Operational Risk events (Table 5.4) to economic sensitivities

P&L & balance sheet		Level 2 – examples	Sensitivity to Bank of England economic factors
Lost revenues or charges (P&L)	Uncollected revenues due to an Operational Risk event.	▪ Uncollected revenues, e.g. failure to claim revenues to which a firm is entitled and loss of entitlement to revenues.	
	Impairments and settlements, to the bank's P&L accounts due to an Operational Risk event.	▪ Restitution/compensation payments linked to a firm's business profile and third-party relationships (Figure 2.1), e.g.:	
		– *Customers & investors*, e.g.: ▪ Credit and Market Risk losses suffered; ▪ Frauds suffered by customers; and ▪ Loss of client assets in safe custody. – *Counterparties, customers and suppliers:* Interest on monies owed.	▪ Rising defaults – both PDs and LGDs. ▪ Falling asset values. ▪ Market moves.[14]
		– *Suppliers:* Breach of contract or licencing agreements e.g. data.	
		– *Employees (current & potential),* e.g.: ▪ Lost historical earnings e.g. due to payroll errors; and ▪ Lost future earnings for an inappropriate dismissal. – *Visitors (e.g. customers, suppliers, etc.):* third-party liability.	▪ Rising unemployment.
		▪ Regulatory action: fines and penalties. ▪ Tax incurred, e.g.: – On behalf of others, e.g. clients or employees; and – Loss of treatment, e.g. failed tax arbitrage/avoidance schemes.	

---

[14]Operational Risk is sensitive to both falling interest rates (e.g. the SME interest rate derivative litigation in the UK following the Global Financial Crisis), and also rising interest rates (e.g. the litigation following the collapse of Orange County in 1994). What seems important is the rapidity and significance of changes in markets, either up or down.

TABLE 11.2 *(Continued)*

P&L & balance sheet		Level 2 – examples	Sensitivity to Bank of England economic factors
	Additional expenses or foregone expenditure with a direct link to the Operational Risk event.	■ Legal liabilities. ORX include legal expenses that relate to Operational Risk events both for when firms act as the plaintiff as well as the defendant.	
		■ Other third-party expenses, e.g. accountants, office cleaners (COVID-19)	
		■ Additional staff costs, e.g.: – Incentives and overtime payments for employees; and – Third-party contractor costs.	
		■ Additional costs, e.g. temporary offices and recovery sites.	
	Costs of repair or replacement, incurred to restore the position that was prevailing before the Operational Risk event.	■ Physical assets: – Buildings; – IT equipment; and – Fixtures & fittings, but avoid double counting with write-downs.	
		■ Costs of improving controls*	
Write-off of assets (balance sheet)	Write-downs of assets due to an Operational Risk event: ■ Theft: asset stolen; ■ Fraud: asset never existed; ■ Extortion; ■ Accidental asset transfers ■ Damage; and ■ Loss of recourse.	■ Market Risk losses or gains (mark-to-market) for the Bank, arising from an Operational Risk event, e.g. rogue trading or fat-fingered typing.	■ Increased volatility. ■ Market moves.
		■ Financial and physical assets: – Cash and bearer bonds; – Securities; – Physical commodities; – Buildings; – IT equipment; and – Fixtures & fittings.	
		■ Loans: Credit Risk losses, exacerbated by operational failures, e.g. failure to perfect security; put in place netting agreements or to call margin.*	■ Rising defaults – both PDs and LGDs.

* These impacts are not included in gross loss (Basel Committee, 2017).

(Continued)

TABLE 11.2   (*Continued*)

P&L & balance sheet		Level 2 – examples	Sensitivity to Bank of England economic factors
Reputational impacts (Stakeholders listed on Figure 2.1)	Authorities	▪ Higher fines, if a repeat offender (Table 9.1). ▪ Additional capital requirements, lowering return on equity. ▪ Licence restrictions on ability to conduct new activities. ▪ *Operational Resilience:* Threat to the financial system, requiring risk mitigation plans.	
	Investors: Bondholders	▪ Higher funding costs if a firm's credit rating is downgraded (Figure 13.11).	
	Investors: Shareholders	▪ Higher costs of capital if existing investors sell shares and the price falls (Figure 13.9).	
	Infrastructure and counterparties	▪ *Operational Resilience:* Disorderly operation of markets. ▪ *Operational Resilience:* Threaten a firm's safety and soundness, e.g. loss of revenues and liquidity.	
	Suppliers and outsourcers	▪ Adverse reaction.	
	Customers	▪ *Operational Resilience:* Intolerable levels of harm to a firm's clients. ▪ Loss of future customer and client revenues (Figure 13.10) – EBA stress testing only (EBA, July 2018).	▪ Rising defaults – third-party suppliers.
	Employees: current & future	▪ Impact on staff morale and inability to retain existing employees. ▪ Inability to recruit new employees.	
	Criminals	▪ Higher levels of fraud if a firm has a poor reputation for fraud prevention.	

3. Assess how behavioural changes and the economic factors lead to losses occurring

Firms need to then consider how the identified behavioural changes and sensitivities to various economic factors, result in existing losses being exacerbated; historical failures being uncovered; and inappropriate responses of banks and stakeholders that can lead to new loss events. Table 11.3 provides a mapping of examples to the earlier event taxonomy (Table 5.2). This underpins the 3.2× increase in the occurrence of large losses (≥$0.1 billion) pre and post the Global Financial Crisis (Formula 11.1).

Existing losses are exacerbated (1st and 3rd Laws) Firms need to assess how behavioural changes already described will alter the occurrence of their existing losses, e.g. changes for demand for products by customers; changes in the behaviour of criminals (Figure 11.3); and changes in investor demand/market activity. Banks also need to consider how changes in economic metrics will impact the scale of loss events, e.g. as described previously increased market volatility will both exacerbate the scale of any fat-fingered typing losses (Figure 11.7), both in terms of day-to-day losses and tail events.[15]

Uncovering historical failures (2nd and 4th Laws) Banks should stress test current and historical sales of products to customers, counterparties or investors reflecting again the 9th Law of Risk Transference, Transformation and Conservation and the Real Option Model (Figure 3.4). The scale of losses/lost opportunity is important, as if these are low then there will be no litigation.[16] In assessing the scale of the impacts of economic shocks on products sold to customers, banks need to consider the duration of the potential exposure, e.g. as noted earlier the US Securities Act (1933) provides investors a "right of recovery" within three years of the issuance of the securities (Table 11.4). Where banks identify customers, counterparties or investors that may suffer significant losses or lost opportunities, then banks should assess, through sampling, the completeness and appropriateness of their documentation, and hence their ability to rebut any claims of mis-sale. The quality of a bank's documentation may vary for different cohorts of sales, again as noted by the Bank of England. Similarly, for loan documentation and security, banks need to review various cohorts of loans to establish the completeness of, for example, their netting agreements and charges over assets, as an input into their LGD estimates. Asset sales to reduce RWAs may also act as a catalyst for the discovery of past documentation issues.

---

[15] Anecdotally, the value of fat-finger typing losses rose during the period of increased volatility at the start of the COVID-19 pandemic.

[16] Consequently, these Operational Risks may display a non-linear risk profile, i.e. there may be a tipping point for the scale of investor/customer losses above which litigation may result. This may hinder the calculation of correlations to economic factors.

TABLE 11.3   Examples of the mapping of the nature of events (Table 5.2) to economic sensitivities

	Nature of events (Table 5.2)	Existing losses are exacerbated, (1st and 3rd Laws)	Historical failures are uncovered, (2nd and 4th Laws)	New losses arising from responses, (1st and 3rd Laws)
Internal events	**People:**			
	▪ Mistakes and omissions	Second-order effect driven by changes in customer and/or investor demand	Discovery of past documentation failures, e.g. missing documents	
	▪ Misconduct by individuals		Discovery of past misconduct	Manipulation of Gilt prices during a Bank of England QE auction
	▪ Systemic misconduct		Discovery of historical mis-representation of prior MBS issuances	Inappropriate foreclosure in the US
	▪ Malicious acts		Discovery of rogue traders revealed by market turbulence	Traders who disguise losses, e.g. CS ABS traders at start of GFC
	Systems:			
	▪ Disruption of software			
	▪ Application malfunctions			
	▪ Hardware failures			
	▪ Disruption of data & storage			
	▪ Disruption of own infrastructure			
	Process:			
	▪ Design/systematic failure			

TABLE 11.3 *(Continued)*

Nature of events (Table 5.2)	Existing losses are exacerbated, (1st and 3rd Laws)	Historical failures are uncovered, (2nd and 4th Laws)	New losses arising from responses, (1st and 3rd Laws)
External events ▪ Third-party	Defaults by key suppliers and outsource service providers		
▪ Malicious acts	Criminals increase activity to exploit greater uncertainty	Discovery of historical second-party frauds	New customer frauds driven by financial "need"
▪ Acts of God			

| Key: | Sensitivity driven by economic factors | | Sensitivity driven by behaviour[17] | |

Responses to economic shocks (1st and 3rd Laws) Banks need to consider how their actions, including planned management actions,[18] and those of their staff may lead to new Operational Risk losses, e.g. increased employment tribunal claims from staff who have been made redundant or customers in financial difficulties who claim to have been treated unfairly.

The CPBP losses that are sensitive to economic cycles, discussed in Chapter 10, primarily relate to the uncovering of historical failures and the responses to economic shocks.

4. Estimate occurrence and impacts

Based upon the identified sensitivities to behavioural changes and economic factors, banks should:

- Estimate stressed values of expected losses, primarily for the higher volume risks (Figure 1.3), i.e. External Fraud and EDPM;

---

[17] Stakeholders may either increase or decrease their existing activities and/or undertake new activities.

[18] The Basel Committee includes examples of typical management actions in response to a stress scenario: increases in capital; RWA reduction, e.g. asset sales and tighter lending criteria; and reductions in expenses, e.g. staff layoffs (Basel Committee, 2017b).

- Assess how stressed economic factors may impact their existing pipelines of customer compensation claims, i.e. where the level of compensation is linked to the transfer of Market or Credit Risk by banks, to their customers, or counterparties, or investors. As noted earlier, this sensitivity is specifically highlighted by the Bank of England within their guidance; and finally
- Stress their scenarios for the behavioural changes and sensitivities in economic factors. Examples of how economic factors[19] link to occurrence, detection and velocity, are also set out in Table 11.4.

In order to illustrate this process, two of the examples of scenario analysis, set out earlier in Chapter 9, have been repeated below and stressed for economic shocks. Figure 11.6 relates to the post-underwriting litigation scenario. It is a revision of the Fault Tree Analysis set out in Figure 9.3, but uses corporate default rates from 2008, the height of the Global Financial Crisis, instead of the more benign 2005.

The scale of the change from stressing the Fault Tree Analysis in this way depends on the extent to which the original scenario reflected some degree of economic shock, e.g. if the original scenario had used a 10-year average default rate, rather than an individual year, then the impact would be more limited. The impacts can also be stressed, for example, for this scenario by considering annual defaulted corporate bond recoveries pre and during the Global Financial Crisis. For 2005 the value of recoveries relating to defaults for senior unsecured bonds is 54.9% vs 33.5% for 2008, based on traded prices (Moody's, 2018). This data can then be used to stress estimates of any related compensation settlements.

Similarly, regarding the fat-fingered typing scenario, the estimation techniques described in Chapter 9 can be also stressed for both market/price volatility and also behavioural changes, e.g. the volume of trade activity. Comparing price and volume data for the FTSE 100 for H1 2019 and H1 2020 reveals a 160% increase in price volatility (STD of daily movements in the FTSE 100 index) and an approximate 50% increase in trade volume. Figure 11.7 illustrates how the formula used for estimating the likelihood and severity in a fat-fingered typing error in Chapter 9 can be stressed for these factors.

Behavioural changes Estimating the future occurrence of loss events, due to changes in behaviour of a firm's stakeholders, (Figure 2.1) is clearly inherently challenging. There are, however, several potential guides for firms. As noted earlier, analysis of the motivation of convicted fraudsters in the UK reveals the key motivating factors for malicious acts are "greed" and "need" (BDO, 2018). Economic shocks typically result in new and additional financial pressures on previously honest individuals, as well as providing new opportunities for professional criminals. For example, in

---

[19]The range of factors are noticeably broader than the key variables used by the Federal Reserve (Table 11.1).

TABLE 11.4 Examples of sensitivities of scenarios to economic factors and duration of exposure and lags in settlements

	Economic factors	Relevant scenarios	Factors stressed (1st, 2nd and 3rd Laws)	Duration of exposure (4th Law)	Lags in settlements[20] (5th Law)
Exacerbate existing losses	■ Increased market volatility (VIX).	■ Fat-fingered typing (Figures 9.2 and 11.7). ■ Intra-day unauthorised trading (Figure 9.1).	■ *Occurrence:* Changes in customer/investor behaviours leads to increased trade volumes. ■ *Velocity:* One day market movements.	N/A	< 1 year
Responses of banks & stakeholders	■ Rising unemployment.	■ Employee litigation – in response to redundancies (Figure 11.5).	■ *Occurrence:* The number of claims against a firm increases.	3 months[21] after redundancy	6 months to 1 year
Responses of banks & stakeholders	■ Increased mortgage delinquency and defaults. ■ Decline in property indices.	■ Treating customers fairly in financial difficulties.	■ *Occurrence:* Increased customer defaults leading to increased claims. ■ *Velocity:* Loss given default.	< 5 years	2 to 10 years[22]
Historical failures uncovered	■ Rising corporate defaults/ credit spreads.	■ Post-underwriting litigation (Formula 9.1 and Figures 9.3 and 11.6). ■ Mis-sale of Collateralised Loan Obligations (CLOs).	■ *Detection:* Increased customer defaults leading to increased claims of mis-sale. ■ *Velocity:* Compensation driven by the scale of Loss Given Default.	3 years	>3 year

(Continued)

---

[20]This lag is between occurrence and settlement.

[21]The deadline for lodging an unfair dismissal claim is defined in clause 111(2a) of the Employment Rights Act, 1996.

[22]In June 2020 LBG was fined $64 million for failures in its handling of mortgage arrears between 2011 and 2015. In addition LBG will pay an additional £300 million in redress.

TABLE 11.4   (*Continued*)

Economic factors	Relevant scenarios	Factors stressed (1st, 2nd and 3rd Laws)	Duration of exposure (4th Law)	Lags in settlements[20] (5th Law)
▪ Rising bond yields. ▪ Falling asset values.	▪ Mis-sale of higher risk yielding invest-ments.[23] ▪ Mis-sale of equity linked products (MBS case study in Chapter 2).	*Detection & Velocity:* Revalue investments reflecting: ▪ Rising yields; ▪ Rising delinquency; ▪ Decline in property indices; and ▪ Falling equity values.	>3 years[24]	4 to 6 years
▪ Directional moves in interest rates.	▪ Mis-sale of interest rate derivatives (Figure 11.4).	▪ *Detection:* Lost opportunity. ▪ *Velocity:* Scale of market moves.	>10 years[25]	>3 years

evidence to the Public Accounts Committee the UK Government disclosed that it had assumed an "error or fraud rate" of between 5% and 10% on its emergency COVID-19 loans. In written evidence to the same committee, the administrators of the Bounce Back Loan scheme disclosed that 20 lenders had blocked a total of 26,933 fraudulent applications between May and October 2020, with a value of £1.1 billion (£40 billion of loans had been advanced).

In addition, firms can also review behavioural changes that have been observed in response to previous economic shocks, for example changes in customer demand for products, such as mortgages for house purchases. Figure 11.8 illustrates that these changes can be quite dynamic, i.e. in 2007 new mortgages financing house purchases declined in anticipation of the UK going into recession, whilst the sudden nature of

---

[23]In a low interest rate environment higher yields could be achieved through funds selling interest rate options; or introducing greater leverage or investing in higher risk/yield securities (Figure 13.6). These first two strategies are reminiscent of some of the Operational Risk losses that arose in 1994.

[24]In 2011 the FHFA launched litigation against the arrangers of MBS issued between 2005 and 2007.

[25]In June 2012 the FSA/FCA agreed with four major banks (RBS, Barclays, LBG and HSBC) that they would review their derivative sales since December 2001. This was 3 ½ years after UK interest rates fell to 0.5%.

FIGURE 11.6 Stressing Fault Tree Analysis to estimate the likelihood of a post-underwriting litigation scenario for an economic shock (Revision of Figure 9.3)

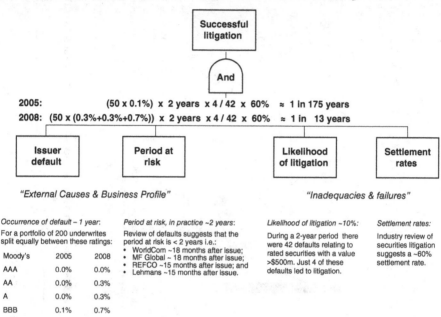

2005: (50 x 0.1%) x 2 years x 4 / 42 x 60% ≈ 1 in 175 years
2008: (50 x (0.3%+0.3%+0.7%)) x 2 years x 4 / 42 x 60% ≈ 1 in 13 years

"External Causes & Business Profile"   *"Inadequacies & failures"*

Occurrence of default – 1 year:
For a portfolio of 200 underwrites split equally between these ratings:

Moody's	2005	2008
AAA	0.0%	0.0%
AA	0.0%	0.3%
A	0.0%	0.3%
BBB	0.1%	0.7%

Period at risk, in practice ~2 years:
Review of defaults suggests that the period at risk is < 2 years i.e.:
- WorldCom ~18 months after issue;
- MF Global ~ 18 months after issue;
- REFCO ~15 months after issue; and
- Lehmans ~15 months after issue.

Likelihood of litigation ~10%:
During a 2-year period there were 42 defaults relating to rated securities with a value >$500m. Just 4 of these defaults led to litigation.

Settlement rates:
Industry review of securities litigation suggests a ~60% settlement rate.

FIGURE 11.7 Estimating the impacts and likelihoods for fat-fingered typing using Market Risk techniques (Revision of Figure 9.2)

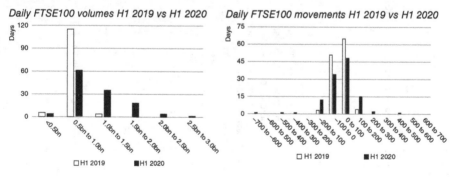

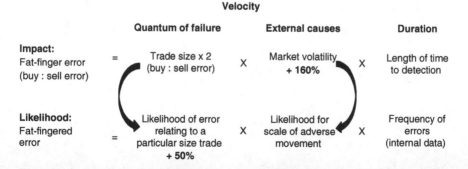

FIGURE 11.8 Comparison of UK GDP during the Global Financial Crisis (2007 to 2009) and COVID-19 (2019 and 2020) and changes in quarterly volume of new mortgages for UK house purchases

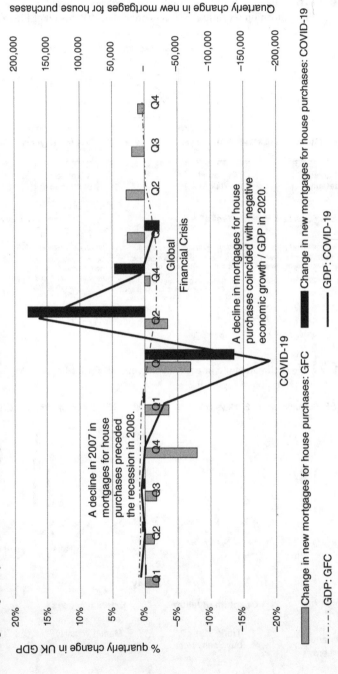

A decline in 2007 in mortgages for house purchases preceded the recession in 2008.

Global Financial Crisis

A decline in mortgages for house purchases coincided with negative economic growth / GDP in 2020.

COVID-19

Change in new mortgages for house purchases: GFC

GDP: GFC

Change in new mortgages for house purchases: COVID-19

GDP: COVID-19

Quarterly change in new mortgages for house purchases

% quarterly change in UK GDP

the 2020 COVID-19 pandemic recession meant that the decline in demand for mortgages to finance new house purchases coincided with negative GDP. As a consequence, identifying and estimating changes in the behaviours of stakeholders should involve workshops similar to other forms of Operational Risk scenario analysis.

The outputs of these different activities, i.e. stressing expected losses; existing pipelines of customer compensation claims; and scenarios; can then be compared to the profile of losses suffered by firms following the Global Financial Crisis (Figure 11.1). This may be misleading, however, because of the 8th Law: Risk Homeostasis, i.e. the losses arising from the economic shock caused by the COVID-19 pandemic may be less significant due to the enhancement of firms' controls following previous misconduct scandals.

5. Assess lags in the settlement of losses (4th and 5th Laws)

Firms then need to consider both the timescales over which different losses occur and also crystallise. Analysis of ORX loss data of the average lags between detection and settlement for losses >€20k (Figure 11.9) shows variations between events types (BIS, 2020). Additionally, as noted previously, analysis of losses after the Global Financial Crisis reveals patterns of initial decline and subsequent increases and peaks, which vary between event types (Cope and Carrivick, 2013). This reflects the overlay of a variety of economic or behavioural effects previously described.

The lags between occurrence and detection (4th Law); and detection and settlement (5th Law) are on average significantly longer for larger CPBP loss events (≥$0.1

FIGURE 11.9　Average lags (in years) between occurrence and detection (4th Law); and between detection and settlement (5th Law)

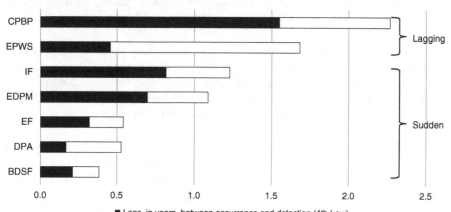

■ Lags, in years, between occurrence and detection (4th Law)
□ Lags, in years, between detection and settlement (5th Law)

billion) as suffered by 31 current and former G-SIBs for the period 2008 to 2017,[26] i.e. respectively 5.2 years and 3.8 years (see Table 11.4 for examples). The 5th Law states that these extended lags between detection and settlement are often linked to incidents involving systemic misconduct; regulatory involvement; litigation; sensitivity to economic cycles; and the distribution of compensation to customers.

6. Capital requirements and correlation

Banks can update their Operational Risk capital models to reflect their stressed scenarios and to incorporate increases in expected losses. In the EBA stress tests, the impacts of stressing Operational Risk capital models tend to be quite limited (as described earlier) due to Pillar 1, Minimum Capital Requirements, already reflecting some degree of procyclical losses. Obviously this would not be the case if banks adopted the hourglass approach described in Chapter 10 (Figure 10.4 is repeated as Figure 11.10), which envisages roughly comparable amounts of Pillar 1 and 2B capital, i.e.:

> *Sudden losses and that are insensitive to economic cycles:* These could primarily be reflected in Pillar 1 capital requirements, using either the new Standardised Approach or AMA-style models. Pillar 2A would also capture emerging risks (Chapter 15), risk concentrations and changes in business models.

> *Lagging losses that are insensitive to economic cycles:* These could simply be accrued as they crystallise over many years and are generally uncorrelated with Market and Credit Risks. The 20% of these large losses that crystallise within 12 months would be reflected within the Pillar 1 capital requirements.

> *Lagging losses that are sensitive to economic cycles:* These primarily drive Pillar 2B. These risks need to be modelled utilising the modified scenario analysis techniques, described in this chapter, for impacts that are sensitive to economic cycles, and AMA-style models, set out in Chapter 10.

In addition to producing a stressed capital requirement, reflecting an economic shock, Operational Risk capital models can also be run at lower confidence intervals, e.g. 50%. The results can then be compared to management's bottom-up estimates of the stressed values of expected losses, as part of validation. This primarily relates to the higher volume risks, i.e. External Fraud and EDPM (Figure 1.3).

Correlations The impacts on correlations should also be considered. Analysis of ORX data (losses >€20k) in the aftermath of the Global Financial Crisis showed increases in the occurrence of losses relating to External Fraud, EDPM and CPBP

---

[26]This data is sourced from the IBM FIRST Risk Case Studies.

FIGURE 11.10 Operational Risk capital requirements should look like an hourglass (Repeat of Figure 10.4)

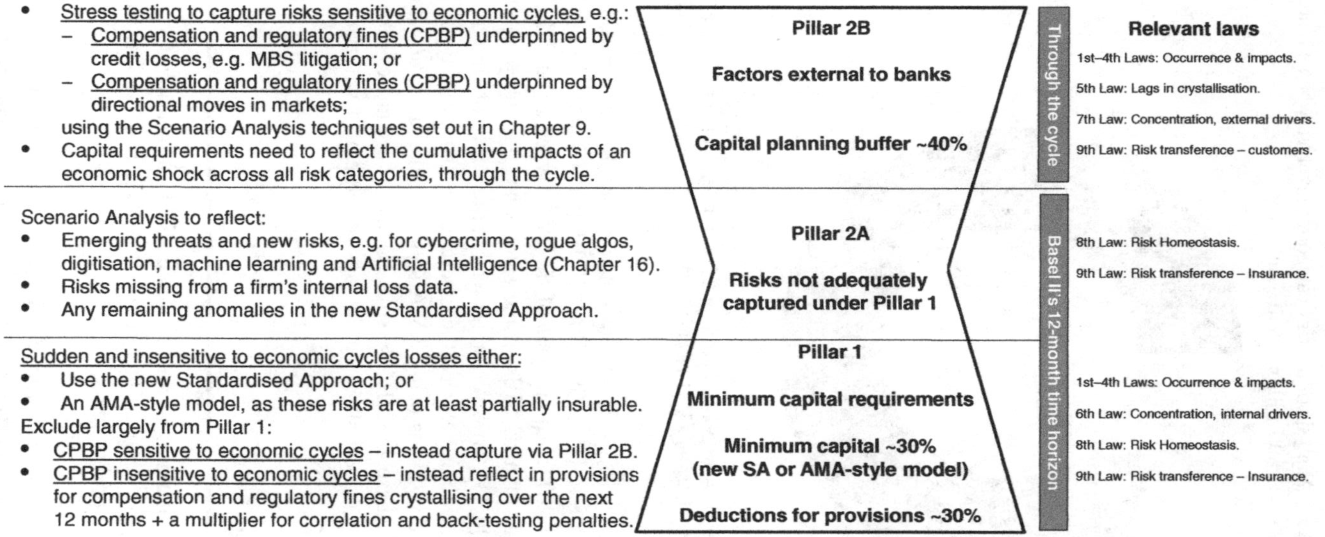

Through the cycle

Basel II's 12-month time horizon

Relevant laws

1st–4th Laws: Occurrence & impacts.
5th Law: Lags in crystallisation.
7th Law: Concentration, external drivers.
9th Law: Risk transference – customers.

8th Law: Risk Homeostasis.
9th Law: Risk transference – Insurance.

1st–4th Laws: Occurrence & impacts.
6th Law: Concentration, internal drivers.
8th Law: Risk Homeostasis.
9th Law: Risk transference – Insurance.

Pillar 2B

Factors external to banks

Capital planning buffer ~40%

Pillar 2A

Risks not adequately captured under Pillar 1

Pillar 1

Minimum capital requirements

**Minimum capital ~30%
(new SA or AMA-style model)**

Deductions for provisions ~30%

- Stress testing to capture risks sensitive to economic cycles, e.g.:
  - Compensation and regulatory fines (CPBP) underpinned by credit losses, e.g. MBS litigation; or
  - Compensation and regulatory fines (CPBP) underpinned by directional moves in markets;
  using the Scenario Analysis techniques set out in Chapter 9.
- Capital requirements need to reflect the cumulative impacts of an economic shock across all risk categories, through the cycle.

Scenario Analysis to reflect:
- Emerging threats and new risks, e.g. for cybercrime, rogue algos, digitisation, machine learning and Artificial Intelligence (Chapter 16).
- Risks missing from a firm's internal loss data.
- Any remaining anomalies in the new Standardised Approach.

Sudden and insensitive to economic cycles losses either:
- Use the new Standardised Approach; or
- An AMA-style model, as these risks are at least partially insurable.
Exclude largely from Pillar 1:
- CPBP sensitive to economic cycles – instead capture via Pillar 2B.
- CPBP insensitive to economic cycles – instead reflect in provisions for compensation and regulatory fines crystallising over the next 12 months + a multiplier for correlation and back-testing penalties.

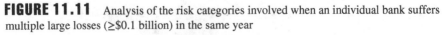

FIGURE 11.11 Analysis of the risk categories involved when an individual bank suffers multiple large losses (≥$0.1 billion) in the same year

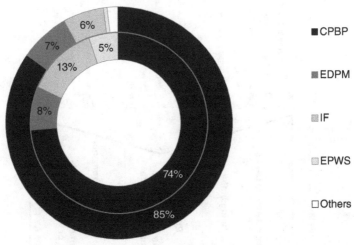

Key:
- Inner ring: Losses ≥$0.1 billion for 31 current and former G-SIBs 1996 to 2006; and
- Outer ring: Losses ≥$0.1 billion for 31 current and former G-SIBs 2007 to 2017.

(Cope and Carrivick, 2013), but, as noted earlier, External Fraud and EDPM peaked between H1 2008 to H1 2009, whilst CPBP peaked in the late crisis period between H2 2009 to H2 2011. An analysis of the event types of large losses (≥$0.1 billion) suffered by individual G-SIBs in the same year, pre and post the Global Financial Crisis (Figure 11.11), however, suggests that there are only limited changes in the correlation of frequencies between the Operational Risk event types. The diversification benefit obtained by firms using AMA-style models, however, should diminish when the inputs into these models are stressed, as the frequency of occurrence of more severe events increases, although the lags in settlement will partially act to diminish this effect.

CONCLUSIONS

Forecasting the impacts of an economic shock on a firm's Operational Risk losses and capital requirements is inherently subjective. The Ten Laws of Operational Risk provide some helpful insights:

- *Occurrence and Detection (1st & 2nd Laws):* The 7th Law states that the impacts of business cycles arise from a combination of changes in economic factors and stakeholder behaviours (Table 11.3). A firm's business profile (summarised in Figure 2.1) defines the scope of its stakeholders, whose behaviours may change, e.g. stakeholders may either increase or decrease their existing activities and/or undertake new activities. Operational Risk losses may rise as some existing losses are exacerbated; historical failures are uncovered; and the responses of banks, bankers, investors, customers and criminals alike to a crisis may lead to new losses (Figure 11.5). Analysis of losses after the Global Financial Crisis reveals complex changes in the profile of Operational Risk losses, with a pattern of initial decline and subsequent increases and peaks (Cope and Carrivick, 2013). These patterns vary between event types, and reflect the overlay of a variety of different economic and behavioural effects.

- *Severity (3rd and 4th Laws):* A number of the potential impacts resulting from Operational Risk events are sensitive to business cycles, as illustrated in Table 11.2. Additionally, sharp movements in some economic measures can both act as a trigger for the uncovering of historical failures, as well as exacerbating the scale of any resulting losses, e.g. the mis-sale of interest rate swaps to UK SMEs (Figure 11.4). The complexity of the differing sensitivities of impacts of Operational Risk events to economic factors, combined with the long and variable lags between detection and settlement (Table 11.4), makes identifying correlations between the severity of losses and economic factors inherently challenging.[27] The failure to identify mathematically significant correlations, however, does not mean that the severity of some losses are not sensitive to economic factors.

- *Correlations (7th Law):* Operational Risk is generally procyclical, and hence is correlated with Market and Credit Risk losses (Figure 3.5). Analysing the nature of multiple large ($\geq$\$0.1 billion) loss events suffered by the same firms in the same year, however, indicates that the relative proportions of the number of loss events for different Operational Risk event types remain fairly stable (Figure 11.11).

- *Lags in settlement (5th Law):* The lags between detection and settlement vary between different Operational Risk event types (Figure 11.9 and Table 11.4). Analysis of large losses ($\geq$\$0.1 billion) suggests that these lags are significantly longer than average for larger CPBP losses (Figure 2.5).

- *Risk Homeostasis (8th Law):* A firm's historical loss experiences may seem to be a good starting point for estimating its stressed losses, and in Chapter 3 it was noted that the banks in the top tercile of G-SIBs, based on large loss experience ($\geq$\$0.1 billion), were unchanged pre and post the Global Financial Crisis. The enhancement of Conduct Risk related controls over the last decade, in response

---

[27]The relative significance of some of these different external causes is illustrated in Table 6.2.

to these earlier losses, may mean, however, that Operational Risk losses arising from the COVID-19 pandemic may be lower than those occurring after the Global Financial Crisis. This is despite the COVID-19 recession being potentially more severe.

Ultimately, a better understanding of the nature and sensitivities of Operational Risk to both behavioural changes and economic factors, combined with the techniques described in this chapter (and also Chapters 9 and 10) should make stress testing estimates both more systemic and informative.

CHAPTER 12

Reverse Stress Testing and the Transfer of Risks via Insurance

This chapter utilises the business profile of firms to identify key vulnerabilities that could make a firm's business model unviable. The techniques described in Chapter 9 can then be used to assess the likelihood of predefined outcomes, through reverse stress testing. This chapter also considers the criteria as to whether an Operational Risk event can be transferred via insurance policies (or catastrophe bonds)[1] to third parties, via the 9th Law: Transference, Transformation and Conservation. The chapter utilises the event and impact taxonomies set out in Tables 5.2 and 5.4 to illustrate the coverage of different insurance policies, and concludes with the regulatory criteria for obtaining a reduction in the Operational Risk capital requirements of banks.

REVERSE STRESS TESTING

Reverse stress testing is the process of assessing predefined adverse outcomes for a firm, e.g. a breach of regulatory capital or liquidity ratios; and identifying the possible scenarios that could lead to such adverse outcomes. Reverse stress testing can help firms to understand the underlying risks and vulnerabilities in their businesses and products that pose a threat to their viability and also helps them to identify situations that could threaten resilience. (Basel Committee, 2017b). Whilst reverse stress tests are conducted across all risk types, the failure of firms due to Operational Risks are relatively rare.

---

[1]Catastrophe bonds are high-yielding securities, where the principal is forgiven by the holders if a trigger event occurs, e.g. an earthquake or hurricane. They are typically issued by insurers, reinsurers, banks and governments. Catastrophe bonds cover insurable events that are both remote and potentially quite catastrophic, and hence the volume issued is relatively low.

REGULATORY GUIDANCE

The PRA requires firms, as part of their business planning and risk management obligations, to conduct reverse stress testing, i.e. scenarios that test their business plans to failure. This involves firms:

1. Identifying a range of adverse scenarios which would cause a business plan to become unviable;
2. Assessing the likelihood that such events could occur; and
3. Adopting effective arrangements, processes, systems or other measures (e.g. cyber insurance) to prevent or mitigate unacceptably high risks of business failure, relative to appetite (PRA, 2020).

The EBA's guidance additionally includes a requirement for firms to identify feedback and non-linear effects, taking into account the dynamics of risk, i.e. the combinations and interactions between and across risk types. When developing the narrative for their scenarios, firms should consider external events, such as economic shocks; an industry crash; political events; litigation cases; and natural disasters. They should also consider risk factors such as Operational Risk, concentrations and correlations, Reputational Risk and loss of confidence, and combinations of these events and factors (EBA, July 2018). This is consistent with the later observations in Chapter 15 of domino effects and feedback loops associated with emerging risks (Figure 15.1).

IDENTIFYING REVERSE STRESS TESTING SCENARIOS

The identification of reverse stress scenarios should begin with the consideration of business profile.

Based upon the business profile of firms and an analysis of both Operational Risk events that have led (or nearly led) to either the closure of a firm or its rescue and also emerging risks (Figure 15.1), then a number of potential points of failure can be identified (Figure 12.1):

1. *Operational Resilience:* Business Continuity Plans contemplate the denial to firms of key resources, typically: staff (people); technology (systems); buildings (infrastructure); and third- (and fourth-) parties, e.g. outsourcers and utility providers; all leading to the disruption of processes.
2. *Regulatory licences:* In order to operate firms must have regulatory licences, which require both adequate systems and controls and financial resources, i.e. both capital and liquidity.
3. *Business plans:* Firms that consistently make losses will eventually fail, without ongoing support from their key stakeholders, e.g. shareholders, bondholders, customers and market counterparties.

FIGURE 12.1 Potential points of business plan failure (Revision of Figure 2.1)

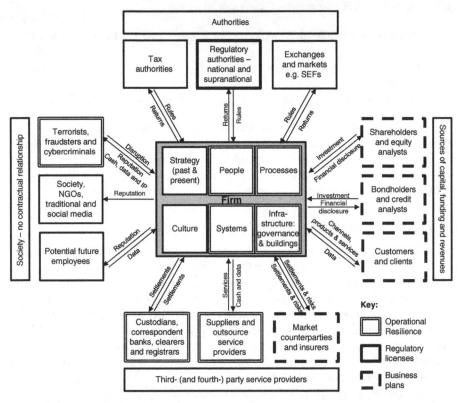

1. Operational Resilience

One of the criteria[2] for defining important business services is if their disruption poses a risk to a firm's safety and soundness (PRA, 2021). There are relatively few instances of firms failing due to losses of staff and infrastructure. The closest examples include the tragic loss by Cantor Fitzgerald of 658 staff members on 9/11 (69% of the firm's New York office staff).[3] There are also instances of bitcoin exchanges filing for bankruptcy following cyber thefts, e.g. the South Korean bitcoin exchange Youbit

---

[2]The other criteria are disruption that would cause intolerable levels of harm to any one or more of the firm's clients; or threaten the UK's financial system; or the orderly operation of markets.
[3]*The Evening Standard*, (9th September 2011) "Cantor Fitzgerald...the City firm that rose from the 9/11 ashes".

in December 2017. Additionally, there have been a number of instances of banks suffering extended IT disruption of a week or more e.g.:

- Danske Bank's wholesale banking systems were disrupted for 1 week in March 2005;
- RBS's retail banking systems were disrupted for 1 to 3 weeks in June/July 2012; and
- TSB's retail banking systems were disrupted for 3 to 4 weeks in April/May 2018.

Whilst none of these IT disruption events threatened the existence of these three banks, issues with Northern Rock's website in September 2007, may have exacerbated the existing concerns of its customers and led to longer queues outside of the Bank's very limited number of branches, i.e. just 56. This last example is an illustration of the EBA's observation as to how different risks may combine and interact.

2. Regulatory licences

There are more examples of firms failing due to insufficient financial resources, i.e. capital and/or liquidity, as a result of an Operational Risk event. For example, the rescue of Barings in 1995 by ING following catastrophic rogue trading losses;[4] Knight Capital undertook an emergency fund raising four days after its high velocity rogue algo losses in 2012; and the collapse of the commodities broker, REFCO, in 2005, following the discovery of significant historical client trading losses and bad debts that had been hidden by its CEO.[5] In some instances rescues may involve existing shareholders, for example, SocGen launched a €5.5 billion rights issue 2½ weeks after announcing a €4.9 billion rogue trader loss in January 2008.

In addition, there are a number of examples of regulators removing a firm's licence due to weaknesses in their systems and controls leading to systemic regulatory breaches. For example, in 1991 the Bank of Credit & Commerce International (BCCI)[6] was simultaneously closed down across seven countries following the discovery of its widespread involvement in money laundering and the existence of very significant hidden losses. Similarly, in 2013, Wegelin & Co, Switzerland's oldest private bank at the time, announced its closure, after the firm admitted charges of conspiracy in helping US citizens to evade taxes between 2002 and 2010.[7]

---

[4]Barings suffered £827 million of rogue trader losses, which far exceeded its capital base of just £412.5 million.

[5]REFCO's futures and options business was subsequently sold to Man Financial.

[6]BCCI was referred to as the "Bank of Crooks & Cocaine International" by the UK satirical magazine, Private Eye, *prior* to its closure, following its earlier conviction of money laundering in the US in 1990.

[7]*The Telegraph*, (4th January 2013) "Switzerland's oldest bank Wegelin to close after pleading guilty to aiding US tax evasion".

3. Business plans

Firms that consistently make losses will eventually fail without continued support from key stakeholders. Failures often involve loss of confidence by customers, investors and depositors alike. There are only a few examples of such failures involving Operational Risk events. In 1988, Drexel Burnham Lambert (Drexel) agreed a $650 million[8] settlement regarding six felony charges to which it submitted an Alford plea, i.e. it pleaded guilty, whilst still asserting its innocence. The combination of the subsequent crash of the junk bond market, the scale of the settlement,[9] and reports of an $86 million loss going into the Q4 1989 resulted in the firm's Commercial Paper rating being cut in late November.[10] The firm entered Chapter 11 bankruptcy protection on 13th February 1990, when it was reportedly unable to repay $100 million of short-term loans that fell due.[11]

Similarly, Enron[12] filed for Chapter 11 bankruptcy protection seven weeks after disclosing a $618 million loss and a $1.2 billion reduction in shareholder funds in October 2001, partly driven by the unwind of its Raptor partnerships. During this period a series of damaging disclosures regarding its off-balance sheet partnerships led to the credit rating for its senior unsecured debt falling from Baa1 to Ba2 (sub-investment grade), triggering collateral calls on a loan note. As Enron was the central counterparty for Enron Online, its customers deserted its online commodities trading platform, as its credit rating fell.

ASSESSING REVERSE STRESS TESTING SCENARIOS

When conducting reverse stress tests, firms should modify the techniques set out in Chapter 9, i.e. the impacts need to be set at a predefined level, which would make the firm's business model unviable. For example, for rogue trading, firms would determine the scale of an unauthorised position, its duration and market volatility (velocity) required to erode their capital bases (Figure 9.1). Firms can then assess the likelihood of this occurring, using either judgement or Fault Tree Analysis (Figure 9.3).

---

[8]$350 million of this settlement was to be paid by Drexel over a 3-year period into an escrow account to compensate its junk bond investors. Drexel paid $200 million in September 1989 but filed for Chapter 11 prior to paying the remaining $150 million.
[9]At the time, the $650 million settlement was the largest ever settlement imposed under the Securities Act (1933) and the Securities Exchange Act (1934).
[10]In December 1989, Groupe Bruxelles Lambert, a Belgian holding company which owned 35% of Drexel, reportedly turned down the investment bank's request for more capital.
[11]*The Economist*, (17th February 1990) "The death of Drexel".
[12]Whilst Enron was not a financial institution, in addition to owning gas pipelines, power stations and water companies through Enron Capital & Trading, it operated an online commodities trading platform, Enron Online.

Whilst any of the predefined outcomes described above can be assessed in this way, the European Central Bank's (ECB) recent survey of ICAAP practices observes that firms primarily used a breach of total Supervisory Review and Evaluation Process (SREP) capital requirements. This practice is actually quite a narrow interpretation of reverse stress testing. Maybe as a consequence, the ECB notes as good practices both constructing reverse stress tests with a predefined outcome of a breach of liquidity ratios and also developing stress scenarios in which key vulnerabilities combine to lead to non-viability of the business model (ECB, 2020). The importance of the interaction of key vulnerabilities is a feature of the summaries of the demise of both Drexel and Enron.

When conducting reverse stress tests firms can also apply historical catastrophic events to their own vulnerabilities. This is illustrated in Figure 12.2, which shows the capital structure of a US G-SIB, at the end of 2019, as a percentage of RWAs, and compares this to historical rogue trader losses, also represented as a percentage of the RWAs of the banks involved, at the time of these events.

Similar analysis can also be undertaken for other impacts, for example, the duration of an extended systems outage that disrupts the ability of a firm's treasury to borrow can be compared against the combination of the firm's Liquidity Asset Buffers (LAB) and cash ladders to determine how long the firm can survive. The impacts of Operational Risk events that lead to reputational damage and loss of client revenues can also be assessed. Figure 12.3 analyses the revenues and operating expenses of a US investment bank. It then applies the percentage reduction in revenues experienced by two firms for *specific* investment banking businesses, to illustrate the potential erosion of profitability. The examples used are Nomura, which suffered a 45% reduction in equity underwriting in Japan in 2012 following regulatory action on its abuse of customer

FIGURE 12.2   Comparison of capital with a reverse stress scenario and historical rogue trader events

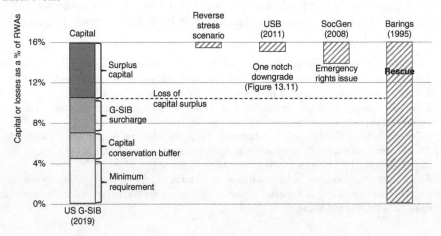

FIGURE 12.3   Comparison of revenues and operating expenses with a reverse stress scenario and historical reductions in the client revenues

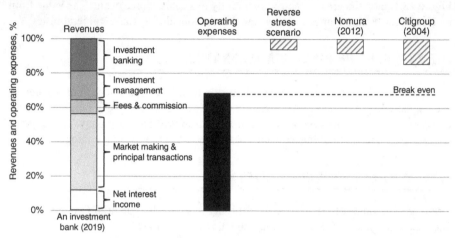

data, and Citigroup, which suffered a 78% reduction in European government bond underwriting following its "Dr Evil" trading strategy in 2004 (Chapter 13).

The frequency of occurrence of an historical event that could make a firm's business model unviable can be calculated using a modified version of Formula 9.7 from Chapter 9 (Formula 12.1):

Formula 12.1 (modified)   Calculation of industry frequency of events that threaten viability utilising public loss data

$$\frac{\text{Number of public domain peer losses that threaten viability}}{\text{Number of peer firms} \times \text{years of data}} = \begin{array}{c} \text{Historical frequency of} \\ \text{losses} \\ \text{that threaten viability} \\ \text{suffered by peers} \end{array}$$

As per scenario analysis, the outputs of reverse stress testing should be reviewed by a "Wise-man" Panel, Risk Committees and ultimately the Board, to help mitigate the influences of the various biases.

CONCLUSIONS

In practice, the vulnerability of firms to these types of catastrophic events is determined by the diversity of their business models, i.e. customer base; product lines; offices and geographical footprints;[13] sources of liquidity; reliance on third (and fourth)

---

[13]Cantor Fitzgerald was able to continue to operate after 9/11, in part, due to the rerouting of its electronic trading operation from its New York data centre into its London office.

parties, etc., as well as their potential misfortune for Operational Risk to combine with other risk types. The more concentrated a firm is in any of the factors described in Figure 12.1, then the greater their vulnerability to a catastrophic event. The value from reverse stress testing comes from systematically considering these vulnerabilities.

THE TRANSFER OF RISKS VIA INSURANCE

Insurance policies can transfer a portion of the financial consequences of a range of events, including mistakes and omissions; malicious acts; third-party failures and natural disasters, from a firm exposed to these risks to an insurance company. These events are clearly a subset of the inadequacies or failures that comprise Operational Risk.

DETERMINANTS OF INSURABILITY

There are a number of criteria for determining whether the potential financial consequences of these events are insurable, reflecting the Ten Laws:

Occurrence and Detection (1st & 2nd Laws)

1. *Defined event:* An insurable event must typically take place at a known time and place,[14] allowing it to be attributed to a specific insurance policy. Consequently, events that occur over an extended period are typically excluded, or require a specialist policy.
2. *Nature of event:* An event which triggers an insurance claim has to be outside of the control of the beneficiary of the insurance policy. Hence a malicious act committed by an employee may be insurable but typically not if it is committed by a director of a company. Insurance policies will detail the specific events that are either insured or excluded.
3. *Law of large numbers:* Typically insurance relates to risks to which a large number of firms are exposed, although the occurrence is rare. This allows insurers to benefit from the law of large numbers, enabling them to predict effectively the frequency of occurrence of large losses over time.

Severity (3rd and 4th Laws)

4. *Nature of impacts:* Insurance policies specify the financial consequences/losses of an insurable event that are either insured or excluded, e.g. typically insurance cannot compensate firms for regulatory fines and penalties. The FCA has expressly forbidden this for any fines that it imposes.

---

[14]Famously there was litigation after the 9/11 attacks on the World Trade Centre, as to whether the attack constituted either one or two insurable events.

5. *The scale of impacts* arising from an event must be economically material to the beneficiaries of the insurance policy, i.e. insurance primarily relates to the risks which generate the high value : low volume Operational Risk losses on the right-hand side of Figure 1.1.

Concentration due to external drivers (7th Law)

6. *Uncorrelated:* Insurable risks are ideally uncorrelated. Insuring correlated events, (for example, losses arising from earthquakes, hurricanes, pandemics and cyber-crime due to systemic industry weaknesses) requires combinations of additional diversification of an insurer's underwriting; transference to re-insurers; and significantly higher premiums, due to the risk to the insurer of multiple simultaneous claims.

Risk Transference, Transformation and Conservation (9th Law)

7. *Affordable premium:* Insurance premiums need to cover the expected cost of losses (the number of claims × the average value of claims), the insurer's administration costs and their cost of capital, i.e. both providing returns to its shareholders and also allowing for the accretion of capital (see the rearranged version of Formula 12.2). If the likelihood of an insured event is high for an individual firm (rather than an industry as a whole), then the annual insurance premium would simply approximate to or exceed the actual losses that the firm suffered each year, plus the insurers' costs. These losses can effectively be excluded by insurance policies setting higher thresholds for the transfer of risks to the insurer. These thresholds are variously known as retention or the deductible or the excess.

As a consequence, it is uneconomic to insure the risks which generate the low value : high volume Operational Risk losses[15] on the left-hand side of Figure 1.1.[16]

Formula 12.2   Rearrangement of Formula 9.8.

$$\begin{array}{c} \text{Annual insurance premium} \\ + \text{ investment returns} \end{array} > \begin{array}{l} \text{(Number of claims pa} \times \text{average value of} \\ \text{claims)} + \\ \text{annual admin costs} + \text{cost of capital} \end{array}$$

---

[15] A paper by a Federal Reserve Economist highlights that, although loss making, an insurance policy that mitigates expected losses could reduce a bank's Operational Risk capital requirement under the new Standardised Approach (Migueis, 2021).

[16] The value of both deductibles and the level of cover provided by an insurance policy should reflect a firm's risk appetite.

EFFECTIVENESS OF INSURANCE POLICIES AS AN OPERATIONAL RISK MITIGANT

The results of QIS-2 (Basel Committee, 2002) revealed that the level of recoveries from insurance and other sources for the participating 30 banks was really quite low, i.e. approximately 5% of net losses (Table 12.1). Insurance recoveries were most relevant to DPA and EPWS, i.e. loss and destruction of physical assets and the bodily injury of staff members, whilst working.

Similarly, the Basel Committee's 2008 loss data collection exercise (Basel Committee, 2009a) found that the median value of insurance recoveries as a percentage of losses was just 3.0%, and the median values for all risks were zero, apart from External Fraud and DPA. This low level of recovery reflects that insurance is based on pooling, i.e. low value:high volume losses[17] are excluded. Additionally, fines and penalties are also excluded; as are some events linked to employee misconduct, e.g. professional indemnity insurance may exclude events arising from employee dishonesty, fraud and

TABLE 12.1 Percentage of individual loss events with non-zero reported recoveries by event type (1998 to 2000)

Recoveries / Basel II events	Percentage of the total number of events (%)			Value of losses		Relevant insurance policies
	% total events	Insurance recoveries	Other recoveries	% of value of losses	Recovery as % value	
EDPM	38.6%	0.2%	12.1%	34.7%	4.4%	▪ Crime.*
EF	37.8%	1.3%	9.0%	20.1%	3.0%	▪ Crime; and ▪ Cyber.
CPBP	8.7%	0.1%	6.2%	27.8%	2.0%	▪ Professional indemnity.
IF	4.7%	1.4%	27.4%	10.8%	19.6%	▪ Crime; and ▪ Rogue trader.
DPA	4.1%	**20.1%**	2.4%	3.0%	6.7%	▪ Cargo; and ▪ Property & Contents.
EPWS	3.4%	**33.7%**	0.5%	2.9%	14.9%	▪ Public liability; and ▪ Employers' liability.
BDSF	2.7%	0.0%	4.5%	0.8%	1.0%	▪ Business interruption.
Total	**100.0%**	**2.6%**	**10.1%**	**100.0%**	**5.4%****	

* Theft of inadvertently misdirected funds can be insured via a Crime Policy.
** The sum of: the % of value of losses × % recovery by risk type.

---

[17]As noted previously, AMA banks can obtain a deduction from their Operational Risk capital requirement for their expected losses, if they can demonstrate that they are adequately captured in their internal business practices (Basel Committee, 2004) e.g. budgeting and/or product pricing.

malicious acts. Finally, whilst rogue trader insurance is available, underwriting capacity is limited.

MAPPING OF INSURANCE COVERAGE TO EVENTS AND IMPACTS

As described earlier, insurance policies define both the nature of events and the associated financial consequences/impacts which are either insured or not. Consequently, to illustrate the scope of Operational Risk events and financial consequences that can be transferred via insurance Table 12.2 combines the event and impact taxonomies (Tables 5.2 and 5.4), and overlays the coverage of various insurance policies. This illustrates that whilst most of the financial consequences of Operational Risk events (the rows from Table 5.4) are insurable, with two exceptions, this is only the case in certain circumstances (the columns from Table 5.2).

The key features of the insurance policies included in Table 12.2 are summarised below:

Business interruption insurance will compensate firms for loss of gross revenues, as well as additional expenses/cost of working (capped at the revenues that would be lost if these costs were not incurred) arising from the disruption of their use of a building, e.g. its damage or destruction; or Government restrictions; or loss of utilities, such as water, electricity, sanitation and telephony; or infectious diseases; or terrorism. An example of a successful claim is reflected in Cantor Fitzgerald's 2002 financial statements. They include $12.8 million of income arising from a successful claim on its business interruption policy, as a consequence of 9/11.

Professional indemnity insurance will reimburse third-party claims for errors and omissions relating to the provision of a firm's services, and associated costs. An example of a successful professional indemnity claim is Mizuho reaching a confidential settlement in its favour, in 2006, with its insurers. This related to the settlement of litigation, under the US Securities Act (1933), regarding Mizuho's role, in 2001, as one of the 17 underwriters of WorldCom securities, prior to its collapse in 2002.[18]

Employers' liability insurance[19] covers compensation and associated costs arising from injury sustained by staff members in the course of their employment. Purchasing this insurance is a statutory requirement for employers in many jurisdictions. This may potentially include mental health issues arising from remote working during the COVID-19 pandemic.

---

[18]Note 8 in Mizuho International plc's 2006 financial statements.
[19]Firms with an international footprint that covers riskier locations may also take out Kidnap & Ransom insurance. This covers negotiations with kidnappers; delivery of a ransom; reimbursement of a ransom once paid; evacuation; and appropriate care.

TABLE 12.2 Mapping of insurance coverage to events and impacts

Impact taxonomy (Table 5.4) / Event taxonomy (Table 5.2)	Internal						External		
	Mistakes & omissions,20 inc accidents	Individual misconduct	Systemic misconduct	Malicious acts*	Systemic process failure	Various system failures	Third-party	Malicious acts	Acts of God**
Lost revenues							Business interruption		
Regulatory actions: Fines & penalties				N/A					
Compensation — ■ Customers	Professional indemnity				Professional indemnity			Cyber	
■ Staff	Employers' liability								
■ People	Public liability						Public liability		
Additional expenses — ■ Customers	Professional indemnity				Professional indemnity		Public liability		
■ Staff	Employers' liability								
■ People	Public liability						Tax liability	Cyber	
■ Other costs				Business interruption			Business interruption		

[20] An insurer is more likely to use the phrase "errors and omissions".

TABLE 12.2 (Continued)

Impact taxonomy (Table 5.4)	Event taxonomy (Table 5.2) — Internal						Event taxonomy (Table 5.2) — External		
	Mistakes & omissions, inc accidents	Individual misconduct	Systemic misconduct	Malicious acts*	Systemic process failure	Various system failures	Third-party	Malicious acts	Acts of God**
Tax incurred							Tax liability		
Market Risk				Rogue trader					
Write-down of financial assets	Crime***			Crime				Crime	
Write-down of physical assets	■ Property ■ Contents			■ Property ■ Contents ■ Crime			Cargo	■ Property ■ Contents ■ Crime ■ Cargo	Cargo
Loss of recourse	N/A								

* Typically the malicious acts of directors are excluded.

** Insurance companies may further subdivide acts of God between isolated events, e.g. a fire, and events that could lead to a concentration of insurance claim losses, e.g. an earthquake; or a hurricane; or a pandemic.

*** Theft of inadvertently misdirected funds can be insured via a Crime Policy.

Public liability insurance protects firms against claims made by clients, contractors, and members of the public (third-party claims) for accidental injury or damage to their property, including due to a firm's negligence/misconduct. The insurance typically covers both the compensation costs and legal expenses.

Cyber insurance covers the cost of repairing and restoring systems, data and websites and associated legal costs, following a cyberattack. An example of a successful claim by a financial institution is Equifax, a provider of consumer credit scores, which suffered a theft of personal details relating to 143 million consumers between May and July 2017. Equifax had a cybersecurity policy which provided $125 million of cover, reportedly from Lloyds of London, with a $7.5 million deductible. Equifax successfully made a full claim on the policy; however, its value was only a fraction of its total related losses.

Tax liability insurance protects against differing interpretations of tax law, and hence can facilitate corporate reorganisations, asset purchases, liquidations, etc. Losses covered include the tax suffered, defence costs and interest on unpaid taxes.

Rogue trader insurance: At least one Lloyds syndicate has offered insurance to cover losses sustained as a result of concealed trading or trading which is falsely recorded in a bank's records. This includes trading in excess of limits, with unauthorised instruments and with unapproved counterparties.

Crime: These policies cover both dishonest, fraudulent and malicious acts carried out by employees to obtain an improper financial gain (NB this excludes rogue trading, as the employee is not directly obtaining a financial gain). Crime policies can also cover a range of other internal and external events, including forgeries; counterfeits; extortion (e.g. ransomware); fraudulent payment instructions (e.g. SWIFT cyber-payment frauds, such as befell Bangladesh Bank in 2015); and fraudulently induced instructions. An example of a successful claim is provided by Standard Bank plc, relating to a loss, due to fraudulent activity, on the valuation of commodity financing transactions in respect of physical aluminium held as collateral in bonded warehouses in Shandong Province (China) in 2014.[21]

Cargo insurance is relevant to banks that take title to physical commodities. Policies cover loss, damage or contamination due to accidents, malicious acts (e.g. piracy) and natural disasters. It excludes misconduct by the insured.

Property and Contents insurance covers losses suffered by the owner of a building and/or its contents due to either theft of damage. An example of a successful claim is provided by the Depository Trust & Clearing Corporation (DTCC).

---

[21] Standard Bank plc's financial statements for 2014.

In October 2012, Hurricane Sandy led to its lobby and underground floors, including its vault, being engulfed in floodwaters, in its headquarters located on Water Street, in Lower Manhattan. This led to damage to DTCC's physical assets; business disruption; and also damage to its clients' physical securities that it was holding as a custodian in the flooded vault. By 2014, DTCC had received $39.3 million in payments against insurance claims relating to property damage, business interruption and damage or destruction of its clients' securities.[22]

In addition to these standard products, some banks have also arranged more bespoke products, for example, in 2016, Credit Suisse took out a five-year Operational Risk insurance policy with Zurich Insurance.[23] The policy provided CHF300 million of cover, but the retention value was high, i.e. CHF3.5 billion. The language in the insurance policy is specifically tailored to meet the Basel II capital offset criteria.

The examples provided above demonstrate that in certain remote circumstances insurance can be an effective mechanism for the transference of Operational Risk. Some of these examples, however, additionally highlight the criticality of determining the appropriate levels of insurance cover required. This can be done using a combination of scenario analysis (Chapter 9) and capital modelling (Chapter 10) for

FIGURE 12.4 Operational Risk capital models can be rerun for insurable impacts for specific insurable events/scenarios, to determine the potential for a firm to suffer impacts in excess of insurance

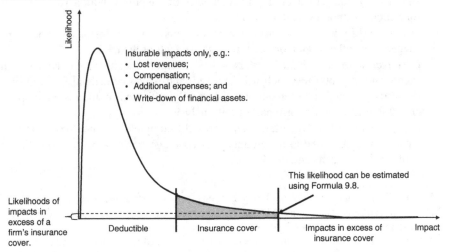

---

[22]Note 23 DTCC's 2013 financial statements.
[23]Zurich Insurance obtained reinsurance from a Bermudan SPV, Operational Re LTD, which financed the reinsurance through the issuance of catastrophe bonds to investors.

difficult-to-estimate impacts, i.e. not Property and Contents, as the value of a firm's physical assets is quite objective. Capital models can be run at different confidence intervals for a particular insurable event/risk (e.g. malicious acts or misconduct), based on specific scenarios, and including only the impacts that are insurable (e.g. including lost revenues, compensation, additional expenses and the write-down of financial assets but excluding regulatory fines and penalties) to indicate the range of potential impacts in excess of a firm's insurance cover (Figure 12.4). The same analysis can also be performed under stressed economic conditions, which, per the 7th Law, may increase both the likelihood of occurrence and the associated impacts.

DEDUCTIONS FROM OPERATIONAL RISK CAPITAL REQUIREMENTS

Basel II currently allows AMA banks to reduce their Pillar 1 capital requirements[24] as a consequence of the transference of some of their Operational Risks via insurance (Basel Committee, 2004), if a number of criteria are met, i.e.:

- *Creditworthiness:* The insurance provider must be an independent third-party (i.e. it cannot be a captive insurer)[25] that has a good credit rating, i.e. a minimum of A.
- *Term:* The insurance policy must have an initial term of no less than one year. For policies with a residual term of less than one year, the banks must make appropriate haircuts reflecting the declining residual term of the policy, with a 100% haircut for policies with a residual term of 90 days or less.
- *Default of the insured:* The insurance policy cannot have exclusions or limitations triggered by either regulatory actions or the default of the bank.
- *Effectiveness of risk mitigation:* A bank has to demonstrate how the risks (i.e. both events and impacts) to which it is exposed, and which contribute to its Operational Risk capital requirement, are specifically mitigated by the insurance policies. Table 12.2 would form part of this analysis.
- *Pay-out uncertainty:* Uncertainty over both the completeness and timing of pay-outs, for example, due to uncertainty over coverage[26,27] or a bank's compliance with a policy's terms and conditions.

---

[24] Anecdotally, regulators may also allow deductions for insurance from Pillar 2A Operational Risk capital requirements for non-AMA banks, if the banks can demonstrate that they also meet these criteria. This may well persist even after the imminent demise of AMA.

[25] A captive insurer is a licensed insurance company established to provide insurance cover to its parent. Captive insurers can reduce their parents' insurance costs; insure difficult risks; and enable direct access to reinsurance markets.

[26] The litigation relating to whether the 9/11 attacks on the World Trade Centre were either one or two insurable events took almost six years to conclude, and the outcomes varied depending upon the precise wording of the different insurance policies.

[27] In July 2020, the FCA brought a test case to ascertain whether 17 sample wordings for Business Interruption insurance policies covered the COVID-19 pandemic, specifically relating to competing causes of loss. In January 2021, the UK Supreme Court predominantly found in favour of the FCA and the policy holders, and against the insurers.

Although the maximum level of Pillar 1 capital deductions for insurance is limited by Basel II to 20%, generally, the level of deductions are lower. The Basel Committee's 2008 loss data collection exercise (Basel Committee, 2009a) identified the median insurance offset for 42 AMA banks was zero, and that the 75th percentile was still only 3.7%, which is comparable to the levels of loss recovery from insurance policies noted earlier.[28]

Whilst Basel III also recognises the role of insurance in risk mitigation, by allowing banks to reduce the value of their losses for insurance recoveries within the Internal Loss Multiplier calculation, this is only once the monies have been received from the insurers. Even after the new Standardised Approach is introduced, however, banks may still be able to offset insurance policies against Pillar 2A capital requirements for risks not adequately captured via Pillar 1.

CONCLUSIONS

Over an extended period of time, the cost of insurance premiums should always exceed the value of market insurance claims, unless the policy has been mispriced. Consequently, the value of insurance is in transferring a large unpredicted financial consequence that occurs over a 12-month time horizon. As a mitigant of Operational Risk, insurance will always be restricted to the losses on the right-hand side of Figure 1.1, and a relatively small percentage of the total value of Operational Risk losses in any particular year. Understanding better the nature of a firm's Operational Risk profile through scenario analysis and capital modelling may enhance the procurement of insurance policies, with more appropriate coverage, i.e. the financial value of the cover; retention levels; and the range of risks covered.

Reverse stress testing and procuring insurance both involve firms making decisions based upon assessments of the likelihood and severity of specific, very remote events. A deeper understanding of the Ten Laws that govern Operational Risk should support more systematic decision making.

---

[28]Credit Suisse's bespoke insurance policy tailored to Basel II reportedly led to a CHF150 million or 2.8% reduction in the bank's Operational Risk capital requirement. This implies a 50% haircut to the value of even this most tailored insurance policy.

CHAPTER 13

Day-to-Day Operational Risk Management

Whilst the tools described in Chapters 8 to 12 are utilised periodically, this chapter details how five day-to-day activities of Operational Risk managers can be enhanced through the consideration of Ten Laws of Operational Risk. These five day-to-day risk management activities all fall under the 8th Law: Risk Homeostasis, i.e. by either preventing exposures that are outside of appetite or by responding to events to bring a firm back within appetite:

1. Incident management and root cause analysis.
2. Control assurance and the nature of control failures.
3. Predictive metrics.
4. Change management, including the implementation of new technology, new product and transaction approval and product stress testing.
5. Reputational Risk quantification and management.

It is these activities which typically fill the days of Operational Risk managers, and generate value by supporting firms to:

- Maximise returns, whilst staying within appetite now, and also in the future, through providing assurance over the operation of controls; obtaining early warning through predictive metrics; and learning lessons from incidents;
- Grow their businesses both quickly and safely through the management of change; and
- Meet the expectations of their stakeholders through all of these day-to-day activities, as well as the proactive and reactive management of reputation.

1. INCIDENT MANAGEMENT AND ROOT CAUSE ANALYSIS

When Operational Risk incidents occur, then firms naturally need to respond in a proportionate manner, in order to curtail immediate losses (1st Law); determine the quantum of failure (3rd Law); and mitigate the potential impacts of recurrence (1st Law). The prioritisation of these actions should be sequenced from right to left in the revised butterfly diagram (Figure 6.3), i.e.:

1st: Corrective/resilience actions which restrict the scale of losses. For example, if a bank has an accidental market risk exposure, then the first action of a trader is to close out the unwanted position! If the position is deliberate and unauthorised (i.e. a malicious act) then management would take control of this process. Similarly, if monies have been misappropriated, then Operations and Legal will act immediately to freeze the funds in the accounts of the recipient banks. Equally, IT will respond to the discovery of a cyber intrusion by removing any malware that has been introduced into the firm. If sufficiently critical, these responses may be co-ordinated by a Crisis Management Committee. Depending on the nature of the incident, firms may also need to decide whether communications are required to some of the various stakeholders set out in Figure 2.1. For example, in the European Union, under the General Data Protection Regulations (GDPR), the leakage of personal data may require notification to the relevant regulator within 72 hours of discovery. Whilst Principle 11 and SYSC 13.4 of the FCA's handbook are rather more all-encompassing, requiring firms to be "... open and cooperative" and to "... notify the FCA immediately of any operational risk matter of which the FCA would reasonably expect notice" including any "significant failure in the firm's systems or controls."

2nd: Detective actions: This involves determining the extent of the incident, i.e. the quantum of failure. For example, the discovery of an error in the design or documentation for a structured product, will initiate a detailed review of other transactions to identify any systemic failure.[1] Similarly, the discovery of cyber intrusion would initiate a detailed review of systems' logs to establish the extent of any malicious activity, e.g. the theft of data.

3rd: Preventive actions to limit the potential impacts of recurrence, including additional preventive, detective and corrective/resilience controls. These final actions are typically co-ordinated by Operational Risk management to ensure objectivity. These actions would include both the enhancement of the design or operation of existing controls and the introduction of new controls, to plug any existing gaps. There may also be actions focused on addressing the causes of the incident (see below).

---

[1] Structuring desks may re-use documentation for other similar transactions. As a consequence, it is possible that a single mistake or omission can be subsequently copied into a number of transactions, becoming a systemic failure. McConnell uses the term "Replication" to describe "corruption that is copied from elsewhere..." (McConnell, 2017).

Depending on the nature of the incident, some degree of HR action may also result. If action is taken this may range in severity from inclusion in a staff member's annual performance review with an associated reduction in their bonus; to disciplinary action; and in extremis dismissal and reflection in the former staff member's regulatory reference. The involvement of Operational Risk management in these processes can be problematic, as the second line often seeks to engender a culture of openness and honesty, which may be incompatible with their contribution to any subsequent disciplinary process.

Root cause analysis is the process of systematically ascertaining the underlying causes of an incident. Techniques that are commonly employed include: the "5 Whys" and Fishbone diagrams.[2] The 5 Whys, involves repeatedly asking "Why?" until a workshop arrives at the root cause of an incident. The first four laws, however, suggest that the belief in a single root cause is a misconception, i.e. as noted in Chapter 5, causes can variously influence occurrence and velocity, as well as the failure of preventive, detective and corrective/resilience controls. Consequently, systematically recording causes (and also control failures, see later) using a fishbone diagram is probably more effective (Figure 13.1). The causal taxonomy (Appendix III) can also be used to improve completeness.

Conclusions

Incident management is the reimposition of control in the aftermath of an incident, and hence the actions can be categorised using the different types of controls, i.e. corrective/resilience, detective and preventive. The first four Laws of Operational Risk illustrate that causes can variously influence occurrence, velocity and the effectiveness of preventive, detective and corrective/resilience controls.

FIGURE 13.1 Fishbone diagram reflecting the first four Laws of Operational Risk

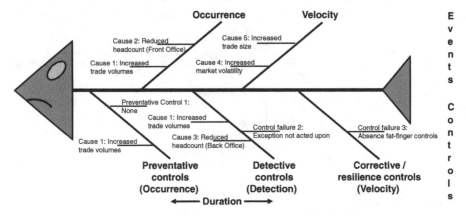

---

[2]These were developed by Kaoru Ishikawa in the 1960s.

2. CONTROL ASSURANCE AND THE NATURE OF CONTROL FAILURES

Firms need to have mechanisms for monitoring the effectiveness of the controls that mitigate their highest inherent risks. This should be grounded upon an understanding of how controls fail.

Analysing the nature of control failures described in well-documented Operational Risk events, reveals them to be a subset of the event taxonomy set out in Chapter 5 (Table 5.2), i.e. a combination of mistakes and omissions, misconduct and malicious acts, etc. For example, staff members may fail to carry out a control or fail to investigate and escalate exceptions properly (mistakes and omissions). Controls may also be circumvented due to the misconduct or the malicious acts of staff members. In addition, controls may fail through ineffective design (Process), e.g. a control may be manual and end of day, when it needs to automated and real-time to be effective; or a control may be missing altogether from a firm's control framework. Additionally, controls may fail through disruption to software and application malfunctions, e.g. the failure of intrusion detection software (Systems). Finally, there may be external drivers for control failures, e.g. a fraudster circumventing controls either acting alone or in collusion with a firm's staff, or the failure of a third (or fourth) party to operate its controls effectively, e.g. an outsourcer. Figure 13.2 is James Reason's Swiss Cheese Model of accident causation annotated with examples of the nature of control failures. Real-world examples are set out in Table 13.1 and Appendix I.3. Similar to events (Table 2.1), the Author expects that the most common control failures will be due to mistakes and omissions, rather than misconduct and malicious acts.

FIGURE 13.2   Swiss Cheese Model annotated for the nature of control failure

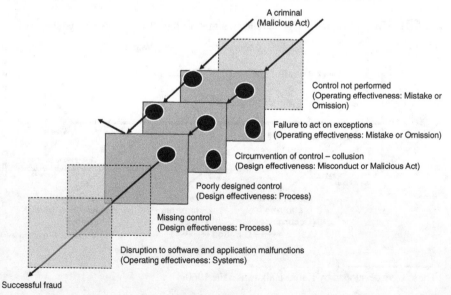

TABLE 13.1 Taxonomy of inadequacies or failures – the nature of the control failures (Appendix I.3)

The nature of control failures				Definitions or examples from various public sources
Internal Control failures	People – Operating effectiveness	Mistakes and Omissions		*Controls not performed*, e.g.: ■ "... the managers responsible ... were unaware that their staff had stopped following agreed procedures [checks on internal trades]." *Control incorrectly or partially performed*, e.g.: ■ "... in a number of instances, maker/checker controls were not properly evidenced and did not identify errors." ■ "Multiple limit breaches were routinely signed-off without rigorous investigation or actions taken to reduce positions." *Failure to act*, e.g.: on exceptions: ■ "Operations did not have the reflex to inform their ... supervisors or Front Office supervisors of ... anomalies." ■ "Certain control functions failed to escalate in a timely manner price testing variances that were identified ..."
		Misconduct and Malicious Acts		The mistakes and omissions described above can also occur deliberately. In addition: *Circumvention of controls – falsification*, e.g.: ■ The FSA received complaint files which had been "altered improperly" in "the form of amendments to existing documents". ■ "To hide his losses and the size of his positions, he created fictitious options." ■ *Circumvention of controls – breach of segregation of duties*, e.g.: A bank clerk made two fraudulent transfers with a total value of €90 million. "Two of [his] colleagues, whose passwords were used to carry out and approve the transactions, were initially questioned but soon declared innocent." ■ *Circumvention of controls – collusion*, e.g.: A trader "... sent a list of four AAA bonds to his bond salesman contact [at another bank] ... and requested month-end prices for the bonds. At approximately the same time, [he also] communicated to his contact the desired prices on the bonds."

(Continued)

TABLE 13.1   *(Continued)*

The nature of control failures		Definitions or examples from various public sources
	Process – Design effectiveness	*Poorly designed controls* for achieving Completeness; Accuracy; Existence; Valuation; Cut-Off; Rights & Obligations; and Presentation & Disclosure, e.g.: ■ "The identification of suspicious trading patterns had to be performed manually. However, it was not generally feasible for...desk supervisors to perform this task for high volume trading desks..." ■ The bank "extracted the relevant trading data for reconciliation purposes from its systems at different points in time which created timing gaps". *Missing controls*, e.g.: ■ The bank "... had no specific systems and controls relating to its LIBOR or EURIBOR submissions processes until December 2009". ■ The firm "...did not have...a control to compare orders leaving SMARS with those that entered it."
	Systems – variously design or operating effectiveness	■ *Disruption of software*, e.g.: "...while [the firm] had installed a tool to inspect network traffic for evidence of malicious activity, an expired certificate prevented that tool from performing its intended function of detecting malicious traffic." ■ *Application malfunctions*, e.g.: "...due to the concerns over the reliability of the VaR calculation, the VaR limit breaches in currency options was removed from the front page of the report..." ■ *Disruption of data & storage*, e.g.: controls fail due to being fed incomplete, or inaccurate data, or data in the wrong format, or untimely data.
External control failures	Third- (and fourth-) party failures	■ *Any of the above*, e.g.: Non-Functional Testing "...had been constrained by the test environments...and...had been conducted at lower volumes than originally planned".
	Malicious acts	■ *External circumvention of controls*, e.g.: "...the attackers removed the data in small increments, using standard encrypted web protocols to disguise the exchanges as normal network traffic."

As noted in Chapter 8, whilst the design effectiveness of controls is relatively stable, and can be assessed through RCSAs, the operating effectiveness of controls is more dynamic. Hence firms should establish regular attestation processes, through which the owners of certain key controls can confirm that they have operated correctly during the month or quarter. If they have not operated correctly, then the owners should set out remedial actions, with appropriate timescales.

Operational Risk management can both report on the current operating effectiveness of these key controls against high inherent risks (Table 13.2) to assess their

TABLE 13.2 Illustration of the monitoring of the operating effectiveness of key controls that mitigate a high inherent risk for business disruption

Preventive controls	Attestation	KCIs	Second line	Detective controls	Attestation	KCIs	Second line	Corrective/ resilience controls	Attestation	Second line	Third line – Internal Audit findings
▪ Batch-scheduling software				▪ Monitoring of the overnight batches				▪ Business Continuity Plans (BCP)			
▪ Application development standards				▪ Capacity monitoring data				▪ Incident management			
▪ Change requirements				▪ Capacity monitoring network				▪ Disaster recovery site			
▪ Project plans				▪ Capacity monitoring applications				▪ System back-ups			
▪ Project governance				▪ Intrusion detection software				▪ Uninterrupted Power Supply (UPS)			
▪ Firewalls				▪ Change management testing requirements				▪ Run-books for migration weekends			
▪ Antiviral software				▪ User Acceptance Testing				▪ Business interruption & cyber insurance			

Key:

Effective ■ (black) Needs improvement ■ (dark grey) Ineffective □ (light grey)

significance and also validate these first-line attestations by sample checking the supporting evidence. This second-line validation should dovetail with other testing activity, e.g. Compliance Monitoring, and Sarbanes–Oxley (Figure 14.1), in order to avoid duplication. As the most common control failures arise from mistakes and omissions, a key element of second-line validation is checking that exceptions highlighted by control processes are investigated and appropriately actioned. Examples of exceptions may include breaks on reconciliations; mismatched confirmations; limit excesses; and unusual business patterns, etc. The importance of the responses of staff to exceptions is emphasised by the FSA's suggestion that investment banks could consider "... including fictitious transactions in production systems and even the involvement of real market counterparties ... " to test how their systems highlight these exceptions and *their staff members react* (FSA, 2008). The Author is aware that many investment banks are interested in adopting this approach: however, only a few firms use this technique in practice due to concerns over accidentally hedging or settling a fictitious trade, or being accused of attempting to manipulate a market! The objective of investment banks booking these fictitious trades is analogous to the use of mystery shopping to test sales processes in retail banks or fake phishing exercises. Informing staff that a firm is using these approaches may, of itself, also be a very effective approach to changing their behaviours.

When there are issues within a firm that lead to significant Operational Risk events, then subsequent investigations often reveal that the issues were known to a number of staff members. For example, when Deutsche Bank reached a settlement with the US authorities in 2015 for sanctions breaches relating to Iran and Libya the Head of the New York Department of Financial Services (NYDFS) observed: "... bank employees in many overseas offices, in different business divisions, and with various levels of seniority were actively involved or knew about it."[3] Similarly, at Kweku Adoboli's trial, the court heard that two junior members on UBS's Exchange-Traded Funds desk were told of the existence of secret, off-books trades, several months before Adoboli was arrested, but that they failed to escalate this information.[4]

In addition to these regular control attestations and second-line validation, there are other softer approaches to improving the identification of ongoing incidents; controls that are not being properly undertaken; and issues that are not being appropriately addressed. For example, engaging with junior staff who are closer to issues and whose concerns may not be being escalated; providing training and external case studies illustrating "good" and "bad" behaviours; and rotating staff between first and second lines. In terms of identifying ongoing bad practices, then low staff turnover can actually be an indicator of potential issues, due to the absence of regular "fresh pairs of eyes"!

---

[3] *The Financial Times*, (5th November 2015) "Deutsche settles US sanctions claims".
[4] *The Times*, (28th September 2012) "Former UBS trader stabbed in the back by colleagues".

Conclusions

Control assurance, in combination with KCIs (see next section), provides a more up-to-date status of the operating effectiveness of key controls. This information supplements a firm's understanding of the design effectiveness of its controls obtained through the RCSAs (Chapter 8). Understanding the occurrence and nature of control failures helps second-line functions to both better target their validation activities and provide more insightful reporting.

3. PREDICTIVE METRICS

Identifying predictive metrics, such as KRIs and KCIs, is a Holy Grail for the Operational Risk profession, as these metrics would enable them to take pre-emptive action to limit losses. Fortunately the Ten Laws of Operational Risk can provide some insights both into why identifying these metrics has proved challenging, and also the events for which it is feasible for KRIs and KCIs to be genuinely predictive.

Challenges of identifying predictive metrics

Analysis of patterns in Operational Risk losses (Chapter 1) and the first seven Laws of Operational Risk highlight a number of challenges to identifying predictive metrics:

- *Differing frequencies:* The frequencies of occurrence/detection differ significantly for the seven Basel II event types (Figure 1.3), i.e. External Fraud and EDPM have higher frequencies of occurrence/detection, whilst Internal Fraud and DPA are much rarer. This reflects the underlying nature of these events (Table 2.1), i.e. External Fraud events are malicious acts generally perpetrated by professional criminals, and EDPM events predominantly arise from the mistakes and omissions of a firm's staff. In contrast internal frauds are malicious acts committed by a firm's own staff and DPA events include acts of God. It is obviously more difficult to demonstrate a predictive relationship between metrics and the occurrence of events, when those events are generally infrequent.
- *Complexity of causal factors:* Large loss events are associated with multiple causal factors. For the sample of 16 well-documented events analysed in Table 2.2, the average is 4½ causal factors per event. The complexity illustrated in the revised butterfly diagram (Figure 13.3) is quite representative of these large loss events. This complexity means that, with a few exceptions, individual metrics related to these larger losses are very unlikely to be predictive, with any precision, on their own.
- *Lags in settlement:* Five of the seven Basel II event types have both relatively short durations (i.e. between occurrence and discovery, 2nd Law) and lags between

FIGURE 13.3 Butterfly diagram annotated for what KRIs and KCIs may predict (Revision of Figure 6.3)
The dotted lines reflect the causes; control failures and impacts of a well-publicised mis-marking incident from 2008.

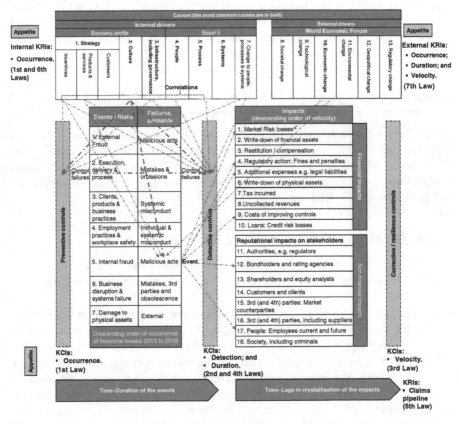

discovery and settlement (5th Law), see Figure 11.9. As a consequence, for these five risks, there can be an immediacy between metrics and the occurrence of events and their crystallisation into losses. For CPBP and EPWS, however, the lags between occurrence and settlement are significantly longer, i.e. measured in years rather than months. The lags for large CPBP losses (i.e. ≥$0.1 billion) are even longer still, for the period 2008 to 2017, for 31 current and former G-SIBs, the lags between occurrence and discovery; and discovery and settlement of losses were respectively 5.2 years and 3.8 years. So a firm's current large CPBP losses will typically reflect its KRIs and KCIs from 4 to 9 years ago!

Predictive powers of KRIs and KCIs

The first seven Laws of Operational Risk suggest metrics linked to business profile (KRIs), internal and external causal factors (KRIs); and the operation of controls (KCIs) can be informative regarding the future occurrence/detection; duration and velocity of loss events for both individual risks and Operational Risk as a whole, specifically:

- KRIs linked to business profile and internal causes may be predictive of the occurrence/detection of loss events (1st & 6th Laws);
- KRIs linked to external causes (e.g. increased volatility, market moves (e.g. interest rates), rising default rates and falling asset values [Table 11.2]) may be predictive of increased occurrence/detection, duration and velocity of losses (7th Law);
- KCIs relating to the operating effectiveness of:
  - *Preventive controls* may be predictive of the increased occurrence of losses (1st Law), especially when these controls mitigate persistent threats, such as human errors and external fraud;
  - *Detective controls* may be predictive of the detection and duration of losses (2nd and 4th Laws), i.e. a weakening of these controls may lead to a short-term reduction in the detection of loss events, but eventually, longer durations will result in larger impacts when finally discovered; and
  - *Corrective/resilience controls* may also be predictive of the severity of losses (3rd Law), i.e. a weakening of these controls may exacerbate any loss events that do occur.

These relationships are summarised in an annotated butterfly diagram (Figure 13.3). Interestingly, as the nature of internal Operational Risk events and control failures are the same (Tables 5.2 and 5.3), then factors that increase the likelihood of occurrence may also increase the likelihood of the failure of the various mitigating controls. This can also be seen in Figure 13.3, e.g. the culture causes links, in this example, to both the nature of the event and the failure of the mitigating controls.

1st & 6th Laws – Predicting occurrence Formula 13.1, which describes the occurrence of Operational Risk events, contains a number of factors that may be the basis of predictive metrics, including business profile, internal and external causes

Formula 13.1 Occurrence of Operational Risk events (Repeat of Formula 2.1)

Occurrence $\approx f$ (Business profile, Internal & external causes, Inadequacies or
of events   failures)
                 – (Preventive controls, Inadequacies or failures, Internal causes)

and the effectiveness of preventive controls.[5] The different event types are considered in turn below:

- *Mistakes and omissions* can result in both Operational Risk events and also the failure of preventive controls. Metrics relating to stretch, such as increased activity levels (business profile) and/or reduced resourcing levels due to unfilled vacancies and staff turnover etc (internal causes) may be predictive of increases in the number of loss events involving human errors. For risks with short lags between occurrence and discovery; and discovery and the settlement of losses (e.g. EDPM, see Figure 11.9) then metrics relating to stretch and business profile may be quite predictive. These relationships are typically linear until firms reach a capacity constraint, when the relationship can become more of a "hockey stick", although encountering such tipping points is quite rare.[6] Weaknesses in preventive controls will also be predictive of future losses due to the persistent nature of human errors.

- *External malicious acts:* Metrics relating to the effectiveness of controls that prevent the persistent external threat of malicious acts (e.g. cybercrime) will also be highly predictive of losses, as any weaknesses in a firm's layers of controls are likely to be identified and exploited by professional criminals. Relevant controls for preventing cybercrime and associated KCIs, may include the status of firewalls (e.g. results of penetration tests); the coverage of intrusion prevention and detection software; and the completeness of patching. Business profile metrics may also be predictive, e.g. an increase in the volume of new loans written may lead to increases in the absolute number of successful fraudulent loan applications.

- *Internal misconduct and malicious acts:* It is obviously impossible to predict when humans will behave inappropriately.[7] It is also challenging to detect its occurrence, hence firms often use portfolios of metrics focused on KRIs highlighting suspicious patterns of business activity and personal behaviours, and also the status of key controls (Table 13.3). The use of a portfolio of metrics can help to address the number of different causal factors, as noted previously, that may contribute to a loss event. AI and machine learning can also facilitate the detection of ongoing incidents.

---

[5]These are consistent with the four categories of indicators defined by Chapelle, i.e. Exposure; Stress; Failure and Causal (Chapelle, 2018).

[6]The Author has seen this twice during his career, once relating to the maximum volume of change without impacting system performance, and the other relating to the sensitivity of the manual processing of securities to trade volumes.

[7]The 2002 film *Minority Report* envisaged a world in which it is possible to predict when humans will commit a crime, known as "pre-crime". At the time of writing this concept remains science fiction!

TABLE 13.3 Illustration of rogue trading Red Flags – detective rather than predictive metrics (Grimwade, 2016)

Nature	Metrics and examples
Suspicious business activity	Large proportion of P&L produced by just one trader, e.g.: ■ Barings: Nick Leeson was responsible for ~25% of Barings 1994 P&L. ■ SocGen: Jerome Kerviel's declared P&L in 2007 constituted 59% of his desk's P&L. Excessive funding demands, e.g.: Barings famously had advanced more than its entire share capital and reserves to support the activities of just one trader in Singapore. Unexplained or unusual P&L, e.g.: ■ AIB failed to review John Rusnak's daily P&L, which swung wildly and frequently breached daily stop-loss limits. ■ Credit Suisse: IPV breaks were not promptly resolved. Systematic late trades, e.g.: ■ AIB: John Rusnak used late trades or "held-over trades" to manipulate his P&L. ■ UBS: Kweku Adoboli only partially recorded the details of many of his trades. Systematic & unexplained cancel & amends, e.g.: ■ NAB's 4 FX option traders persistently cancelled and amended either fictitious trades or trades with incorrect rates. ■ SocGen: Jerome Kerviel persistently cancelled and amended fictitious trades. Persistent unconfirmed trades, e.g.: ■ UBS: Kweku Adoboli had ~$3.57 billion of unconfirmed trades when his hidden positions were discovered. ■ AIB: John Rusnak was able to bully and cajole Operations staff into not confirming all of his trades.[8] Trading of unapproved products, e.g.: ■ NAB's FX options desk engaged in transactions before New Product Approval was granted. Regular limit breaches, e.g.: ■ NAB's four rogue option traders persistently breached VaR limits throughout 2003. ■ AIB: John Rusnak regularly traded with counterparties without credit limits.
Suspicious personal behaviours	Not taking 10-day block leave, e.g.: ■ SocGen: Jerome Kerviel took only 4 days of vacation during 2007. ■ AIB: John Rusnak rarely took days off and often traded on his laptop whilst on holiday. Own account trading breaches, e.g.: ■ UBS's Legal & Compliance Departments twice warned Kweku Adoboli for failing to disclose his spread betting account.

---

[8] *The New York Times*, (15th March 2002) "Bank report said trader had bold plot".

- Weaknesses in the design or operating effectiveness of a firm's controls for mitigating CPBP and Internal Fraud will not necessarily be exploited by staff members, in the same way that professional criminals will exploit control weaknesses. Consequently, metrics highlighting weaknesses in controls that mitigate CPBP and Internal Fraud will not automatically predict the occurrence of events, but they may be more likely.
- Finally, as noted previously, the significant lags between the occurrence and discovery, and the discovery and the settlement of CPBP (and also EPWS) losses (Figure 11.9), means that a firm's current KRIs and KCIs will be unrelated to its current CPBP and EPWS loss experiences.

- *Process: Design/systemic failure:* The nature of these events means that relevant metrics are actions arising from RCSAs linked to specific risks.
- *Systems: Disruption of software; application malfunctions; disruption of data & storage and disruption of own infrastructure:* Whilst disruption is common, large Operational Risk losses arising from these events are relatively rare (Figure 1.3). Common causes of systems' events include the volume of change; capacity constraints, e.g. data, processing, and networks; and the age of a firm's technology.[9]
- *Acts of God:* By definition these are infrequent events, although Climate Change may increase the occurrence of Physical Risks in the future (Chapter 16).
- *Third- (and fourth-) party failures:* Outsource service providers can suffer from all of the events described above but their customers will typically lack the necessary metrics to predict the occurrence of these events, other than to observe adverse trends in service levels.

2nd and 4th Laws – Predicting detection and duration Formula 2.2 indicates that metrics alerting to deficiencies in detective controls will predict short-term reductions in Operational Risk loss events, but increased future discoveries. The longer duration of these events, when they are finally discovered, will lead to the resulting losses being more severe (Figure 2.4). Additionally, as noted in Chapter 2, internal and external changes can also act as catalysts for the discovery of historical and ongoing Operational Risk events through serendipity. Consequently, Operational Risk managers should predict that increases in the detection of Operational Risk loss events will occur following internal changes (e.g. a system's migration); industry-wide incidents (e.g. SOREs); and economic shocks (see 7th Law below).

---

[9] A survey of 296 firms conducted by the FCA during 2017 and 2018 on cyber and technology resilience identified change management as the most important root cause. Other causes included capacity management and hardware issues (FCA November 2018).

5th Law – Predicting settlement There are some categories of Operational Risk where there are defined workflows for processing potential losses. For example, a proportion of customers' complaints received by a firm will eventually be settled and become loss events. So a spike in complaints in one year will be highly predictive of an increase in the payment of compensation to customers in subsequent years, although clearly at the point in time when this is identified, it is probably already too late to prevent the occurrence of these losses. Effective corrective/resilience controls, however, may help to ameliorate some of the resulting losses from these claims/litigation pipelines and also any associated reputational damage.

7th Law – Predicting occurrence/detection, and severity from correlations with business cycles Review of Figure 11.1 suggests that the most important predictive metrics will be economic factors (Table 11.1), with CPBP losses being the most sensitive to business cycles (Figure 1.4). The resulting Operational Risk losses may, however, not peak for a further five years (Figure 3.5), making their relationship to metrics difficult to determine. As described in Chapter 11, the interactions between Operational Risk and business cycles are very complex:

- *Occurrence/Detection:* The 7th Law states that the impacts of business cycles arise from a combination of changes in economic factors and stakeholder behaviours (Table 11.3). Operational Risk losses may rise as some existing losses are exacerbated; historical failures are uncovered; and the responses of banks, bankers, investors, customers and criminals alike to a crisis may lead to new losses. Analysis of losses after the Global Financial Crisis reveals complex changes in the profile of Operational Risk losses, with a pattern of initial decline and subsequent increases and peaks (Cope and Carrivick, 2013). These patterns vary between event types, and reflect the overlay of a variety of different economic and behavioural effects.
- *Severity (Velocity × Duration):* A number of the potential impacts resulting from Operational Risk events are sensitive to business cycles, as illustrated in Table 11.2. Additionally, sharp movements in some economic measures can both act as a trigger for the uncovering of historical failures, as well as exacerbating the scale of any resulting losses (Figure 11.4).

Table 13.4 is a revised version of Table 2.1 that has been reordered by the frequency of events from left to right, per Figure 1.3, and annotated to highlight three categories of risks based upon ORX data and the Author's views. The categorisations by frequency are driven by a mixture of the horizontals, the nature of events, e.g. all acts of God are infrequent; and the verticals, the Basel II event types, e.g. External Frauds are frequent:

1. *Frequent events, with impacts typically within one year* (Figure 11.9). EDPM losses are predominantly mistakes and omissions, and hence predictive metrics

TABLE 13.4 The applicability of metrics based upon the nature of events and their frequency

Basel II event taxonomy — Nature of the events (Table 5.2)	EDPM	EF	CPBP	EPWS	IF	BDSF	DPA
People — Mistakes and omissions	Stretch Business profile Preventive KCIs			Stretch Business profile Preventive KCIs		Stretch Business profile Preventive KCIs	N/A
People — Systemic misconduct			Economic KRIs Portfolios of detective KCIs Claims pipeline	Portfolios of detective KCIs Claims pipeline			
People — Misconduct by individuals							
People — Malicious acts					Portfolios of detective KCIs	Detective KCIs	
Systems[10] — Disruption of software			Portfolios of detective KCIs				
Systems[10] — Application malfunctions						Portfolios of predictive KRIs: ■ Change ■ Capacity ■ End of Life KCIs	
Systems[10] — Hardware failures							
Systems[10] — Disruption of data & storage							
Systems[10] — Disruption of own infrastructure							
Process — Design/systemic failure	RCSAs Detective KCIs		RCSAs Detective KCIs	RCSAs Detective KCIs			
External — Third- (and fourth-) party failures	Trends in performance		Trends in performance			Trends in performance	
External — Malicious acts		Business profile Preventive KCIs		N/A (Terrorism)		Preventive KCIs	N/A (Terrorism)
External — Acts of God				N/A		N/A	N/A

Based upon Figures 1.3 and 11.9: ▮ Frequent, with lags < 1 year ▮ Frequent, but with lags > 1 year ▯ Infrequent events

---

[10] System and process failures often also arise from human failures in designing these systems and processes. System failures may also arise from failures of operation.

244

will be linked to factors that make human errors more likely, e.g. stretch and business profile, and also the effectiveness of preventive controls, due to the persistent nature of human errors. Whilst External Frauds are malicious acts, the persistence of the threat also means that the status of KCIs for preventive controls will be predictive of future losses.

2. *Frequent events, but with lags of over a year* (Figure 11.9). For CPBP the nature of the events are typically individual or systemic misconduct. Consequently, the relevant metrics will be portfolios of detective, rather than predictive, metrics. The significant lags between and discovery and settlement means that a firm's current losses will reflect its historical controls and its pipeline of claims and litigation. The sensitivity of CPBP to business cycles, in particular, as a result of the responses of both banks and stakeholders to economic shocks, can also make economic factors predictive indicators.

3. *Infrequent events* that are sudden and inherently unpredictable, e.g. acts of God leading to Damage to Physical Assets obviously do not lend themselves to predictive metrics! For BDSF, firms typically suffer a plethora of minor IT issues with limited financial impacts. The causal factors that can be used as predictive metrics include capacity, the volume of change, hardware issues, e.g. the prevalence of end of life/end of support technology. These metrics, however, lack precision regarding the occurrence of infrequent but much more disruptive BDSF events. Finally, internal frauds are malicious acts for which the relevant metrics are again portfolios of detective, rather than predictive, metrics.

Conclusions

Whilst predictive metrics are not quite as unattainable as the Holy Grail, neither are they universal. The predictive powers of metrics are driven by the nature of the underlying events primarily mistakes and omissions; misconduct and malicious acts; and the associated lags, i.e. for CPBP and EPWS a firm's current losses will reflect its historical controls and its pipeline of claims and litigation. KRIs highlighting stretch may be doubly predictive, because stretch can both lead to an increase in events involving mistakes and omissions and also the failure of mitigating controls (Tables 5.2 and 5.3). The status of preventive controls will also be predictive regarding persistent threats, e.g. in the form of both human errors and professional criminals. Finally, the most important driver of Operational Risk losses is business cycles, making economic factors predictive KRIs. The 7th Law describes, however, the complexity of the relationships between business cycles and Operational Risk and indicates that only some of the consequences can be prevented, with prompt action, for example, losses arising from the inappropriate responses of banks, bankers, customers and criminals to economic shocks.

4. CHANGE MANAGEMENT

The Basel Committee's recent consultation document on sound practices for the management of Operational Risk includes greater prescription regarding the management of change. In particular paragraph 37 is new:

> 37. A bank should have policies and procedures defining the process for identifying, managing, challenging, approving and monitoring change on the basis of agreed objective criteria. Change implementation should be monitored by specific oversight controls. Change management policies and procedures should be subject to independent and regular review and update, and clearly allocate roles and responsibilities in accordance with the three-line-of-defence model, in particular:
>
> (a) The first line of defence should perform operational risk and control assessments of new products and initiatives.
> (b) The second line of defence [Corporate Operational Risk Function or CORF] should:
>   – Challenge the operational risk and control assessments of first line of defence, as well as
>   – Monitor the implementation of appropriate controls or remediation actions.

CORF should cover all phases of this process, from the identification and evaluation of the required change, through the decision-making and planning phases, to the implementation and post-implementation review. In addition, CORF should ensure that all relevant control groups (e.g. finance, compliance, legal, business, ICT [Information and Communication Technology], risk management) are involved as appropriate." (Basel Committee, 2020).

This guidance is sensible and reflects the significance of both products and services, and change as causal factors (Table 2.2). Change can be either day-to-day (Run The Bank, RTB) or more significant (Change The Bank, CTB). The range of initiatives are defined by the components of Figure 2.1, for example, the implementation of new technology and the retirement of end of life technology (Systems); the re-engineering of processes (Processes); the outsourcing and offshoring of activities (third and fourth parties); the opening and closure of offices (Infrastructure); a range of cost reduction initiatives; the introduction of new products and services, businesses and channels (Customers); and the disposal and wind-down of businesses.[11] This section considers

---

[11] The FCA's rulebook requires notification of " . . . any proposed restructuring, reorganisation or business expansion which could have a significant impact on the firm's risk profile or resources . . . " and " . . . any action which a firm proposes to take which would result in a material change in its capital adequacy or solvency . . . " (FCA Rulebook, SUP 15.3.8).

two types of change to a firm's business profile: the implementation of new technology and the introduction of new products, services and transactions.

1. Business profile – Implementation of new technology (Grimwade, 2016)

All change initiatives increase the Operational Risk profile of a firm in the short term, through their impacts on Business As Usual (BAU) processes and the risks associated with migrations. Change initiatives can also alter, "...for better, for worse..."[12] a firm's risk profile after each migration, and permanently with the final end-state. This is described below, and illustrated in Figure 13.4:

1. *Stresses on BAU activities (People: Mistakes and Omissions):* This may arise from either the redirection of experienced resources onto projects, leading to stretch, and/or through the delay of other initiatives that are required to enhance a firm's control framework.
2. *Risks of transition (Systems: Disruption of Software; Application Malfunction; or Data Corruption or Integration Failures):* Every time there is a change there is a risk that it will fail, e.g. the application fails or malfunctions; or migrated data

FIGURE 13.4   Illustration of the alteration of business and Operational Risk profiles due to change (Grimwade, 2016)

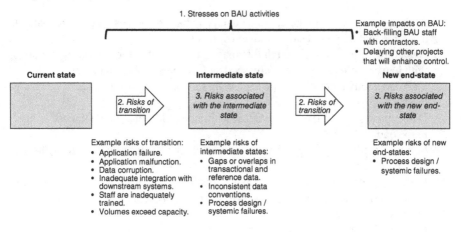

---

[12]An extract from the Church of England's marriage ceremony from the Book of Common Prayer.

is incomplete or inappropriate; or that the downstream systems are inadequately integrated. In addition there can be incidents caused by the lack of adequate staff training regarding new processes; or that new volumes may unexpectedly exceed planned capacity of either staff members or the new technology. In addition the migration process may also detect past Operational Risk incidents, e.g. trades that were incorrectly booked many years earlier.

3. *Risks associated with the intermediate and end-states (Process: Design/Systemic Failures):* Each intermediate state, as well as the end-state have new Operational Risk profiles, with the potential for losses arising from process design/systemic failures. The intermediate stages are potentially riskier, as to reduce the impacts of the risks of transition, described above, project managers often phase implementations. This means that firms may simultaneously run end of life and strategic applications with their data split between the two. This can lead to issues from gaps or overlaps in transactional data and inconsistencies in reference data and conventions (e.g. the treatment of Public Holidays) or end of day cut-off times. These can also have knock-on impacts on downstream systems if inadequately integrated.

Unfortunately, project managers traditionally focus on "Project Risks", i.e. the risks that the project will fail to deliver the required functionality, on time and to budget. These are not Operational Risks, however, common responses of project managers to initiatives that are running late tend to increase all of the risks described above, e.g.:

- Adding resources, with increased demands on RTB resources, as they are instantly available and may not lead to budget overruns.
- Extending milestones, although this may not be possible for regulatory initiatives with hard deadlines, or if the delivery date has been publicly announced, (See the TSB case study below), or if the firm wishes to Go Live prior to a year-end change freeze.
- De-scoping some of the functionality, leading to additional manual work arounds in the end-state.
- Splitting technology releases into more, smaller packages, leading to additional intermediate states.
- Reducing the levels of User Acceptance Testing (UAT) and raising the appetite of projects for the significance of open issues that are acceptable at Go Live, increasing risks of transition.
- Rescheduling tasks in parallel that were previously planned as sequential.
- Reducing contingency time to resolve issues identified through UAT testing.

CASE STUDY: 2018 TSB BANKING SYSTEM MIGRATION

Over the weekend of 21st and 22nd April 2018, TSB transferred approximately five million customers to a new platform. Unfortunately, customers immediately began to experience problems because the platform was not ready; and the third-party operator (TSB's parent, SABIS) was also unready to operate the system (Slaughter & May, 2019).

Go Live was the culmination of a complex programme, which began in March 2016, and had an original delivery date of September 2017. This first date was missed due to delays to Functional Testing. At the end of September 2017, a re-plan was completed and TSB announced that the migration would take place in Q1 2018. Unfortunately this deadline was also missed, and 22nd April 2018 was the next proposed Go Live date.

Following Go Live, approximately two million customers suffered significant impacts, for several months, including no access to online facilities, such as balance details and payments; and there were also breaches of customer confidentiality.[13] TSB suffered £330 million of additional costs including £125.2 million in customer compensation and £49.1 million in opportunistic fraud and operational losses.

There were a number of underlying causes to these issues. Firstly, Functional Testing was meant to be completed seven months prior to Go Live, allowing time for Performance Testing (capacity) and Data Migration testing. Functional Testing overran, however, leading to it being undertaken in parallel with the other testing, only ending a week before Go Live. As a result, substantially less Functional Testing was executed than planned. For the Performance Testing there was no dedicated test environment, and as a consequence it had to be undertaken in the production environment, which limited its scope. As a result, TSB failed to identify that their two "identical" data centres were not configured identically! In addition, the Performance Testing targets were lowered when the original targets could not be met.

Weaknesses in the management of the programme meant that the RAG status of the testing was misreported to give a more positive picture of progress. For example, two weeks prior to Go Live readiness was initially rated "Red" but was changed to "Grey – tbc", at the request of the CIO. Ten days later, Go Live

(Continued)

---

[13]NB GDPR only came into force on 25th May, 2018. Consequently, any penalties arising in the UK for data privacy breaches would be under the previous UK regime.

readiness was upgraded to "Green" from "Grey" by the CIO, despite some of the tests still being outstanding. Slaughter & May also analysed the bugs recorded, relating to the project, and identified that the backlog rose steadily in advance of the Go Live (Figure 13.5). Slaughter & May concluded that a report to the Board, prior to Go Live, did not present an "accurate picture" of outstanding bugs.

FIGURE 13.5   Open bugs on TSB's 2018 banking system migration[14]

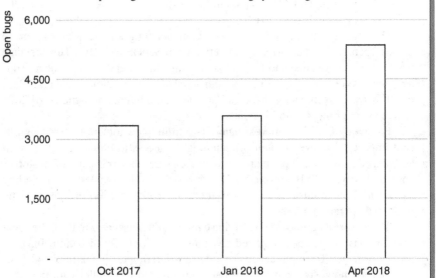

Both the Operational Risk management team (second line) and Internal Audit (3rd line) failed to provide effective challenge. The list of 22 programme risks remained unchanged for approximately 18 months despite the programme undergoing significant change. The risks on the register were also largely generic, e.g. "Management stretch" and specific risks were not identified. The lack of sufficient second-line resources with the necessary capabilities was a contributing factor. Additionally, whilst Internal Audit reviewed a number of areas that turned out to be very important, they either failed to identify key issues or the resulting actions were not followed through.

---

[14]TSB disagreed with Slaughter & May's analysis, and the parties failed to agree on how many bugs were live due to the disorganised recording of the bugs by the project.

Approaches to managing the Operational Risk arising from change initiatives

As per the Basel Committee's guidance, the risks arising from change need to be assessed by the first line. The second line should undertake both review and challenge and monitor the appropriateness of "... controls or remediation actions."

As the second line lacks the resources to review every change initiative within a firm, then it must prioritise the initiatives which are either inherently more risky (e.g. changes that relate to a firm's important business services (re: Operational Resilience) or higher risk products), or residually risky, due to issues with the quality of execution of the change initiative, e.g. an initiative that is persistently rated as "Red" and which has a hard deadline.

The framework for managing these risks must involve the identification of how change can alter a firm's business and Operational Risk profiles (Figures 2.1 and 13.4) and assessing the effectiveness of the mitigations. For example, for technology change:

1. *Stresses on BAU activities:* This can be monitored through trends in KRIs and KCIs focused upon signs of stretch, e.g. lags in performing regular tasks and resolving remedial actions; the status of key control attestations; and regular discussions with Department Heads. The impacts on BAU may be as a result of either an individual change initiative and/or the overall portfolio of change.

2. *Risks of transition:* The second line should assess the relevant preventive, detective and corrective/resilience controls, i.e.:
   - *Preventive controls:* These include requirements documents, project plans and associated planning assumptions, governance (steering committees and status reports) and logs of risks, issues and interdependencies. The second line should also review the adequacy of the projects budget and hence resourcing, i.e. what aspects of the project have not been funded. In reviewing these controls the second line needs to assess the quality of these controls (Table 13.1), for example, as noted in the TSB case study, that project had a risk log but the risks on it remained unchanged for 18 months.
   - *Detective controls:* These are focused on identifying issues with the effectiveness of the planned implementation, for example, progress with UAT testing and trends in bugs (Figure 13.5). The second line needs to identify reductions in the level of testing being conducted; the basis for any downgrades in open issues; and/or the basis of their assessment as being tolerable.
   - *Corrective/resilience controls:* These include run-books for Go Live weekends with "go/no-go" decision points and contingency plans for responding to post-Go Live issues.

3. *Risks associated with the new intermediate or end-states:* The first line should identify changes, e.g. in processes and/or data flows and put in place appropriate controls. The second line needs to review and challenge these assessments

and mitigations. The second line should in particular consider controls relating to any additional new manual processes introduced as a consequence of a failure to deliver the full scope of the requirements.

2. Business profile – Introduction of new products, services and transactions

Similar to other change initiatives, the risks associated with new products, services and transactions clearly need to be assessed (e.g. can a new product be: booked? confirmed? valued? settled? etc). Additionally, when firms are selling products to customers that involve the transference of Market and Credit Risks, then per the 9th Law on Risk Transference, Transformation and Conservation, they should understand the risks to their clients/investors. Figure 13.6 illustrates the Market Risk profiles of three quite different products:

- *Lower Risk*, e.g. a capital guaranteed deposit. A client's investment is used predominantly to purchase highly rated securities, and a small proportion is used to purchase options on an index, that will only be exercised if they are in the money. At worst the investor may lose a small and known percentage of their investment, but they may significantly benefit from a favourable market move. The risk of litigation on these products is low because an investor's potential losses are both limited and known in advance.
- *Medium Risk*, e.g. a long only fund. The value of an investment moves up and down with markets. The product is simple and easy to understand, but the investor could suffer significant losses, depending on the nature of the underlying assets.
- *Higher Risk*, e.g. precipice bonds. Investors in these products could receive a "high headline rate of return", as the funds write put options. If, however, following market falls the put options are exercised, then the investors could suffer significant losses. For example, the Extra Income and Growth Plan designed by Scottish Widows and distributed by Lloyds TSB between October 2000 and July 2001 (i.e. pre-9/11 and the bursting of the dot.com bubble) protected investors from an initial 33% fall in the price of the 30 individual underlying equities. But larger market falls led to investors losing at least 2% of their total investment for every 1% downward movement in the index.[15] By September 2003 investors had lost between 30% and 48% of their capital (FSA, 2003).

---

[15] *The Independent*, (12th April 2003) "The perils of precipice bonds".

FIGURE 13.6 Varying Market Risk profiles of products

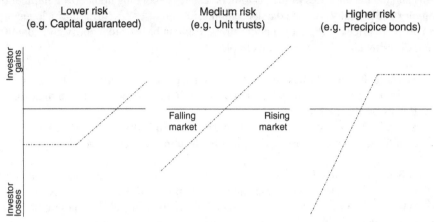

A product-specific stress test – a case study on equity release products

A product-specific stress test is designed to assess the impact of an adverse scenario on an institution's exposure to a financial product or portfolio, rather than at the enterprise or other aggregate level. Product-specific stress test scenarios can include but are not limited to liquidity constraints, client behaviour, cash flows, credit ratings or contract covenants. These stress tests can help identify and quantify risks associated with new or modified products/portfolios (Basel Committee, 2017b).

Equity release products address the challenge of an aging population, with increasing life expectancy, which may be asset rich but cash poor. There are two current versions of these products:

- *Lifetime Mortgages:* The customer takes out a mortgage which is repaid through the sale of their property on death or admission to residential care. Interest on the mortgage, which is fixed, compounds over the life of the mortgage, although it is capped at the eventual value of the property.
- *Home Reversion Plans:* The customer sells a percentage of their house at an under-value in return for a lump sum or an annuity. The bank receives its percentage of the proceeds of the eventual sale.[16]

---

[16]The Author's limited research into these products, by posing as a potential customer, seems to suggest that the pricing for these two products is similar, which is surprising, as providers of Home Reversion Plans have the same downside risks but they also benefit from upward movements in property prices.

There can be a range of favourable and less favourable outcomes for both the firms and the beneficiaries of the customers' estates depending upon how a number of complex and partially correlated risks combine, i.e. interest rates (firms only), longevity and property prices.[17] Product-specific stress tests can be used to identify and quantify these differing circumstances, for example:

1. Scenario 1: Interest rates stay low and house prices rise abruptly. The premature death of a customer can lead to a firm benefiting from a windfall gain on a Home Reversion Plan; whilst
2. Scenario 2: Interest rates rise and house prices fall. If a customer benefits from significantly increased longevity, then the firm may suffer a loss (Figure 13.7).

Adverse outcomes for customers and their beneficiaries may lead to claims of mis-sale of the product and/or unfair interest rate break costs on Lifetime Mortgages, especially as the product is sold to a potentially more vulnerable demographic. The industry mitigates these CPBP risks through customers receiving independent advice from both a financial adviser and a solicitor, although this does not mitigate Reputational Risk arising from client outcomes which are disproportionally beneficial to the firm.

The COVID-19 pandemic may potentially generate some losses for firms writing these products if it leads to the following combination of outcomes: falling house prices; low/negative interest rates; and raised morbidity rates. As a consequence, there will be higher break costs on any swaps (rather than options) that firms have taken out to hedge their fixed interest rate risk exposures on Lifetime Mortgages.

Conclusions

Change is a key causal factor for large Operational Risk losses. The very nature of change means that Operational Risk management tools need to be used in a much more dynamic and flexible manner than the usual periodic assessments. This involves variously identifying how the business profile of a firm is changing and mitigating the associated risks, whilst for new products and transactions firms must additionally assess the scale of risks of their customers suffering adverse outcomes in different economic situations. The value of in-flight second-line review and challenge is that Operational Risk management can both advise on the management of risks, to support safe business growth, and if necessary veto a new initiative, in order to support keeping the firm within appetite.

---

[17]The pricing should be similar to an annuity, but with a discount for the uncertainty over future property prices.

FIGURE 13.7 Different scenarios for equity release products

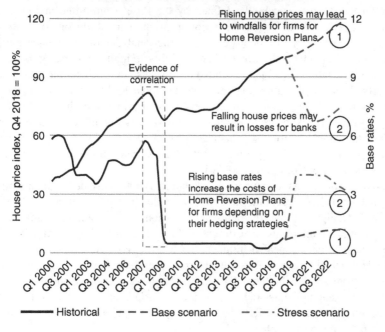

UK house price index and base rates:
Historical and BofE base and stress scenarios

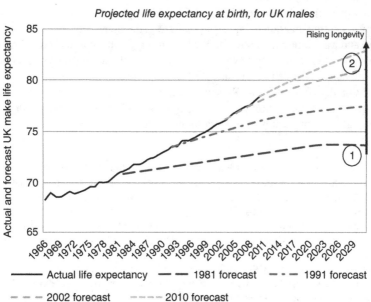

Projected life expectancy at birth, for UK males

5. REPUTATIONAL RISK QUANTIFICATION AND MANAGEMENT

Reputational Risk was succinctly defined by the Basel Committee in July 2009 as "... the risk arising from negative perception on the part of customers, counterparties, shareholders, investors, debt-holders, market analysts, other relevant parties or regulators that can adversely affect a bank's ability to maintain existing, or establish new, business relationships and continued access to sources of funding (e.g. through the interbank or securitisation markets). Reputational Risk is multidimensional and reflects the perception of other market participants. Furthermore, it exists throughout the organisation and exposure to Reputational Risk is essentially a function of the adequacy of the bank's internal risk management processes, as well as the manner and efficiency with which management responds to external influences on bank-related transactions." (Basel Committee, 2009c).

The range of internal and external stakeholders (both individuals and institutions) with which firms have a reputation is more completely captured in a revised version of Figure 2.1 (Figure 13.8). Incidents and decisions with reputational impacts alter the behaviours of all of these different stakeholders, including criminals and the different stakeholders can also influence each other, e.g. the actions/campaigns of Non-Governmental Organisations (NGOs) may alter the behaviours of shareholders.

Reputational Risk is both a risk that firms can proactively take and also an impact arising from a range of other risk events, including Operational Risk (Table 5.4). As a consequence, Reputational Risk has similarities to Operational Risk, in that it can originate from any part of a firm.

Firms proactively take Reputational Risk through the decisions that they make regarding accepting customers; agreeing loans (e.g. the financing of the Dakota Access Pipeline) and transactions; locating and relocating call centres; and closing branches,[18] etc. Even though a firm may have done nothing legally wrong these decisions may adversely impact a firm's reputation with certain of its stakeholders.

Additionally, Reputational Risk can result from incidents involving other categories of risks, i.e. Operational, Credit,[19] Market and Liquidity Risk.[20] For example, Reputational Risk can result from Operational Risk through the actions and misdeeds

---

[18]For example, an article in the FT (30th October 2015) entitled "RBS reneges on promise to safeguard 'the last bank in town'" stated that 165 RBS and NatWest branches that fitted the "last bank in town" criteria had been closed over the past two years, leaving those communities affected without a high street bank.

[19]For example the media coverage of Credit Suisse's losses following the collapses of Greensill Capital and Archegos in March 2021, and its credit rating outlook moving from "Stable" to "Negative".

[20]For example the disclosure by the BBC on 13th September 2007 that the Bank of England had agreed to provide Northern Rock with emergency financial support, as its lender of last resort, may have contributed the subsequent run on the Bank.

FIGURE 13.8 Internal and external stakeholders with whom firms have reputations (Revision of Figure 2.1)

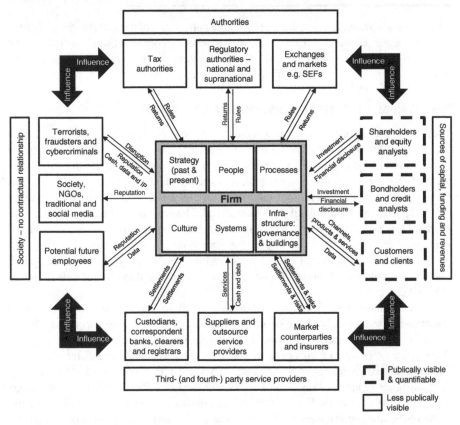

of staff (e.g. rogue traders and the rigging of LIBOR); human errors (e.g. fat-fingered typing); hacking incidents and systems failures (e.g. RBS's extended technology issues in 2012).[21] The remainder of this section focuses upon:

- Examples of quantification of reputational damage caused by Operational Risk events;
- Other measures of reputational damage; and
- Frameworks for managing Reputational Risk.

---

[21] As noted earlier, SYSC 13.4 of the FCA's handbook requires firms to "...notify the FCA immediately of any operational risk matter of which the FCA would reasonably expect "notice" including any" "significant failure in the firm's systems or controls."

QUANTIFICATION OF REPUTATIONAL DAMAGE ARISING FROM OPERATIONAL RISK EVENTS

As incidents with reputational impacts alter the behaviours of the stakeholders of firms, these consequences can be difficult to observe outside of organisations. The exceptions are the right-hand side of Figure 13.8, i.e. stakeholders that are sources of capital, funding or revenues. Examples of each are considered below:

Shareholders/investors – changes in behaviours

There have been various studies looking at the impacts of unexpected Operational Risk incidents on the market capitalisations of financial institutions. Analysis undertaken prior to the Global Financial Crisis indicated that the initial impact of the announcement of an unexpected Operational Risk loss is equivalent to the scale of the loss, but that over the subsequent 6 months the total return to shareholders, relative to a market index, declined by a multiple of the loss suffered. The scale of the impacts of returns to shareholders varied depending on the nature of the event. Operational Risk incidents which had the most significant impacts on shareholder returns included instances of deceptive sales practices and concealment; antitrust violations (e.g. price fixing and market manipulation); failures of regulatory compliance; and internal frauds (Dunnett et al, 2005).

Unexpected Operational Risk incidents have these impacts on total shareholder returns because they either have or are perceived to have a genuine impact on a firm's business. The charts below contrast the apparent impact (or lack of impact) on the share prices, relative to their peers, of two banks that both suffered differing sudden Operational Risk incidents. In September 2016, Wells Fargo was fined $185 million by the Consumer Financial Protection Bureau and the OCC for its staff members opening approximately two million unauthorised customer accounts in the US. Despite the value of the fine representing just 0.1% of the Bank's total equity, six weeks after the announcement Wells Fargo's share price was down approximately 15% in comparison to three peer banks. In contrast the announcement in January 2004 by NAB of A$360 million (1.4% of the Bank's total equity) of unauthorised trading losses incurred by four FX option traders led to no discernible impact on the Bank's share price relative to its three peers, despite the losses representing a higher percentage of NAB's total equity (Figure 13.9).

This illustrates that the impact of an incident on share price is driven by a variety of factors, not just scale of the unexpected Operational Risk losses. In these cases the relevance of the losses to the business strategies of the two banks may have been significant, i.e. cross-selling was core to Wells Fargo's strategy, whilst FX option trading was not core to NAB's strategy.

Finally, in some instances the share price of a firm impacted by a reputationally damaging incident may actually rise, possibly reflecting that the wounded firm has become a takeover target.

FIGURE 13.9 The differing impacts of Operational Risk events on share prices

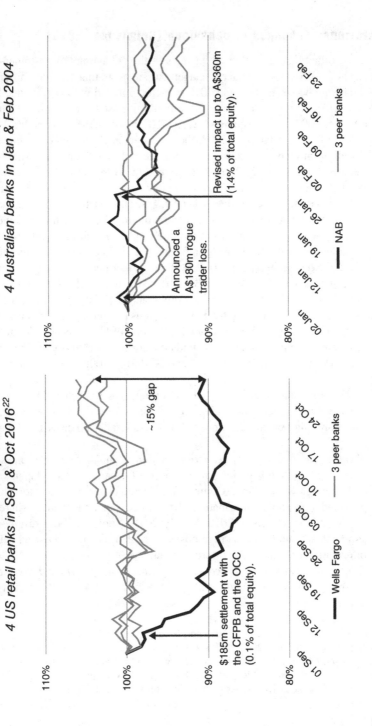

Movements in the share prices of 4 US retail banks in Sep & Oct 2016[22]

Movements in the share prices of 4 Australian banks in Jan & Feb 2004

~15% gap

$185m settlement with the CFPB and the OCC (0.1% of total equity).

Announced a A$180m rogue trader loss.

Revised impact up to A$360m (1.4% of total equity).

Wells Fargo — 3 peer banks

NAB — 3 peer banks

[22]Thaler's model for the reaction of market prices to information involves an initial under-reaction, followed by adjustment and overreaction.

Customers – changes in behaviour (Grimwade, 2016)

There is limited data available on changes in the behaviours of customers, however, a review of UBS's assets under management suggests that the firm suffered reputational damage between 2008 and 2010, which coincided with two events. Significant losses on US subprime which led UBS initially to raise CHF13 billion from investors in December 2007,[23] followed by a further CHF16 billion through a rights issue in June 2008,[24] and finally in October 2008, the Swiss government agreed to inject a further CHF6 billion into the Bank through the purchase of mandatory convertible notes.[25]

Separately, in February 2009, UBS agreed to settle criminal charges with the US Justice Department through a $780 million payment and to reveal the identities of 280 clients that it assisted to seriously evade US taxes. This disclosure of the names required the Swiss regulators to draft an emergency regulation. Subsequently, in June 2010, the Swiss Parliament agreed a treaty with the US enabling their tax authorities to provide the US authorities with the details of a further 4,450 US customers. This enabled UBS to settle civil charges in August 2010, without further penalties.[26,27]

During this 2½-year period UBS suffered a net outflow of ~CHF200 billion in assets from its Wealth Management division, potentially reflecting the combined effects of this US case and also the Bank's various capital injections during the Global Financial Crisis. As illustrated (Figure 13.10), one of UBS's peers, Credit Suisse, did not experience a similar outflow of funds during this period, maybe because it only raised an additional CHF10 billion of capital during 2008 from a group of strategic investors.

As Wealth Management firms and Asset Managers often charge fees based on their assets under management, the P&L effect of this outflow can be readily estimated.

There are other examples of misconduct visibly altering customer behaviours:

- *Nomura suffered a 45% reduction in equity underwriting* in Japan in 2012 following regulatory action on its abuse of customer data. Japan's Securities & Exchange Surveillance Commission found that employees for Nomura had provided non-public information about three separate planned share offerings to institutional clients in 2010. In July 2012, Nomura's CEO resigned after the company said there was a "high possibility" that its employees had leaked inside information on other share offerings to clients.
- *Citigroup suffered a 78% reduction in European government bond underwriting* following its "Dr Evil" trading strategy in 2004, i.e. its market share fell

---

[23] *Reuters*, (10th December 2007) "UBS gets Singapore capital injection".
[24] UBS website, (13th June 2008) "UBS AG successfully completes its rights offering".
[25] *The Financial Times*, (16th October 2008) "Swiss to fund $60bn 'bad bank' for UBS".
[26] *Reuters*, (9th April) Special Report: "How the U.S. cracked open secret vaults at UBS".
[27] *Reuters*, (17th June 2010) "Swiss parliament approves UBS-U.S. tax deal".

FIGURE 13.10 "A heavy two-year outflow of funds from its wealthy clients"[28] (Grimwade, 2016)

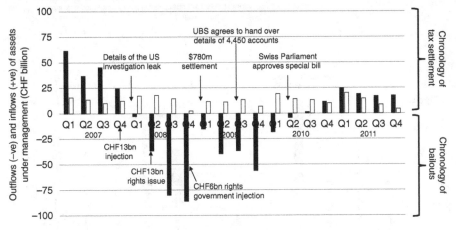

■ UBS Wealth & Asset Management   □ Credit Suisse Wealth & Asset Management

from 10.1% to 2.3%. The "Dr Evil" strategy involved Citigroup building up a large position in European government bonds and then selling them rapidly – €11 billion were sold in just 18 seconds on the MTS platform (FSA, 2005). One of the stated objectives was that "...over time, [it] may help to kill off some of the smaller dealers."[29,30]

Bondholders/credit rating agencies – changes in behaviour

Operational Risk incidents can also impact a firm's credit rating. These can be assessed by reviewing the impacts of sudden and material Operational Risk incidents on a firm's credit rating[31] (Figure 13.11). The analysis below focuses on 12 such incidents spread over a decade, and shows that whilst the scale of loss and its proportion of shareholder's equity is important they are not the only factors considered.

---

[28] *The Wall Street Journal*, (27th October 2010) "UBS stanches outflow of funds".

[29] *The Financial Times*, (1st February 2005) "Citigroup bond trading memo revealed".

[30] *Bloomberg*, (23rd July 2006) "Citigroup Haunted by Dr. Evil, Fails to Gain Governments' Trust".

[31] This reflects the most significant response from one of two credit ratings agencies reviewed.

FIGURE 13.11   Impacts of unexpected Operational Risk events on credit ratings

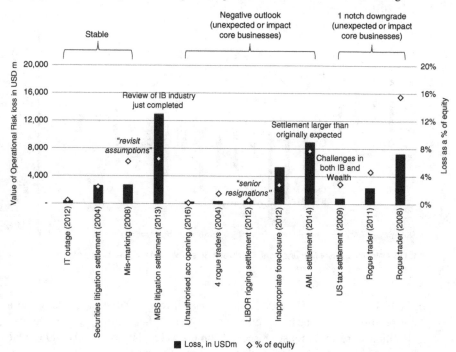

The incidents that have greater impact on credit ratings are high velocity (3rd Law) and unexpected (i.e. they have short lags, 5th Law) and impact a firm's core business. Conversely, events that are low velocity and have extended lags and that relate to non-core activities seem to be less impactful.

Other measures of reputational damage

Whilst other impacts may be both less visible to the outside world, they can be equally impactful. A firm's track record and reputation with its regulators may also impact the scale of fines and penalties that may be imposed. As mentioned earlier, the FCA's process for determining the financial penalties that it imposes on firms involves the assessment of "Mitigating and aggravating factors" (Step 3, see Table 9.1). Aggravating factors might include the firm's responsiveness to regulatory warnings, and fines imposed on other institutions, as well as previous final notices imposed on the firm. If a firm loses credibility with its regulators, then this may result in the visible departure of senior staff, much closer regulatory supervision (e.g. Section 166 reviews) and higher Pillar 2A capital add-ons; however, most of these will be invisible outside of the firm.

Other less tangible impacts, such as reductions in staff morale, may be evidenced through increasing absenteeism and staff turnover and unfilled vacancies, as attracting new staff is more difficult.

Observable impacts of societal pressure, e.g. media coverage or NGO campaigns (Grimwade, 2016)

The media coverage of firms can also have an impact on the behaviour of managers within banks. For example, at the height of the Global Financial Crisis the LIBOR submissions of firms were seen as a barometer of their ability to raise funds readily from other firms. An article on Bloomberg in September 2007 entitled "Barclays takes a money market beating" included the phrase "what the hell is happening at Barclays and Barclays Capital securities unit that is prompting its peers to charge it premium interest rates in the money market?" In the aftermath of the run on Northern Rock in September 2007, the questioning of Barclay's high LIBOR submissions by the media caused concern amongst Barclays' senior management. This in turn was translated by less senior managers into instructions to the LIBOR submitters at Barclays to lower their submissions in late 2007 and early 2008, so that they were in line with other firms... "just set it where everyone else sets it, we don't want to be standing out". (Recording of a conference call, on 19th March, 2008, two days after the rescue of Bear Sterns by JPMorgan Chase).

Similarly, in August 2015, Standard Chartered withdrew from an advisory role on the development of the Carmichael Coalmine in Queensland, Australia, after a concerted campaign by the NGO Greenpeace and legal actions against the project's approval by the federal government.

Observable impacts of expected reputational damage

One of the lessons learnt for the Basel Committee from the Global Financial Crisis was that firms attempted to support off-balance sheet structures that they had established *beyond* their contractual obligations. These types of off-balance sheet vehicles and structures include securitisation structures such as Asset-Backed Commercial Paper conduits and Structured Investment Vehicles (SIVs); structured products manufactured by a bank and distributed to its customers; sponsorship of money market mutual funds; in-house hedge funds; and real estate investment trusts. Examples of this support include, in November 2007, Bank of America announcing that it planned to set aside $600 million to cover potential losses in two money market funds managed by a subsidiary.

Across the industry, the support of these structures, in order to protect the reputations of individual firms, exposed banks to additional and unexpected Credit, Market and Liquidity Risks. Bringing these assets onto their balance sheets also put significant pressure on their financial profiles and capital ratios. As a consequence, the Basel

Committee expects that the processes for approving new products or strategic initiatives should consider the potential provision of implicit support, and that this should be reflected in firms' ICAAPs (Basel Committee, 2009c).

Frameworks for managing Reputational Risk

The similarities between Reputational and Operational Risk (i.e. they can both be proactively and passively taken and they can both arise from any part of a firm) means that the frameworks for their management are both similar (Figure 17.5) and overlapping.

Proactive management: (Grimwade, 2016)

The proactive management of a firm's reputation may involve:

- *Change:* Escalation and approval of Reputational Risks associated with key changes, e.g. new products (Figure 13.6); transactions (e.g. Climate Change, Transition Risks [Chapter 16]); markets; business changes (e.g. branch closures) and customers.
- *Scenario analysis,* i.e. includes the identification of impacts that may be damaging to a firm's reputation. As noted earlier, changes in behaviour are obviously unpredictable; however, firms can utilise historical examples of reputational damage to estimate the range of potential impacts and the associated drivers.
- *Stress testing* to understand the consequences and second round orders of Reputational Risk. As described above, this could include stressing special purpose vehicles for which the firm has no legal obligations to provide support, but may do so to protect its reputation, or circumstances in which customers are disproportionately disadvantaged and firms are disproportionately advantaged (Figure 13.7).
- *Reverse stress testing,* i.e. inclusion of scenarios that are damaging to a firm's reputation and consequently may impact the viability of a firm's business plan (Figure 12.3). Probably, with the run on Northern Rock in mind, the Basel Committee expects firms to consider the impact of Reputational Risk on their overall liquidity position, and specifically how increases in the asset side of the balance sheet can be funded following "...possible restrictions on funding, should the loss of reputation result in various counterparties' loss of confidence".
- *Monthly or quarterly reporting:* A Senior Management committee should periodically receive details of incidents and decisions that have the potential to affect a firm's reputation, and any actions taken to protect the firm's reputation (e.g. transactions rejected where reputation was a consideration) and emerging threats. In addition, firms can define for each of their groups of stakeholders KRIs which may indicate the direction of travel of the firm's reputation, e.g. reputation with current staff members may be inferred by tracking trends in staff turnover and staff

satisfaction surveys, whilst the firm's reputation with potential staff members may be inferred from the duration of unfilled vacancies. Equally, retail banking firms can survey customer satisfaction (e.g. % of sampled customers that "Would recommend the bank to a friend?") and firms can monitor trends in positive and negative media coverage.

Reactive management

The reactive management of a firm's reputation involves incident management. A firm's response to any material incident will involve a consideration of the potential impacts on a firm's stakeholders. Research has shown that the way firms communicate details of unexpected Operational Risk events can variously delay or exacerbate the market's response (Dunnett et al, 2005). The communications that form part of a firm's response to an incident constitute corrective/resilience controls.

CONCLUSIONS

The key success factors for managing Reputational Risks are to embed its consideration within existing risk management processes and to provide training to staff on what is and is not acceptable.

OVERALL CONCLUSIONS

The essence of all of these day-to-day risk management processes is that they involve Operational Risk managers dynamically assessing risks and controls and making judgements, leading to actions. These may be reactive, e.g. relating to incident management, the status of key controls and predictive metrics. They may also be proactive, i.e. Operational Risk management's role in approving and monitoring change. Combined, they assist firms to stay within appetite through the 8th Law: Risk Homeostasis.

Consequently, they represent some of the most valuable activities that Operational Risk managers undertake. Understanding the nature of Operational Risk, i.e. the laws governing occurrence, detection/duration and velocity and the associated controls can underpin these assessments and judgements.

The content of this chapter illustrates how the Ten Laws can be used to enhance these tools through a better understanding of the behaviours of Operational Risk.

CHAPTER 14

Conclusions

The ambition of Part Two has been to utilise the Ten Laws to redesign for success the Operational Risk management profession's tools. This brief final chapter will consider the nature of both the tools used by the profession and the enhancements that are proposed.

Articulating Risk Appetite (Chapter 7) serves two broad purposes, i.e. to "evaluate opportunities for appropriate risktaking" and as a trigger for action in response to "excessive risk-taking" (FSB, 2013) for proactively taken Operational Risk or excessive passive risk exposures (10th Law). The value derived from the various Operational Risk management tools reflects the effectiveness with which they support these two purposes. Chapter 7 describes the extent to which different measures of appetite are most useful for specific categories of risk and also proactive or reactive decision making.

Overview of the Operational Risk management profession's tools

The tools listed in this section (and other books on Operational Risk management) are dominated by periodic risk assessment activities, i.e. RCSAs, scenario analysis, capital modelling and stress and reverse stress testing. Although, in practice, Operational Risk managers spend the majority of their time carrying out the day-to-day activities listed in Chapter 13 (Figure 14.1).

The tools that are used periodically all assess and articulate a firm's Operational Risk profile in terms of likelihood and severity, focused upon the more remote risks and the associated controls. RCSAs do this qualitatively, whilst scenario analysis, capital modelling, stress testing and reverse stress testing are all quantitative assessments. This may reflect both the regulatory focus on quantification (enshrined in both Basel II and III) and the extent to which estimating likelihoods is inherently difficult for humans due to the existence of various biases (Chapter 4), and hence the need for well-defined and systematic approaches.

In contrast the tools used dynamically on a more day-to-day basis are designed to keep a firm within appetite regarding higher frequency risks/day-to-day losses. These

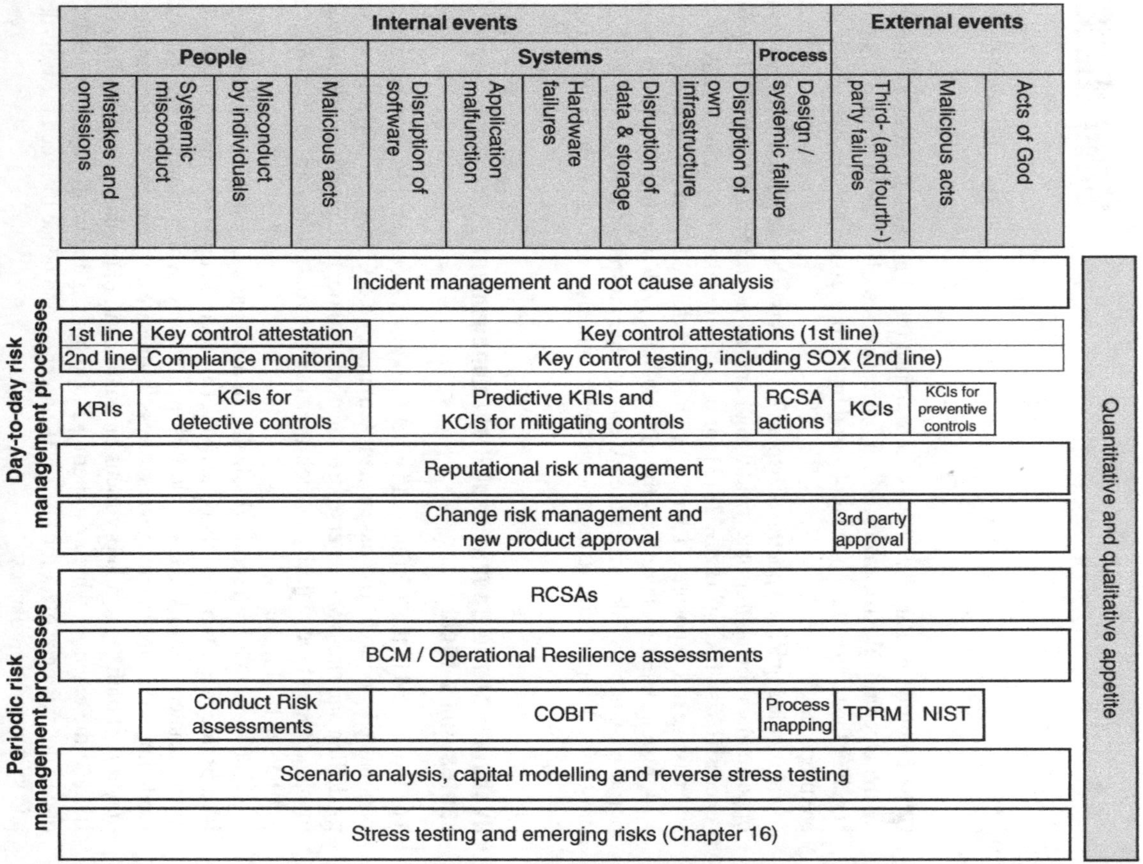

FIGURE 14.1 Integrating the Operational Risk management tools with other specialist tools

activities are a mixture of proactive and reactive responses, i.e.: conducting root cause analysis on incidents (reactive); monitoring trends in KRIs (proactive) and KCIs (reactive); undertaking control assurance (proactive); reviewing business change (e.g. IT change and new products); and advising/signing-off on the appropriateness of the proposed controls (proactive). Additionally, they also involve tracking the progress of remedial actions, confirming their completion and reporting on their firm's Operational Risk profile to key stakeholders. These day-to-day tools underpin the 8th Law: Risk Homeostasis, through the identification and the remediation of current issues and by ensuring that risks associated with new activities are appropriately mitigated.

Enhancements to day-to-day Operational Risk management tools (Chapter 13)

The key learnings taken from the part one of this book for these day-to-day activities are as follows:

Incident management: The first three laws imply that there are potentially three categories of actions that firms should take in the aftermath of an incident, linked to the three types of controls, i.e. they should be prioritised from right to left in the revised butterfly diagram (Figure 6.3):

1. *Corrective/resilience actions* immediately taken to curtail any further losses;
2. *Detective actions* to identify the scope of the incident/issue, e.g. is the incident an isolated mistake or omission or an example of systemic failure due to a badly designed process or systematic misconduct; and
3. *Preventive actions* to limit the likelihood and the impacts of recurrence.

Root cause analysis: Reviewing the first four laws indicates that causal factors relating to Operational Risk incidents can be grouped under one of more of the following five headings:

1. Occurrence (1st Law), i.e. why the event occurred?
2. Preventive controls (1st Law), i.e. why these controls failed, allowing the incident to occur?
3. Detective controls/duration (2nd Law), i.e. why these controls failed, allowing the incident to persist?
4. Velocity (3rd Law), i.e. why the losses were incurred so rapidly?
5. Corrective/resilience controls (3rd and 4th Laws), i.e. why these controls failed to limit the scale of loss?

   Patterns in causes should also be tracked as internal causal factors may be both correlated (Figure 5.2) and also reinforce each other, producing feedback loops and domino effects, driving the concentration of loss events in individual firms (6th Law). The strongest correlations seem to be between strategy; culture; governance; people; and processes.

Control assurance and the nature of control failures: The nature of the inadequacies or failures which constitute events (1st Law and Table 2.1) are the same as the nature of controls failures (Table 5.3). This should drive the types of tests undertaken, as part of control assurance work, in particular focusing on operational effectiveness/control failures due to mistakes and omissions, such as the failure to perform a control or to act upon an exception.

Predictive metrics: The effectiveness of metrics at predicting the occurrence of events are clearly more readily demonstrable for those that occur more frequently (1st Law and Figure 1.3) and also those with short lags between detection and settlement (5th Law and Figure 11.9). In these circumstances, metrics linked to causal factors that drive occurrence will be predictive, e.g. metrics for signs of stretch may be predictive of the occurrence of both events and control failures involving mistakes and omissions. Metrics relating to the effectiveness of controls that prevent a persistent external threat of malicious acts (e.g. cybercrime) will also be highly predictive of the occurrence of these events, as any control weakness is likely to be exploited.[1] Metrics linked to the operational effectiveness of detective and corrective/resilience controls will be predictive of the duration (2nd Laws) and scale of loss events (3rd and 4th Laws), but this is contingent on an event occurring. Finally, review of Figure 11.1 suggests that the most important predictive metrics will be economic factors (Table 11.1), with CPBP losses being the most sensitive to business cycles (Figure 1.4), although the relationships are very complex.

Change management: Assessing the Operational Risks arising from change involves considering the different states of a firm's business profile: the stresses on BAU activities; the risks of transition/migration and the intermediate and end-states. For both the risks of transition and the intermediate and end-states, Operational Risk managers should assess the appropriateness of the preventive, detective and corrective/resilience controls (1st, 2nd and 3rd Laws). For new business approval, Operational Risk managers should pay particular attention to products and transactions that transfer Market and Credit Risks to their customers (9th Law) and the profile of these risks (Figure 13.6).

---

[1]In December 2020 the Reserve Bank of New Zealand suffered a data breach relating to a File Transfer Application provided by a vendor, Accellion. The vendor detected a vulnerability in mid-December and advised its customers to install a patch which was deployed on 24th December. The Reserve Bank of New Zealand was breached the next day, Christmas Day, most likely prior to implementing the patch. The very act of Accellion notifying its clients of the vulnerability may have alerted criminals.

Reputational Risk: The stakeholders with which a firm has a reputation are set out in Figure 2.1. The potential impacts involve changes in stakeholder behaviours, i.e. both changes in existing behaviours and/or new behaviours (Table 5.4). These may change as a result of either proactive decisions taken by firms, e.g. regarding their customers and products, etc., or as a consequence of events, such as an IT outage, or a rogue trader event or a regulatory settlement (Figure 13.11). The proactive taking of Reputational Risk and its reactive management after an event can be managed in a comparable manner to Operational Risk.

Enhancements to periodic Operational Risk management tools

As previously noted, estimating the likelihood and severity of Operational Risks is inherently difficult due to the existence of human biases, but fortunately by providing insights into the behaviour of Operational Risk, the Ten Laws can improve RCSAs, scenario analysis, capital modelling and stress and reverse stress testing.

RCSAs (Chapter 8) The 2019 ORX survey (ORX, 2020) highlighted a number of issues with RCSAs, i.e. they are often out of date, are not informative enough, and the process is inefficient. The key enhancements proposed to RCSAs relate primarily to the scope of the exercise, in order to obtain more value:

- *Scope – business profile:* RCSAs should be driven from the business profiles of firms (Figure 2.1, 1st Law) to ensure the completeness of the scope of the exercise. Operational Risk managers should in particular focus on businesses that provide services as proactively taking Operational Risk is "disproportionately risky" (10th Law).
- *Scope – causes:* RCSAs should include the identification of the most important internal causes, as these increase the occurrence of inadequacies or failures that constitute both events and control failures (Figure 6.3, 1st to 5th Laws).
- *Scope – prioritise risks* that lead to either high velocity losses (3rd Law) or the slow accretion of larger losses over time (4th Law), through systemic failure (Table 5.4). Ensure that the regularity of the mitigating controls are aligned to the velocity of the risks (Figure 2.3).
- *Scope – deprioritise risks* that generate high volume:low value losses arising from mistakes and omissions that will naturally be remediated through the day-to-day Operational Risk management practices (8th Law).
- *Inadequacies or failures* (both events and control failures): The natures of events or control failures need to be identified, as this indicates the relative likelihood of occurrence, for example, mistakes and omissions are commonplace; systematic misconduct is rarer; and acts of God are even more remote (Table 2.1, 1st Law).

- *Duration of events:* A firm's current year's losses may be driven by weaknesses in both its current and historical preventive controls and also its current detective controls (2nd Law). Consequently, Operational Risk managers should avoid *just* undertaking trigger-based RCSAs.
- *Design effectiveness:* The focus should be on the design effectiveness of controls, which is relatively stable and drives remedial actions. Whilst operating effectiveness should be assessed through the day-to-day control assurance activities described in Chapter 13.
- *Risk profile:* Representing complex risks as just two data points for inherent and residual risks is overly simplistic. The use of spectrum diagrams (Figure 8.2) may better capture the continuous or discontinuous nature of some key Operational Risks.

Scenario analysis (Chapter 9) The first four laws describe the drivers for both the occurrence of events (inadequacies or failures) and their impacts (velocity × duration). The nature of the events and of the impacts can drive more tailored and systematic approaches for their estimation:

- *Impacts:* The nature of the different impacts (Table 5.4, 3rd Law) allows for bespoke techniques to be used for their estimation, whether Market Risk boundary losses; restitution/compensation; theft of assets; or regulatory fines.
- *Likelihood – nature of events:* Similarly the techniques for estimating likelihood are specific to the particular nature of the events (Table 5.2, 1st Law) e.g. mistakes and omissions, systematic misconduct and acts of God.
- *Likelihood – persistent threats:* For cybercrime, due to the persistent nature of the threat, the design and operational effectiveness of the preventive controls can be used to assess the likelihood of a systematic control failure and hence the occurrence of a successful cyberattack.

Capital modelling (Chapter 10) An approach to capital modelling is proposed that reflects the Ten Laws, primarily the sensitivity of Operational Risk to economic cycles (7th Law) and the very significant lags between detection and settlement of CPBP losses (5th Law) which leads to a distribution of capital that resembles an hourglass:

- *Pillar 1:* Includes Operational Risk losses that crystallise suddenly and are insensitive to economic cycles (Figures 11.1 and 11.9).
- *Pillar 2A:* Includes risks not adequately covered in Pillar 1, e.g. emerging risks, risk concentrations and changes in business models.
- *Pillar 2B:* Includes risks that are sensitive to economic cycles (7th Law) and that also demonstrate significant lags (5th Law). This is again illustrated in Figures 11.1 and 11.9.

Risks that are both insensitive to economic cycles and display significant lags could simply be accrued, as they crystallise over many years and are generally uncorrelated with Market and Credit Risk losses.[2]

Stress testing (Chapter 11) Despite the extensive regulatory guidance on stress testing, there is a dearth of detail on the mechanism by which an economic shock leads to spikes in Operational Risk losses. The Ten Laws provide insights:

- *Mechanism:* The 7th Law states that after an economic shock, some Operational Risk losses rise: existing losses are exacerbated, historical failures uncovered and responses to a crisis may lead to new losses. Occurrence, velocity and duration of Operational Risk losses all increase. Losses arising from the uncovering of historical misconduct can be explained through the Real Option Model (Grimwade, 2016).
- *Occurrence:* The increase in the occurrence of Operational Risk events results from a combination of direct sensitivities to specific economic factors and changes in stakeholder behaviours over time (Table 11.3).
- *Impacts:* The increase in the value of Operational Risk losses results from the direct sensitivity of specific impacts to economic factors (Table 11.2).
- *Lags in settlement:* The 7th Law states that after a severe downturn losses come in waves: first Market, then Credit and finally Operational Risk (Figure 11.2). These lags between detection and settlement vary between different Operational Risk event types (Figure 11.9 and Table 11.4). Analysis of large losses ($\geq$\$0.1 billion) suggests that these lags are significantly longer than is usually reflected in stress tests.
- *Risk Homeostasis (8th Law):* The enhancement of CPBP-related controls over the last decade, in response to these earlier losses, may mean, however, that Operational Risk losses arising from subsequent economic slowdowns (e.g. due to COVID-19) may be lower than those occurring after the Global Financial Crisis. This is despite the COVID-19 recession being potentially more severe.

Through a better understanding of the mechanism by which economic shocks alter Operational Risk losses, firms can produce more structured and meaningful stress test results.

Reverse stress testing and transference of Operational Risk via insurance (Chapter 12) The ECB has recently noted that when undertaking reverse stress testing firms primarily focus on breaches of SREP. Utilising the summary of the business profiles of firms indicates a more complete range of threat categories

---

[2]The observation that regulatory fines declined in 2020 may indicate that they are in fact negatively correlated with stressful events, in the short term (Risk.net, July 2020).

(Figure 12.1) relating to Operational Resilience; regulatory licences; and business plans (e.g. loss of customer revenues). Pleasingly, these can all be linked to real-world examples of incidents that have threatened the viability of the business plans of specific firms. Scenario analysis techniques described in Chapter 9 can also be applied to reverse stress testing.

As a mitigant of Operational Risk, insurance will always be restricted to the losses on the right-hand side of Figure 1.1, and a relatively small percentage of the total value of Operational Risk losses in any particular year. Understanding better the nature of a firm's Operational Risk profile through scenario analysis and capital modelling, and the extent to which events and impacts are insurable (Table 12.2) may enhance the procurement of insurance policies, with more appropriate coverage relative to appetite, i.e. the financial value of the cover; retention levels; and the range of risks covered.

CONCLUSIONS

As described in Chapter 6, the Ten Laws of Operational Risk are underpinned by three pillars:

1. *The business profiles of firms*, which determine both the profile of their risks and the potential quantum of failure (Table 2.5 and Figure 6.2).
2. *The nature of the three taxonomies*, i.e. inadequacies or failures; causal factors and impacts. The taxonomy of inadequacies or failures covers both the occurrence of events and also the failure of controls (Table 13.1).
3. *Human and institutional behaviours* influence the activities of a firm's stakeholders altering the occurrence of inadequacies or failures, such as misconduct and malicious acts. Human biases can also alter the assessment of remote risks and the extent to which firms learn lessons and consequently suffer fewer Operational Risk loss events over time (8th Law).

Whilst this is very intuitive, this section has attempted to apply systematically these self-evident truths[3] to enhance the Operational Risk management profession's tools to better assess these risks, relative to appetite and to "evaluate opportunities for appropriate risktaking" and act as a trigger for action in response to "excessive risk-taking" (FSB, 2013).

---

[3]This is a paraphrasing of the opening of the second paragraph of the US Declaration of Independence which begins with the statement from the Founding Fathers that "We hold these Truths to be self-evident...".

Three

Predictions of the Future Behaviours of Operational Risk

INTRODUCTION

It is emerging Operational Risks that are habitually cited as keeping executives awake at night. Consequently, Chapter 15 sets out techniques for more systematically identifying emerging risks, whilst Chapter 16 focuses on four current internal and external threats and utilises the Ten Laws to explain and predict how Operational Risk may respond in the future. The four current internal and external threats are:

1. Pandemics;
2. Climate Change;
3. Cybercrime; and
4. Technological advances, including algos, AI and machine learning.

CHAPTER 15

Identifying Emerging Risks

In Chapter 1 it was noted that over time certain categories of Operational Risk appear to be dynamic. The 7th Law states that the occurrence, velocity and duration of loss events can all be driven by external causes. The 8th Law also observes that "...for emerging risks, control expenditure will rise in anticipation of increased future losses". Hence the identification of emerging risks, whether changing existing risks or new risks[1] is an important activity for Operational Risk managers and should be focused upon the six[2] categories of external threats/causes set out, both below and previously in Table 2.2:

1. Society; **3.** Economic cycles; **5.** Geopolitics;
2. Technology; **4.** Environment; **6.** Regulation.

As a consequence of Example Bias (Chapter 4), humans find it more difficult to identify and assess events of which they have no direct experience. Consequently, Operational Risk managers need to adopt more systematic approaches for identifying emerging risks (Grimwade, 2019), i.e. they should consider:

1. *"What current trends will persist or accelerate?"* Some currently observable trends may continue to grow, e.g. the automation of banking driven by the confluence of technological and societal change, i.e. big data; AI and machine learning; changes in customer behaviours, especially Generations Y and Z, towards technology and social media.[3] The COVID-19 pandemic may have

---

[1] In 2016, ORX prepared an aggregated definition of emerging risks by reviewing the definitions of its members: "Emerging risks are either new or evolving existing risks. They have the potential to cause significant negative impact and could prevent the firm from meeting its business objectives" (ORX, 2016).
[2] Five of these threats reflect the World Economic Forum's high level risk categories, i.e. Economic; Environmental; Geopolitical; Societal, and Technological. Other sources of external threats include the analyses annually produced by the FCA and the IMF.
[3] Social media may both expand the number of individuals within a "herd" and accelerate the Herd Behaviour response.

further accelerated the existing industry trend towards online/mobile banking and contactless payments and away from branch banking, cheques and cash. This trend has been accompanied by the continued evolution of cybercrime. Whilst outside of financial services, in the wider environment, pathogens will continue to evolve drug resistance (Environment).

2. *"How may history repeat itself?"*[4] Similar economic circumstances may lead to the same outcomes (the 7th Law), e.g. in:

- 1988/89: A sharp movement (up) in GBP rates led to the Hammersmith & Fulham interest rate derivative (swaps) litigation;
- 1994: A sharp movement (up) in US rates led to the collapse of Orange County, and also interest rate derivative (swaps with embedded options) litigation;
- 2008/09: A sharp movement (down) in GBP rates also led to interest rate derivative (swaps and floors) litigation;
- 2001: The bursting of the dot.com bubble led to both regulatory action and securities (IPOs) litigation; and
- 2007/2008: The bursting of the US housing bubble also led to both regulatory action and securities (MBS and CDO) litigation.

    Based on these historical patterns, a sharp fall in economic activity and asset values, associated with a pandemic, or the bursting of an asset bubble, such as bitcoin(?), may also be expected to lead to litigation and Operational Risk losses (Economic cycles).

3. *"What trends in other markets may move into banking?"* Comparisons can be drawn with other markets, e.g. the dramatic impacts of disruptors, such as Uber, may be predictive of the changes that may be wrought upon banking by peer-to-peer lending, cryptocurrencies and other fintech ventures (Technology).

4. *"What are our 'known knowns'?"*[5] Some aspects of the future are actually quite certain in terms of both their occurrence and their timing, e.g. the human population will increase to 8.5 billion by 2030 (Society), whilst populations will contract and age in the developed world (Society); and the world will warm by at least 1 ½ to 2° C (Environment). Other aspects of the future are certain in terms of their occurrence but not their timing, e.g. solar weather will periodically disrupt communications and power transmission; and pandemics of varying intensities will regularly occur (Environment).

Firms should then identify any single points of failure e.g. SITEs,[6] and the interrelationships between these different external threats/causal factors that can impact

---

[4]When Karl Marx said "History repeats itself, first as tragedy, second as farce" he was referring to the accessions of Napoleon I and III.

[5]"There are known knowns – there are things we know we know." Donald Rumsfeld, US Secretary of Defence, February 2002.

[6]SITEs: Strategic Information Technology Enterprises, which are necessary for a firm's systems to operate. Other single points of failure include the undersea cables that support the internet and communications between countries and continents.

their Operational Risk profiles (Figure 15.1). Understanding these interrelationships is critical, as for example, the Commodity Futures Trading Commission (CFTC) notes regarding Climate Change that "... transition and physical risks – as well as climate and non-climate-related risks – could interact with each other, amplifying shocks and stresses" (CFTC, 2020). The complexity of Figure 15.1, is indicative of the challenges for firms of understanding these emerging threats.

A prominent feature of Figure 15.1 is the extent to which these various external threats/causes almost all impact economic cycles, and as a consequence the Operational Risk profiles of firms, through the 7th Law. As noted previously, some of these interrelationships reinforce each other, exacerbating their impacts and accelerating the pace of change by creating feedback loops; the combination of new technology and societal change is one such positive feedback loop, which also influences the behaviours of cybercriminals. Meanwhile, other emerging threats behave more like falling dominos/migration paths, i.e. the occurrence of one emerging threat naturally makes other events more likely to occur. For example, Brexit may lead to the break-up of the UK, followed by a sterling crisis and then an economic shock.

Once identified, firms need to consider the time horizons over which these emerging threats may crystallise (Figure 15.2). The World Economic Forum's 2021 report (World Economic Forum, 2021) categorises threats into three groups, i.e. clear and present dangers/short-term risks (0 to 2 years); knock-on effects/medium-term risks (3 to 5 years);[7] existential threats/long-term risks (5 to 10 years). Figure 15.2 highlights that the time horizons of some of these threats are both uncertain and may extend over many decades. For example in the case of Climate Change the full impacts may crystallise outside of many current business planning horizons (PRA, April 2019).

Figure 15.2 also illustrates how some of these emerging threats may be permanent features of the future (e.g. population growth and Climate Change) whilst others may recurrently emerge, peak and then decline, e.g. pandemics of different intensities are recurrent, whilst Y2K was anticipated and mitigated, at the turn of the century, with few incidents through significant industry effort and expenditure (8th Law).

Similarly the man-made hole in the Ozone Layer, which was discovered by the British Antarctic survey in 1985, should be closed by the mid-2030s, due to the rapid action taken in the late 1980s.[8]

Operational Risk managers additionally need to consider how these threats translate into management actions, e.g. the reduction in returns on equity, post the Global Financial Crisis, led banks to scale back or to close capital intensive businesses; to accelerate automation; to outsource and reduce headcount; and to expand fee generating businesses (Brei, 2019). Operational Risk managers must also consider how these threats will alter the behaviours of their various stakeholders (Figure 2.1). For example,

---

[7]Three to five years was the period highlighted in Q&A guidance from the FSA on reverse stress testing in April 2011.
[8]Margaret Thatcher, a chemist by training, was seen as being instrumental in persuading other world leaders to take action.

FIGURE 15.1   An illustration of the interrelationships between emerging threats, and their feedback loops and domino effects

NB Climate Change Transition Risks appear twice in Figure 15.1 as they can be driven by both Geopolitics, e.g. governments setting targets, and also by Society, e.g. people changing their purchasing decisions (Chapter 16). The economic factors are those stressed by the Bank of England in their stress tests (Chapter 11).

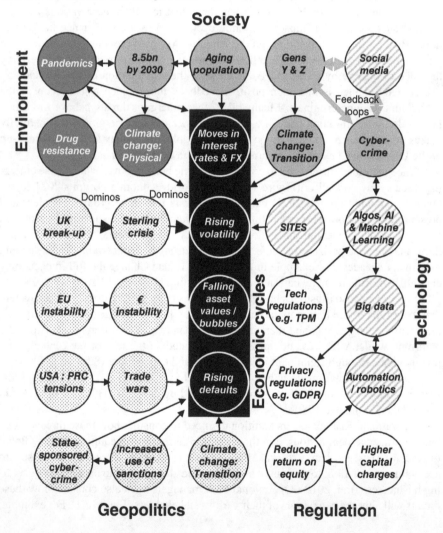

FIGURE 15.2 The differing time horizons of a sample of past and present emerging threats

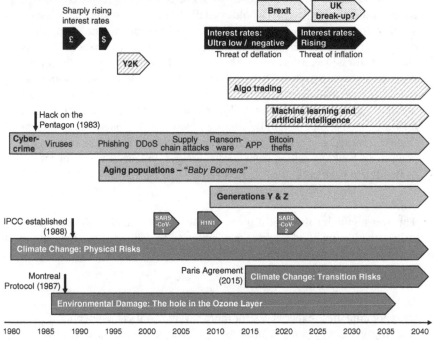

Viruses and pandemics: The SARS-CoV-1 coronavirus caused the SARS pandemic (2003); a strain of the H1N1 flu virus caused the Swine Flu pandemic (2009/10); and the SARS-CoV-2 coronavirus caused the COVID-19 pandemic (2020/21).

there may be changes in the fines imposed by regulators (Figure 4.2); the activity of criminals (Figure 11.3); and customer demand for products (Figure 11.8).

Finally, firms need to identify how these emerging threats and the responses of management may impact their Operational Risk profiles through both the creation of new risks and the exacerbation of existing risks, by utilising the Ten Laws to determine the impacts on occurrence, detection/duration and velocity. Whilst predicting the future behaviours of Operational Risk may sound an impossibility, in his earlier book the Author slightly prophetically wrote on the subject of pandemics:

> The World Bank predicts that a severe pandemic could reduce global wealth by around US$4 trillion, i.e., around 5% of global GDP. Although between 1997 and 2009 there were six major outbreaks of airborne infections, including SARS [SARS-CoV-1] and H1N1, none approached the scale of the 1918–19 Spanish flu pandemic [also a strain of H1N1], which infected

around 500 million people and killed between 50 and 100 million, or 3% to 5% of the world's then population.[9]

The impact of a major pandemic would be consistent with the effects of a sharp economic slowdown. It would crystallise latent misconduct issues, such as mis-sale claims relating to life-insurance policies and investment products that did not respond well to falling interest rates, as well as fixed-rate loans and interest-rate swaps, as central banks would try to stimulate the world's economy by cutting rates. There would also be specific business disruption risks, e.g., the challenges of trying to maintain a branch network when staff are ill or are caring for children following the closure of schools, or are just unwilling to risk their health by coming to work. Additionally, professional fraudsters would also probably take advantage of perceived weaknesses in the controls of banks, resulting from staff shortages, to launch wave after wave of fraudulent payments.

(Grimwade, 2016).

This text highlights that whilst predicting when a pandemic will occur is clearly impossible, the likelihood of a severe pandemic can be estimated by analysing recent history (Figure 15.2), and predicting the impacts of a severe pandemic is readily achievable by:

- Leveraging previous experiences of recent mild pandemics;
- Extrapolating these experiences for more severe historical pandemics;
- Drawing parallels from the impacts of recent economic shocks, although not caused by a pandemic, on the behaviours of the key stakeholders of firms; and
- Assessing how Operational Risk will respond, by utilising the Ten Laws.

Applying this in practice is explored further in Chapter 16 for four current internal and external threats.

---

[9] At the time of writing, COVID-19 had officially infected 221 million and killed 4.6 million (WHO COVID-19 Dashboard), although The Economist has estimated that the number of deaths is more accurately between 15 and 18 million (The Economist "The pandemic's true death toll", September 2021).

Predictions of the Future Behaviours of Operational Risk in Response to Four Emerging Threats

This chapter focuses on four current internal and external threats and utilises the Ten Laws to explain and predict the responses of Operational Risk. The four current internal and external threats are:

1. Pandemics;
2. Climate Change;
3. Cybercrime; and
4. Technological advances.

The nature of each of these threats is described and illustrated with relevant case studies. Predictions regarding the future behaviours of Operational Risk are systematically made by mapping the nature of these threats to the Ten Laws of Operational Risk.

1. PANDEMICS

This section describes the range of direct and indirect impacts of a pandemic, and uses the Ten Laws to illustrate their potential impacts on the Operational Risk profiles of firms. Given that the COVID-19 pandemic is still in progress at the time of writing, it is only the final section, which describes the timescales over which losses may crystallise, which may prove to be predictive, rather than just descriptive.

The direct impacts of pandemics on firms include the physical welfare of their staff. The indirect impacts are, however, much more varied and arise from a mixture of changes in the behaviours of a firm's stakeholders, as set out in Figure 2.1, including the actions taken by authorities, and the resulting economic consequences. Each will be considered in turn:

Authorities (e.g. governments and regulators): The responses of governments to stop the spread of pandemics, for which there are initially neither vaccines nor effective treatments (e.g. antibiotics or antiviral drugs), have largely remained unchanged over the centuries. For example, in the seventeenth century, King Charles II issued an order, in response to the Great Plague, which will be familiar to those experiencing the COVID-19 pandemic 350 years later, i.e. it mandated that:

- All houses were to be kept clean;
- No stranger was allowed to enter a town unless they had a certificate of health;
- No public gatherings, such as funerals, were to be held;
- Sick people were to be isolated in "pest-houses" on the edge of town to protect their families;
- The houses of the sick were to be sealed for 40 days. Warders were appointed to find the occupants "necessaries" and "to keep them from conversing with the sound"; and
- Parishes that could no longer maintain their poor would receive financial relief from neighbouring parishes (King Charles II, 1666).

The modern day national lockdowns, implemented by many governments during the COVID-19 pandemic, have meant that the majority of bank staff have had to work remotely. The closure of schools also reduces the working capacity of staff members who are the parents or carers for younger children, whilst the introduction of financial support for businesses through government-backed loans, e.g. the UK's COVID-19 Bounce Back Loans,[1] can create spikes in new business activity.

As noted previously in Chapter 11, there is also some evidence of changes in the behaviours of regulators, i.e. during the first wave of the COVID-19 pandemic, the number and value of regulatory settlements declined, maybe as a result of regulators redirecting their focus to supporting firms, rather than fining them for their past misconduct.

Sources of funding and/or revenues (e.g. customers): The uncertainty caused by pandemics may lead to a reduction in customer driven activity. For example, Figure 11.8 highlighted that a sharp reduction in the quarterly volume of UK mortgages for house purchases coincided with the commencement of the COVID-19 pandemic in 2020. There may also be changes in customer behaviour, i.e. the lower footfall in bank branches due to lockdown will result in compensating increases in the volume of customer traffic via other channels, i.e. call centres, mobile apps and online banking.

---

[1] Bounce Back Loans were launched by the UK Government in May 2020. They were a fast-track loan scheme to support Britain's sole traders and small to medium-sized businesses. The loans were unsecured and 100% UK Government guaranteed.

Third parties (e.g. market counterparties and investors): Pandemics will naturally also alter the behaviours of market counterparties and investors. As noted in Chapter 11, the COVID-19 pandemic drove dramatic changes in trade volumes in some markets, e.g. the volumes of UK equities traded increased 140% in March 2020 (44.8 million trades) in comparison to March 2019 (18.4 million trades). There was also an observable flight to assets traditionally seen as secure, for example, between 1st January and 30th June 2020 the value of gold rose by 24%, whilst the value of the FTSE 100 fell by 19%.

Society (including fraudsters and cybercriminals): As will be discussed later in this chapter, professional cybercriminals are rational,[2] they will seek to optimise the rewards that they obtain for the resources at their disposal. As previously noted in Chapter 11, the Global Financial Crisis led to reductions in new business volumes, leading criminals to change their attack vectors, i.e. away from application fraud and towards account takeover frauds (Figure 11.3). Whilst the outbreak of the COVID-19 pandemic has also been marked by a spike in account takeover frauds and ransomware attacks, in addition criminals have targeted emergency COVID-19 loans.[3]

Economic consequences

The economic consequences of a pandemic are many and varied, and arise from disruption to both supply caused by government restrictions, and reductions in demand due to changes in the behaviours of consumers and investors. The knock-on consequence crystallises over a range of time horizons.

In the short term this includes increased market volatility and directional moves of markets and asset values both up and down, as described earlier for both gold and equities. There may also be occurrences of market dislocations, e.g. the May WTI future hit levels of minus $40 per barrel(!) as producers began to run out of storage space for oil, as demand fell more rapidly than reductions in production. Falls in demand for oil impacted the currencies of major oil producing countries, e.g. the Russian Rouble depreciated by 32% against the USD between 1st January and 31st March 2020. These market consequences may then lead to defaults of market counterparties/trading houses that are unable to meet margin calls. Bricks and mortar retailers of non-essential goods also suffered from the loss of footfall due to lockdowns, leading to high-profile defaults. Monetary policy may become even looser than in the aftermath of the Global Financial Crisis, e.g. interest rates in the UK dropped to their lowest ever rate of 0.1% in March 2020, with the Monetary Policy Committee discussing in September 2020 "the effectiveness of negative policy rates".

---

[2] In Q4 2019, 98% of companies that paid a ransomware ransom received a working decryption tool (Coveware, 2020).

[3] In evidence to the Public Accounts Committee the UK Government disclosed that it had assumed an "error or fraud rate" of between 5% and 10% on its emergency COVID-19 loans.

In the medium term, a global economic slowdown, as forecast by the International Monetary Fund (IMF), would result in rising unemployment and defaults by both personal and corporate banking clients. The resulting reduction in tax receipts, accompanied by expanding government expenditure in unemployment benefits, would also lead to burgeoning deficits and falling debt yields, unless the possibility of sovereign default becomes a concern.

Applying the Ten Laws

As noted earlier, pandemics have both direct and indirect impacts on the Operational Risk profiles of firms. In addition to influencing the occurrence of events and the velocity of losses, pandemics can also lead to both the weakening of current controls and also the detection of historical events.

Direct impacts of the pandemic

Occurrence (1st Law): Direct impacts of the pandemic include the risks to the physical well-being of staff members (acts of God), and the associated costs incurred by firms to make their office environments as safe as possible. Medical safeguards include preventive controls, such as disinfection of offices and air-conditioning systems, personal protective equipment (PPE) and the deployment of Plexiglas barriers, and also detective controls, such as thermo-scanners and home and office test kits (EBA, 2020).

Indirect impacts of the pandemic: changes of behaviour of authorities (governments and regulators) The actions of governments in imposing lockdowns require firms to introduce a largely remote working operating model (Business Profile), whilst the closure of schools reduces the resources available to firms, as the working capacity of some staff members may be restricted by the need to care for younger children (Controls).

Occurrence (1st Law): The reduction in staffing levels and the fragmentation of manual processes, due to the use of remote working operating models, may increase the occurrence of both events and control failures (Table 13.1) through mistakes and omissions. This may be exacerbated by reduced response times due to poor connectivity/latency issues arising from the quality of individual staff members' Wi-Fi services. The heavy reliance on remote working also introduces a new single point of failure for firms, i.e. their remote access service provider. Firms may also incur additional costs in order to operate effectively via a remote working operating model, e.g. additional IT expenditure (EBA, 2020).[4] Some of these additional costs may be offset by claims against Business Interruption insurance policies (Chapter 12). Remote working by bank staff may also provide new

---

[4] Anecdotally Lloyds Banking Group bought ~20,000 laptops for its staff.

opportunities for criminals, e.g. through the deployment of key logging malware if staff members are using their own PCs to access bank systems.

Lags (5th Law): Any delays in regulators imposing penalties on firms, as appeared to occur in the early stages of the COVID-19 pandemic, will increase the lags between discovery and settlement.

Indirect impacts of the pandemic: changes in the behaviour of customers

Occurrence (1st Law): A reduction in some customer activities (e.g. the taking out of new loans) will naturally alter a firm's business profile and reduce the occurrence of events resulting from mistakes and omissions, primarily EDPM. The increase in the volume of customer traffic via call centres, mobile apps and online banking will, however, place greater pressure on the resilience of this infrastructure.

Indirect impacts of the pandemic: changes in the behaviour of investors and market counterparties

Occurrence (1st Law): Changes in the activities of investors and market counterparties may variously lead to both increases and reductions in transaction volumes, and hence alter the occurrence of primarily EDPM loss events arising from mistakes and omissions.

Indirect impacts of the pandemic: changes in the behaviour of fraudsters and cybercriminals

Occurrence (1st Law): As noted earlier, professional criminals are rational, and consequently will seek to optimise their rewards by exploiting, through their malicious acts, the new circumstances, i.e. customer uncertainty; the requirement for banks to fast-track the approval of emergency loans; and remote working operating models, whilst reduced bank staffing levels may weaken the effectiveness of their preventive and detective controls.[5]

Indirect impacts of the pandemic: economic consequences

Per the 7th Law, the economic consequences of a pandemic will lead to raised Operational Risk losses through:

- Exacerbating existing risks;
- Inappropriate responses of banks and stakeholders alike; and
- Uncovering of historical Operational Risk events (Tables 11.1 and 11.2).

Exacerbating existing risks

Occurrence (1st Law) and Velocity (3rd Law): An example of how the economic consequences of a pandemic can exacerbate existing losses, is how higher

---

[5]ORX'S Annual Banking Loss Report (ORX, 2021) reveals a €2 billion increase in External Fraud in 2020 when compared to average External Fraud losses over the previous five years (€2.1 billion).

market volatility will increase any losses (and gains) arising from fat-fingered typing errors[6] by increasing the velocity of losses (3rd Law). Economic consequences can also increase the occurrence of existing risks, such as the default of third-party suppliers (1st Law).

Inappropriate responses

Occurrence (1st Law) and Velocity (3rd Law): Banks, bankers and customers can respond inappropriately to an economic shock. For example, financial need[7] may drive previously law-abiding customers to desperation crimes (external malicious acts). Similarly, staff members may respond inappropriately to adverse financial outcomes, for example, mis-marking their trading books to disguise loss making positions that would otherwise have breached their stop-loss limits (internal malicious acts). The identification of such incidents may also be delayed during a pandemic, through a weakening of detective controls due to the combination of reduced staffing levels and the undermining of Front Office supervision by remote working. Rising unemployment and insolvencies will force banks to have to deal with increasing numbers of customers in financial difficulties. Failing to do so appropriately can lead to litigation, regulatory sanction and compensation.[8] Sometimes, however, the inappropriate response of a firm is a "sin of omission" e.g. private banks and fund managers have a fiduciary duty to respond to changing market circumstances and to rebalance discretionary portfolios appropriately and to provide fresh advice to clients. The scale of any potential Operational Risk losses for firms may variously reflect the Market and Credit Risk exposures of these funds/their clients, via the 9th Law: Risk Transference, Transformation and Conservation.

Uncovering of historical Operational Risk

Detection (2nd Law) and Velocity (3rd Law): Economic shocks can also reveal latent events. For example, negative prices and interest rates can highlight the existence of log normal functions within models that are unable to deal

---

[6]For example, anecdotally in 2021 the LME had to increase its dynamic price limits for tin on LME Select due to increased market volatility, increasing the consequences of any fat-finger errors by its members, due to a combination of external events including disruption to production due to COVID-19.

[7]As noted in Chapter 2, BDO's FraudTrack 2018 Survey splits the motivations of fraudsters between "Greed" and "Need".

[8]The FCA noted in their press release accompanying their £26 million fine of Barclays (FCA, 2020) for failures in relation to their treatment of customers in arrears or experiencing financial difficulties, that banks faced challenges in this area due to COVID-19, "... which only heightens the importance of firms treating customers in financial difficulty fairly and appropriately."

with negative values, as well as the absence of floors in structured products (Chapter 2). Similarly customer defaults may lead to the discovery of second-party ("bookkeeper") frauds perpetrated by client staff, as well as deficiencies in transaction documentation, e.g. missing security documentation and netting agreements (Credit Risk : Operational Risk boundary losses). Finally, sharp market movements and rising defaults may lead to claims of mis-sale of both investment products and derivatives used for hedging purposes, as explained by the Real Option Model (Figure 3.4). The value of such claims will be driven by economic factors, such as the scale of market movements (Market Risk) and/or the prevalence of defaults (Credit Risk).

These various impacts are summarised in Table 16.1.

Reputational Risks Table 16.1 also indicates that how firms respond to a pandemic will influence their reputation with a range of stakeholders, specifically:

- *Staff members:* Their perception as to the efforts made by firms to ensure that their working environments are safe, i.e. both in the office, regarding the risk of COVID-19 infection, and also at home, regarding their mental health and also their physical well-being, through the provision of appropriate desks and chairs, and keyboards and monitors.
- *Criminals:* As noted previously, criminals are rational, and consequently they will rapidly ascertain the relative strengths of firms in preventing application frauds relating to the government-backed fast-track emergency loans.
- *Customers:* During the early stages of a pandemic customers will have formed a view as to the rapidity with which banks approved the government-backed fast-track emergency loans. In the aftermath of a pandemic the focus will be on how banks deal with their customers that are in financial difficulties.

Timescales and conclusions

Consideration of the 5th and 9th Laws of Operational Risk (i.e. lags and risk conservation) suggest that the most significant losses that firms will suffer relating to COVID-19 will actually crystallise several years after the pandemic is finally over. These losses will arise from either:

- Discoveries of deficiencies in loan and transaction documentation (Credit : Operational Risk boundary losses); or
- Failing to treat customers in financial difficulties fairly; or
- Fraud-related litigation: fiduciary failures relating to frauds suffered by either customers or government guarantors of COVID-19 emergency financing; or
- Litigation claiming past mis-sales relating to both derivatives purchased by customers for hedging purposes and investment products (9th Law: Risk Transference, Transformation and Conservation).

TABLE 16.1 The mapping of Pandemic Risks to Basel II

Basel II Operational Risks and the nature of events (Appendix I.1)	Direct and indirect risks arising from a pandemic		
	Direct consequences	Behavioural changes, including lockdowns	Economic consequences
1. EPWS: ■ Acts of God.	*Occurrence*: ■ Physical well-being of staff members; and ■ Costs of PPE, deep-cleaning, etc.	*Occurrence:* ■ Physical and mental well-being of staff members working remotely.	
2. BDSF ■ Third- (fourth-party) failures.		*Occurrence & Velocity:* ■ Reduced connectivity/latency; ■ Vendor failures; and ■ Costs of enhanced BCP.	*Occurrence*: ■ Vendor defaults.
3. EDPM: ■ Mistakes and omissions.		*Occurrence*: ■ Reduced bank resourcing due to school closures; ■ Fragmentation of manual processes due to remote working; ■ Changes (up and down) of customer activity; ■ Fast-track provision of emergency loans; and ■ Changes (up and down) in investor activity.	*Occurrence*: ■ Negative prices and rates: Disruption to models. *Detection*: ■ Uncovering of historical documentation issues, e.g. relating to loans/security. *Velocity*: ■ Increased market volatility increases the impacts of fat-fingered typing.
4. EF: ■ Malicious acts.		*Occurrence*: Exploitation of: ■ Changes in customer behaviour; and ■ Reductions in bank resourcing and remote working/weakening of controls.	*Occurrence*: ■ Desperation frauds, i.e. customer frauds driven by financial need. *Detection*: ■ Second-party fraud uncovered by clients.

TABLE 16.1 (*Continued*)

Basel II Operational Risks and the nature of events (Appendix I.1)	Direct and indirect risks arising from a pandemic		
	Direct consequences	Behavioural changes, including lockdowns	Economic consequences
5. IF: ■ Malicious acts.			*Occurrence & Velocity:* ■ Weakened surveillance controls due to remote working; and ■ Mis-marking in response to market falls.
6. CPBP – Government, investor and client litigation: ■ Misconduct.			*Occurrence & Velocity:* ■ Inappropriate responses: 　■ Treating customers unfairly in financial difficulties; and 　■ Failure to rebalance discretionary funds. ■ Fiduciary failures allowing customers and governments to suffer frauds. *Detection & Velocity:* ■ Uncovering of historical misconduct; and ■ The value of misconduct is exacerbated by market volatility.
7. DPA:	■ N/A	■ N/A	■ N/A
Reputational risk due to: ■ Responses of banks.	■ *Staff members:* Perception of efforts of firms to make the office environment safe.	■ *Staff members:* Home working environment and mental health. ■ *Criminals:* Reputation for fraud detection. ■ *Customers:* Rapidity of approving emergency loans.	■ *Customers:* Treatment of customers in financial difficulties; and responses to victims of fraud.

The losses that firms suffer as a result of risk transference/conservation following the COVID-19 pandemic may be less significant than the losses that firms suffered after the Global Financial Crisis due to various control enhancements that have been implemented, reflecting the 8th Law: Risk Homeostasis. The potential claims from governments relating to whether banks exercised appropriate care and attention in their fast-track dispersal of emergency loans (9th Law: Risk Conservation) is an entirely new risk and, as such, the 8th Law is less relevant for this pandemic as opposed to the next.

The last two categories may be particularly long-dated due to the observation that insolvencies in the world's 13 largest economies are lower than expected, in comparison to the Global Financial Crisis. Usually, insolvencies rise in the quarters following reductions/negative GDP, but IMF data suggests that the reverse happened, i.e. insolvencies reduced sharply.[9] There may be a number of causes for this observation, including the level of support provided by these governments. In addition, as noted above, from a reputational perspective banks may be reticent about foreclosing on customers during a pandemic. Finally, the reduction in the staffing levels of banks, due to the closure of schools, may also mean that they currently lack the necessary resources to foreclose on large numbers of customers, even if they wished to do so.

Figure 16.1 highlights three key features regarding pandemics and the risk profiles of firms:

1. Pandemics come in waves. For example, the Spanish flu pandemic of 1918 to 1920 came in four waves. Even with the deployment of COVID-19 vaccines, the propensity of this virus to mutate means that there may be subsequent waves of at least partially resistant variants.
2. A severe pandemic can generate a more complex range of Operational Risks than a simple economic slowdown. As a consequence, the correlations between causal factors associated with individual large loss events (Figure 5.2) will look significantly different in the coming years.
3. The most severe Operational Risk impacts of a pandemic are only likely to crystallise in the years following the ending of the pandemic.

2. CLIMATE CHANGE

This Part describes the range of Climate Change risks, i.e. both Physical and Transition Risks, and uses the Ten Laws to illustrate their potential impacts on the Operational Risk profiles of firms. Whilst the BIS correctly states that the sensitivity of Operational Risk to Transition and Physical Risks seems less significant than for other risks, it narrowly only highlights direct exposures, i.e. the impacts of Physical Risks on a bank's

---

[9]*The Financial Times*, (3rd February 2021) "Keeping zombie companies alive is the right call".

FIGURE 16.1 Applying the Ten Laws to the COVID-19 pandemic

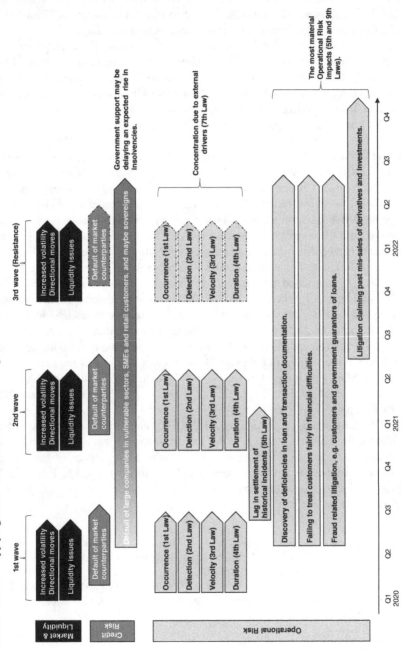

offices or data centres and those of other institutions across its value chain (BIS, January 2020). This section will demonstrate that unfortunately the impacts of Climate Change on the Operational Risk profiles of firms may be much broader.

In the 11,000 years before the Industrial Revolution, the average temperature across the world was largely stable at around 14° C.[10] The burning of fossil fuels to power the Industrial Revolution, however, began to release greenhouse gases, such as carbon dioxide, methane and nitrous monoxide, which are forming a "blanket" around the planet, trapping energy from the Sun, causing the Earth to heat up.

This effect was first noticed in the 1980s, and in 1988 the International Panel on Climate Change (IPCC) was set up to provide governments with information to tackle Climate Change. In December 2015, parties to the United Nations Framework Convention on Climate Change (UNFCCC) reached an agreement (the Paris Agreement) to combat Climate Change and to accelerate the actions and investments needed for a sustainable low-carbon future. The Paris Agreement's central aim is to keep the global temperature rise this century to below 2° C above pre-industrial levels and to pursue efforts to limit the temperature increase even further to 1.5° C (Article 2).[11] The Paris Agreement establishes binding commitments to Nationally Determined Contributions (NDC) supported by domestic measures to achieve them. For example, in November 2016, the EU committed that its members would reduce greenhouse gas emissions by 40%, relative to 1990 emissions, by 2030. This represented a significant progression beyond the EU's previous undertaking of a 20% emission reduction by 2020. The parties to the Paris Agreement are also required to communicate their NDCs every five years, and each successive NDC will represent progress beyond the previous one (Article 4). For example, in February 2020, Norway was one of the first countries to update its NDC with a target of a 50% to 55% reduction, relative to 1990 levels for the time frame of 2021 to 2030. This is progress from Norway's original NDC of a 40% reduction.

The wide-ranging consequences of Climate Change are typically divided between the direct effects of an increase in global temperatures of between 1.5° C to 2° C envisaged under Article 2, i.e. Physical Risks, and the consequences of the humanity's transition towards a low-carbon economy, in line with Article 4, i.e. Transition Risks. Whilst considered separately, Physical and Transition Risks are unfolding in parallel (CFTC, 2020).

---

[10]There were extended climate cycles, however, during this period, e.g. the Medieval Warm Period, which was followed by the Little Ice Age, leading to Frost Fairs on the Thames in London during the seventeenth and eighteenth centuries.
[11]The Earth's human population was 7.4 billion when the Paris Agreement was reached in 2015, and is projected to increase by approx. 50% to almost 11 billion by 2100, demonstrating the scale of the task facing humanity.

Physical Risks of Climate Change

Global warming will result in more extreme weather events (e.g. storms, flooding, drought, wildfires and extreme heat), as well as gradual changes to the Earth's climate (e.g. rising temperatures and sea levels).

Extreme weather events By increasing average atmospheric and ocean temperatures, Climate Change is adding energy to the Earth's weather, leading to more extreme weather events. For example, hurricanes are fuelled by heat in the top layers of the ocean and require sea-surface temperatures greater than 26° C to form. Since 1995 there have been 17 above-normal Atlantic hurricane seasons, as measured by National Oceanic and Atmospheric Administration's Accumulated Cyclone Energy (ACE) Index. This is the longest stretch of above-normal seasons on record. Similarly, research by NASA suggests that every 1° C rise in sea-surface temperatures increases the number of extreme storms by about 21%. Additionally, there is research to indicate that wave power is also increasing, i.e. wave power has increased globally by 0.4% per year since 1948, and this is again correlated with the rising sea-surface temperatures, both globally and in individual oceans (Reguero et al., 2019). This may be contributing to an observed (US Coast Guard) increase in the size of rogue waves (waves that are twice the height of the background waves), although there was a slight decrease in their frequency. At their most destructive, rogue waves have been blamed historically for the loss of shipping.

The warming of the Earth's climate may also result in heatwaves and droughts, as weather patterns change, leading to increased water stress and disruption to food production. The types of impacts that global warming may cause are illustrated by El Niño, which is a recurrent climate pattern, involving the warming of the tropical Pacific that occurs every two to seven years, triggering predictable weather disruptions. Generally, El Niño produces more intense cyclones, heavier rains and warmer weather in South America, but drier weather in Southeast Asia and parts of Australia. Crops affected include cocoa in Côte d'Ivoire, palm oil in Malaysia and rice across Southeast Asia. In the summer of 2015, a late monsoon in India led to the so-called "dahl shock", following a 40% reduction in rainfall, which caused a 13% drop in pea production and prices to be pushed to record highs.[12]

Gradual/chronic changes to the Earth's climate Ongoing temperature rises will also lead to the melting of glaciers and ice sheets, adding more water to the oceans, causing rising sea levels. Oceans absorb 90% of the extra heat from global warming, causing water to expand, exacerbating further rising sea levels. This combination

---

[12]*The Economist*, (20th June 2015) "Commodities and El Niño: The Mocha Hedge".

increases the risk of flooding in coastal cities. A joint study by the World Bank and OECD in 2013 forecast that average global flood losses will rise from $6 billion pa in 2005 to $52 billion pa by 2050. The study highlighted that the cities where flood risk will increase most are not necessarily the cities where the risk is particularly high today. In terms of the overall cost of damage, New York is one of the top ten cities at the greatest risk, and others include Miami, New Orleans, Mumbai, Shenzhen and Osaka.

Long-term increases in temperature may also lead to extreme heat exposure and reduced life expectancy (CFTC, 2020). Additionally in temperate parts of the world, Climate Change may lead to increases in the prevalence of disease-transmitting species, such as ticks and mosquitoes. For example, in the UK, Climate Change is likely to enable the populations of invasive species to become established, particularly mosquito species. Higher temperatures typically decrease the time it takes for mosquitoes to become infectious, potentially allowing more opportunities for transmission when feeding, prior to breeding, i.e. a 1° C average rise in mean temperature, expected between 2030 and 2050 could lead to an approximate one to two week extension of adult mosquito activity in Southern England. Increases in rainfall and humidity could also further support mosquito breeding levels (Medlock and Leach, 2015). Gradual changes in temperature and precipitation may also cause disruption to agriculture (Basel Committee, 2021).

Whilst called Physical Risks, extreme weather and ongoing Climate Change may also cause economic shocks, as a consequence of disruption to agriculture; damage to physical infrastructure and interruption to supply chains, leading to increased market volatility;[13] long-term changes in asset values; rising defaults in affected sectors (e.g. agriculture and sectors with physical infrastructure); and changing stakeholder behaviours (e.g. investors, customers and criminals).

Applying the Ten Laws

The impacts of Physical Risks on Operational Risk will be assessed using the relevant Ten Laws, and illustrated with the criteria for identifying emerging threats, set out in Chapter 15, i.e. existing trends; history repeating itself; trends in other industries; and "known knowns".

1st Law Occurrence   The 1st Law states that the occurrence of incidents is driven by business profile; the nature of inadequacies or failures; preventive controls and internal and external causes. The influence of Physical Risks on inadequacies or failures are considered below.

---

[13] Hurricane Harvey, in August 2017, caused widespread flooding and led to the closure of almost a quarter the US's refining capacity. This coincided with average gasoline prices rising by 8%, i.e. from $2.33 to $2.52 per gallon.

The nature of inadequacies or failures *Acts of God*, which could include the consequences of extreme weather, contribute, per Table 2.1, to the occurrence of DPA, BDSF and EPWS. An example of the consequences of extreme weather events is Hurricane Sandy, which hit New York on 29th October 2012. In anticipation the city suspended all subway, bus and commuter rail services, and the schools were also closed. The storm surge flooded streets and subway lines and also disrupted power supplies (see below). In addition to the NYSE suspending trading on 29th and 30th October,[14] some firms were more directly impacted. For example, the storm flooded the underground floors, including the vault, of DTCC's headquarters in Lower Manhattan. This led to business disruption and damage to both DTCC's fixtures and fittings, as well as its clients' physical securities that DTCC was holding, as a custodian, in its flooded vault.

Third- (and fourth-) party failures may also be caused by Physical Risks. For example, also in the aftermath of Hurricane Sandy, on 31st October 2012, when the NYSE resumed trading, at 11.15 a.m Knight Capital had to redirect its customers to other brokers after its back-up generators failed. Knight Capital was relying on back-up power after Hurricane Sandy disrupted electricity supplies for large parts of the US east coast. A quite different example of the impacts of Physical Risks on third- (and fourth-) party suppliers is the filing for Chapter 11 bankruptcy protection by the Pacific Gas and Electric (PG&E) on 14th January 2019.[15] Its bankruptcy filing was the result of its potential financial liabilities for environmental damage following the California Department of Forestry and Fire Protection, concluding that 12 wildfires that blazed in October 2017 "were caused by electric power and distribution lines, conductors and the failure of power poles" owned by PG&E.[16] These third- (and fourth-) party failures may contribute, per Table 2.1, to the occurrence of BDSF, EDPM and CPBP.

Business profile The constituents of a firm's business profile were defined in Figure 2.1, and reflect both its internal operating model and its external commercial relationships and stakeholders. As noted in Chapter 11, the Operational Risk profile of firms can be altered by changes in the behaviour of its stakeholders in response to Physical (and also Transition) Risks. This may include changes in fraudulent activities, as criminals will act to exploit new situations. This behaviour is illustrated by the recent changes in fraud patterns, i.e. the average daily rate of UK payment fraud (the number of attempted frauds as a proportion of overall transactions) was up 117% between 1st October and 15th November 2020, in comparison with the same period a year earlier, as criminals attempted to exploit the huge growth in online shopping due to the

---

[14]Similarly on 16th October 1987 London markets closed early due to disruption caused by the "Great Storm", which was an extratropical cyclone, with hurricane-force winds.

[15]NB this did not, however, disrupt the supply of electricity to PG&E's customers.

[16]In 2018, insurance companies decided to drop fire coverage from over 88,000 residents in California due to the scale of the 2017 wildfire season (EIOPA, December 2020).

COVID-19 pandemic.[17] Business profile also includes a firm's physical infrastructure (e.g. offices and data centres), which, as already mentioned, may be vulnerable to extreme weather events.

3rd Law: Velocity   Velocity "…is driven by the quantum of inadequacies or failures; causes; and the nature of the impacts generated by the event". The nature of the impacts of Physical Risks makes them high velocity events, i.e. the duration of extreme weather events may be quite short but the resulting losses could be high. For example, the velocity of the losses suffered by DTCC, pre-insurance, as a consequence of Hurricane Sandy in 2012 is approximately $20 million per day (Figure 2.3).

7th Law: Concentration due to external drivers   As noted previously, Physical Risks can create economic shocks, through disruption to agriculture; damage to physical infrastructure and interruption to supply chains. This typically results in increased market volatility; long-term changes in asset values; rising defaults in affected sectors (e.g. agriculture and sectors with physical infrastructure) and changing stakeholder behaviours, leading to Operational Risk losses:

- Existing losses are exacerbated, for example, increased market volatility from disorderly price adjustments (e.g. a fire-sale of stranded assets) would increase the severity of any fat-fingered typing errors. The behaviours of various stakeholders may also change, e.g. increased demand from customers and investors for certain products and asset classes (e.g. green and safe-haven assets), whilst, as noted above, criminals will act to exploit both uncertainty and changing consumer demand;
- Historical failures may be uncovered, e.g. deficiencies in loan documentation revealed by customer defaults caused by physical events and the historical mis-sale of products revealed by disorderly price adjustments (e.g. increased market volatility or long-term changes in asset values, through the Real Options Model [Chapter 3]) again caused by physical events; and
- Responses to a crisis may lead to new losses, as firms attempt to execute new strategies, such as closing businesses and withdrawing support for clients in affected sectors. Firms will need to ensure that they treat customers in financial difficulties fairly through these changes.

8th Law: Risk Homeostasis   In response to increased risks to BDSF, then, the 8th Law predicts that firms should respond by enhancing their corrective/resilience controls. This will mean firms diversifying their infrastructure and suppliers and considering geographical proximity/concentration of both their physical assets and those of their suppliers. For example, traditionally, banks had at least two physical data centres that were mirrored. The real-time mirroring of the data centres meant that they tended

---

[17] *The Financial Times*, (28th/29th November, 2020) "Online fraud surges ahead of Black Friday".

to be located in reasonable proximity, i.e. tens of miles apart rather than hundreds of miles. The growing trend of banks using the cloud will increase their resilience to these Physical Risks, but at the potential expense of increased risks of cybercrime and third- (and fourth-) party failure.

9th Law: Risk transference and conservation The Physical Risks of Climate Change may also alter the scope and/or availability of business interruption, property and contents insurance due to acts of God (Table 12.2). This is a consequence of the determinants of insurability listed in Chapter 12, specifically the extent to which insurable events should ideally be uncorrelated (allowing risks to be pooled following the Law of Large Numbers) and the premiums affordable. An increase in both the number and the scale of extreme weather events would naturally result in both more and larger correlated insurance claims, driving up the premiums, through annual re-pricing,[18] that insurance companies must charge in order to cover claims, administration and capital costs (Formula 12.2). Finally, in an environment in which the Earth's climate continues to change, insurance companies may need to price their insurance policies on the basis that claims in the following year will probably be even greater than the current year's claims, undermining their actuarial models. The European Occupational Pensions and Insurance Authority (EIOPA) highlights these issues in its recent discussion paper (EIOPA, December 2020).

Control effectiveness Finally, in extreme Climate Change scenarios control effectiveness may be weakened through a combination of the spreading of tropical diseases into previously temperate regions and also the impacts of heat stress on staff members.

Transition Risks from humanity's response to Climate Change

The PRA notes that there are a range of factors that will influence transition towards a low-carbon economy, e.g. policy and regulation; the emergence of disruptive technology or business models; shifting sentiment and societal preferences; and evolving legal interpretations (PRA, April 2019). Transition will result in changes in demand, which will drive the supply and the value of assets, for example:

- Falling demand for fossil fuels may drive down either supply and/or prices.[19] The CFTC (2020) additionally highlights the potential for these price adjustments to be "disorderly";

---

[18] Similarly, in 2021, insurance premiums in the London market for Business Interruption insurance anecdotally rose by 20% as firms repriced to reflect potential unexpected correlated claims arising from the COVID-19 pandemic.

[19] The EU's hard coal production fell from 368 million tonnes in 1990 to just 78 million tonnes in 2018, but over the same period the EU's hard coal consumption only fell from ~500 to 226 million tonnes (Eurostat). The combination of these changes means that the absolute levels of the EU's imports of hard coal have actually marginally increased during this period, i.e. the EU's production of hard coal has fallen more rapidly than its consumption.

- Falling demand for some products may lead to rising default rates in adversely impacted sectors of the economy, e.g. those most closely linked to fossil fuels; and
- Rising demand for more environmentally friendly products and technologies will either push up prices and/or increase the supply of commodities needed for new these technologies, e.g. for rare earth metals that are required for the magnets used in wind turbines.[20]

Additionally, transitioning from existing to new technologies may also increase the risks of business disruption, e.g. wind power can be a less reliable method of generating electricity than fossil fuels.

Applying the Ten Laws

The impacts of Transition Risks on Operational Risk will also be assessed using the relevant Ten Laws, and illustrated with the criteria for identifying emerging threats, set out in Chapter 15, i.e. existing trends; history repeating itself; trends in other industries; and "known knowns".

1st Law Occurrence   The 1st Law states that the occurrence of incidents is driven by business profile; the nature of inadequacies or failures; preventive controls and internal and external causes. The influence of Transition Risks on inadequacies or failures are considered below.

Third- (and fourth-) party failures may be caused by Transition Risks. Many European countries are closing their coal power stations to meet their NDC targets under the Paris Agreement and expanding less reliable wind farms,[21] potentially making electricity supply increasingly less certain. For example, on 4th November 2020, the UK's National Grid sent out a Margin Notice for more power stations to come on line as a combination of plant outages and *low wind farm output* increased the risk of blackouts. The National Grid had forecast a shortfall of 1.5% of its desired power plant capacity to meet both unexpected demand and plant break downs. These third- (and fourth-) party failures may contribute, per Table 2.1, to the occurrence of BDSF, EDPM and CPBP.

3rd Law: Velocity   The velocity of losses suffered from Transition Risks may increase over time as humanity's response to Climate Change accelerates. The economic impacts of Transition Risks will be considered under the 7th Law.

7th Law: Concentration due to external drivers   As noted previously, Transition Risks can create economic shocks, through business disruption to infrastructure (e.g. power generation) and changing stakeholder behaviours leading to increased

---

[20]Rare earth metals production increased from ~64,000 tons in 1994 to ~214,000 by 2019 (Statista).
[21]*The Financial Times*, (13th October 2015) "European Energy".

market volatility; long-term changes in asset values; and rising defaults in affected sectors (e.g. fossil fuel dependent sectors), and Operational Risk losses that overlap with Physical Risks, i.e.:

- Existing losses are exacerbated, for example, increased market volatility from disorderly price adjustments would increase the severity of any fat-fingered typing errors. The behaviours of various stakeholders may also change e.g. increased demand from customers and investors for certain products and asset classes (e.g. green and safe-haven assets), whilst, as noted above, criminals will act to exploit both uncertainty and changing consumer demand;
- Historical failures may be uncovered e.g. deficiencies in loan documentation revealed by defaults of customers with businesses linked to fossil fuels and the historical mis-sale of products revealed by increased market volatility and long-term changes in asset values due to transition through the Real Options Model (Chapter 3); and
- Responses to a crisis may lead to new losses, as firms attempt to execute new strategies, such closing businesses and withdrawing support for clients in impacted sectors. Firms will need to ensure that they treat customers in financial difficulties fairly through these changes. Failing to respond to Climate Change may also expose firms to litigation.

The Global Financial Crisis provides an example of the types of litigation that may arise relating to the historical transactions. Due to the rise in the oil price from 2003, the Ceylon Petroleum Corp, Sri Lanka's state-owned importer, refiner and retailer of crude oil, entered into ~30 oil derivative transactions between February and October 2008 (Figure 16.2). These hedging trades were zero cost collars, locking the Ceylon Petroleum Corp into paying a range of prices for its oil. As a result of the Global Financial Crisis in 2008, the price of oil collapsed below the floors of Ceylon Petroleum Corp's collars, and it suspended payments, claiming, with mixed success, that it had relied on its banks for advice and guidance.

10th Law: Active and passive risk taking

Fee generation: The assessment of exposure of funds to Climate Change risk will increasingly become a critical component of the due diligence undertaken by investment managers. A 2015 survey conducted by the Asset Owners Disclosure Project (AODP) Global Climate of the top 500 asset owners, identified almost half (232) of them were doing nothing material to manage the financial risks associated with Climate Change (ADOP, 2015). Awareness of the importance of Climate Change, however, has clearly increased, as by 2019 630 investors, managing more than $35 trillion of assets, signed the "Global Investor Statement to Governments on Climate Change" which called on governments to improve climate-related financial reporting. The potential financial consequences of Climate Change to funds was highlighted

FIGURE 16.2   How the movement of the oil price drove derivative litigation

in December 2020, when EIOPA published an assessment of the impacts of
Transition Risks on the investment portfolios of European insurers. Based
on its assumptions and scenarios its report estimated losses of up to 25% on
equity holdings in high-carbon sectors (EIOPA, December 2020). It is quite
conceivable, that in the near future, failing to consider the financial risks of
Climate Change may be seen as a breach of fiduciary duty, and hence a basis
for litigation, similar to not managing effectively other risks within investment
portfolios.

Customers' carbon footprint: Transition Risks may also include the impacts on a
firm's reputation with its stakeholders from either not responding to concerns
about Climate Change or proactively supporting industries that are damaging
to the environment. For example, in response to an AGM resolution criticising
its financing of the coal industry, Mizuho announced in April 2020 that it
would cut its ¥300 billion ($2.8 billion) of loans to coal power projects by
half by 2030 and to zero by 2050. The AGM resolution was sponsored by
the Kiko Network, a Japanese activist group that focuses on coal, and it had
support from a number of investment funds. Climate campaigners had also
placed a full-page advert in the *Financial Times* in March 2020, calling on
Mizuho to exit coal financing.[22]

---

[22]*Reuters*, (16th April 2020) "Mizuho to stop lending to new coal power projects".

Conclusions

Figure 16.3 is an expansion of Environmental Risks from Figure 15.1. It illustrates that whilst Physical Risks obviously include damage to infrastructure and disruption to the supply chains of firms, they may also lead to increased market volatility; long-term changes in the value of financial assets and wider economic shocks, including raised default rates in affected sectors (e.g. agriculture and sectors with physical infrastructure), through physical damage and supply-side disruption.

In contrast, the impacts of Transition Risks are primarily demand-driven. They arise from changes in the behaviours of authorities, investors, and consumers/customers, and again lead to increased market volatility; long-term changes in the value of financial assets; and raised default rates in affected sectors (e.g. fossil fuel dependent sectors). In addition, like Physical Risks, Transition Risks can also lead to risks of some instances of supply-side disruption due to the transition from old to new technologies, e.g. the transition from coal to wind power.

The behaviour of criminals will also change in response to the opportunities presented by both Physical and Transition Risks, i.e. both changes in customer/consumer behaviours and any disruption caused to firms e.g. a reduction in control effectiveness in extreme Climate Change scenarios.

Earlier analysis (Figure 2.3) indicates that whilst physical damage to assets have higher velocities, events that lead to compensation payments have higher magnitudes, although typically with longer lags between detection and settlement (5th Law). Losses that involve the transformation of Credit and Market Risks into Operational Risks (9th Law) historically have been the most significant. Consequently, it is the economic consequences of Climate Change that will ultimately generate the largest Operational Risk losses.

Finally, as noted in the Introduction, Transition and Physical Risks cannot be considered in isolation. The CFTC has observed that "... transition and physical risks – as well as climate and non-climate-related risks – could interact with each other, amplifying shocks and stresses" (CFTC, 2020). Three potential scenarios involve:

- Strong and immediate actions to mitigate Climate Change, which whilst limiting Physical Risks would increase Transition Risks;
- Delayed and weak actions to mitigate Climate Change would eventually lead to higher Physical Risks; and
- Delayed actions followed by very strong actions in an attempt to catch up, which would probably lead to both higher Physical Risks and subsequently higher Transition Risks, due to the economic consequences being both rapid and significant.

These relationships are reflected in Figure 16.3 by a feedback loop between Climate Change and changes in the behaviour of the stakeholders listed in Figure 2.1. The sheer complexity of these interrelationships means that stress testing, using different potential Climate Change scenarios, is really the only option for quantification. The Laws of Operational can be used, as part of these exercises, to assess the impacts of Climate Risk on Operational Risk, with Table 16.2 providing a summary of the different Physical and Transition Risks and their direct and indirect impacts on a firm's Operational Risk profile.

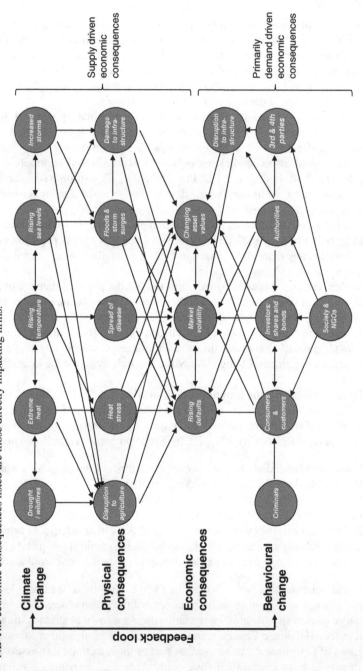

FIGURE 16.3 The interrelationships between the physical and economic consequences of Climate Change

NB The economic consequences listed are those directly impacting firms.

TABLE 16.2 The mapping of Transition and Physical Risks to Basel II

Basel II Operational Risks and the nature of events (Appendix I)	Transition Risks		Physical Risks	
	Examples of direct impacts	Examples of direct and indirect Operational Risks	Examples of direct impacts	Examples of direct and indirect Operational Risks
1. BDSF ■ Acts of God; and ■ Third- and fourth-party failures.	■ Retirement of coal-fired power stations within Europe and North America.	*Occurrence & Duration:* ■ Increased risk of power outages due to the variability of renewables, such as wind power. ■ Third- and fourth-party failures.	■ Rising temperatures. ■ Extreme heat. ■ Rising sea levels and larger rogue waves. ■ Increased storms. ■ Increased flooding and storm surges. ■ Droughts and wildfires.	*Occurrence & Duration:* ■ Physical disruption to services, e.g. staff unable travel to work. ■ Heatwaves will place increased demand for electricity for air conditioning. ■ Third- and fourth-party failures.
2. DPA: ■ Acts of God; and ■ Third- and fourth-party failures.	■ N/A	■ N/A	■ Rising temperatures. ■ Extreme heat. ■ Rising sea levels and larger rogue waves. ■ Increased storms. ■ Increased flooding and storm surges. ■ Droughts and wildfires.	*Occurrence & Velocity:* ■ Physical damage to infrastructure of firms and third and fourth parties, e.g. offices and data centres. ■ Physical damage to assets owned by commodity banks, e.g. oil on water and land. ■ Third- and fourth-party failures.

(*Continued*)

TABLE 16.2 (*Continued*)

Basel II Operational Risks and the nature of events (Appendix I)	Transition Risks		Physical Risks	
	Examples of direct impacts	Examples of direct and indirect Operational Risks	Examples of direct impacts	Examples of direct and indirect Operational Risks
3. CPBP – Investor and client litigation: ■ Misconduct.	Increased market volatility and changing long-term asset values: ■ Energy prices. ■ Commodity prices. ■ Interest and FX rates. ■ Security values. Rising defaults in affected sectors. Expansion of regulation.	*Detection/ Duration and Velocity:* Customer and investor litigation arising from: ■ Losses; and/or ■ Lost opportunities. *Lags* would be significant. Not treating customers in financial difficulties fairly. Regulatory breaches.	Increased market volatility and changing long-term asset values: ■ Energy prices. ■ Commodity prices. ■ Interest & FX rates. ■ Security values. Rising defaults in affected sectors.	*Detection/ Duration and Velocity:* Customer and investor litigation arising from: ■ Losses; and/or ■ Lost opportunities. *Lags* would be significant. Not treating customers in financial difficulties fairly.
4. EF: ■ Malicious acts.	Change in criminal behaviours, i.e. opportunistic frauds exploiting: ■ Customer uncertainty. ■ Disruption to banks.	*Occurrence:* ■ Customer and investor litigation if these losses arise from bank negligence. ■ Direct losses suffered by firms e.g. ransomware.	Change in criminal behaviours, i.e. opportunistic frauds exploiting: ■ Customer uncertainty. ■ Disruption to banks.	*Occurrence:* ■ Customer and investor litigation if their losses arise from bank negligence. ■ Direct losses suffered by firms, e.g. ransomware.
5. EPWS ■ Acts of God.	■ N/A	■ N/A	■ Extreme weather, e.g. heat stress. ■ Spread of diseases to temperate zones.	*Occurrence & Detection:* ■ Reduced resource levels due to higher levels of sickness.

TABLE 16.2 (*Continued*)

Basel II Operational Risks and the nature of events (Appendix I)	Transition Risks		Physical Risks	
	Examples of direct impacts	Examples of direct and indirect Operational Risks	Examples of direct impacts	Examples of direct and indirect Operational Risks
6. EDPM: ■ Mistakes and omissions.	■ Disorderly price adjustments. ■ Changing customer and investor behaviours.	*Occurrence & Velocity:* ■ Fat-fingered typing errors more expensive. ■ Changing transaction volumes may increase error rates.	■ Disorderly price adjustments. ■ Changes in customer and investor behaviours.	*Occurrence & Velocity:* ■ Fat-fingered typing errors more expensive. ■ Changing transaction volumes may increase error rates.
7. IF	■ Economic disruption	*Occurrence:* ■ Inappropriate responses. *Detection:* ■ Historical frauds.	■ Economic disruption	*Occurrence:* ■ Inappropriate responses. *Detection:* ■ Historical frauds.
Reputational risk due to: ■ Proactive risk taking (10th Law).	■ Financing carbon intensive industries.	*Occurrence & Duration:* ■ *Societal* disapproval. ■ *Investor* changes in behaviour, e.g. increased costs of capital and funding. ■ *Authorities* may act to increase capital requirements.	■ N/A	■ N/A

3. CYBERCRIME

Cybercrime is perpetually described as an emerging risk as criminals and financial institutions seem to be locked in an unending battle of innovation. This section provides a brief history of cybercrime; and then applies the 8th Law: Risk Homeostasis to explain observed patterns in SWIFT cyber-payment fraud and data theft; and then utilises Zoology's Optimal Foraging Theory (OFT) to understand the behaviour of cybercriminals, in order to make predictions of the future.

A brief history of cybercrime

Cybercrime regularly appears near the top of industry surveys of emerging risks[23] and yet a brief history of the reported first appearances of new methods of cybercrime (Figure 16.4) shows that some of these risks have already been with the industry for a generation. The nature and objectives of cybercrime have, however, changed over the decades, i.e. from initial curiosity, to disruption caused by viruses and Denial of Service attacks; to most recently thefts of data, intellectual property and assets (e.g. Bitcoins); and extortion. Hacks against the Pentagon provide an illustration as to how the perpetrators have changed over time. In 1983, a 17-year-old reportedly successfully hacked into ARPANET, the Pentagon's computer network. More recently, in 2020, it was reported that the Pentagon, like 18,000 other institutions, had installed an infected version of the SolarWinds Orion software that was released between March and June 2020. The perpetrator is believed to be a highly sophisticated nation state that targeted a supplier to very secure institutions, in order to gain access.

8th Law: Risk Homeostasis

The 8th Law predicts that a firm's expenditure on controls will increase in order to keep its expected Operational Risk losses in equilibrium with its appetite. This section considers evidence of the 8th Law provided by patterns in SWIFT cyber-payments frauds and data thefts.

SWIFT cyber-payments fraud   The first publicly disclosed SWIFT cyber-payment fraud seems to have taken place in 2015. But, as is generally the case with emerging risks, there was a forerunner of this fraud, i.e. in 2004 there was an attempted fraud against a Japanese bank in London using a key logging device, rather than malware. The criminals attempted to steal £229 million through 10 fraudulent SWIFT messages. They were thwarted by errors in their payment instructions which resulted in these payments not being processed.

Analysing SWIFT cyber-payment frauds in the public domain (Bouveret, 2018, Risk.net, 2019 and IBM FIRST Risk Case Studies) reveals that the thefts relate to emerging market banks and are quite infrequent, given the number of SWIFT users (>11,000). Recovery rates range between 20% and 100%, reflecting a combination of the sophistication of criminals in laundering the money and the varying speeds of response from the banks. Finally, the trend in the success of these frauds is downwards (Figure 16.5), in line with the 8th Law, reflecting industry-wide responses to the first frauds, e.g. the launching by SWIFT of the Customer Security Programme in 2016

---

[23]The first- and second-placed risks on Risk.net's top-10 risks for 2018 were "IT disruptions", including cyberattacks and "Data compromise" including cyber-theft (Risk.net, March 2019).

FIGURE 16.4 A brief history cybercrime firsts and some of the most notorious cyberattacks[24]

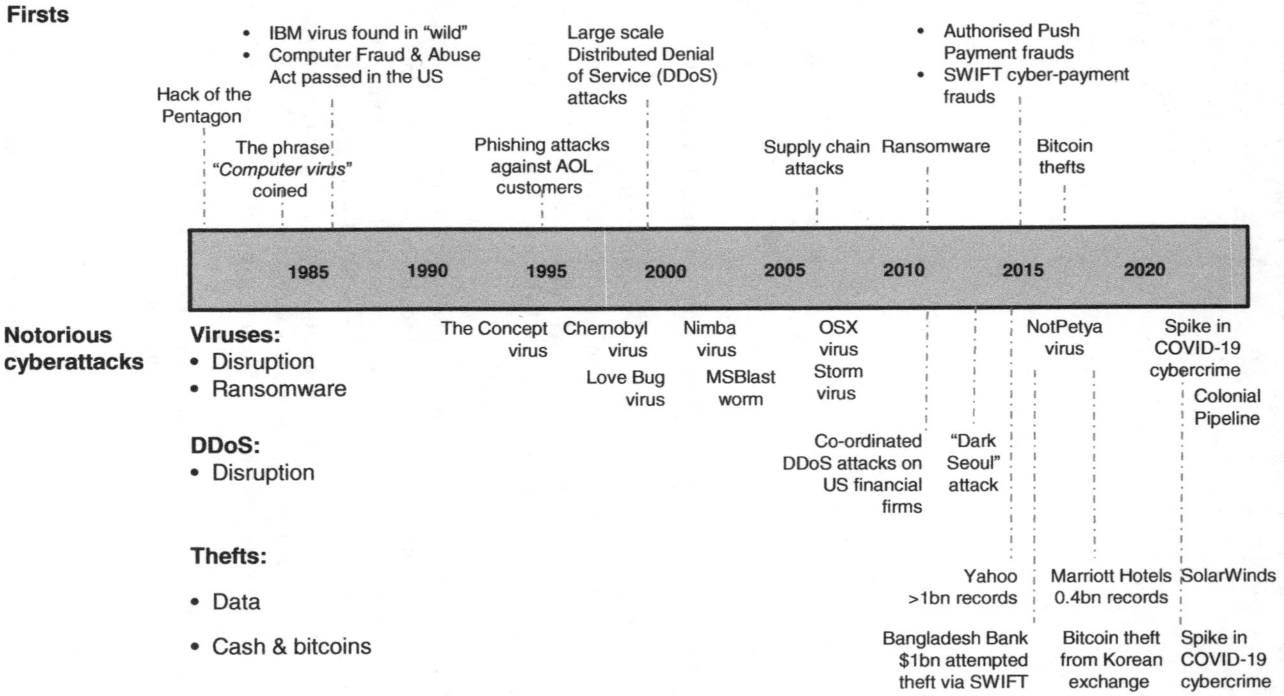

Firsts

- IBM virus found in "wild"
- Computer Fraud & Abuse Act passed in the US
- Large scale Distributed Denial of Service (DDoS) attacks
- Authorised Push Payment frauds
- SWIFT cyber-payment frauds

Hack of the Pentagon

The phrase "Computer virus" coined

Phishing attacks against AOL customers

Supply chain attacks   Ransomware

Bitcoin thefts

| 1985 | 1990 | 1995 | 2000 | 2005 | 2010 | 2015 | 2020 |

Notorious cyberattacks

Viruses:
- Disruption
- Ransomware

The Concept virus   Chernobyl virus   Nimba virus   OSX virus   Storm virus   NotPetya virus   Spike in COVID-19 cybercrime

Love Bug virus   MSBlast worm

Colonial Pipeline

DDoS:
- Disruption

Co-ordinated DDoS attacks on US financial firms   "Dark Seoul" attack

Thefts:
- Data
- Cash & bitcoins

Yahoo >1bn records   Marriott Hotels 0.4bn records   SolarWinds

Bangladesh Bank $1bn attempted theft via SWIFT   Bitcoin theft from Korean exchange   Spike in COVID-19 cybercrime

[24] Sourced from various industry lists.

FIGURE 16.5   Gross and net losses from public SWIFT cyber-payments frauds (Grimwade, 2019)

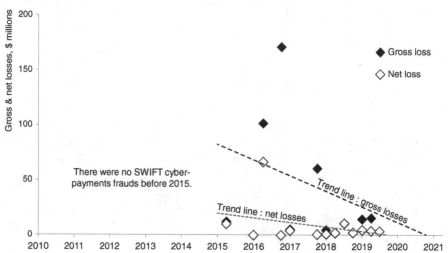

and the publication in 2017 of a Customer Security Controls Framework, which has subsequently been updated annually.

SWIFT believe that the cybercriminals have evolved their techniques in response to these controls enhancements, i.e. up until early 2018, SWIFT typically saw, per fraudulent transaction, amounts of ten/tens of millions. Since then, however, average fraudulent transaction amounts have reduced to between $0.25 million to $2 million (SWIFT, 2019).

Data thefts   The absence of a consistent industry data set for cyber data thefts clearly hinders tracking of trends. Figure 16.6 focuses on large-scale data thefts (>50 million records), for which information is consequently more complete. This analysis reveals that they began a few years earlier than SWIFT cyber-payment frauds, and are much more common, as criminals generally target less-regulated sectors, i.e. social media, retail and technology, "because that's where the data is".[25] The trend in these *large-scale data* thefts also appears to be beginning to decline,[26] again probably reflecting industry-wide investments in cyber defences and encryption in line with the 8th Law, and also responses to new data regulations, e.g. the EU's GDPR regulations relating to personal data that came into force in May 2018.

---

[25] Asked why he robbed banks, the Depression era bank robber Willie Sutton said "...because that's where the money is".

[26] As larger firms enhance their controls cybercriminals may focus more on the smaller/"weaker members of the herd", see later in this chapter.

FIGURE 16.6 Scale and severity of data hacks >50 million records over the last decade[27]

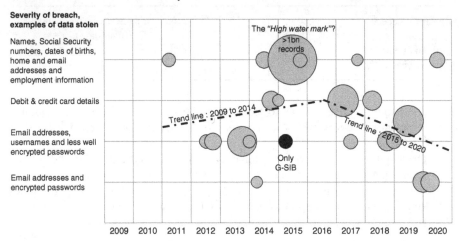

Motivations of criminals

Zoology, the Author's first profession, has identified that predators are driven by the optimisation of effort and benefit. This has been articulated through the theory that animals will naturally evolve Optimal Foraging Theory.[28] For example, oystercatchers have been observed to optimise their foraging for mussels based upon both population density, i.e. the time it takes them to find mussels of different sizes, and the thickness of the mussel shells, i.e. the time it takes for them to exploit food sources once located.[29] As professional cybercriminals are rational[30] they will also seek to optimise the rewards that they obtain (i.e. the gaining of either financial assets or data) for the resources at their disposal (i.e. their manpower or previously phished data). That OFT can explain the behaviour of criminals was first proposed over a decade ago (Bernasco, 2009). Formula 16.1 is the Author's adaptation of an OFT formula to cybercrime, i.e. a criminal's reward/proceeds of crime in a year is driven by:

- The average value of each successful fraud, which reflects the victim's financial or data scale;

---

[27] Sourced from various listings, including https://informationisbeautiful.net/visualizations/worlds-biggest-data-breaches-hacks/.

[28] A key proponent of Optimal Foraging Theory is Professor Lord John Krebs, who was a lecturer at Oxford University when the Author was an undergraduate in the Zoology Department in the mid-1980s.

[29] The optimal size of mussel shells for an oystercatcher turns out to be between 30 and 45 mm.

[30] In Q4 2019, 98% of companies that paid a ransomware ransom received a working decryption tool (Coveware, 2020).

Formula 16.1 Optimal Foraging Theory formula customised to cybercrime

Reward/proceeds of crime, $ or data items per year	=	Average value of each fraud, $ or data.	×	Fraudster's resources, i.e. manpower (man-days)
				$$\frac{}{(\text{Time to locate victims} + \text{Time to exploit victims})}$$

- The length of time it takes to locate a victim, which is driven by the number of potential victims, which in turn may be influenced by any changes in their behaviours;
- The length of time it takes to exploit each victim once located, which is driven by the adequacy of the victim's controls, e.g. COVID-19, led to an increase in bank staff working remotely. Unless well controlled, this may allow new opportunities for criminals to penetrate IT systems (BIS, 2021); and
- The resources available to a criminal e.g. the number of man-days.

Figure 16.7 provides a visualisation of the application of Optimal Foraging Theory to cybercrime, reflecting the "prey density" in terms of the number of potential

FIGURE 16.7 Visualisation of the application of Optimal Foraging Theory to cybercrime[31]

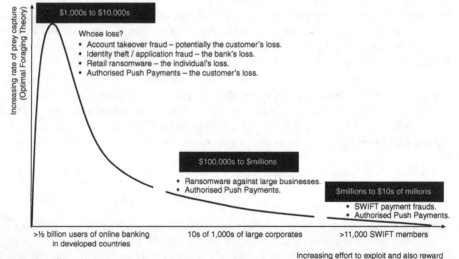

[31]Online banking penetration of G-7 is highest in the UK, 78%, EU and North America (various sources). The value of ransomware attacks varied in Q4 2019, with an average ransom payment

victims of differing financial scales and hence the potential value of successful frauds. Consequently, the cybersecurity of potential victims should increase with their financial scale.

If Figure 16.7 was redrawn for data thefts, then the far right-hand side would not be populated by banks, but instead it would contain the social media, retail and technology firms that retain hundreds of millions/billions of items of personal data.

Conclusions

The combination of the 8th Law: Risk Homeostasis and the application of Optimal Foraging Theory to cybercrime has resulted in "...the complexity of the attacks...evolving almost daily."[32] The 8th Law and Optimal Foraging Theory also lead to the following predictions:

- In order to be effective, it is not necessary for a bank's cybersecurity controls to be invulnerable. Instead they simply need to be sufficiently robust so that a criminal concludes that targeting a weaker firm will be a more productive use of their resources. It may not be a coincidence that almost all of the banks that have been victims of SWIFT cyber-payment frauds are from emerging markets.
- The success of any new form of cybercrime will subsequently decline, once potential victims become aware of the method of attack and can put in place appropriate countermeasures. This is driver behind the profiles of both Figures 16.4 and 16.5. This will lead to cybercrime related losses coming in waves, driven by criminal innovation, followed by troughs, driven the innovation of their potential victims.[33]
- In response to these countermeasures, criminals may further enhance and change their tools and techniques (e.g. the observed reduction in the value of attempted fraudulent SWIFT payment instructions); alternatively, they may simply redeploy their existing technology against weaker, less valuable, but more numerous victims.

---

of $84k, and the largest ransom demand observed by Coveware was $780k, although the ransom reportedly paid by the Colonial Pipeline in May 2021 was significantly larger, i.e. $4.4m. Ransomware attacks against small businesses may be as low as $1.5k (Coveware, 2020). The number of SWIFT members is sourced from the SWIFT website, and the value of frauds is taken from Figure 16.5.

[32] Brigadier Alan Hill, Head of Operate and Defend at the MoD in "The Ministry of Defence fends off 'thousands' of daily cyberattacks", *The Financial Times*, 25th June, 2015.

[33] FDIC and OCC proposed in December 2020 rules requiring US banks to notify their regulators about major computer security incidents within 36 hours. This may facilitate industry-wide responses to new threats.

- Any factors which weaken a potential victim's controls, reducing the time to exploit a victim, or alter its behaviour, increasing the ability of cybercriminals to locate victims will lead to an increase in fraud, e.g. the COVID-19 pandemic.
- It was inevitable that cybercriminals would target supply chains,[34] e.g. Solar-Winds, "Due to the fact a single MSP [Managed Service Providers] can service a large number of customers" (US Secret Services, 2020). Consequently, per Formula 16.1, successfully breaching the defences of an MSP can both massively accelerate the location of victims and reduce the time taken to exploit them.

Finally, Optimal Foraging Theory cannot be applied to state-sponsored cyber-criminals as political motivations will trump the optimisation of benefit and effort. This is important as sophisticated tools developed for espionage may subsequently become commercialised by criminal groups. For example, the Stuxnet virus, which was discovered in 2010, and reportedly was developed by the USA and Israel to disrupt Iran's nuclear programme, has reportedly subsequently been modified by criminal groups.

4. TECHNOLOGICAL ADVANCES, INCLUDING ALGOS, AI AND MACHINE LEARNING

Technological advances are perpetual. Over the last decade, however, the exponential growth in computing power and the amount of data that can be processed has accelerated this trend. This will ultimately transform the Operational Risk profiles of firms. This section provides an overview of the current usage of AI and machine learning in financial services. It then reviews examples of Operational Risk losses caused by the operation of models, before applying the first five laws to predict how the Operational Risk profiles of firms may be changed.

Overview of key technological advances

The Bank of England and the FCA defined the following terms in their 2019 survey of machine learning: (Bank of England and FCA, 2019):

- *Algos* are rules-based code where the human programmer explicitly decides what decisions are being taken in different circumstances.
- *Artificial Intelligence* is the development of computer systems able to perform tasks which previously required human intelligence. AI is a broad field, of which machine learning is a subcategory.

---

[34]MSPs are companies that provide management services for a customer's IT infrastructure using remote administration tools.

- *Machine Learning* is a methodology whereby computer programmes fit a model or recognise patterns from data, without being explicitly programmed and with limited or no human intervention.

Current usage in financial services Financial services firms are primarily utilising machine learning to obtain new analytical insights, e.g. improve the combatting of fraud and money laundering; automate decision making; streamline processes; and personalise automated customer experiences (Bank of England and FCA, 2019). Specific examples include:

- *New analytical insights – AML and fraud prevention and detection:* Firms can utilise machine learning to analyse millions of documents and check details against "blacklists" for the KYC checks before the onboarding process begins.[35] Post-onboarding firms can use machine learning to assess the likelihood of a customer posing a financial crime risk. Additionally, when customers make payments, firms can use machine learning to identify suspicious activities and flag potential cases, for review by bank staff (Bank of England and FCA, 2019).
- *Operational efficiency/streamlining of processes:* Automation of "low value processes" e.g.:
  - JPMorgan Chase has introduced COIN (Contract Intelligence), a platform that uses machine learning to analyse legal documents and to extract important data;[36]
  - Trading & Sales: Firms are using machine learning to increase the speed and accuracy of processing orders; and
  - BNY Mellon has deployed >220 automated computer programs/"bots". The activities undertaken include responding to audit letters and correcting errors in fund transfer requests.[37]
- *Personalised automated customer experience:* Banks are using chatbots to interact with customers and solve simple problems and provide "day-to-day transactions", e.g. account information and password resets.[38] Machine learning can facilitate faster identification of customer requirements and also, if necessary, transfer the

---

[35]This aspect is not new. When the Author worked for a universal bank, several decades ago, the second-hand vehicle financing business assessed new applications submitted by car dealerships within seconds. This included cross-checking to industry-wide databases of names, addresses and mobile numbers previously used in frauds. Applications that were scored as being higher risk by the algorithm were referred to a staff member. Unlike with machine learning, however, the algorithm was updated manually based on human analysis of successful application frauds.

[36]Page 49 of JPMorgan Chase's 2016 Annual Report.

[37]*Reuters*, (10th May 2017) "BNY Mellon advances artificial intelligence tech across operations".

[38]*Forbes*, (28th October 2016) "Meet Erica, Bank of America's New Voice AI Banking System".

customer to a human agent more quickly. The aim of these chatbots tools is to fulfil efficiently a customer's request. Machine learning allows the model to learn from the feedback of previous interactions with customers. Machine learning can also be used to profile customers for precision-targeted offers and to identify customers with a higher likelihood of dissatisfaction (Bank of England and FCA, 2019).

▪ *Decision making – Credit Risk:* Credit approvals for retail customers have long been automated and based on scorecards. Machine learning is starting to be used for wholesale transactions, for example, the Author is aware of a European bank that is exploring using machine learning for assessing and approving commercial real estate loan applications.

▪ *Decision making – Sales & Trading:*
  – *Pricing:* Machine learning models can combine a large number of market time-series to arrive at an estimate of a short-term fair value; and
  – *Execution:* Machine learning models can evaluate venue, timing and order size choices to optimise the filling of equity orders (Bank of England and FCA, 2019).

Machine learning can also be used to provide suggested portfolio decisions to fund managers; and price general insurance products, such as motor and building and contents.

Looking forward, the survey of 106 UK financial institutions in 2019 conducted by UK regulators (Bank of England and FCA, 2019) found that respondents expect to more than double their usage of machine learning applications over the next three years.

Operational Risk losses arising from the operation of models

Whilst there seem to be no examples of AI and machine learning leading to Operational Risk losses, there are a number of examples of losses arising from either malfunctioning algos or algos designed to automate systemic misconduct, illustrating the types of risks that may be generated by AI and machine learning.

Decision making – trade execution: Malfunctioning algo at Knight Capital

In July 2012, Knight Capital implemented some new code for its order routing system, which was intended to replace a piece of redundant code that had been unused since 2003. Whilst this change was implemented successful in the code on seven servers, on an eighth server it was not only omitted, but the legacy code on this server was accidentally reactivated (SEC, 2013).

At 8.01am on 1st August the Knight Capital's order routing system began generating automated email messages, 97 in total, indicating that there was a problem, but these messages were not treated as alerts and were ignored by the IT function. When markets opened at 9.30 a.m. the reactivated legacy code on the eighth server began attempting to fulfil some retail orders. Unfortunately, the code that should have stopped it sending out orders once the customer' requests were filled had been deleted in 2005. So it just kept on sending out orders. The IT function's initial attempts at addressing the problem by reversing the code drop were unsuccessful. Finally, at 10.15 a.m. the order router was switched off, but only after 212 small retail orders had led to the firm executing ~4 million trades, generating a $460 million loss. As a consequence, Knight Capital had to undertake an emergency $400 million issuance of convertible preferred stock to a small group of investors on Sunday 5th August.

Decision making – trade execution: Automation of systemic misconduct – asymmetrical last look Barclays was fined[39] $150 million in November 2015 by the NYDFS for abusing the last look FX trading practice on its BARX electronic trading platform between 2009 and 2014 (NYDFS, 2015). Last look enables firms to ensure that high-frequency traders have not detected a move in a market a few milliseconds before the bank, enabling them to arbitrage the bank's marginally less nimble trading platforms. Last look imposes a hold period between the receipt of a customer's order and its acceptance and execution, in order to protect a bank from this type of arbitrage. Barclays had, however, implemented last look in an asymmetrical fashion, i.e. trades that moved in the customer's favour, above a threshold, were rejected by BARX, but not if they had moved in the bank's favour!

Decision making – trade execution: Automation of systemic misconduct – spoofing In October 2014, the SEC reached a $1 million settlement with a New York based high frequency trading firm – Athena Capital Research – for placing a very large number of aggressive, rapid fire trades in the final two seconds of almost every trading day between June and December 2009, in order to manipulate the closing prices of thousands of NASDAQ-listed stocks. The SEC had found that Athena used an algo to buy and sell stocks just before the close, allowing its trades to make up over 70% of the total NASDAQ trading volume in the affected stocks in the final seconds of trading, almost every day (SEC, 2014).

Decision making – trade execution: Mispricing of illiquid equities Credit Suisse in Australia was fined in May 2016 by the Australian Securities & Investments Commission (ASIC) because its automated order-processing system failed to recognise that two stocks were illiquid. As a result there was neither a "last traded price" nor an "opening price", leading the algo to execute trades at a price well above the previous days' trading prices, artificially raising the price of the stocks (AISC, May 2016).

---

[39] Although Barclays did not admit wrongdoing.

Decision making – credit ratings: Coding error in a ratings model In early 2007, Moody's in Europe discovered a coding error in a model for rating certain Constant Proportion Debt Obligation (CPDO) notes. The impact was that 11 CPDO notes with a value of just under $1 billion were overrated by between 1.5 to 3.5 notches. The issue was only identified when an US investment bank involved in a transaction queried why Moody's credit rating was out of line with its own internal credit rating model (SEC, 2010).

Decision making – credit approvals: Coding error in the affordability calculator In September 2016, the AISC Commission fined Commonwealth Bank of Australia (CBA) for breaching responsible lending laws when providing personal overdraft facilities, due to a coding error in the Bank's affordability calculator. As a consequence, between July 2011 and September 2015, CBA approved 9,577 customers for overdrafts which would have otherwise been declined. CBA wrote-off AUD2.5 million in overdraft balances (AISC, September 2016).

Interestingly, all of these examples of losses arising from either malfunctioning algos or algos designed to automate systemic misconduct, relate to decision making.

Applying the Ten Laws

It is the first five laws which are most relevant to Operational Risk losses arising from AI and machine learning.

1st Law: Occurrence Formula 2.1 indicates that the occurrence of Operational Risk events involving machine learning is driven by a combination of a firm's business profile; the nature of inadequacies or failures; and the effectiveness of preventive controls. The business profile for AI and machine learning reflects a firm's usage of these tools, e.g. decision making vs providing a personalised customer experience. The nature of the inadequacies or failures may variously include issues relating to the appropriateness of the data being analysed by the model, or the model engineering not performing as intended. The relevant preventive controls include: validation of the data inputs; model validation and approval prior to deployment; and ongoing outcome monitoring and having a "human in the loop".

2nd Law: Detection Formula 2.2 indicates that the detection of inadequacies or failures is driven by the effectiveness of detective controls, which for AI and machine learning includes, as noted above, outcome monitoring. Controls, as previously discussed, are not always effective (Appendix I.3: Control failure taxonomy). This is illustrated by the failure of Moody's to identify the coding error in their CPDO rating model, described above, until a US investment bank involved in a transaction, queried the outputs (Figure 16.8).

FIGURE 16.8 Duration of inappropriate outcomes of decision-making models, consequences and lags (Grimwade, 2019)

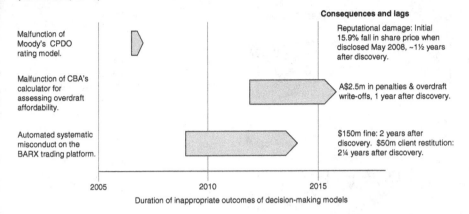

Consequences and lags

Malfunction of Moody's CPDO rating model.	Reputational damage: Initial 15.9% fall in share price when disclosed May 2008, ~1½ years after discovery.
Malfunction of CBA's calculator for assessing overdraft affordability.	A$2.5m in penalties & overdraft write-offs, 1 year after discovery.
Automated systematic misconduct on the BARX trading platform.	$150m fine: 2 years after discovery. $50m client restitution: 2¼ years after discovery.

2005   2010   2015

Duration of inappropriate outcomes of decision-making models

3rd Law: Velocity Formula 2.3 indicates that the rapidity with which losses accrete (velocity) is driven by the quantum of inadequacies or failures; the nature of the impacts; external causes; and the effectiveness of corrective/resilience controls.

The quantum of failure can be measured in terms of the scale of an unexpected market position created by a rogue algo, e.g. Knight Capital's rogue algo firm executed ~4 million trades, which resulted in a net $3.5 billion long position on 80 stocks and a net $3.15 billion short position on another 74 stocks in just 45 minutes. CBA's mis-coded affordability calculator led to the inappropriate approval of overdraft facilities for 9,577 customers over a four-year period.

The nature of impacts included in the various case studies include: Market and Credit Risk exposures; regulatory fines and penalties; client restitution; and reputational damage. The scale of losses arising from an unintended Market Risk exposure may clearly be exacerbated by higher market volatility. In the case of Knight Capital the malfunctioning algo itself added to the day's volatility, as it generated >50% of the trade volume for 37 shares, contributing to >10% share price movements. This aspect of malfunctioning algos makes this risk both very fat-tailed and non-linear, i.e. the losses generated from a major malfunction may be disproportionately large in comparison to smaller events (Figure 16.9).

The key corrective/resilience controls relate to the operation of "kill switches" for models that expose firms to very high velocity risks, i.e. primarily Market Risk.

4th Law: Severity Formula 2.4 indicates that the scale of losses is driven by the combination of the velocity, which includes the quantum of inadequacies or failures and external causes; and duration. The interaction of these different factors are observable in Figure 16.9.

FIGURE 16.9   Drivers of the impacts of individual malfunctioning trading algos (Grimwade, 2019)

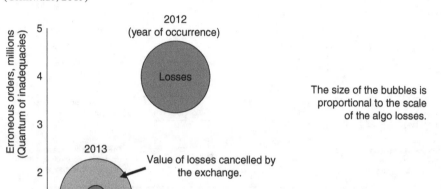

At the time, malfunctioning trading algos were far from uncommon, as when, in the aftermath of the Knight Capital incident, the Chicago Federal Reserve interviewed 30 market participants they discovered that half of the clearers, two thirds of the proprietary trading firms and all of the exchanges had experienced errant algos (Chicago Federal Reserve, 2012). Figure 16.9 highlights that the prevalence of algo malfunctions, however, appears to have subsequently declined since then. This may reflect responses to these high-profile events by both firms and regulators alike, e.g. the requirements set out in MiFID II. This represents a further illustration of the 8th Law: Risk Homeostasis.

5th Law: Lags   The 5th Law observes that "the length of time between detection and settlement is linked to systemic misconduct; regulatory involvement; litigation; sensitivity to economic cycles; and the distribution of compensation to customers. Almost three quarters of large losses crystallise over a year after detection." This is consistent with the small sample of events included in this section and Figure 16.8.

Conclusions

The Laws of Operational Risk indicate that the usage of AI and machine learning in decision making will lead to significant Operational Risk losses due to the combination of both the quantum of potential inadequacies or failures, caused by a systematically malfunctioning model, and the potential nature of the impacts, i.e. Market and Credit Risk exposures. For both risks, the scale of losses are also heavily influenced by the speed of detection, although this variously ranges between minutes and months, given the relative velocities of these two key impacts.

CONCLUSIONS

The four emerging threats/causes described in this chapter have some similarities and differences in both the natures of the threats and their impacts (Table 16.3). Climate Change and technological advances will create permanent changes to the Operational Risk profiles of firms for the remainder of the working lives of Operational Risk managers. Pandemics and cybercrime will also be a perpetual feature of the future but the profile is very different. Driven respectively by mutation and natural selection and by innovation and greed, the profile of both pandemics and cybercrime will tend to come in waves, with initial success for pathogens and criminals followed by troughs caused by the deployment of effective countermeasures, whether vaccines or better cyber defences. These waves can be seen in Figure 15.2.

In terms of Operational Risk consequences, the most significant for both pandemics and Climate Change arise from impacts of economic cycles on a firm's existing business profile, i.e. current customers and historical sales in the form of losses arising from deficiencies in loan documentation, revealed following customer defaults; claims of mis-sale; failing to treat customers fairly in financial difficulties; and desperation frauds carried out by customers (7th Law: Concentration due to external drivers). The impacts of pandemics and Climate Change on the Operational Risk profiles of banks is also heavily driven by behavioural changes of key stakeholders. In contrast, cybercrime is characterised by losses directly arising from disruption and theft of data, potentially linked to extortion; fraud; and theft of financial assets and intellectual property. The Operational Risks generated by technological advances differ as their most significant impacts relate to automated decision making regarding the taking of both Market and Credit Risks. Hence, the inappropriate operation of AI and machine learning models may generate Market and Credit Risks : Operational Risks boundary losses through the 9th Law: Risk Transference, Transformation and Conservation. Although there are currently no loss events in the public domain, in the future, the pattern of losses may resemble the industry's experience with algos (Figure 16.9), i.e. the occurrence of some very high-profile losses prior to firms deploying enhanced control frameworks (8th Law: Risk Homeostasis).

The financial services industry seems to be entering a third era of Operational Risk (Grimwade, 2019). The first era (the 1990s) was a period of largely idiosyncratic losses, whilst the second era (2001 to 2015) was marked by misconduct-related losses linked to the bursting of both the dot.com and the US housing bubbles and by Systemic

Operational Risk Events (Figure 11.1). The burgeoning third era (2015 onwards) will be driven by feedback loops between cybercrime, societal change (i.e. Generations Y and Z) and technological advances (e.g. social media), whilst the increasing use of AI and machine learning in decision-making models within banking will systematically expose firms to Market and Credit Risks : Operational Risk boundary losses.

Whilst this third era of losses may never come to an end (Figure 15.2), it may ultimately be overtaken by a fourth era (2030 onwards?) in which Operational Risk losses are driven by Transition and Physical Climate Change risks.

TABLE 16.3 Mapping these emerging risks to the impact taxonomy (Appendix II)

P&L	Level 2 – examples	Pandemics	Climate Risk – Transition Risks	Climate Risk – Physical Risks	Cybercrime	Technological advances
Lost revenues or charges (P&L) — Uncollected revenues due to an Operational Risk event.	▪ Uncollected revenues, e.g. failure to claim revenues to which a firm is entitled and loss of entitlement to revenues.	Revenue disruption	Revenue disruption	Revenue disruption	Ransomware	
Impairments and settlements to the bank's P&L accounts due to an Operational Risk event.	▪ Restitution/compensation payments linked to a firm's business profile and third-party relationships (Figure 2.1), e.g.: ▪ Customers and investors, e.g.: ■ Credit and Market Risk losses suffered; ■ Frauds suffered by customers; and ■ Loss of client assets in safe custody. ▪ Counterparties, customers and suppliers: Interest on monies owed.	Various, e.g. fiduciary duty to prevent customers suffering fraud	Various, e.g. claims of misconduct regarding historical sales	Various, e.g. treating customers in financial difficulties unfairly	Various, e.g. compensation for data leaks	Various, e.g. compensation for automated misconduct and systematic processing errors
	▪ *Suppliers:* Breach of contract or licencing agreements, e.g. data.					
	▪ *Employees (current and potential), e.g.:* ■ Lost historical earnings, e.g. due to payroll errors; and ■ Lost future earnings for an inappropriate dismissal.	Sickness, mental health and death		Sickness, mental health and death		

(continued)

TABLE 16.3 (Continued)

P&L	Level 2 – examples	Pandemics	Climate Risk		Cybercrime	Technological advances
			Transition Risks	Physical Risks		
	■ Visitors (e.g. customers, suppliers, etc.): third-party liability.					
	■ Regulatory action: fines and penalties.		Penalties for breaching new regulations.		Personal data leaks	Automated misconduct
	■ Tax incurred, e.g.: ■ On behalf of others, e.g. clients or employees; and ■ Loss of treatment, e.g. failed tax arbitrage/ avoidance schemes.					
Additional expenses or foregone expenditure[40] with a direct link to the Operational Risk event.	■ Legal liabilities. ORX include legal expenses that relate to Operational Risk events both for when firms act as the plaintiff as well as the defendant.	Costs of litigation	Costs of litigation	Costs of litigation	Costs of litigation	Costs of litigation
	■ Other third-party expenses, e.g. accountants, office cleaners (COVID-19), etc.	Staff welfare costs		Staff welfare costs		

[40] An unexpected impact of COVID-19 was a reduction in budgeted travel & entertainment expenditure for international banks.

Additional staff costs, e.g.: ■ Incentives and overtime payments for employees; and ■ third-party contractor costs.		
Additional costs, e.g. temporary offices and recovery sites.	WFH costs	
Physical assets: ■ Buildings; ■ IT equipment; and ■ Fixtures and fittings, but avoid double counting with write-downs.[41]		Repairs due to extreme weather
Costs of repair or replacement, incurred to restore the position that was prevailing before the Operational Risk event.		
■ Costs of improving controls*		

(continued)

---

[41] In supplementary guidelines published by the Committee of European Banking Supervisors CEBS, July (2010) the costs to repair or to replace an asset were included in Direct Charges rather than External Costs, reducing the potential for double counting.

TABLE 16.3 *(Continued)*

| Balance sheet and stakeholders | Level 2 – examples | Pandemics | Climate Risk | | Cybercrime | Technological advances |
			Transition Risks	Physical Risks		
Write-off of assets (balance sheet) — Write-downs of balance sheet assets due to an Operational Risk event, e.g.	Market Risk losses or gains (mark-to-market) for the Bank, arising from an Operational Risk event e.g. rogue trading or fat-fingered typing.	Fat-fingers	Fat-fingers	Fat-fingers		Trade decision-making software
■ Theft: asset stolen ■ Fraud: asset never existed; ■ Extortion; ■ Accidental asset transfers; ■ Damage; and ■ Loss of recourse.						
	■ Financial assets: ■ Cash and bearer bonds; and ■ Securities.	Cyber-criminals exploit new situations	Cyber-criminals exploit new situations	Cyber-criminals exploit new situations	Cyber-criminals exploit new situations	Cyber-criminals exploit new technologies

Reputational Impacts (Stakeholders listed on Figure 2.1)						
		Physical assets: ■ Physical commodities; ■ Buildings; ■ IT equipment; and ■ Fixtures & fittings.			Destruction caused by extreme weather	Credit decision-making software
		■ Loans: Credit Risk losses, exacerbated by operational failures, e.g. failure to perfect security; put in place netting agreements or to call margin. *	Uncovering latent issues	Uncovering latent issues	Uncovering latent issues	
	Authorities	■ Higher fines, if a repeat offender (Table 9.1). ■ Additional capital requirements, lowering return on equity. ■ Licence restrictions on ability to conduct new activities. ■ *Operational Resilience:* Threat to the financial system, requiring risk mitigation plans.		Capital penalties for exposures to Climate Change		
	Investors: Bondholders	■ Higher funding costs if a firm's credit rating is downgraded (Figure 13.11).		Changing investment decisions		
	Investors: Shareholders	■ Higher costs of capital if existing investors sell shares and price falls (Figure 13.9).				

(continued)

TABLE 16.3 *(Continued)*

Balance sheet and stakeholders	Level 2 – examples	Pandemics	Climate Risk		Cybercrime	Technological advances
			Transition Risks	Physical Risks		
Infrastructure and counterparties	■ *Operational Resilience:* Disorderly operation of markets. ■ *Operational Resilience:* Threaten a firm's safety and soundness, e.g. loss of revenues and liquidity.					
Suppliers and outsourcers	■ Adverse reaction.					
Customers	■ *Operational Resilience:* Intolerable levels of harm to a firm's clients. ■ Loss of future customer and client revenues (Figure 13.10) – EBA stress testing only. Not an Operational Risk loss for capital calculations (EBA, July 2018).	Support during pandemic	Reduced share of wallet			
Employees: current & future	■ Impact on staff morale and inability to retain existing employees. ■ Inability to recruit new employees.	Support during pandemic				
Criminals	■ Higher levels of fraud if a firm has a poor reputation for fraud prevention.				Reputation of cyber-security	
Society	■ Adverse reaction.		Social media and NGOs			

* Not an Operational Risk loss for capital calculations.

PART

Four

Conclusions

This final section consists of Chapter 17, which concludes the book by reprising the key themes and by considering how the various tools should be integrated into an holistic Operational Risk strategy to provide commercial value to firms.

Conclusions and Operational Risk Strategy

The Author once worked at a bank in which staff in the Group Risk function would often bemoan the Risk department not having "a seat at the table" – this metaphorical table being the one at which decisions were made. The Author's view was (and remains) that staff from Risk departments will proactively be invited to decision-making meetings only if they are seen as having valuable insights.[1] With this focus on providing value, this chapter provides a summary of:

1. The behaviours of Operational Risk;
2. The Ten Laws of Operational Risk;
3. An explanation of the underlying drivers of the behaviours of Operational Risk;
4. The key enhancements to Operational Risk management tools; and
5. Alternative strategies to meet the objectives of Operational Risk managers.

1. SUMMARY OF THE BEHAVIOURS OF OPERATIONAL RISK

The analysis of various industry loss data collection exercises in Chapter 1 highlights that Operational Risk displays a range of behaviours at differing levels, i.e. the overall Operational Risk level; the seven risk subcategories; business lines; and individual banks:

- *Profile of Operational Risk losses:* The largest number of Operational Risk loss events have relatively low impacts, whilst a small number of loss events have disproportionately high impacts (Figures 1.1 and 1.2).

---

[1]Cynically, second-line staff may still be invited to decision-making meetings, even if they do not have anything interesting to say, as a mechanism of dispersing any resulting blame in the event of a loss being subsequently suffered!

- *Trends and dynamism:* There is a spike in number and value of Operational Risk loss events ≥€10 million that coincides with the aftermath of the Global Financial Crisis (Table 1.1 and Figures 1.1, 1.2 and 11.1). The main driver of this is CPBP (Figures 1.3 and 1.4).
- *Frequency and stability:* Some of the seven subcategories of Operational Risk are consistently more frequent than others, in particular EDPM and EF. The frequencies of some of these subcategories also appear to be quite stable over time, e.g. EDPM, IF, BDSF and DPA (Figure 1.3).
- *CPBP's disproportionate impacts:* The losses generated by this risk subcategory are disproportionately large (Figure 1.4) and as noted above it is more dynamic than many of the other subcategories of Operational Risk (Figure 1.3 and 1.4).
- *Profile of different business lines:* The risk profiles of Trading & Investment and Banking business lines are actually quite similar with the exception that the Banking business line is more exposed to External Fraud loss events (Figure 1.4).
- *Profile of individual banks:* The risk profiles of banks seem to differ quite markedly in terms of the volume of Operational Risk loss events that they suffer (Figure 1.5).

Chapter 6 demonstrated how these observed behaviours of Operational Risk can all be explained through the Ten Laws.

2. OVERVIEW OF THE TEN LAWS OF OPERATIONAL RISK

The Ten Laws are far from a random list of statements. The first five laws (the left-hand-side of Table 17.1) relate to the occurrence, detection and the financial significance of

TABLE 17.1 The coverage of the Ten Laws of Operational Risk and their units

Describe individual events	Describe patterns in events and interrelationships
1. Occurrence of events (events)	6. Concentration due to internal drivers (ratio of losses for different banks)
2. Detection of events (events over time)	7. Concentration due to external drivers (ratio of losses pre & post the GFC)
3. Velocity of losses (incurred losses ($) over time)	8. Risk Homeostasis (losses ($) over time)
4. Duration and severity of events (incurred losses ($))	9. Risk transference, transformation and conservation (events over time) and (losses ($) over time)
5. Lags in settlement (settled losses ($) over time)	10. Proactive taking of Operational Risk (losses ($) over time)

individual loss events, whilst the final five laws (the right-hand-side of Table 17.1) relate to the patterns in events and their interrelationships.

More specifically, the first five laws identify the nature of the inadequacies or failures that constitute both Operational Risk events and control failures; the business profile of firms; the underlying internal and external causes; and assess their varying relevance to different categories of Operational Risk. Business profile is systematically defined in terms of a firm's strategy, culture, and infrastructure, including governance, processes, people and systems, and its external relationships with authorities, e.g. regulators; its sources of capital, funding and revenues; third- (and fourth-) party service providers; and society. Business profile influences both the risks to which firms are exposed and the quantum of inadequacies or failures (Figure 17.2). The first five laws also cover the rapidity (velocity) with which different categories of impacts accrete; the duration of events; and the lags between the detection of events and their subsequent crystallisation into losses.

The final five laws describe the interactions between Operational Risk and other factors. The 6th and 7th Laws cover the concentration of losses in firms driven by either internal or external causes, respectively. The 6th Law identifies that internal causes primarily drive the occurrence of Operational Risk events, whilst the most important external cause, economic change, increases the occurrence and detection of Operational Risk events, as well as their velocity and duration (7th Law). The ubiquitous role of causes in many of these laws is reflected in a revised version of the profession's butterfly diagram (Figure 17.1).

The 8th Law: Risk Homeostasis describes how firms will naturally respond to losses (both actual and anticipated) outside of their appetite, by enhancing their controls.[2] As a consequence, the 8th Law implies that past losses may not always be a good guide to the future loss experiences of a firm. The 9th Law deals with the ability of firms to transfer risks to other entities. It describes how Market and Credit Risks can be transformed into Operational Risk, through the "granting" of Real Options, and that the absolute quantum of risk is conserved through this process. Operational Risk can also be transferred via insurance. Finally, the 10th Law explains how firms can proactively take Operational Risk by selling products and providing services, in return for fee income. It demonstrates that this source of revenue generates disproportionate Operational Risks.

---

[2]This is consistent with the 1960s Japanese manufacturing concept of poka-yoke or "mistake-proofing", which involves both the prevention of defects from occurring, and the amendment of processes, when defects do occur, to avoid their recurrence.

FIGURE 17.1 A revised butterfly/bow-tie diagram (Repeat of Figure 6.3)
The dotted lines reflect the causes; control failures and impacts of a well-publicised
mis-marking incident in 2008

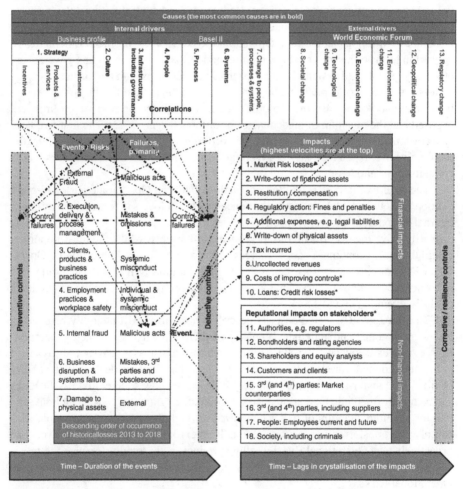

The criticality of time – revised butterfly diagram

Across the bottom of the revised butterfly/bow-tie diagram (Figure 17.1) is time,
emphasising the importance of both the duration of events[3] and the lags that can occur
in settlement (Figures 2.4 and 2.5, and also Figure 11.9). As a consequence, time

---

[3]The time elapsed between the failure of preventive controls and the success of detective controls.

features more significantly in risk appetite (Chapter 7), capital modelling (Chapter 10) and stress testing (Chapter 11).

An overarching formula

The Ten Laws can also be represented as a single overarching formula (Formula 17.1). There are a number of interesting aspects of Operational Risk highlighted in this formula. It describes losses suffered by a firm in a particular year, which is influenced by not just occurrence (1st Law), but also the detection of events (2nd Law) and the lags in settlement (5th Law). The formula also makes clear that the Operational Risk losses suffered by a firm will arise from a combination of proactively taken Operational Risks, as well as other risks to which the firm is passively exposed (10th Law). As noted above, the level of losses suffered by firms should equilibrate over time to their risk appetites through the 8th Law: Risk Homeostasis. The three taxonomies described in Chapter 5 are very influential. Causal factors are all-pervasive. Internal causes drive the concentration of Operational Risk events (6th Law), whilst external causes can drive occurrence, detection/duration, velocity, and lags (7th Law). The taxonomy of inadequacies or failures describes both events and control failures and hence influences both occurrence and impacts, whilst the nature of different consequences described in the impact taxonomy influences the velocity of losses. Finally, the 9th Law (Risk transference and conservation), is an important factor in both the velocity of some losses, and also recoveries through insurance.

The spans of the influence of both human and institutional behaviours and biases, and business profile are also highlighted in Formula 17.1.

3. THE UNDERLYING DRIVERS OF THE BEHAVIOURS OF OPERATIONAL RISK

Whilst Chapter 6 demonstrated that the Ten Laws can clearly explain how Operational Risk behaves, they do not necessarily explain why these patterns exist. The Author believes that there are three underlying pillars that drive these patterns:

1. *The business profiles of firms* determine both the profile of their risks and the potential quantum of failure (Table 2.4 and Figure 6.2);
2. *The nature of the three taxonomies* described in Chapter 5, i.e. inadequacies or failures (both events and control failures); causal factors and impacts; and
3. *Human and institutional behaviours and biases* influence the activities of a firm's stakeholders altering the occurrence of inadequacies or failures, such as misconduct and malicious acts. They can also alter the assessment of remote risks and the extent to which firms learn lessons and consequently suffer fewer Operational Risk loss events over time.

Formula 17.1 An overarching formula for Operational Risk

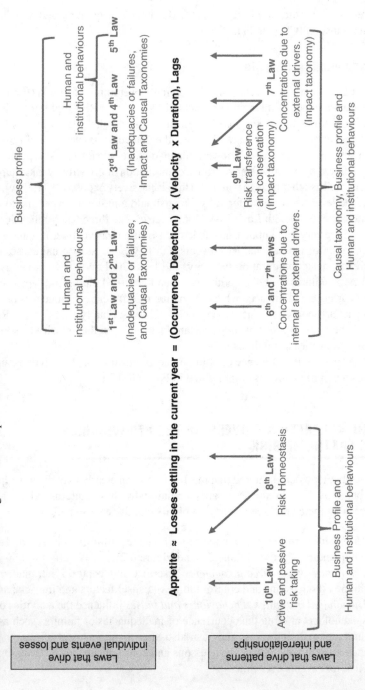

Appetite ≈ Losses settling in the current year = (Occurrence, Detection) x (Velocity x Duration), Lags

1. The business profiles of firms

A firm's business profile can be articulated in terms of the relevant authorities, e.g. regulators in various jurisdictions; its sources of capital, funding and revenues; its various third- (and fourth-) party service providers; and society. These reflect the firm's strategy (both past and present), which also influences its culture; people, processes; systems; and infrastructure, including governance. The influence of strategy can be seen in Figure 17.2, which compares some of these factors for Banking and Trading & Investment businesses, i.e. the numbers of customers; channels; volume and value of transactions; and geographical/jurisdictional footprint. It is the business profiles of ORX members, that is a key contributing factor to the shapes of both Figures 1.1 and 1.2, by influencing, in particular, the occurrence and scale of losses through several of the Ten Laws, i.e. 1st Law: Occurrence; 3rd Law: Velocity; 6th and 7th Laws: Concentration due to internal and external causes; 9th Law: Risk Transference, Transformation and Conservation; and 10th Law: Active and passive risk taking. Finally, aspects of a firm's business profile can also drive both causal factors and staff behaviours.

2. The nature of the three taxonomies

The influence of these three taxonomies are considered in turn.

1. Taxonomy of causal factors Although not obvious in Table 17.1, the first seven laws and the 9th Law all include implicitly or explicitly either internal or external causes, which can influence the occurrence of events; the effectiveness of preventive, detective and corrective/resilience controls and the scale of any consequential financial impacts. This is reflected in Figure 17.1, a revised butterfly/bow-tie diagram, which illustrates the all-pervasive nature of causes by listing them across the top of the diagram, rather than on the left-hand side. The dotted lines in Figure 17.1 reflect the influences of causes on occurrence, control failures and impacts based upon a well-publicised mis-marking incident from 2008. Additionally, the various causal factors are not all independent, instead some of them appear to be correlated exacerbating their influence (Figure 17.3). Finally, as highlighted in Figure 17.1, the same causal factors may have multiple influences. These causal factors contribute to both the observed concentrations of Operational Risk losses in individual firms and also industry-wide trends.

2. Taxonomy of inadequacies or failures Inadequacies or failures constitute the nature of both events and control failures. A review of the volume of incidents recorded against the seven Basel II subcategories suggests that the most common loss events arise from human mistakes and omissions. Systemic misconduct by groups of staff members/firms seems to be less common, whilst malicious acts by staff members are orders of magnitude rarer still. The BDO FraudTrack report (BDO, 2018) highlights

FIGURE 17.2 The business profile of a firm annotated for factors driving the differences between Banking and Trading & Investment business lines (Repeat of Figure 8.1)

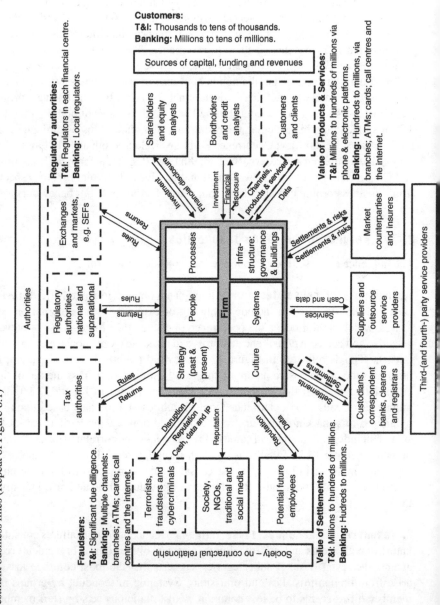

Customers:
T&I: Thousands to tens of thousands.
Banking: Millions to tens of millions.

Sources of capital, funding and revenues

Regulatory authorities:
T&I: Regulators in each financial centre.
Banking: Local regulators.

Shareholders and equity analysts

Bondholders and credit analysts

Customers and clients

Value of Products & Services:
T&I: Millions to hundreds of millions via phone & electronic platforms.
Banking: Hundreds to millions, via branches; ATMs; cards; call centres and the internet.

Authorities

Exchanges and markets, e.g. SEFs

Regulatory authorities – national and supranational

Tax authorities

Firm
Processes
People
Strategy (past & present)
Infrastructure: governance & buildings
Systems
Culture

Market counterparties and insurers

Suppliers and outsource service providers

Custodians, correspondent banks, clearers and registrars

Third-(and fourth-) party service providers

Terrorists, fraudsters and cybercriminals

Society, NGOs, traditional and social media

Potential future employees

Fraudsters:
T&I: Significant due diligence.
Banking: Multiple channels: branches; ATMs; cards; call centres and the internet.

Society – no contractual relationship

Value of Settlements:
T&I: Millions to hundreds of millions.
Banking: Hudreds to millions.

Investment

Financial disclosure

Channels, products & services

Data

Settlements & risks

Cash and data

Services

Settlements

Rules

Returns

Rules

Returns

Rules

Returns

Disruption

Reputation Cash, data and IP

Reputation

Reputation

Data

Settlements & risks

FIGURE 17.3 Correlations between causal factors associated with individual large loss events (Repeat of Figure 5.2)

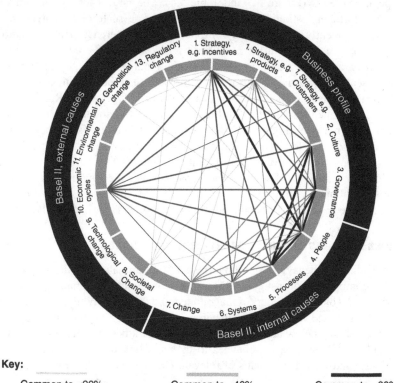

Key:

| Common to <20% of incidents in sample (Table 2.2) | Common to <40% of incidents in sample | Common to <60% of incidents in sample |

the importance of alternatively "Greed" and "Need" in motivating staff members to commit malicious acts. The exception is obviously professional criminals (Chapter 16).

In the revised butterfly diagram (Figure 17.1) the seven Basel II subcategories of Operational Risk are ordered based upon their frequency (Figure 1.3). In addition the primary nature of the associated inadequacies or failures has been added to each risk (Table 2.1). Finally, as inadequacies or failures are not only the nature of events (1st Law), but also the nature of control failures, then their influence also spans the first seven laws and the 9th Law. This has been reflected in the butterfly diagram by indicating the existence of more than one inadequacy or failure relating to a single event, i.e. whilst there can only be one inadequacy or failure that constitutes the event itself, other inadequacies or failures have been included that relate to the failure of the mitigating controls. This reflects the Reason's Swiss Cheese Model (Figure 13.2, Chapter 13).

3. Taxonomy of the nature of impacts The nature of the impacts arising from an Operational Risk event are clearly also critical to understanding the behaviours of Operational Risk (Figure 2.3 and Table 5.4). The largest losses that firms suffer are in the form of restitution and compensation. The scale of the largest of these impacts is frequently driven by the 9th Law: Risk Transference, Transformation and Conservation, i.e. when Market and Credit Risks are *transferred* to customers and clients, they are both *transformed* into Operational Risk for the arranging firm, and their scale is *conserved*.[4] This relationship between Operational Risk and Market and Credit Risks is also one driver for the sensitivity of Operational Risk to economic cycles, as explained through the 7th Law: Concentration due to external causes and the Real Option Model (Figure 3.4). The existence of Market Risk : Operational Risk boundary losses also leads to the existence of potentially very high velocity losses. Typically, impacts from events may be either high velocity or large-scale, but not both. Finally, the nature of some of the impacts drives the length of lags (5th Law), i.e. those involving "... misconduct; regulatory involvement; sensitivity to economic cycles; and the distribution of compensation to customers" have longer lags.

3. Human and institutional behaviours and biases

Understanding the behaviour of all but the simplest animals is challenging due to the complex combination of instinct and learning. Consequently, human and institutional behaviours and biases are orders of magnitude more complex. Whilst a detailed exploration of human and institutional behaviours and biases is beyond the scope of this book, summarised below are the various influences on both the behaviour of a firm's stakeholders (Figure 2.1), i.e. changes to their existing behaviours, as well as new behaviours; and their assessments of relevant Operational Risks. Each is considered in turn:

> *Professional criminals:* Chapter 16 put forward the theory that the behaviour of criminals can be explained through Zoology's Optimal Foraging Theory, i.e. that criminals will seek to optimise their returns for the effort that they expend in illegally obtaining assets. This implies that firms do not need to invest in foolproof cybersecurity, but they do need to ensure that they are not the "weakest in the herd".

> *Customers and investors:* Chapters 11 and 16 observed the impacts on the behaviour of customers and investors of the COVID-19 pandemic, e.g. new mortgages to finance house purchases initially declined (Chapter 11) and the flight of investors to "safe-haven" assets, e.g. gold (Chapter 16). There is some evidence in the responses of investors to the COVID-19 pandemic of Thaler's model for the reaction of market prices to information, i.e.

---

[4]Figure 11.1, in Chapter 11, highlights the relative significance of Market and Credit Risks on Operational Risk.

under-reaction, is followed by adjustment and overreaction (Chapter 13). The overreaction phase may also reflect the Herd Behaviour Bias (see Group Polarisation Bias below).[5] This bias was neatly articulated by the former governor of the Bank of England, Sir Mervyn King, talking about the Global Financial Crisis "it was not rational to start a bank run, but rational to participate in one, once it has started".

Authorities (Institutions), including regulators: Regulators have stated objectives, for example the FCA's include financial stability, consumer protection, integrity and competition. In the aftermath of the Global Financial Crisis the FSA/FCA imposed a series of record fines to encourage firms to comply with these objectives (Figure 4.2). In 2020, however, the FCA appeared to curtail imposing fines, possibly because it was prioritising financial stability over its other objectives (Chapter 16).

Staff members: The majority of inadequacies or failures arise from human failings whether events or control failures. Misconduct and malicious acts are rarer, with the BDO 2018 Fraud Track Survey revealing that the motivations for internal frauds can be split into two main groups, i.e. "Greed" and "Need". This seems intuitively correct, i.e. people are generally honest but do make mistakes.

Firms (Institutions): The 8th Law: Risk Homeostasis (Chapter 4) predicts that control expenditure will increase to keep firms within appetite both now, and also in the future (e.g. Y2K). In assessing a firm's current and future risk exposures, however, staff members (and authorities) are prone to a series of behavioural biases that may distort their conclusions and actions. For example, when individuals form subjective estimates, they start with a point of reference, a possibly arbitrary value, and then adjust away from it (Anchoring/Proximity Bias). The more easily people can recall examples, the more common they judge a thing to be (Example Bias). This means that Operational Risk managers and regulators may be susceptible to overestimating the likelihood of Operational Risk, as they are constantly exposed to these events. Similarly, the very act of contemplating an event occurring, may lead to the overestimation of the likelihood of the event actually occurring (Imagination Inflation).

Being in groups can further influence how people assess risks, for example, when people who share beliefs get together in groups, they become more convinced that their beliefs are correct, and they also become more extreme in their views. People will also conform to the Group's view and express opinions which are clearly incorrect (Group Polarisation Bias). Unfortunately, once a belief is in place, humans will screen what

---

[5]This may also explain the irrational bulk buying of toilet rolls in the UK at the outset of the COVID-19 pandemic. As noted earlier, social media may both expand the number of individuals within a "herd" and accelerate the Herd Behaviour response.

they see and hear, in a biased manner, to ensure that their beliefs are proven correct (Confirmation Bias).

These biases are particularly important to the periodic risk management processes that involve the assessment and articulation of a firm's Operational Risk profile, as they can distort the effectiveness of the 8th Law: Risk Homeostasis, to respond in "...anticipation of increased future losses".

Finally, it is important to note that these three underlying pillars that drive the Ten Laws should not be viewed in isolation. Instead they dynamically interact with each other as illustrated in Figure 17.4.

FIGURE 17.4   Illustration of the interactions between the three pillars driving the Ten Laws (Repeat of Figure 6.4)

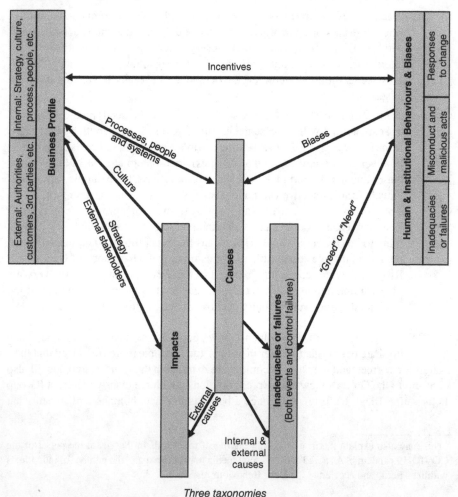

4. SUMMARY OF KEY ENHANCEMENTS TO OPERATIONAL RISK MANAGEMENT TOOLS

Operational Risk appetite should be articulated both quantitatively and qualitatively. The Ten Laws facilitate an understanding of the appropriate use of different Operational Risk appetite measures and tools (Table 7.1) to enable firms to "evaluate opportunities for appropriate risk taking and act as a defence against excessive risk-taking" (FSB, 2013). The proposed enhancements to the profession's tools, in Section II, are all based on a better understanding of the behaviours of Operational Risk relating to its occurrence; the velocity of losses; the nature of the mitigating controls; behavioural changes of stakeholders and the importance of time. For example:

Incident management: The order in which actions should be prioritised after an incident should reflect the order of controls on the revised butterfly diagram (Figure 17.1) reading from right to left, i.e. corrective/resilience actions to curtail immediate losses and secure recoveries; detective actions, to ascertain the scope of the issue; and preventive actions to limit recurrence.

Root cause analysis: Causes can increase the occurrence of loss events and their velocity, and also weaken controls (1st to 4th Laws), hence root cause analysis should utilise the causal taxonomy (Appendix III) to group causes into five categories based upon: occurrence, velocity and failures of preventive, detective and corrective/resilience controls.

Predictive metrics: The effectiveness of metrics at predicting the occurrence of events are clearly more readily demonstrable for risks that occur more frequently (1st Law and Figure 1.3) and also those with short lags between detection and settlement (5th Law and Figure 11.9). In these circumstances, metrics linked to causal factors that drive occurrence will be predictive, e.g. metrics for signs of stretch may be predictive for the occurrence of events involving mistakes and omissions. Metrics relating to the effectiveness of controls that prevent a persistent external threat of malicious acts (e.g. cybercrime) will also be highly predictive of the occurrence of these events, as any control weakness is likely to be exploited. Finally, review of Figure 11.1 suggests that the most important predictive metrics will be economic factors (Table 11.1), with CPBP losses being the most sensitive to business cycles (Figure 1.4), although the relationships are very complex.

Change management: Assessing the Operational Risks arising from change involves considering the different states of a firm's business profile: the stresses on BAU activities; the risks of transition/migration and the intermediate and end-states. For both the risks of transition and the intermediate and end-states Operational Risk managers should assess the appropriateness of the preventive, detective and corrective/resilience controls (1st, 2nd and 3rd Laws). For new business approval, Operational Risk managers should pay particular attention to products and transactions that transfer Market and Credit Risks to their customers (9th Law) and the profile of these risks (Figure 13.6).

Reputational Risk: The stakeholders with which a firm has a reputation are set out in Figure 2.1, and the potential impacts (Table 5.4), which involve changes in stakeholder behaviours. These may change as a result of either proactive decisions taken by firms, e.g. regarding their customers and products, etc., or as a consequence of events, such as an IT outage, or a rogue trader event or a regulatory settlement (Figure 13.11). The proactive taking of Reputational Risk and its reactive management after an event can be managed in a comparable manner to Operational Risk.

RCSAs should include the identification of the most important internal causes, as these both increase the occurrence of inadequacies or failures that constitute both events and control failures (Figure 6.3, 1st to 4th Laws). RCASs should prioritise risks that lead to either high velocity losses (3rd Law) or the slow accretion of larger losses over time (4th Law), through systemic failure (Table 5.4). Equally, RCSAs should deprioritise risks that generate high volume:low value losses arising from mistakes and omissions that will naturally be remediated through the day-to-day Operational Risk management practices (8th Law). RCSAs should also focus upon products and services that are particularly sensitive to economic shocks, and may involve the transfer of Market and Credit Risks to customers and investors (7th and 9th Laws) and also businesses that generate fee income through the provisions for services, as these are disproportionately risky (10th Law).

Scenario analysis: The techniques used for estimating the likelihood and severity of a scenario should not be driven by the Basel II event types, but instead by the frequency of the occurrence of the event (the inadequacy or failure, Appendix I) or the nature the impacts (Appendix II) respectively. These techniques can also be used for reverse stress testing. By utilising the 1st, 3rd and 4th Laws systematically, firms can facilitate the mitigation of the influences of the various behavioural biases.

Capital modelling should reflect the sensitivity of Operational Risk to economic cycles (7th Law) and the very significant lags between detection and settlement of CPBP losses (5th Law), which leads to a more realistic distribution of capital. Pillar 1 includes Operational Risk losses that crystallise suddenly and are insensitive to economic cycles. Pillar 2A includes risks not adequately covered in Pillar 1, e.g. emerging risks, risk concentrations and changes in business models. Pillar 2B includes risks that are both sensitive to economic cycles (7th Law) and also demonstrate significant lags (5th Law). Pillars 1 and 2B are significantly larger than Pillar 2A, creating an "hourglass" shape (Figure 10.4). Risks that are both insensitive to economic cycles and display significant lags can simply be accrued.

Stress testing: The mechanisms for an economic shock, causing some Operational Risk losses to rise are that existing losses are exacerbated, historical failures are uncovered and the responses to a crisis may lead to new losses (7th Law). Occurrence, velocity, duration and lags in Operational Risk losses all increase. Underpinning an increase in Operational Risk events is a combination of direct sensitivities to specific economic factors and changes in stakeholder behaviours, whilst the increase in the value of Operational Risk losses is the direct sensitivity of specific impacts to economic factors. Consequently, stress testing needs to involve an assessment of the impacts of an economic shock on both the behaviours of stakeholders (Table 11.3) and the scale of impacts (Table 11.2). The lags between detection and settlement vary between different Operational Risk event types (Figure 11.9 and Table 11.4), and are significantly longer than is usually reflected in stress tests.

Reverse stress testing: The ECB has recently noted that when undertaking reverse stress testing firms primarily focus on breaches of SREP. Utilising the summary of the business profiles of firms indicates a more complete range of threat categories (Figure 12.1) relating to Operational Resilience; regulatory licences; and business plans (e.g. loss of customer revenues). Pleasingly, these can all be linked to real-world examples of incidents that have threatened the viability of the business plans of specific firms. Scenario analysis techniques described in Chapter 9 can also be applied to reverse stress testing.

Insurance: As a mitigant of Operational Risk, insurance will always be restricted to the losses on the right-hand side of Figure 1.1, and a relatively small percentage of the total value of Operational Risk losses in any particular year. Understanding better the nature of a firm's Operational Risk profile through scenario analysis and capital modelling, and the extent to which events and impacts are insurable (Table 12.2) may enhance the procurement of insurance policies, with more appropriate coverage in line with risk appetite, i.e. the financial value of the cover; retention levels; and the range of risks covered.

Emerging risks: The Ten Laws can be applied to understand the Operational Risk consequences of emerging threats. For example, the extent to which they directly alter the occurrence of events (e.g. cybercrime and Climate Change's Physical Risks); increase the quantum of inadequacies or failures (e.g. AI and machine learning); change the behaviours of stakeholders (e.g. Climate Change's Transition Risks); and lead to economic shocks (e.g. Climate Change, both Physical and Transition Risks).

5. ALTERNATIVE STRATEGIES TO MEET THE OBJECTIVES OF OPERATIONAL RISK MANAGERS

The purpose of Operational Risk management must be to provide commercial value to firms through:

1. Maximising returns, whilst staying within appetite now, and also in the future (Chapter 7).
2. Growing their businesses both quickly and safely (Figure 13.4).
3. Meeting their stakeholders' expectations (Figure 13.8).

The various tools described in Section II assist firms to stay within appetite both currently and in the future through the 8th Law: Risk Homeostasis. The essence of the day-to-day risk management processes is that they involve Operational Risk managers dynamically assessing risks and controls and making judgements, leading to actions. These may be either proactive regarding the approval of new products or the execution of change or reactive, i.e. remedial actions in response to incidents or an adverse trend in KRIs and KCIs.

The periodic risk management processes are more focused on managing remote and emerging risks. For example, scenario analysis, capital modelling and reverse stress testing involve assessing remote risks to which a firm is currently exposed, whilst stress testing and identifying emerging risks involves the assessment of risks that may crystallise in future circumstances. Figure 17.5 maps the various day-to-day and periodic tools to these three objectives and highlights the extent to which they are either proactive or reactive. It also includes other specialist assessments. Obviously, the objectives achieved by these tools are not binary, i.e. tools for growing both quickly and safely will also help meet the expectations of stakeholders!

Whilst Figure 17.5 is generic for all firms, the appetite statements of individual firms for Operational Risk losses will determine the frequency and granularity with which these day-to-day and periodic tools will be used. Firms with lower appetites for Operational Risk losses will typically have lower thresholds for reporting incidents; conduct more granular root cause analysis; have higher numbers of predictive metrics; higher levels/more frequent testing of key controls; and will dynamically update their RCSAs. Alternative strategies are summarised in Table 17.2.

The Boards of firms have to decide whether the effort expended in these activities is justified by the benefit obtained.

IN CONCLUSION

The difficulty in understanding Operational Risk is its complexity, i.e. it is driven by the dynamic interaction of the business profiles of firms; human and institutional behaviours; and the nature of the taxonomies for inadequacies or failures, causes and

FIGURE 17.5 Linking Operational Risk management tools to objectives (Revision of Figure 14.1)

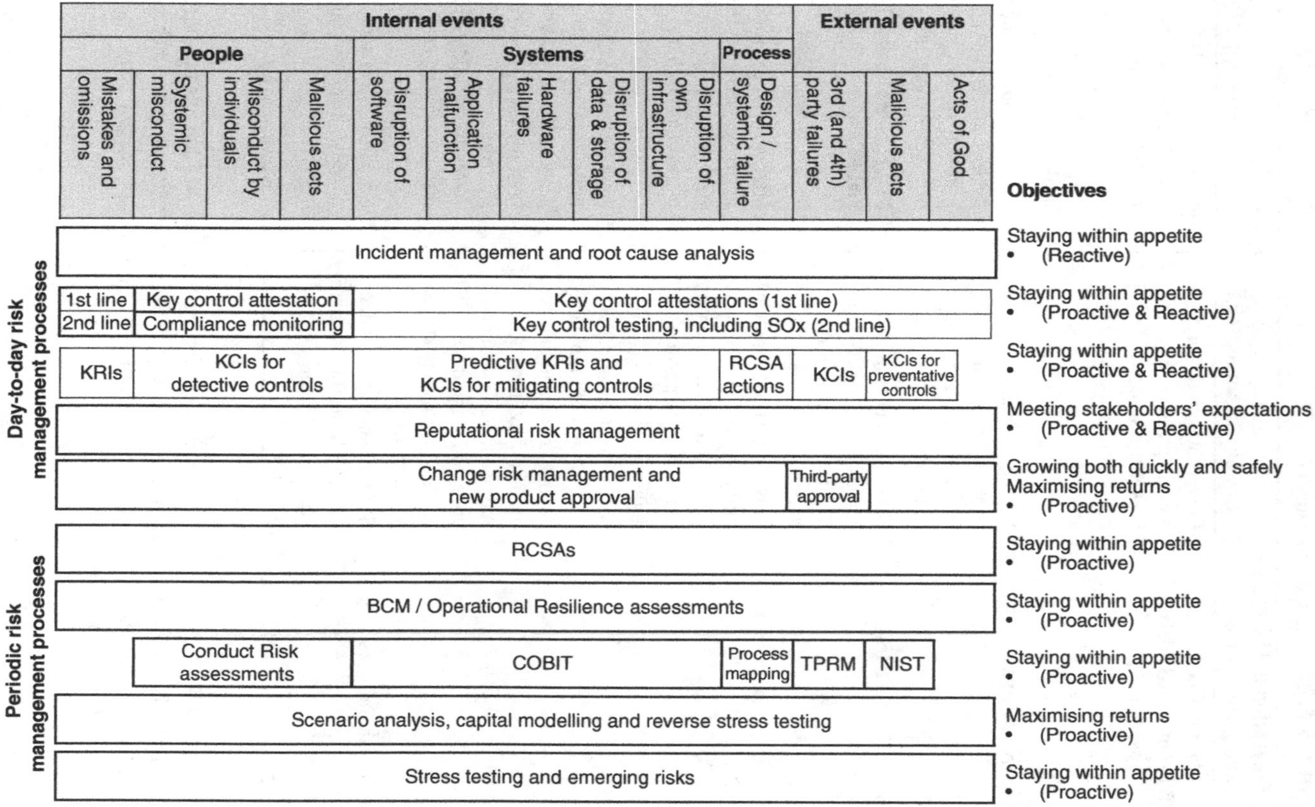

	People				Systems				Process	External events		
	Mistakes and omissions	Systemic misconduct	Misconduct by individuals	Malicious acts	Disruption of software	Application malfunction	Hardware failures	Disruption of data & storage	Disruption of own infrastructure	Design / systemic failure	3rd (and 4th) party failures	Malicious acts	Acts of God

Internal events / **External events**

Objectives
- Staying within appetite (Reactive)
- Staying within appetite (Proactive & Reactive)
- Staying within appetite (Proactive & Reactive)
- Meeting stakeholders' expectations (Proactive & Reactive)
- Growing both quickly and safely / Maximising returns (Proactive)
- Staying within appetite (Proactive)
- Staying within appetite (Proactive)
- Staying within appetite (Proactive)
- Maximising returns (Proactive)
- Staying within appetite (Proactive)

Day-to-day risk management processes

- Incident management and root cause analysis
- 1st line: Key control attestation / Key control attestations (1st line)
- 2nd line: Compliance monitoring / Key control testing, including SOx (2nd line)
- KRIs: KCIs for detective controls / Predictive KRIs and KCIs for mitigating controls / RCSA actions / KCIs / KCIs for preventative controls
- Reputational risk management
- Change risk management and new product approval / Third-party approval

Periodic risk management processes

- RCSAs
- BCM / Operational Resilience assessments
- Conduct Risk assessments / COBIT / Process mapping / TPRM / NIST
- Scenario analysis, capital modelling and reverse stress testing
- Stress testing and emerging risks

347

TABLE 17.2 Alternative strategies

Operational Risk management tools	Lower risk appetite	Higher risk appetite
Incident management and root cause analysis	■ Lower thresholds for reporting losses, e.g. zero. ■ Lower thresholds for conducting root cause analysis.	■ Higher thresholds for reporting losses, e.g. €20,000. ■ Higher thresholds for conducting root cause analysis.
Control assurance	■ Higher numbers of key control attestations. ■ Higher frequency of testing of the key controls.	■ Lower numbers of key control attestations. ■ Lower frequency of testing of the key controls.
Predictive metrics	■ Higher numbers of KRIs and KCIs. ■ Mandated period for remediation.	■ Lower numbers of KRIs and KCIs.
Change management	■ Lower threshold for change initiatives being reviewed. ■ Lower threshold for changes to products requiring approval.	■ Higher threshold for change initiatives being reviewed. ■ Higher threshold for changes to products requiring approval.
RCSAs	■ Assessments conducted at lower levels of granularity, i.e. both risks and units of measure, e.g. processes. ■ Assessments dynamically updated for incidents, KRIs, KCIs, control attestations and actions.	■ Assessments conducted at higher levels of granularity/top-down, i.e. both risks and units of measure. ■ Assessments updated in response to triggers.
Scenario analysis	■ Scenario analysis conducted at lower levels of granularity, i.e. both risks and units of measure.	■ Scenario analysis conducted at Group level.

impacts. This means that its management and measurement will always be more challenging and involve more subjectivity than for the other risk categories. Hopefully, though, the Ten Laws articulated in this book will support Operational Risk managers in their noble endeavours.

Taxonomy of Inadequacies or Failures: Events and Control Failures

APPENDIX I.1 MAPPING THE NATURE OF INADEQUACIES OR FAILURES (EVENTS) TO BASEL II

Nature of the events \\ Basel II event taxonomy	Execution, delivery & process management	Clients, products & business practices	Employment practices workplace safety	External fraud	Internal fraud	Business disruption & systems failure	Damage to physical assets
People							
▪ Mistakes and omissions	Inaccurate data entry errors, e.g. fat-fingered typing.		Accidents at work: "slips, trips & falls".			Mis-sequencing batches.	Accidents at work.
▪ Systematic misconduct		Mis-sale PPI, swaps & MBS; LIBOR & FX manipulation; market timing; antitrust and sanctions breaches.	Class action against firm's hiring, compensation and promotion practices.				
▪ Misconduct by individuals		Mis-sale of products. Market manipulation. Leaking personal data.	Discrimination by individual managers.				
▪ Malicious acts				Collusion with external fraudsters, e.g. providing client data.	Rogue traders. Payment frauds. Procurement frauds.	Collusion with external fraudsters, e.g. providing client data.	

Category	Item						
Systems	■ Disruption of software					Extended retail banking IT outage (2018).	
	■ Application malfunctions		Trade & transaction reporting fines.			Trading algo malfunction (2012).	
	■ Hardware failures					Printer and disk failures.	
	■ Disruption of data & storage					Data quality and storage.	
	■ Disruption of own infrastructure					Networks and middleware.	
Process	■ Design/ systemic failure	Improper foreclosure practices (2012).	Weak systems & controls, e.g. failure to comply with Client Asset rules (2015).	Systemic design failures in bonus schemes/processes.			
External	■ 3rd (and 4th) party failures	All of the above	Some of the above, e.g. data leaks.			All of the above	
	■ Malicious acts			Terrorism e.g. 9/11 (2001).	Application fraud. Theft of assets. Ransomware.	NotPetya (2017). WannaCry (2017).	Terrorism e.g. 9/11 (2001).
	■ Acts of God			Pandemics, e.g. COVID-19.		Extreme weather and pandemics.	Hurricane Sandy's damage of DTCC's vault (2012).

APPENDIX I.2: TAXONOMY OF INADEQUACIES OR FAILURES: THE NATURE OF EVENTS

<table>
<tr>
<th colspan="3">The nature of events</th>
<th>Definitions or examples
from various public sources</th>
</tr>
<tr>
<td rowspan="2">Internal</td>
<td rowspan="2">People</td>
<td>Mistakes and omissions primarily relate to data, both physical and electronic, and its:

■ Communication;
■ Capture;
■ Storage;
■ Interpretation.

As well as the loss of assets.</td>
<td>■ Miscommunication (e.g. Completeness, Accuracy, Cut-off) of information.
■ Omissions (Completeness), e.g. failure to populate all required data-fields in a payment system (2020) or to include floors in structured products.
■ Failure to meet a deadline (Cut-off), e.g. settlements, corporate actions, or submissions.
■ Inaccuracies (Accuracy): e.g.
  ■ Drafting, e.g. an incorrect waterfall incorporated in a CDO's documentation (1999).
  ■ Selection, e.g.: payment to the wrong legal entity in a group in Chapter 11 (2008).
  ■ Transposition, e.g. ordering 610k shares at ¥16 instead of 16 shares at ¥610k (2001).
  ■ Replication, e.g. data "corruption that is copied from elsewhere" (McConnell 2017).
  ■ Duplication, e.g. trader submitted an order 145 times by leaning on his F12 key (1998).
■ Misinterpretation (Rights & Obligations), e.g. authorities' statutes, rules and regulations.
■ Loss (Existence), e.g. foreclosure processes were undermined by missing physical documents (2010) or a bank lost five tapes containing electronic customer data (2004).
■ Accidents, e.g. "slips, trips & falls".</td>
</tr>
<tr>
<td>Misconduct by individuals</td>
<td>■ Individual staff members can act inappropriately e.g. the FCA " ... concluded that [the trader's] trading ... was designed to move the price of the Bond, in an attempt to sell it to the Bank of England at an abnormal and artificial level" (2014).</td>
</tr>
</table>

The nature of events		Definitions or examples from various public sources
Process	Systemic misconduct	▪ Groups of staff members can act inappropriately because it is the practice of either their firm or their industry in general, for example, mis-sale of PPI; the systemic breaching of sanctions; and the facilitation of tax evasion.
	Malicious acts	▪ *Staff members may commit a criminal act*, e.g. theft, fraud, forgery and acting dishonestly.
	Design / systematic failure	▪ *Systemic failures* due to a poorly designed process. ▪ *Regulatory penalties* for poorly designed processes, e.g. a fine in the UK for poor "systems & controls".
Systems (Appendix IV.2)	Disruption of software	▪ *Disruption of software*, e.g. disruption of internet banking for >1 week, including slow performance, crashes, inability to log-on and access to other customers' data! (2018).
	Application malfunctions	▪ *System miscalculations*, e.g. error calculating end-capital for personal insurance policies over a 10-year period (2005). ▪ *Incorrect decisions*, e.g. the calculator used to assess the affordability of overdrafts from 2011 to 2015 failed to consider some housing and living expenses. ▪ *System generated duplicated or erroneous transactions*, e.g. erroneous orders generated by order router leading to a $460 million trading loss (2012). ▪ *System mispricing*, e.g. malfunction of an investment bank's electronic trading system led to ~16,000 erroneous, mispriced orders being placed on major exchanges (2013).
	Hardware failures	▪ *Printer failure*, e.g. multiple statements in the same envelope (2010). ▪ *Disk failure*, e.g: trading halted on an exchange by data corruption caused by destroyed server disk drives (2018).

The nature of events			Definitions or examples from various public sources
Systems* (Appendix IV.2)		Disruption of data & storage	▪ *Quality*, e.g. failings in a bank's prudential reporting, included "credit ratings data was not feeding correctly into the LRR system…" (2019). ▪ *Storage*, e.g. a bank's currency system failed to settle roughly 22,000 FX trades due to insufficient disk space (2003).
		Disruption of own infrastructure	▪ *Batch-scheduler failures*, e.g. delays for ~1 week to processing debit cards transactions, ATM withdrawals and other electronic banking services due to disruption of the batch-scheduling software (2010). ▪ *Networks & middleware failures*, e.g. a 7-hour systems-wide outage due to the incorrect replacement of a cable connecting the data-storage system to the mainframe (2010).
External		3rd (and 4th) party failures	▪ *Telecoms & internet*, e.g. a 12-hour outage of mobile devices (2007). ▪ *Utilities, e.g. power outages & surges*, e.g. a data storage disk system experienced an electrical outage, which corrupted its data. Wholesale payment and securities transactions were disrupted for ~1 week (2003).
		Malicious acts	▪ *3rd party may commit a criminal act*, e.g. theft, fraud, forgery, extortion and acting dishonestly. (See Appendix IV.1 for a more detailed cybercrime taxonomy.)
		Acts of God	▪ *Isolated natural disasters*, e.g. a fire. ▪ *Systemic events, with multiple impacts*, e.g. an earthquake, a hurricane or a pandemic.

*System and process failures often also arise from design failures. System failures may also arise from failures of operation.

There are two aspects of this taxonomy that link to other professions:

1. *Auditors:* Mistakes and omissions can be linked to the control testing objectives of auditors;[1] and
2. *Insurers:* The nature of the inadequacies or failures that constitute events is similar to how insurance companies categorise incidents.

---

[1] When the Author trained as an accountant in the late 1980s/early 1990s, his firm had seven defined objectives for audit tests, i.e.: Completeness; Accuracy; Existence; Valuation; Cut-Off; Rights & Obligations; and Presentation & Disclosure.

APPENDIX I.3: TAXONOMY OF INADEQUACIES OR FAILURES: THE NATURE OF THE CONTROL FAILURES

The nature of control failures			Definitions or examples from various public sources
Internal control failures	People – operating effectiveness	Mistakes and omissions	*Controls not performed*, e.g.: ■ "... the managers responsible ... were unaware that their staff had stopped following agreed procedures [checks on internal trades]."[a] *Control incorrectly or partially performed*, e.g.: ■ "... in a number of instances, maker/ checker controls were not properly evidenced and did not identify errors".[b] ■ "Multiple limit breaches were routinely signed off without rigorous investigation or actions taken to reduce positions".[a] *Failure to act*, e.g. on exceptions: ■ "Operations did not have the reflex to inform their ... supervisors or Front Office supervisors of ... anomalies"[c] ■ "Certain control functions failed to escalate in a timely manner price testing variances that were identified ..."[d]
		Misconduct and malicious acts	The mistakes and omissions described above can also occur deliberately. In addition: *Circumvention of controls – falsification*, e.g.: ■ The FSA received complaint files which had been "altered improperly" in "the form of amendments to existing documents".[e] ■ "To hide his losses and the size of his positions, he created fictitious options."[f] *Circumvention of controls – breach of segregation of duties*, e.g.: ■ A bank clerk made two fraudulent transfers with a total value of €90 million. "Two of [his] colleagues, whose passwords were used to carry out and approve the transactions, were initially questioned but soon declared innocent".[g]

The nature of control failures	Definitions or examples from various public sources
	Circumvention of controls – collusion, e.g.: ■ A trader "...sent a list of four AAA bonds to his bond salesman contact [at another bank]...and requested month-end prices for the bonds. At approximately the same time, [he also] communicated to his contact the desired prices on the bonds".[h]
Process – design effectiveness	*Poorly designed controls* for achieving Completeness; Accuracy; Existence; Valuation; Cut-Off; Rights & Obligations; and Presentation & Disclosure, e.g.: ■ "The identification of suspicious trading patterns had to be performed manually. However, it was not generally feasible for...desk supervisors to perform this task for high volume trading desks..."[i] ■ The bank "extracted the relevant trading data for reconciliation purposes from its systems at different points in time which created timing gaps".[j] *Missing controls*, e.g.: ■ The bank "...had no specific systems and controls relating to its LIBOR or EURIBOR submissions processes until December 2009".[k] ■ The firm "...did not have...a control to compare orders leaving SMARS with those that entered it."[l]
Systems – variously design or operating effectiveness	■ *Disruption of software*, e.g.: "...while [the firm] had installed a tool to inspect network traffic for evidence of malicious activity, an expired certificate prevented that tool from performing its intended function of detecting malicious traffic."[m] ■ *Application malfunctions*, e.g.: "...due to the concerns over the reliability of the VaR calculation, the VaR limit breaches in currency options was removed from the front page of the report...".[a] ■ *Disruption of data & storage*, e.g. controls fail due to being fed incomplete, or inaccurate data, or data in the wrong format, or untimely data.

The nature of control failures		Definitions or examples from various public sources
External control failures	3rd (and 4th) party failures	■ *Any of the above*, e.g. Non-Functional Testing "...had been constrained by the test environments...and...had been conducted at lower volumes than originally planned".[n]
	Malicious acts	■ *External circumvention of controls*, e.g. "...the attackers removed the data in small increments, using standard encrypted web protocols to disguise the exchanges as normal network traffic."[m]

SOURCES FOR APPENDIX I.3

Again, in line with Professor Richard Feynman's advice, at the start of this book, this Control Failure Taxonomy is based upon a review of 14 well-documented incidents (the sources are listed below) and the explicitly described control failures:

a. PwC, "Investigation into foreign exchange losses at the National Australia Bank", 12th March 2004.

b. PRA, "Final Notice Citigroup Global Markets Limited..." et al., 26th November 2019

c. Societe Generale, "Mission Green: Summary Report", 20th May, 2008.

d. FSA, "Final Notice: Credit Suisse International and Credit Suisse Securities (Europe) Limited", 13th August 2008.

e. FSA, "Final Notice: UK Insurance Limited", 17th January 2012.

f. The Ludwig Report, "Report to the Boards of Directors of Allied Irish Banks, P.L.C., Allfirst Financial INC., and Allfirst Bank concerning currency trading losses", 12th March 2002.

g. BBC, "Clerk jailed for £72m bank fraud", 7th July, 2008.

h. SEC, "Securities and Exchange Commission, Plaintiff, v. Kareem Serageldin, David Higgs, Faisal Siddiqii and Salmaan Siddiqui, Defendants." 1st February, 2012.

i. FINMA, "UBS trading losses in London: FINMA finds major control failures", 26th November 2012.

j. SFC, "SFC reprimands and fines The Royal Bank of Scotland PLC $6 million for internal control failings", 22nd April 2014.

k. FSA, "Barclays fined £59.5 million for significant failings in relation to LIBOR and EURIBOR", 27th June 2012.

l. SEC, "SEC Charges Knight Capital With Violations of Market Access Rule", 16th October 2013.

m. US Government Accountability Office, Report to Congressional Requesters "DATA PROTECTION Actions Taken by Equifax and Federal Agencies in Response to the 2017 Breach", August 2018.

n. Slaughter & May, "An independent review following TSB's migration onto a new IT platform in April 2018", October 2019.

Impact Taxonomy and Their Relative Scales and Velocities

P&L & balance sheet		Level 2 – examples	Scale $	Velocity $/day
Lost revenues or charges (P&L)	Uncollected revenues due to an Operational Risk event.	▪ Uncollected revenues, e.g. failure to claim revenues to which a firm is entitled and loss of entitlement to revenues.		
	Impairments and settlements to the bank's P&L accounts due to an Operational Risk event.	▪ Restitution/compensation payments linked to a firm's business profile and 3rd party relationships (Figure 2.1), e.g.: 　– *Customers & investors*, e.g.: 　　▪ Credit and Market Risk losses suffered; 　　▪ Frauds suffered by customers; and 　　▪ Loss of client assets in safe custody. 　– *Counterparties, customers and suppliers:* Interest on monies owed.		

P&L & balance sheet		Level 2 – examples	Scale $	Velocity $/day

Lost revenues or charges (P&L)		– *Suppliers:* Breach of contract or licencing agreements, e.g. data.
		– *Employees (current & potential)*, e.g.:
		  ■ Lost historical earnings, e.g. due to payroll errors; and
		  ■ Lost future earnings for an inappropriate dismissal.
		– *Visitors* (e.g. customers, suppliers etc): 3rd party liability.		

		■ Regulatory action: fines and penalties.		

		■ Tax incurred, e.g.:
		  ■ On behalf of others, e.g. clients or employees; and
		  ■ Loss of treatment, e.g. failed tax arbitrage/avoidance schemes.		

	Additional expenses or foregone expenditure[1] with a direct link to the Operational Risk event.	■ Legal liabilities. ORX include legal expenses that relate to Operational Risk events both for when firms act as the plaintiff as well as the defendant.		Not enough data
		■ Other 3rd party expenses, e.g. accountants, office cleaners (COVID-19), etc.		

		■ Additional staff costs, e.g.:
		  ■ Incentives and overtime payments for employees; and
		  ■ 3rd party contractor costs.		

		■ Additional costs, e.g. temporary offices and recovery sites.		

---

[1] An unexpected impact of COVID-19 was a reduction in budgeted travel & entertainment expenditure for international banks.

P&L & balance sheet		Level 2 – examples	Scale $	Velocity $/day
	Costs of repair or replacement, incurred to restore the position that was prevailing before the Operational Risk event.	■ Physical assets: ■ Buildings; ■ IT equipment; and ■ Fixtures & fittings, but avoid double counting with write-downs.		
		■ Costs of improving controls*		
Write-off of assets (balance sheet)	Write-downs of assets due to an Operational Risk event, e.g. ■ Theft: asset stolen ■ Fraud: asset never existed; ■ Extortion; ■ Accidental asset transfers ■ Damage; and ■ Loss of recourse.	■ Market Risk losses or gains (mark-to-market) for the Bank, arising from an Operational Risk event, e.g. rogue trading or fat-fingered typing.		
		■ Financial and physical assets: ■ Cash and bearer bonds; ■ Securities; ■ Physical commodities; ■ Buildings; ■ IT equipment; and ■ Fixtures & fittings.		
		■ Loans: Credit Risk losses, exacerbated by operational failures, e.g. failure to perfect security; put in place netting agreements or to call margin.*	Not enough data	Not enough data

These impacts are not included in gross losses (Basel Committee, 2017).

P&L & balance sheet		Level 2 – examples	Scale $	Velocity $/day
Reputational impacts (Stakeholders listed on Figure 2.1)	Authorities	■ Higher fines, if a repeat offender (Table 9.1). ■ Additional capital requirements, lowering return on equity. ■ Licence restrictions on ability to conduct new activities. ■ *Operational Resilience:* Threat to the financial system, requiring risk mitigation plans.	Not enough data	Not enough data
	Investors: Bondholders	■ Higher funding costs if a firm's credit rating is downgraded (Figure 13.11).		
	Investors: Shareholders	■ Higher costs of capital if existing investors sell shares and the price falls (Figure 13.9).		
	Infrastructure and counterparties	■ *Operational Resilience:* Disorderly operation of markets. ■ *Operational Resilience:* Threaten a firm's safety and soundness, e.g. loss of revenues and liquidity.		
	Suppliers and outsourcers	■ Adverse reaction.		
	Customers	■ *Operational Resilience:* Intolerable levels of harm to a firm's clients. ■ Loss of future customer and client revenues (Figure 13.10) – EBA stress testing only. Not an Operational Risk loss for capital calculations (EBA, July 2018).		
	Employees: current & future	■ Impact on staff morale and inability to retain existing employees. ■ Inability to recruit new employees.		
	Criminals	■ Higher levels of fraud if a firm has a poor reputation for fraud prevention.		

Key: Scale and velocity of losses (based on Figure 2.3)

Not enough data ☐   £10ms ▢ $100ms ▨ $1bns ▩ $10bns ■

Causal Taxonomy Based Upon a Review of Large, Well-Documented Events

Level 1		Level 2	▪ Examples of causes extracted from various public sources
Business profile causal categories	1. Strategy	Past & present / Sales incentives	▪ "Thousands of employees engaged in improper sales practices to satisfy goals and earn financial rewards under the Respondent's incentive program."[a]
		Business objectives	▪ "Senior management's emphasis on increasing efficiency compromised the effectiveness of certain controls."[b]
		Products & services / Income streams	▪ "Total net PPI income as a percentage of overall profit before . . . tax was on average 14% for 2003 to 2006."[c]
		Complexity	▪ "Inappropriate sales of more complex varieties of interest rate hedging products."[d]
		Customers / Sophistication	▪ ". . . when sold to customers who are likely to lack expertise (i.e. non-sophisticated customers) . . . some interest rate hedging products may be inappropriate."[d]

	Level 1	Level 2	■ Examples of causes extracted from various public sources
Business profile causal categories	2. Culture	Tone from the top	■ "... a widespread sense of complacency, a reactive stance in dealing with risks.... This complacent attitude was seen at the top of the institution."[e]
		Risk takers	■ "Some of the Traders treated aggressively anyone who questioned their activities..."[f]
		Control functions	■ "Certain personnel within control functions... were overly deferential in challenging certain traders."[g]
	3. Infrastructure, including governance	Oversight	■ "Inadequate oversight and challenge by the Board and its committees of emerging non-financial risks."[e]
		Appetite & policy frameworks	■ "A lack of clear articulation of minimum standards in the form of Group-wide policies..."[e]
		Reporting lines	■ "... there were no clear lines of responsibility..."[h]
Basel II internal causal categories	4. People	Expertise	■ "Too much reliance [was] placed on inexperienced and / or junior staff."[g]
		Resourcing levels	■ "A heavy reliance on manual processes and the workload... meant that certain of the existing controls in place were not operating effectively."[i]
		Training	■ "... advisers were not provided with adequate training..."[j]
		Mis-understanding	■ "For reasons that are not clear... the junior staff in Operations interpreted... [the] email to mean that they were no longer required to carry out any checks..."[f]
		Supervision	■ "... management and supervision of traders... were not effective..."[g]

Level 1	Level 2	◼ Examples of causes extracted from various public sources
Basel II internal causal categories 5. Processes[1]	Manual processes	◼ "The booking structure . . . was complex and overly reliant on large spreadsheets . . ."[g]
	Definition of processes	◼ "Failing to establish adequate processes for loan modifications."[k]
6. Systems[2]	Systems' age	◼ ". . . an expired digital certificate contributed to the attackers' ability to communicate with compromised servers and steal data without detection . . ."[l]
	Systems' architecture	◼ "Risk . . . relied upon a number of disparate systems to calculate VaR . . ."[f]
7. Change to the above	People	◼ "Reassignments and reorganisations within certain control functions . . . exacerbated the situation."[g]
	Processes	◼ None in the public domain.
	Systems	◼ IT "upgraded the batch scheduler software . . . because this software could no longer be sufficiently supported . . ."
8. Societal change	Compensation culture	◼ ". . . claims management companies also ramped up their efforts to cash in before August 2019."
9. Technological change	Big data, AI and robotics	◼ None in the public domain.

---

[1]*Processes:* This includes deficiencies in the design of processes, but excludes human errors, which are covered within People.

[2]*Systems:* This includes outages arising from aging systems and poor architectures but, as above, it excludes human errors.

	Level 1	Level 2	▪ Examples of causes extracted from various public sources
External change causal categories	10. Economic cycle	Market moves	▪ "...the greatest volumes [of interest rate hedges] were sold in the period 2005–2008, before the base rate fell sharply to its current, sustained historic low."[m]
		Fall in asset values	▪ "...changing market conditions in late 2007 and during 2008..."[j]
		Increase in defaults	▪ "Under the settlement, roughly 750,000 borrowers who lost their homes to foreclosure between 2008 and 2011 can expect to receive a...cash payment."[n]
	11. Environmental change	Decarbonisation	▪ None in the public domain.
		Extreme weather	▪ Closure of NYSE due to Hurricane Sandy "...to ensure safety of our people and communities."[o]
		Pandemics	▪ The COVID-19 pandemic coincided with operational disruption; market dislocation (e.g. negative future oil prices); an economic slowdown and a spike in cybercrime.
	12. Geopolitical change	New trade sanctions	▪ "When the US imposed heightened sanctions against Iran in mid-1995, the bank developed a practice to manipulate and delete information..."[p]
	13. Regulatory/ statutory change	New requirements	▪ "...the Judicial Review...against, what the industry believed was the creation, and the retrospective application of new requirements by the FSA."[c] ▪ The UK Supreme Court "...considered that the Orient-Express decision...was wrongly decided...and conclude that it should be overruled."[o]

SOURCES FOR APPENDIX III

In line with Professor Richard Feynman's advice, at the start of this book, this Causal Taxonomy is based upon a review of 17 well-documented incidents (the sources are listed below) and the explicitly described causes:

a. Consumer Financial Protection Bureau, Consent Order, Wells Fargo Bank, 8th September 2016.
b. FINMA, "UBS trading losses in London: FINMA finds major control failures", 26th November 2012.
a. Parliamentary Commission on Banking Standards, written evidence from Lloyds Banking Group, 4th January 2013.
b. FSA Update, "Interest rate hedging products Information about our work and findings".
c. APRA, "Prudential Inquiry into the Commonwealth Bank of Australia (CBA) Final Report", 30th April 2018.
d. PwC, "Investigation into foreign exchange losses at the National Australia Bank", 12th March 2004.
e. FSA, "Final Notice UK operations of Credit Suisse", 13th August 2008.
f. FSA, "Barclays fined £59.5 million for significant failings in relation to LIBOR and EURIBOR", 27th June 2012.
g. Société Générale, "Summary of PwC diagnostic review", 23rd May 2008.
h. FSA, "Final Notice Coutts & Co", 7th November 2011.
i. US Dept of Justice, "Federal Government and State Attorneys General Reach $25 Billion Agreement with Five Largest Mortgage Servicers to Address Mortgage Loan Servicing and Foreclosure Abuses", 9th February 2012."
j. US Government Accountability Office, Report to Congressional Requesters "DATA PROTECTION Actions Taken by Equifax and Federal Agencies in Response to the 2017 Breach", August 2018.
k. FCA, "FCA fines RBS, NatWest and Ulster Bank Ltd £42 million for IT failures", 20th November 2014.
l. *Reuters*, "U.S. banks agree to $25 billion in homeowner help", 10th February 2012.
m. CNN, "NYSE and Nasdaq closed as Hurricane Sandy hits", 29th October 2012.
n. US Dept. of the Treasury, "U.S. Treasury Department announces Settlement with Lloyds TSB Bank, PLC", 22nd December 2009.
o. The UK Supreme Court Judgement, "The Financial Conduct Authority (Appellant) v Arch Insurance (UK) Ltd and others", 15th January 2021.

Risk Taxonomies for Cybercrime and IT Operational Risks Based on Analysis of Actual Loss Events

Again, in line with Professor Richard Feynman's advice, these risk taxonomies for cybercrime and IT Operational Risk events are derived from categorising actual events recorded within the IBM FIRST Risk Case Studies.

APPENDIX IV.1 RISK TAXONOMY FOR CYBERCRIME BASED ON AN ANALYSIS OF ACTUAL LOSS EVENTS

Operational Risk		Cybercrime risks, i.e. the risk of loss arising from ...
Level 1	Level 2	

Business disruption and system failures	Systems	■ *Cyber disruption of software*, e.g.:
		  ■ A virus infiltrated an investment bank's internal browser-based trade execution and client system. Brokers were unable to execute trades and access client files (2002).
		  ■ A retail bank closed 70–80 of its branches in Finland for 1 day after a group of workstations were brought down by the MSBlast worm (2003).

		■ *Cyber disruption of data & storage*, e.g. the NotPetya virus scrambled PCs' file systems, rendering all files on a disk unreadable (2017).
		■ *Cyber hardware failures*, e.g. the reported impact of the Stuxnet virus on the Iranian nuclear programme (2010).

Operational Risk		Cybercrime risks, i.e. the risk of loss arising from ...
Level 1	**Level 2**	

		▪ *Cyber disruption of own infrastructure*, e.g. website disruption:
		   ▪ A bank's official web pages were replaced with false ones by an online vandal in the UK, Greece and Spain (2000).
		   ▪ The Anonymous group brought down credit card provider's website site for ~7 hours through a Distributed Denial of Service (DDoS) attack (2010).

		▪ *Cyber disruption of external infrastructure*, e.g. a "slammer" worm disrupted global phone, internet and banking networks by attacking applications utilising Microsoft's SQL Server 2000 database software (2003).

		▪ *Cyber disruption of vendors and suppliers of IT-related services*, e.g.:
		   ▪ A security token provider disclosed that systems related to its token security product had been hacked (2011).
		   ▪ An issuer of digital certificates filed for bankruptcy after being hacked (2011).

External fraud	Theft and Fraud	▪ *Cyber theft of firm's cash*, e.g.:
		   ▪ Fraudulent SWIFT messages (2016).
		   ▪ Whaling (2018).
		 ▪ *Cyber theft of clients' cash from firm*, e.g.:
		   ▪ Hacking the firm, e.g. a Korean cryptocurrency exchange filed for bankruptcy after being hacked and clients' cryptocurrency was stolen (2016).
		   ▪ Cloning of a debit card to make purchases on a client's account (2000).
		 ▪ *Cyber theft of clients' cash via their laptops*, e.g.:
		   ▪ Authorised Push Payments (APP) through interception of emails.
		   ▪ Infection of clients' laptops with trojans, e.g. SEK8 million was transferred from 250 bank customers when they became infected with the Haxdoor Trojan (2006).
		 ▪ *Cyber investment frauds*, e.g. by establishing a clone of a bank's website.

Operational Risk		Cybercrime risks, i.e. the risk of loss arising from ...
Level 1	**Level 2**	

CPBP	Systems Security	■ *Cyber extortion from banks*, e.g.:
		   ■ NotPetya (2017) – ransomware.
		   ■ Hackers stole customer data and then demanded a ransom of CAD1 million not to publish (2018).
		 ■ *Cyber extortion from customers*, e.g. ransomware.

		■ Application fraud using phished data or information obtained from social media.[1]
		■ *Cyber theft of client data from banks*, e.g. theft of 76m retail customers' data (2014).

		■ *Cyber theft of data from banks' suppliers and vendors*, e.g.:
		   ■ 145.5m customer records were hacked from a consumer credit agency (2017).
		   ■ 5.6 million credit card holders' details were hacked from a vendor, which processes transactions for major credit card providers (2003).

		■ *Cyber theft of bank customers' data from unrelated 3rd parties*, e.g. retailers (2006).
		■ *Cyber theft of intellectual property*, e.g. ~800 megabytes of software company's operating system source code was posted on a Russian website (2004).
	Suitability, Disclosure & Fiduciary	■ *Cyber breach of privacy*, i.e. the potential for compensation payments for breach of fiduciary duties following a hack. [Costs should be reflected against "Systems Security".]

	Improper Business or Market Practices	■ *Cyber market manipulation*, e.g.:
		   ■ Buy orders for penny stocks were executed from hacked clients' retail brokerage accounts to "pump-and-dump" low-volume shares (2006).
		   ■ Market-sensitive press releases were hacked from market news companies and were sold to traders in return for a share in the resulting profits (2015).

---

[1]This is an example of a *"cyber-enabled"* fraud rather than a *"cyber-dependent"* fraud.

APPENDIX IV.2: RISK TAXONOMY FOR IT OPERATIONAL RISK EVENTS BASED ON AN ANALYSIS OF ACTUAL LOSSES

Basel II		IT Operational Risks, i.e. the risk of loss arising from . . .
Level 1	**Level 2**	

Business disruption and system failures	Systems	■ *Disruption of software*, e.g.:
		  ■ A 3-day partial outage of the internet banking due to "exceptionally high volumes of traffic" (2009).
		  ■ Disruption of internet banking for >1 week, including slow performance, crashes, inability to log on and access to other customers' data! (2018).

		■ *Disruption of data & storage*, e.g.:
		  ■ Quality: An exchange erroneously placed test orders on active energy and metals markets while it was executing quality assurance (2010).
		  ■ Capacity: A bank's currency system failed to settle roughly 22,000 FX trades due to insufficient disk space (2003).

		■ *Hardware failures*, e.g.:
		  ■ Printer failure: Multiple statements in the same envelope (2010).
		  ■ Disk failure: Trading halted on an exchange by data corruption caused by destroyed server disk drives (2018).

		Disruption of own infrastructure:
		■ *Batch-scheduler failures*, e.g.:
		  ■ Delays for ~1 week to processing debit cards transactions, ATM withdrawals and other electronic banking services due to disruption of the batch-scheduling software (2010).
		  ■ Incorrect customer data for >1 week due to disruption of the batch-scheduler impacting 635 systems (2012).
		■ *Networks & middleware failures*, e.g.:
		  ■ A 7-hour systems-wide outage due to the incorrect replacement of a cable connecting the bank's data storage system to the mainframe (2010).

Basel II		IT Operational Risks, i.e. the risk of loss arising from ...
Level 1	Level 2	

		Disruption of external infrastructure:
		■ *Incompatible operating software*, e.g.:
		  ■ An antiviral software vendor released a data file update to its software, which made inoperable customers' laptops using a variant of the WindowsXP (2010).
		  ■ Denmark's national login solution for services including online banking became inaccessible for customers who had installed a Java 7 version 45 update (2013).
		■ *Telecoms & internet*, e.g.:
		  ■ Telecom failures, e.g. 12 hour outage of mobile device (2007).
		  ■ A bank's website and external email connection were down for 1 day after it failed to renew its domain name (2000).
		■ *Utilities, e.g. power outages & surges*, e.g.:
		  ■ A data storage disk system experienced an electrical outage, which corrupted its data. Wholesale payment and securities transactions were disrupted for ~1 week (2003).
		  ■ All flights were cancelled by an airline from Gatwick and Heathrow Airports for 1 day following a systems failure due to a "power surge" (2017).

		■ *Disruption of vendors and suppliers of IT-related services*, e.g. a custody bank was unable to calculate accurately the net asset values of mutual funds and ETFs due to an issue with an upgrade to an application provided by the vendor (2015).

		System malfunctions:
		■ *System miscalculations*, e.g.:
		  ■ Error calculating end-capital for personal insurance policies over a 10-year period (2005).
		  ■ Error calculating mortgage prepayment charges (2006).

Basel II		IT Operational Risks, i.e. the risk of loss arising from...
Level 1	Level 2	
Execution, Delivery & Process Management	Transaction Capture, Execution & Maintenance	System malfunctions: ■ *Incorrect decisions*, e.g.: 　■ A rating agency's computer models incorrectly awarded triple AAA ratings to ~$1bn of CPDO securities when they should have been graded up to 4 notches lower (2007). 　■ The calculator used to assess the affordability of overdrafts from 2011 to 2015 failed to consider some housing and living expenses. ■ *System generated duplicated or erroneous transactions*, e.g.: 　■ Erroneous orders generated by order router leading to a $460 million trading loss (2012). 　■ Duplicated farm subsidies (€3.4 billion) paid to 350,000 French farmers (2013). ■ *System mispricing*, e.g.: 　■ A trade matching system error between 2008 and 2013 caused it to execute some trades at prices below or above the best available bid or offer on an equity market. 　■ Malfunction of an investment bank's electronic trading system led to ~16,000 erroneous, mispriced orders being placed on major exchanges (2013). ■ *Stale prices* during periods of market turbulence, e.g. the Frankenshock (2015).
External fraud	Theft and Fraud	■ *Theft of firm's cash*, e.g.: 　■ Unsuccessful theft of £229 million using key logging devices (2004). 　■ Successful theft of £1.3 million from a retail branch using a key logging device (2013). ■ *Theft of clients' cash*, e.g. use of card skimming devices in ATMs to obtain clients' passwords to produce cloned cards (2008). ■ *Theft of hardware*, e.g. motherboards (2000) and a laptop containing the entire customer database (2006).

Basel II		IT Operational Risks, i.e. the risk of loss arising from …
Level 1	**Level 2**	
		■ *Fraudulent exploitation of algos*, e.g. a former trader was fined for "spoofing" other market participants that used algos that generated their quotes based upon the current Best Bids and Best Offers in the market (2014).
	Systems Security	■ N/A see cybercrime risks.

Clients, Products & Business Practices	Suitability, Disclosure & Fiduciary	■ *Breach of privacy – errors*, e.g.:
		  ■ Posting client data on the publically accessible section of its website (2000).
		  ■ Unencrypted server containing details of ~1 million bank customers was sold on eBay by an employee of a 3rd party archiving company (2008).
		  ■ A bank was unable to confirm the destruction, by a 3rd party vendor, of two magnetic tapes which contained 16 years/20 million historical customer statements (2018).
		■ *Breach of privacy – exceeds legal authority*, e.g. the granting of inappropriate access to customer data (2018).
		■ *Breach of contract*, e.g. user application licences and data downloads.

	Improper Business or Market Practices	■ *Automation of improper trade/market practices*, e.g.:
		  ■ Fine for a bank for their FX trading platform systematically rejecting customer trades where the market had significantly moved in their favour via "last look" (2015).
		  ■ "Dr Evil" trading strategy (2004).
		  ■ Spoofing (2014).

Damage to Physical Assets	Disasters and other events	■ *Terrorism*, e.g.: 9/11 destroyed a major part of a bank's communications network. The bank's main computers and backup facilities failed and its processing system was slowed for weeks (2001).
	Unauthorised Activity	■ *Malicious breach of privacy*, e.g.: a disgruntled internal auditor at a retailer posted the payroll details of 100,000 staff members online (2014).

Basel II		IT Operational Risks, i.e. the risk of loss arising from ...
Level 1	**Level 2**	

Internal Fraud	Theft and Fraud	▪ *Malicious destruction of assets*, e.g.:
		  ▪ A computer analyst at an investment bank embedded a "logic bomb" in the firm's network before he left the firm (2002).
		  ▪ An employee transmitted a code and command to 10 core bank global control centre routers and erased the running configuration files in 9 of the routers, resulting in a loss of connectivity to about 90% of all the bank's networks across North America (2012).

		▪ *Misappropriation of assets*, e.g.:
		  ▪ *Theft of client data*, e.g. private banks (2005 & 2010).
		  ▪ *Theft of intellectual property*, e.g. theft of computer code used in high-frequency trading by a trader prior to his resignation (2009).
		  ▪ *Procurement frauds by technology staff.*

Glossary

ABS	Asset-Backed Securities
ADOP	Asset Owners Disclosure Project
AI	Artificial Intelligence
AIB	Allied Irish Bank
AISC	Australian Securities and Investment Commission
AMA	Advanced Measurement Approach
APP	Authorised Push Payments
BAU	Business As Usual
BCCI	Bank of Credit & Commerce International
BCM	Business Continuity Management
BDSF	Business Development & Systems Failure
BIS	Bank of International Settlements
CBA	Commonwealth Bank of Australia
CCAR	Comprehensive Capital Adequacy Review
CDOs	Collateralised Debt Obligations
CEBS	Committee of European Banking Supervisors
CET1	Common Equity Tier 1
CFTC	Commodity Futures Trading Commission
CLOs	Collateralised Loan Obligations
COBIT	Control Objectives for Information and Related Technologies
CORF	Corporate Operational Risk Function
CPBP	Clients, Products & Business Practices
CPDO	Consistent Proportion Debt Obligations
CTB	Change The Bank
DFAST	Dodd–Frank Act Stress Test
DPA	Damage to Physical Assets
DTCC	The Depository Trust & Clearing Corporation
EAD	Exposure At Default
EBA	European Banking Authority
ECB	European Central Bank
EDPM	Execution, Delivery & Process Management
EF	External Fraud
EIOPA	European Occupational Pensions and Insurance Authority

EPWS	Employment Practices & Workplace Safety
FCA	Financial Conduct Authority
FHFA	Federal Housing Finance Agency
FSA	Financial Services Authority
FSB	Financial Stability Board
GDPR	General Data Protection Regulations
GFC	Global Financial Crisis
G-SIBs	Global Systemically Important Banks
ICT	Information and Communication Technology
IF	Internal Fraud
IMF	International Monetary Fund
IOR	Institute of Operational Risk
IPCC	International Panel on Climate Change
KCI	Key Control Indicator
KRI	Key Risk Indicator
LAB	Liquidity Asset Buffers
LBG	Lloyds Banking Group
LDA	Loss Distribution Approach
LGD	Loss Given Default
MBS	Mortgage-Backed Security
NAB	National Australia Bank
NDC	Nationally Determined Contributions
NGOs	Non-Governmental Organisations
NIST	National Institute of Standards and Technology
NYDFS	New York State Department of Financial Services
OFT	Optimal Foraging Theory
ORX	Operational Riskdata eXchange Association
PCAOB	Public Company Accounting Oversight Board
PD	Probability of Default
PPI	Payment Protection Insurance
PRA	Prudential Regulation Authority
QE	Quantitative Easing
QIS	Quantitative Impact Studies
RCSA	Risk & Control Self-Assessment
RTB	Run The Bank
RWAs	Risk-Weighted Assets
SEC	US Securities & Exchange Commission
SIV	Structured Investment Vehicle
SMEs	Small & Medium Enterprises
SOREs	Systemic Operational Risk Events
SOX	Sarbanes-Oxley
SPV	Special Purpose Vehicle

SREP	Supervisory Review and Evaluation Process
STD	Standard Deviation
TPRM	Third-Party Risk Management
TSA	The Standardised Approach
UAT	User Acceptance Testing
UNEP	United Nations Environment Programme
UPS	Uninterrupted Power Supply
VaR	Value at Risk
VIX	Chicago Board Options Exchange's Volatility Index

Bibliography

Abdymomunov, A., (2014) *"Banking Sector Operational Losses and Macroeconomic Environment"* Federal Reserve Bank of Richmond (Preliminary and incomplete).

ADOP: Asset Owners Disclosure Project Global Climate 500 Index, 2015. (aodproject.net)

AISC, (20th May 2016) *"Disciplinary Matter – Credit Suisse Equities (Australia) Limited"*.

AISC, (14th September 2016) *"16-308MR CBA pays $180,000 in penalties and will write off $2.5 million in loan balances"*.

Bank of England, (March 2019) *"Stress testing the UK banking system: 2019 guidance for participating banks and building societies"*.

Bank of England and FCA, (October 2019) *"Machine learning in UK financial services survey"*.

Basel Committee on Banking Supervision, (September 1998) *"Framework for Internal Control Systems in Banking Organisations"*.

Basel Committee on Banking Supervision, (June 1999) Consultative paper, *"A new capital adequacy framework"*.

Basel Committee on Banking Supervision, (September 2000) *"Principles for the Management of Credit Risk"*.

Basel Committee on Banking Supervision, (May 2001) *"QIS 2 Operational Risk Loss Data"*.

Basel Committee on Banking Supervision, (September 2001) *"Working Paper on the Regulatory Treatment of Operational Risk"*.

Basel Committee on Banking Supervision, (January 2002) *"The Quantitative Impact Study for Operational Risk: Overview of Individual Loss Data and Lessons Learned"*.

Basel Committee on Banking Supervision, (February 2003) *"Sound Practices for the Management and Supervision of Operational Risk"*.

Basel Committee on Banking Supervision, (March 2003) *"The 2020 Loss data Collection Exercise on Operational Risk: Summary of the Data Collected"*.

Basel Committee on Banking Supervision, (June 2004) *"International Convergence of Capital Measurement and Capital Standards A Revised Framework"*.

Basel Committee on Banking Supervision, (July 2009a) *"Results from the 2008 Loss Data Collection Exercise for Operational Risk"*.

Basel Committee on Banking Supervision, (July 2009b) *"Observed range of practice in key elements of Advanced Measurement Approaches (AMA)"*.

Basel Committee on Banking Supervision, (July 2009c) *"Enhancements to the Basel II framework"*.

Basel Committee on Banking Supervision, (October 2014) *"Review of the Principles for the Sound Management of Operational Risk"*.

Basel Committee on Banking Supervision, (March 2016) *"Consultative Document: Standardised Measurement Approach for operational risk."*

Basel Committee on Banking Supervision, (December 2017a) *"Basel III: Finalising post-crisis reforms"*.

Basel Committee on Banking Supervision, (December 2017b) *"Supervisory and bank stress testing: range of practices"*

Basel Committee on Banking Supervision, (August 2020) *"Consultative Document Revisions to the principles for the sound management of operational risk"*.

Basel Committee on Banking Supervision, (April 2021) *"Climate-related risk drivers and their transmission channels"*.

BDO, (2018) *"FraudTrack Survey"*.

Bernesco, W., (2009) *"Foraging strategies of homo criminalis: lessons from behavioural ecology"* Crime Patterns & Analysis Volume 2, Number 1 pages 5 to 16.

BIS, (January 2020) *"The green swan Central banking and financial stability in the age of climate change"*.

BIS, Working Papers No 840, (February 2020) *"Operational and cyber risks in the financial sector"*.

BIS, Bulletin 37, (January 2021) *"Covid-19 and cyber risk in the financial sector"*.

Bouveret, A., (2018) *"Cyber Risk for the Financial Sector: A Framework for Quantitative Assessment"*, IMF Working Paper No. 18/143.

Brei, M., Borio, C., and Gambacorta, L., (2019) *"Bank intermediation activity in a low interest rate environment"* BIS Working Papers No 807.

Cagan, P., and Lantsman, Y., (2007) *"The cyclicality of Operational Risk"*, Algorithmics white paper.

CEBS, (July 2010) *"Compendium of Supplementary Guidelines on implementation issues of operational risk"*.

CEBS, (October 2010) *"Guidelines on the management of operational risks in market-related activities"*.

Cech, R., (2009) *"Measuring causal influences in operational risk"*, Journal of Operational Risk Vol 4, Number 3, pages 59 to 76.

CFTC, (2020) *"Managing Climate Risk in the U.S. Financial System"*.

Chaparro, M. R., (2013) *"A new dimension to Risk Assessment"*. Centre for Mathematical Sciences Lund University.

Chapelle, A., (2018) *"Operational Risk Management: Best Practices in the Financial Services Industry"*, Wiley.

Chartered Institute of Internal Audit, (2020) *"Controls"*.

Chernobai, A., Jorion, P., and Yu, F., (2011) *"The Determinants of Operational Losses in U.S. Financial Institutions"*, Journal of Financial and Quantitative Analysis (JFQA), **46**(6), pp. 1683–1725, 2011.

Chernobai, A., Ozdagli, A., and Wang, J., (2018) *"Business Complexity and Risk Management: Evidence from Operational Events in U.S. Bank Holding Companies"*.

Chicago Federal Reserve, (October 2012) Letter No 303.

Cope, E., and Carrivick, L., (2013) *"Effects of the Financial Crisis on Banking Operational Risk Losses"*, Journal of Operational Risk Vol. **8**, Number 3.

Coveware, (January 2020) *"Q4 Ransomware Marketplace report"*. Ransomware Costs Double in Q4 as Ryuk Sodinokibi Proliferate (coveware.com).

Curti, F. et al, (2019) *"Cyber Risk Definition and Classification for Financial Risk Manage- ment"*. https://www.richmondfed.org/-/media/richmondfedorg/conferences_and_events/ banking/2019/cyber_risk_classification_white_paper.pdf

Dunnett, R., Levy, C., and Simoes, A., (2005) *"The hidden costs of operational risk"* McKinsey.

EBA, (June 2015) *"EBA draft Regulatory Technical Standards on the specification of the assess- ment methodology under which competent authorities permit institutions to use Advanced Measurement Approaches (AMA) for operational risk in accordance with Article 312(4)(a) of Regulation (EU) No 575/2013"*.

EBA, (31st January 2018) *"2018 EU-wide stress test, methodological note"*.

EBA, (July 2018) *"Guidelines on institutions' stress testing"*, EBA/GL/2018/04.

EBA, (November 2018) *"2018 EU-wide Stress Test, Results"*.

EBA, (December 2020) *"EBA report on the implementation of report on the implementation of selected COVID-19 policies"*, EBA/REP/2020/39 21/12/2020.

ECB, (May 2020) *"Guide on climate-related and environmental risks"*.

ECB, (August 2020) *"ECB report on banks' ICAAP practices"*.

EIOPA, (December 2020) *"Discussion paper on non-life underwriting and pricing in light of climate"*.

FCA, (February 2018) *"Algorithmic Trading Compliance in Wholesale Markets"*.

FCA, (November 2018) *"Cyber and Technology Resilience: Themes from cross-sector survey 2017/2018"*.

FCA, (June 2020) *"FCA fines Lloyds Bank, bank of Scotland and The Mortgage Business £64,046,800 for failures in mortgage arrears handling"*.

FCA, (December 2020) *"FCA fines Barclays £26 million over treatment of customers in financial difficulty"*.

Federal Housing Finance Agency, as conservator for the Federal National Mortgage Associa- tion and the Federal Home Loan Mortgage Corporation, Plaintiff vs JPMorgan, (September 2011).

Federal Reserve Bank, (December 2015) *"Federal Reserve Guidance on Supervisory Assess- ment of Capital Planning and Positions for LISCC Firms and Large and Complex Firms"* Attachment SR 15-18.

Federal Reserve Bank, (December 2015) *"Federal Reserve Guidance on Supervisory Assess- ment of Capital Planning and Positions for Large and Noncomplex Firms"* Attachment SR 15-19.

Federal Reserve System, (2019) *"Dodd–Frank Act Stress Test 2019: Supervisory Stress Test Methodology"*.

Federal Reserve System, (2020) *"Dodd–Frank Act Stress Test 2020: Supervisory Stress Test Results"*.

FSA, (24th September 2003) *"Final Notice Lloyds TSB"*.

FSA, (28th June 2005) *"Final Notice, Citigroup Global Markets Limited"*.

FSA, (October 2008) Market Watch 29.

FSB, (2013) *"Principles for An Effective Risk Appetite Framework"*.

Galbraith, J.K., (1955) *"The Great Crash, 1929"*. Penguin.

Gardner, D., (2009) *"Risk. The Science and Politics of Fear"*, Virgin Books.

Grimwade, M., (2016) *"Managing Operational Risk: New Insights & Lessons Learnt"*. Risk- Books.

Grimwade, M., (2018) *"An alternative to SMA: Using through the cycle loss data to propose an 'hourglass' solution"*, Journal of Risk Management in Financial Institutions, **11**(4) Pages 361 to 380.

Grimwade, M., (2019) *"Applying existing scenario techniques to the quantification of emerging Operational Risks"*, Journal of Operational Risk, Vol **14**, Number 3 Pages 27 to 72.

Grimwade, M., (2020) *"Ten laws of operational risk"*, Journal of Operational Risk, Vol **15**, Number 3 Pages 43 to 95.

Hillson, D., (2005) *"Describing probability: The limitations of natural language"*. Describing probability (pmi.org).

IMF, (2009) *"Global Financial Stability Report Responding to the Financial Crisis and Measuring Systemic Risk World Economic and Financial Surveys"*.

IMF, (2019) *"Global Financial Stability Report: Lower for Longer"*.

King Charles II, (1666) *"Rules and orders to be observed by all Justices of Peace, Majors, Bayiliffs, and other Officers, for the prevention of the spreading of the infection of the Plague"*. The National Archives (SP29/155 f102).

McConnell, P., (2015) *"Modelling operational risk capital: the inconvenient truth"*. The Journal of Operational Risk, Vol **10**, Number 4.

McConnell, P., (2017) *"Two Laws of Operational Risk"*. LinkedIn https://www.linkedin.com/pulse/two-laws-operational-risk-patrick-mcconnell/

Medlock, J.M. and Leach, S.A., (2015) *"Effect of climate change on vector-borne disease in the UK"*, The Lancet Infectious Diseases **15**(6). pp. 721–730.

Migueis, M., (2018) *"Forward-looking and Incentive-compatible Operational Risk Capital Framework"*, Journal of Operational Risk, Vol **13**, Number 3 Pages 1 to 15.

Migueis, M., (2021) *"Regulatory Arbitrage in the Use of Insurance in the New Standardized Approach for Operational Risk Capital"*, Journal of Operational Risk, Vol **16**, Number 1 Pages 1 to 11.

Moody's, (2018) *"Annual Default Study: Corporate Default and Recovery Rates, 1920–2017"*.

Naim, P. and Condamin, L., (2019) *"Operational Risk Modelling in Financial Services"*. Wiley.

NYDFS, (17th November 2015) *"Consent Order: Barclays"*.

ORX, (2016) *"Scanning the Horizon: 2016 Emerging Risk Methodology Report"*.

ORX, (Edition 2017, revised March 2018) *"Operational Risk Reporting Standards (ORRS)"*.

ORX, (2010; 2012, 2014; 2017; 2018; 2019; 2020; and 2021) *"Annual Banking Loss Reports"*.

ORX, (January 2020) *"Optimising Risk and Control Self-Assessment (RCSA)"*.

ORX & Oliver Wyman, (2019) *"The ORX References Taxonomy for operational risk and non-financial risk. Summary Report"*.

ORX & Oliver Wyman, (2020) *"Extended ORX Reference Taxonomy for operational and non-financial risk – Causes & Impacts. Full Report"*.

PCAOB, *"Auditing Standard No. 5, An Audit of Internal Control Over Financial Reporting That Is Integrated with An Audit of Financial Statements"*.

PRA, (2018) Statement of Policy: *"The PRA's methodologies for setting Pillar 2 capital"*.

PRA, (2019) Statement of Policy *"Enhancing banks' and insurers' approaches to managing the financial risks from climate change"*.

PRA, (2020) Supervisory Statement, *"The Internal Capital Adequacy Assessment Process (ICAAP) and the Supervisory Review and Evaluation Process (SREP)"*.

PRA, (2021) Policy Statement, *"Operational resilience: Impact tolerances for important business services"*.

Reason, J., (1990) *"The contribution of latent human failures to the breakdown of complex systems"* Philosophical Transactions of the Royal Society of London of Biological Sciences **327**(1241):475–484.

Reason, J., (2000) *"Human error: models and management"* British Medical Journal. 18 March, 2000; **320**(7237): 768–770.

Reguero, B., Losada, I., and Mendez, F., (2019) *"A recent increase in global wave power as a consequence of oceanic warming"* Nature Communications volume 10, Article number: **205**.

RiskBooks, (1998) *"Operational Risks and Financial Institutions"*.

Risk.net, (September 2016) *"Negative Euribor erodes securitisation profits Implicit floors in notes leave originators facing cost of negative rates on hundreds of tranches"*.

Risk.net, (March 2019) *"Top 10 op risks 2019: theft and fraud"*.

Risk.net, (14th July 2020) *"Op risk data: losses plummet during lockdown"*.

SEC, (31st August 2010) *"Report of Investigation Pursuant to Moody's Investor Services"*.

SEC, (21st June 2011) *"J.P. Morgan to pay $153.6 million to settle SEC charges of misleading investors in a CDO tied to U.S. housing market"*.

SEC, (1st February 2012) *"Litigation Release No. 22247, SEC v. Kareem Serageldin et al"*.

SEC, (16th October 2013) *"Administrative order against Knight Capital"*.

SEC, (16th October 2014) *"Cease & Desist order against Athena Capital Research"*.

Slaughter & May, (2019) *"An independent review following TSB's migration onto a new IT platform in April 2018"*.

SWIFT, (2019) *"Three years on from Bangladesh Tackling the adversaries"*.

UNEP Finance Initiative, (2020) *"Charting a New Climate"*.

US Secret Services, (December 2020) *"Compromised Managed Service Providers"*, GIOC Reference #20-032-I.

Wilde, G., (1998) *"Risk homeostasis theory: an overview"*. Injury Prevention. **4** (2): 89–91.

World Economic Forum, (2021) *"The Global Risks Report 2021"* 16th Edition.

Index